Insights to Performance Excellence 2002

Also Available from ASQ Quality Press:

Insights to Performance Excellence in Healthcare 2001: An Inside Look at the 2001 Baldrige Award Criteria for Health Care
Mark L. Blazey, Joel H. Ettinger, Paul Grizzell, and Linda Janczak

Insights to Performance Excellence in Education 2001: An Inside Look at the 2001 Baldrige Award Criteria for Education
Mark L. Blazey, Karen S. Davison, and John P. Evans

From Baldrige to the Bottom Line: A Road Map for Organizational Change and Improvement
David W. Hutton

Quality Problem Solving
Gerald F. Smith

Root Cause Analysis: Simplified Tools and Techniques
Bjørn Andersen and Tom Fagerhaug

Principles and Practices of Organizational Performance Excellence
Thomas J. Cartin

Six Sigma Project Management: A Pocket Guide
Jeffrey Lowenthal

Six Sigma for the Shop Floor: A Pocket Guide
Roderick A. Munro

The Change Agents' Guide to Radical Improvement
Ken Miller

The Certified Quality Manager Handbook, Second Edition
Duke Okes and Russell T. Westcott, editors

Managing Change: Practical Strategies for Competitive Advantage
Kari Tuominen

To request a complimentary catalog of ASQ Quality Press publications, call 800-248-1946, or visit our Web site at http://qualitypress.asq.org.

Insights to Performance Excellence 2002

An Inside Look at the 2002 Baldrige Award Criteria

Mark L. Blazey

ASQ Quality Press

Milwaukee, Wisconsin

Insights to Performance Excellence 2002:
An Inside Look at the 2001 Baldrige Award Criteria
Mark L. Blazey

ISBN 0-87389-537-1

Acquisitions Editor: Annemieke Koudstaal
Project Editor: Craig S. Powell
Production Administrator: Gretchen Trautman
Special Marketing Representative: David Luth

ASQ Mission: The American Society for Quality advances individual, organizational,
and community excellence worldwide through learning, quality improvement, and
knowledge exchange.

Microsoft is a registered trademark of Microsoft Corporation

Attention Bookstores, Wholesalers, Schools, and Corporations: ASQ Quality Press
books, videotapes, audiotapes, and software are available at quantity discounts with bulk
purchases for business, educational, or instructional use.
For information, please contact ASQ Quality Press at 800-248-1946, or write to ASQ
Quality Press, P.O. Box 3005, Milwaukee, WI 53201-3005.

To place orders or to request a free copy of the ASQ Quality Press Publications Catalog,
including ASQ membership information, call 800-248-1946. Visit our Web site at
www.asq.org or http://qualitypress.asq.org .

Printed in the United States of America

   Printed on acid-free paper

American Society for Quality
ASQ

Quality Press
600 N. Plankinton Avenue
Milwaukee, Wisconsin 53203
Call toll free 800-248-1946
Fax 414-272-1734
www.asq.org
http://qualitypress.asq.org
http://standardsgroup.asq.org
E-mail: authors@asq.org

This book is dedicated to the memory of my father, Everett who taught me the value of continuous improvement, and to my family, who provided support for the continuous search for excellence: my mother, Ann L. Blazey who constantly strives to improve everything she does; my brothers Scott, Brian, and Brent; my children Elizabeth and Mark; and most of all, my lifelong partner and loving wife Karen.

I would also like to remember Karen Hoffman who was the director of the Baldrige-based quality award program at Baxter Incorporated. She was a dedicated, enthusiastic, professional and will be missed.

Table of Contents

Foreword by John Lawrence ix

Acknowledgments xiii

Preface xiv

Introduction xv

Insights to Performance Excellence 1

Changes from the 2000 Award Criteria 73

Organizational Profile 75
    P.1 Organizational Description 76
    P.2 Organizational Challenges 78

Category 1—Leadership 81
    1.1 Organizational Leadership 82
    1.2 Public Responsibility and Citizenship 91

Category 2—Strategic Planning 99
    2.1 Strategy Development 101
    2.2 Strategy Deployment 110

Category 3—Customer and Market Focus 119
    3.1 Customer and Market Knowledge 120
    3.2 Customer Relationships and Satisfaction 126

Category 4—Information and Analysis 137
    4.1 Measurement and Analysis of Organizational Performance 138
    4.2 Information Management 148

Category 5—Human Resource Focus 155
    5.1 Work Systems 156
    5.2 Employee Education, Training, and Development 164
    5.3 Employee Well-Being and Satisfaction 172

Category 6—Process Management 181
    6.1 Product and Service Processes 182
    6.2 Business Processes 195
    6.3 Support Processes 202

Category 7—Business Results 209
    7.1 Customer-Focused Results 210
    7.2 Financial and Market Results 216
    7.3 Human Resource Results 221
    7.4 Organizational Effectiveness Results 225

Tips on Preparing a Baldrige Award Application 233

Scoring System 241

Self-Assessments of Organizations and Management Systems 251

The Site Visit 273

Glossary 289

Clarifying Confusing Terms 297

Appendix A: A Global View of Quality 301

Appendix B: Comparing Baldrige and ISO 9000:2000—

    A Maturity/Excellence Model versus a Compliance Model 305

Appendix C: 2002 Systems Required for Performance Excellence 309

About the Author 317

Index 318

Award Cycle Fees . . . . .CD-ROM

2002 Baldrige Application Template . . . . .CD-ROM

2002 Criteria for Performance Excellence . . . . .CD-ROM

2002 Eligibility Certification Overview . . . . .CD-ROM

2002 Eligibility Forms . . . . .CD-ROM

Application Instructions . . . . .CD-ROM

Malcolm Baldrige National Quality Award Winners and
    Contact Information . . . . .CD-ROM

State and Regional Quality Award Contact Information .CD-ROM

Foreword

Leadership Challenges by John Lawrence

A lot of time and energy is put into the question, "What drives success in business?" The answer is both deceptively simple and hauntingly complex. It's as much a function of the people and the value the business brings to the marketplace as it is the approaches chosen to deliver it. Success in business is a risky, complex, and challenging human endeavor. It takes more than being able to articulate the lessons learned by the successful—the trick is being able to help others incorporate and leverage those lessons in their own approaches, whether it is in the private sector, education, healthcare, or government. Dr. Mark Blazey is doing just that and it is successes in the marketplace that makes this series a continuing best seller.

Traditionally, success in business has involved the pursuit of functional excellence in fields such as sales (IBM), marketing (Coca-Cola), manufacturing (Ford), capital formation (Morgan Stanley), and the improvement of the human condition (Pearl River School District in New York and Chugach School District in Alaska). Today, as important as functional supremacy is, it is not enough. It is how all the elements of a business come together and provide value in the marketplace—to customers—that is the key ingredient to success. Success involves a balancing act. It involves understanding how the system works together that is important. What is the system used to run the most successful businesses? Can all the executives in the business articulate what that system is—can each one draw a picture of that system on a single sheet of paper and explain it to 10 year old children? I once had the CEO of one of the largest transportation companies in North America ask his 35 direct reports to draw a picture of the system they used to run the business on one sheet of paper. He waited five minutes and collected the papers. As he thumbed through the papers I was taken back by the way he just looked at the pieces of paper and kept shaking his head back and forth in disbelief. No two pieces of paper portrayed the same picture. Think of the message that sends. Here are the 35 senior people in a multibillion dollar business and they do not have a uniform view of how the business is run. These executives do not know whether or how they will be able to keep the promises they make to their customers, employees, stockholders, and the communities in which they work and live. Think of what a powerful message would be sent if they all focused on the same themes, pursued the same vision and objectives, and had confidence that the things they asked the people to do were indeed the right things for the business to succeed.

Organizations are formed to accomplish a set of objectives to serve people. It's that simple. Whether the organization is for-profit or not-for-profit, small or large, public or private, manufacturing, service, government, healthcare, or education—the main thing that changes from one *successful* organization to another is the way they keep score. Whether the primary indicator of success is profits, children educated, patients cured, miles of roads paved, or number of overnight packages delivered on time, to be successful they must understand and meet the requirements of the many different customers they have organized to serve.

Like it or not, to be successful organizations must identify and serve customers—although they may choose to call them many other names such as clients, students, patients, families, constituents, communities, voters, rate-payers, passengers, or shoppers, to name a few. The nomenclature changes depending upon the language of the business, but at the end of the day it's those "customers" who are making decisions about whether or not they are going to do business with us. If we can keep the customers we've got and attract new ones, it is a sign that the organization is going to thrive. Clearly, without customers organizations cannot survive.

Strange as it may seem, there are organizations that have not put "delighting customers" at the top of their priority list (or anywhere on the list). Delighted customers are five times more likely to buy from you than those who are simply satisfied. Furthermore, delighted customers usually bring along a friend—enabling the organization to thrive. On the other hand, 80 percent of dissatisfied customers are likely to walk away and not even tell you they were dissatisfied. Worse yet, it costs 10 times as much to regain a lost customer as it does to retain a current one. Worst of all, dissatisfied customers are likely to tell at least 20 of their friends, while only five will hear of the startling news associated with "delight." With the large number of internet-based consumer buying sites in place today, the dissatisfied customer can easily tell thousands of their bad experiences. In the 21st Century, the customer is king. It's a customer economy.

If organizations intend to delight customers, leaders and employees must understand their requirements and expectations. More than ever before, we need to personalize the customer relationship and build loyalty. Horst Schulze, the former CEO of Ritz-Carlton, a hotel chain that forever altered the nature of customer service, points this out very well when he says, "Customers need a reason to be loyal, give them a reason." While CEO, Mr. Schulze took the time to be personally involved in a two-day orientation with all of the staff at the opening of each new Ritz Carlton hotel. Here was the chief executive making sure that everyone in the business understood the objectives and keys to success. His penetrating but simple questions to staff up and down the line would focus on who are your customers; what is important to these customers; how do we make these four or five things that are important to our customers better than anywhere else. To illustrate a typical Ritz-Carlton experience, if a guest has a preference for a hard pillow, a note is entered into the customer data base and wherever the guest goes in the Ritz chain a hard pillow will be on the bed. In another instance, while cleaning the room in the morning, a house keeper found a small teddy bear on the floor among the child's dirty clothes. Upon return the child found the teddy bear sitting at a small table with the Ritz Lion having tea. Now, what do you think went through the minds of the parents and the child?!

To deliver that level of performance consistently, the Ritz-Carlton—or any organization—must put in place a set of processes that focus on customer delight and are capable of delivering consistent results. Again, let's look at the Ritz-Carlton. The person who is recognized as the best at doing a task is the one who documents the process. For three weeks, a new employee follows in the footsteps of an experienced, high-performing employee who volunteers to be a teacher-mentor. At the end of the training period, the new person is tested. Passing means the employee begins to work independently; failing means more training and testing. On-the-job, specific, quantifiable performance goals are set. Goals and timing for "improvement" are then established and progress reported quarterly. Processes are aimed at those things that customers consider important and employees are focused on delivering them at high levels of achievement and they are constantly engaged in an effort to do it better. This creates an environment of true "continuous improvement." The environment of customer-focused continuous improvement keeps customers coming back, and bragging about their delightful experience to their friends. Horst Schulze has figured out that the friends and acquaintances of current customers are the very set of people they were trying to attract to the business in the first place.

When key work processes are capable of producing desired results consistently, the outcomes are predictable. That is why a "process" orientation is important. Too many people in nonmanufacturing disciplines like sales, education, or healthcare believe that using process discipline to carry out work is an outdated manufacturing idea and does not apply in their fast-paced world. The newest winners of the Baldrige Award demonstrate clearly that process orientation is critical for success in nonmanufacturing areas such as fast food restaurants and public school systems. After talking with hundreds of leaders who are concerned with the level of performance in their organizations, it appears that the fear of discipline and accountability that a process orientation brings to the workplace may be the real obstacle to change.

Unfortunately, even when organizations begin to execute processes well, their leaders quickly find that excellence and optimum performance continues to elude them. Organizations can fail to satisfy customers when key work processes have been developed in a vacuum—without tying them to customer requirements. "Internally-focused" processes have often been driven by the desire to do things more efficiently and effectively from the company's point of view—without regard to customer concerns. The resulting organizational arrogance—the belief that we know better than the customer—is almost certain to bring about customer dissatisfaction and ultimate customer revolt, causing customers to demand change. To be successful, organizations must consistently understand and do well those processes that deliver the four or five characteristics that are critical to customer delight. The winners in the highly competitive environment in which we live are the organizations that understand these drivers of customer delight and then design and execute work processes aimed at delivering them better than anywhere else.

Many business leaders find it difficult to determine what customers want, fend off the competition, and satisfy the workers, all within a budget. That is where the development and execution of "strategy" come into play. Strategy is about understanding the direction in which customers are moving, the direction in which the competition is moving, the direction in which the market is moving, and coupling the information with the capabilities of the business—and then identifying the few things to do that are critical to the future success of the business.

Knowing how well all of the factors are working involves having a "dashboard for the business." No one would think of driving a car on a trip or getting on an airplane if the instrument panel were missing. Yet business leaders often make critical decisions with either one-dimensional instruments (financial) or instruments that provide insufficient information about the state of the business (factors measured because they are available but not necessarily important). Relying only on financial instruments is comparable to driving the car by only looking in the rear-view mirror. The good news is the picture is pretty clear. The bad news is that you will crash sooner or later. Of course leaders in every organization must be aware of the organization's financial health. However, that is not enough information to lead the organization effectively through difficult and challenging times. The organization's leaders must also know what is important to customers, how well it is delivering on those things that are important, the

reaction of its customers, the direction in which their expectations are moving and the capability and capacity of its work processes and delivery systems. With this knowledge, leaders are in a much better position to make better decisions about the actions needed to be successful, bring value to the market place, and respond to changing circumstances and new opportunities.

While customer focus, strategic planning, and data to support effective decision making are critical components of the successful organization, these factors combined are still not sufficient to ensure success. Every organization must acquire good people, train them, motivate them, and retain them. Today, to be successful, organizations must attract and develop employees who understand that the customers are the most import aspect of the business. Employees must have the competencies to use facts and information to make good decisions, and to continue learning and contribute to their own growth and development. In a world where product and service superiority lasts only a short period of time, it is the capabilities of the people that will be the source of ongoing excellence.

The ability to make this system come together and work harmoniously is the responsibility of leadership. Basically, leadership has two functions: (1) to use strategy to set the direction very clearly; and (2) to establish the environment in which that direction is consistently carried out to the delight of its customers. Some leaders find it difficult to establish and articulate a clear vision and set of values. When this happens the people in an organization are forced to substitute their own ideas about the "right direction." When many do this, the organization finds itself pulled in different directions. Leaders cannot expect people to know what to do if they have not established and continuously reinforce the norms of desired behavior. Leadership is very much about setting and leading by example—role modeling what the company stands for and living the change expected of all.

The best organizations in every sector have demonstrated that all parts of the system must be effectively integrated to optimize performance. It is not possible to achieve excellence by only doing some of the things that are easy and ignoring the rest of them. It is a concept that is easy to understand but very difficult to execute. On the one hand it's simple. On the other hand, it's very complex.

We live in a rapidly changing world where global issues affect our lives in many ways, excellence is expected, and the customer is king. There is enormous opportunity for those prepared to work both hard and smart in the pursuit of excellence. The approaches used to achieve success have proven effective in all types of organizations: sustained *results* occur from an intense focus on *customers*; the consistent fulfillment of customer expectations derives from capable *work processes* that must be aligned with a market driven *strategy*. The performance of the business is monitored through continuous acquisition and analysis of *information* (the dashboard). None of this works without *people* who are motivated and skilled to consistently execute their work processes. Finally, it is all tied together with *leaders* whose job it is to set the direction, create the environment for continuous improvement and learning, and lead by role modeling desired behaviors and norms—living the values they expect in others.

With his best selling series and his personal involvement, Dr. Mark Blazey has been helping organizations of all types and in all sectors achieve success and develop enviable track records of performance. He has helped them develop practical approaches for continuous improvement that serve as the cornerstone for leadership and organizational success. Mark Blazey helps make a set of complex concepts simple and has made this book a best seller. Insights to Performance Excellence is a book for beginners as well as experts in the field of organizational development and operational excellence. The book delivers the lessons, provides the insights, and sets the framework for a successful journey to performance excellence.

—John Lawrence
Retired Vice President of Quality
Xerox Business Services (1997 Baldrige Winner)

Acknowledgments

Harry Hertz, Curt Reimann, Barry Diamondstone, and the dedicated staff of the Malcolm Baldrige National Quality Award office have provided long-standing support and guidance in promoting quality excellence. The book would not be possible in a timely fashion without the design and layout expertise, dedication, and commitment of Enterprise Design and Publishing. In addition, Karen Davison and John Lawrence provided substantial editorial and analytical assistance. Several others have helped shape my thinking about performance excellence and refine this book, including Joe Sener, Olga Striltschuk, Mary Gamble, Orland Pitts, Ed Hare, April Mitchell, George Bureau, Debra Danziger-Barron, Skip Coggins, Barbara Graham, Bill Hoberg, Geoff Calhoun, Jim Shipley, Tom Kubiak, Patricia Billings, Wendy Brennan, Gerald Brown, Wendy Steager, Beverly Centini, Sheryl Billups, Joe Kilbride, Linda Vincent, Joan Wills, Steve Hoisington, Gary Floss, Jack Evans, Arnie Weimerskirch, Paul Grizzell, Don Cates, Marty Mariner, Andy Downs, Jerry Holt, Bill Mac Lachlan, and George Raemore. I also greatly appreciate the typing and editorial assistance, background research, and proofreading of Jessica Norris. The chapter on site visits, the criteria model and integrated management systems analysis, the management and performance excellence surveys, the performance standard for leadership, the supplemental scoring guidelines, the sections concerning the potential adverse consequences of not doing what the Criteria require, and the application preparation files are used with permission of Quantum Performance Group, Inc. The core values, criteria, selected glossary terms, award winners, and background information in this book are drawn from information in the public domain supplied by the Malcolm Baldrige National Quality Award program. Kevin Hendricks and Vinod Singhal provided research results that were used in this book from their extensive study of financial performance. Data from the Economic Evaluation of the Baldrige National Quality Program by Albert Link and John Scott were prepared for NIST in October 2001. Data from Foundation for the Malcolm Baldrige National Quality Award regarding the perception of chief executive officers from over 300 United States organizations are also included in this book.

—Mark Blazey

Preface

A substantial portion of my professional life has been spent helping people understand the power and benefits of this integrated management system and become examiners for many performance excellence awards. These people come from all types of organizations and from all levels within those organizations. Participants include CEOs, corporate quality directors, state organization chiefs, small business owners, heads of hospitals, teachers, professors, medical doctors, and school superintendents, to name a few.

This book was originally developed for them. It was used as a teaching text to guide their decisions and deliberations as they provided feedback to organizations that documented their continuous improvement efforts using Baldrige Award-type management systems. Many examiners who used this text asked me to publish it in a stand-alone format. They wanted to use it to help their own organizations, customers, and suppliers guide and assess their continuous improvement efforts.

These two groups of readers—examiners of quality systems and leaders of high-performing organizations—can gain a competitive edge by understanding not only the parts of a high-performance management system, but how these parts connect and align. My goal for this book is that readers will understand fully what each area of the quality system means for organizations and find the synergy within the seven major parts of the system: leadership, strategic planning, customer and market focus, information and analysis, human resource focus, process management, and business results.

Organization leaders have reported that this book has been valuable as a step-by-step approach to help identify and put in place continuous improvement systems. As this progresses, improvement efforts in one area will lead to improvements in other areas. This process is similar to experiences we have all encountered as we carry out home improvement: improve one area, and many other areas needing improvement become apparent. This book will help identify areas that need immediate improvement as well as areas that are less urgent but, nevertheless, vitally linked to organizational and operational excellence.

I am continually looking for feedback about this book and suggestions about how it can be improved. Please contact me by phone at Quantum Performance Group, Inc. 315-986-9200; e-mail me at Blazey@QuantumPerformance.com; or visit our Web site at www.QuantumPerformance.com.

Introduction

The Malcolm Baldrige National Quality Award 2002 Criteria for Performance Excellence and scoring guidelines are powerful assessment instruments that help leaders identify organizational strengths and key opportunities for improvement. The primary task of leaders is then to use the information to achieve higher levels of performance.

Building an effective management system capable of driving performance improvement is an ongoing challenge because of the intricate web of complex relationships among management, labor, customers, stakeholders, partners, and suppliers. The best organizations have a management system that improves its work processes continually. They measure every key facet of business activity and closely monitor organizational performance. Leaders of these organizations set high expectations, value employees and their input, communicate clear directions, and align the work of everyone to achieve organizational goals and optimize performance.

Unfortunately, because of the complexity of modern management systems, the criteria used to examine them are also complex and difficult to understand. *Insights to Performance Excellence 2002* helps performance excellence examiners and organization improvement practitioners clearly understand the 2002 Baldrige Performance Excellence Criteria and the linkages and relationships between the items.

Six types of information are provided in this book for each of the 18 items that comprise the criteria:

1. **The actual language of each item, including notes** (presented in the shadow box). [Author's Note: The information in these shadow boxes presents the official Baldrige criteria and serves as the only basis for the examination. The other five types of information presented in this book for each Item (elements 2 through 6 below) provide the author's interpretation of the official Criteria requirements and should not be used as a basis for establishing additional requirements during an examination or performance review.]

2. **A plain-English explanation of the requirements of each Item** with some suggestions about the rationale for the Item and ways to meet key requirements.

3. **A summary of the requirements of each Item in flowchart form.** The flowcharts capture the essence of each item and isolate the requirements of each item to help organizations focus on the key points the item is assessing. Note that most boxes in the flowcharts contain an item reference in brackets [ ]. This indicates that the criteria require the action. If there is no item reference in brackets, it means the action is suggested but not required. Occasionally a reference to "[scoring guidelines]" is included in a box. This means that the authority foe the requirement comes from the scoring guidelines.

4. **The key linkages between each item and the other items.** The major or primary linkages are designated using a solid arrow (——▶). The secondary linkages are designated using a dashed arrow (---▶).

5. **An explanation of some potential adverse consequences that an organization might face if it fails to implement processes required by each Item.** (Examiners may find this analysis useful as they prepare relevant feedback concerning opportunities for improvement. However, these generic statements should be ustomized—based on key factors, core values, or specific circumstances facing the organization being reviewed—before using them to develop feedback comments supporting opportunities for improvements in Categories 1 through 6.)

6. **Examples of effective practices that some organizations have developed and followed consistent with the requirements of the Item.** These samples present some ideas about how to meet requirements. (Remember, examiners should not convert these sample effective practices into new requirements for organizations they are examining.)

Changes to this 2002 edition include:

- New information to help leaders focus on priority opportunities for improvement and understand better the role they must play in refining their management systems and processes

- An analysis of some of the adverse consequences organizations may face by failing to implement processes required by the performance excellence criteria

- Additional definitions to enhance understanding of key words in the Criteria and Scoring guidelines

Insights to Performance Excellence 2002 will strengthen your understanding of the criteria and provide insight on analyzing your organization, improving performance, and applying for the award.

Insights to Performance Excellence

This section provides information for leaders who are transforming their organizations to achieve performance excellence. This section:

- Presents a business case for using the Baldrige Criteria to improve organizational performance

- Describes the core values that drive organizational change to high levels of performance and underlie the Baldrige Criteria

- Provides practical insights and lessons learned—ideas on transition strategies to put high-performance systems in place and promote organizational learning

This section emphasizes themes driven by the 2002 Criteria and core values. It also includes suggestions about how to start down the path to systematic organizational improvement, as well as lessons learned from those who chose paths that led nowhere or proved futile despite their best efforts.

BALDRIGE BEGINNINGS AND ONGOING REFINEMENT

During the decade of the 1980s, many U.S. businesses suffered losses in the marketplace due to stronger international competition. We found that for nearly 30 years, Japanese business leaders were able to improve the performance of their organizations by following the teachings of W. Edwards Deming and striving to meet the requirements of the Deming Prize Criteria. The power of the Japanese recovery from the devastation of World War II to a dominant global economic power was documented in a CBS documentary entitled, *If Japan Can, Why Can't We?*

The documentary explained the strong, positive impact that the prize had on the desire and ability of Japanese business leaders to improve organizational performance. Moreover, it served as a catalyst for the creation of a national quality award for the United States. It was hoped that a similar award would help U.S. business leaders focus on the systems and processes that would lead them to recovery much as the Deming Prize Criteria helped the Japanese.

After nearly five years of work, in 1987, the U.S. Congress created the national quality award named in honor of the Secretary of the Department of Commerce, Malcolm Baldrige, who had died a short time earlier in a rodeo accident. The Malcolm Baldrige National Quality Award or "Baldrige Award" had one key purpose: to help U.S. businesses improve their competitiveness in the global marketplace.

After much debate and discussion, the creators of the award criteria—led by Dr. Curt Reimann of the U.S. Department of Commerce—agreed that the award criteria should not be based on theories of how organizations ought to conduct business in order to win. They had seen too many instances where organizations followed the many piecemeal theories of the management gurus that led nowhere.

On the other hand, some argued that the United States should simply adopt the Deming Prize Criteria which had been in place for 35 years. However, after monitoring the performance of earlier Deming Prize winners, it became apparent that the practices that enabled many of them to achieve high performance in the past were no longer sufficient to ensure high performance in the present. Changes in the marketplace, customer requirements, competition, worker skills and availability, and technology (to name a few) have forced organizations to change the way they manage their business in order to continue to succeed and win.

The designers of the U.S. national award wanted to avoid problems presented by both approaches. Accordingly, the principle was adopted that the criteria must be continually refreshed and be based on the verified management practices of the world's best-performing companies that enabled them to achieve such high levels of performance, productivity, customer satisfaction, and market dominance.

In order to make sure that the Baldrige Criteria for Performance Excellence continue to be relevant, the U.S. Department of Commerce, National Institute of Standards and Technology reviews the drivers of high performance each year. Based on these analyses, the criteria for the Malcolm Baldrige National Quality Award are validated and refined.

In spite of this ongoing renewal, some critics of the Baldrige Criteria argue that the Baldrige standards are "outdated" and "passé." These critics often ask, "If the Baldrige Criteria are updated each year, why don't they reflect the newest management techniques?" They seem to prefer to employ unproven theories of what is needed to be successful in today's global market, pointing to the rising success of e-commerce and the dot-coms. None of these critics, however, have been able to offer any performance-based evidence to support their opinion. In fact, the collapse of thousands of badly managed dot-coms seems to indicate that unproven theories and management fads do no more to build solid performance today than they did in prior decades.

The main reason why the Baldrige Criteria do not require the use of the latest management fads is because a management practice must be a proven driver of high performance before the practice is included as a requirement. Such "proofs" require strong evidence of widespread practice and related performance outcomes.

A new management practice might work well for one organization but not for another. Fact-based evidence must demonstrate that the practice leads to high performance in all types of organizations including, for example, small and large, manufacturing and service, union and nonunion, public and private.

Because it usually takes two or more years for a "promising practice" to prove its value, the Baldrige Criteria will lag behind the newest, unproven fads. However, the rigor of the Baldrige review is part of the value the Baldrige Criteria add to business excellence. The criteria help leaders sort out the fads from the proven techniques. The Baldrige Criteria reflect leading-edge, validated management practices essential to achieving optimum performance.

Finally, it is important to mention that the Baldrige Criteria were never intended to limit innovation and creativity—in fact, the criteria require those traits in an organization. Specifically, the criteria require leaders to promote innovation throughout the organization [1.1a(2)] and in work and jobs [5.1a(1)]. The criteria also require, in many areas, that the organizations keep management techniques current with changing business needs, including: listening to customers [3.1a(3)], building relationships with customers [3.2a(4)], determining customer satisfaction [3.2b(4)], performance measurement system [4.1a(3)], data availability and reliability [4.2a(3)], software and hardware systems [4.2b(2)], work and jobs [5.1a(1)], and business processes [6.1b(5), 6.2a(6), and 6.3a(7)].

The best leaders use the principles described by the Baldrige Criteria as the fundamental way they manage the organization, and then search for ways to refine and enhance their work systems to provide a little more competitive advantage. They experiment with new techniques and are not content to simply follow a "management cookbook." However, they instill a solid management system first, then experiment and improve—not the other way around.

Many of these top leaders use the Baldrige principles and management systems to achieve high performance without any public announcements or fanfare. They have never applied for the award and do not intend to do so. They are content to achieve excellence and win in the business world, rather than compete for a prize.

Nearly all business leaders and managers that reject the value of the criteria out-of-hand do not understand the principles they contain, even those that claim to have "tried Baldrige." The system that effectively drives top performance in organizations is complex. After all, if it was easy to achieve excellence, everyone would do it. The business landscape is littered with companies that never understood or failed to continue using the validated, leading-edge management practices defined by the Baldrige Criteria. This book is for those leaders who are willing and able to commit to becoming effective leaders and optimizing performance.

THE BUSINESS CASE FOR USING THE BALDRIGE PERFORMANCE EXCELLENCE CRITERIA

All leaders know that change is not easy. They will be asked and perhaps tempted to turn back many times. They may not even be aware of these temptations or of the backsliding that occurs when their peers and subordinates sense their commitment is wavering. Those leaders who are dedicated to achieving high performance appreciate examples of success from organizations that are ahead of them on the journey. These are organizations that have held the course despite nagging doubts, organizational turbulence, and attempts at sabotage.

The following section of the book:

- Summarizes perceptions and predictions about business trends and the value of the Malcolm Baldrige Award, based on survey responses of chief executive officers from 308 major U.S. organizations. (This survey was conducted by the Foundation for the Malcolm Baldrige National Quality Award, April 1998.)

- Summarizes research on financial performance of approximately 400 firms that were recognized by local, state, or national awards for quality management practices. (Research results are reported with permission of Dr. Vinod R. Singhal. Research was conducted by Kevin B. Hendricks and Vinod R. Singhal.)

- Describes public and private sector organizations that have gained ground and made rapid strides forward on their journeys, having achieved recognition as winners of the Malcolm Baldrige National Quality Award. It then identifies the core values that have guided these organizations to achieve high levels of performance excellence.

VALUE OF BALDRIGE CRITERIA AND AWARDS

In a report entitled "The Nation's CEOs Look to the Future," 308 CEOs from large, small, and several non-corporate organizations described what they believe lies ahead for business in the United States and the value of the Baldrige Criteria and Award.[1] These trends relate in many ways to the 2002 criteria and will be considered each year as the criteria are revised to reflect the current business environment and the most effective management practices for that environment.

The vast majority (67 percent to 79 percent) of the CEOs believe that the Baldrige Criteria and Awards are very or extremely valuable in stimulating improvements in quality and competitiveness in U.S. businesses. Given the trends and business environment they describe in the survey, and how they see U.S. businesses keeping pace, the criteria provide a valuable competitive advantage.

Major Trends

More than 70 percent of the CEOs reported the trends listed below as major ones that will be likely to effect the business environment significantly in the coming years:

- **Globalization.** This trend, identified as critical by 94 percent of respondents, has implications for all categories, but particularly Strategic Planning, where global competition and alliances must be included in planning, and for Customer and Market Focus, where building and maintaining customer relationships is critical.

- **Improving Knowledge Management.** This trend, identified as critical by 88 percent of respondents, means that knowledge acquisition management is and will continue to be a significant competitive advantage. How Information and Analysis as well as training, education, and sharing of best practices are managed will be key to performance excellence.

- **Cost and Cycle-Time Reduction.** This trend, identified as critical by 79 percent of respondents, is particularly relevant to Process Management. Organizations that effectively manage key product and service design and delivery processes will have a competitive edge in the global marketplace.

---

[1]"The Nation's CEOs Look to the Future: A Survey Conducted for the Foundation for the Malcolm Baldrige National Quality Award." Data collection: February–April 1998. Results tabulated and analyzed by Louis Harris & Associates, Inc.

- **Improving Supply Chains Globally.** This trend, identified as critical by 78 percent of respondents, is a companion to the trend already described as Globalization. As business is increasingly taking place on the global stage, supply chain management needs to improve— either with direct suppliers and partners or beyond to partnerships and alliances. These requirements are particularly important to Process Management.

- **Manufacturing at Multiple Locations in Many Countries.** This trend, identified as critical by 76 percent of respondents, again relates to Globalization and also to Improving Supply Chain Management. To be successful at multiple country manufacturing, one needs to use a systems approach involving all Categories from Strategic Planning to Process Management, with a strong focus on Customers and Markets as well as Human Resources.

- **Managing the Use of More Part-Time, Temporary, and Contract Workers.** This trend, identified as critical by 71 percent of respondents, reflects the rapidly changing environment that businesses operate within. The "hot" skills and technologies of today become out of date quickly. The product and service focus of today is tomorrow's throw away. Organizations must manage successfully with a more flexible and contingent workforce. Yet they must still manage that workforce effectively; they still need the right skills and knowledge, motivation and incentives, and satisfaction from work. This trend is a major challenge particularly relevant to the Human Resource Focus Category.

Other Major Trends

More than 51 percent of the CEOs reported the trends listed below as major ones that will be likely to effect business in the years ahead. These include (from most cited, 69 percent, to least cited, 52 percent):

- Developing new employee relationships based on performance

- Improving human resources management

- Improving the execution of strategic plans

- Developing more appropriate strategic plans

- Ongoing measurement and analysis of organizational processes

- Developing a consistent global corporate culture

- Outsourcing of manufacturing

- Creating a learning organization

These trends, together with the ones listed above, present a picture of what CEOs predict will be major business trends in the coming decade. The case for using the Baldrige Criteria as a way to manage effectively is validated and strengthened by the specific trends, their close relationship to the criteria, and also by the next section, in which the same CEOs rate the competencies that major U.S. industries must possess to take advantage of these trends as a competitive advantage. CEOs report a huge gap between current state competency and future/desired state competency for many major trends. For example:

- Almost all of the CEOs report Globalization as a major trend, but only 18 percent rate major U.S. organization competency as excellent. Seventy percent rated the competency as only fair.

- Improving Knowledge Management was cited by 88 percent of CEO respondents as a major trend, but only 23 percent see U.S. organization competency as excellent. Fifty-five percent rate the competency level as only fair.

- Competency in Cost and Cycle-Time Reduction was rated as excellent by 31 percent and only fair by 52 percent.

These are a sample of competency gaps cited by CEOs in the survey. They reiterate the need to use proven management practices to close these gaps and ensure that U.S. organizations remain or become leaders in the global marketplace to sustain our quality of life.

CEO Skills Needing Improvement

CEOs were asked as part of the survey to reflect on their skills and their peer group's skills and to report on which skills were most in need of improvement. The skills cited below were thought by more than 50 percent to need "a great deal" of improvement. They are key to addressing the major business trends reported earlier in this section. The skills include:

- The ability to think globally and execute strategies successfully

- Flexibility in a changing world

- The ability to develop appropriate strategies and rapidly redefine their business

- The understanding of new technologies

Another 40 to 50 percent of CEOs believe that these skills also need to improve "a great deal." Skills needing improvement include the ability to:

- Work well with different stakeholders

- Create a learning organization

- Make the right bets about the future

- Be a visible, articulate, charismatic leader

- Be a strong enough leader to overcome opposition

Stakeholders and Interests that are Becoming More Important

The majority of CEOs (75 percent or more) think that international customers, consumers, and employees are becoming more important to business success. Over 60 percent believe that suppliers, outside board directors, and institutional shareholders are also becoming more important. Addressing requirements of the Customer and Market Focus Category and Employee Focus Categories is increasing in importance, according to the CEOs surveyed.

Execution of Strategies is Critical

When asked which required more improvement—the development or execution of appropriate strategies, CEOs selected "Execution" by about a three-to-one margin. This means that alignment of work and realis-

tic action plans need to be improved along with accountability. If the organization is pulling in different directions it is more difficult to accomplish individual unit or division priorities—energies and resources are being drained, execution is flawed, and results are suboptimized.

Expanding Market Size is Critical

When asked which is more important—to increase market share or expand market size, CEOs selected "Expanding Market Size" by over a four-to-one margin. This will require improved Leadership, Strategic Planning, and Customer and Market Focus, particularly in the global economy. It will also require a more skilled and diverse workforce and more effective work processes.

The Competition Ahead

CEOs had various ideas about where the most serious competition to their businesses will come from in the next decade. Only a small number (12 percent) thought the toughest competition would come from other Fortune 500 companies. About 33 percent thought it was most likely to come from U.S. companies not yet on the Fortune 500 list. About 30 percent thought their toughest competitors were most likely to be foreign companies. Some saw start-up, entrepreneurial businesses as being the most serious competition. Comparing services and products to the competition and determining what the competition is doing to satisfy its customers is central to Baldrige-based assessments.

It is interesting, though, that most CEOs did not see the most serious competitors as being the major Fortune 500 companies of today. Perhaps this, more than any other CEO opinion, presents a compelling case for using the Baldrige Criteria—the fast and relentless pace of business change where companies on top today are not likely to be on top tomorrow without corresponding changes and improvements in their business.

Research Supports the Business Case

Two researchers were interested in quality award winners and to what extent (if any) quality management impacted financial performance. The research of Dr.

Kevin B. Hendricks from the College of William and Mary, School of Business and Vinod R. Singhal from the Georgia Institute of Technology, Dupree College of Management is the basis for the following piece of evidence that supports the use of the Baldrige Criteria.[2]

Their research looked beyond "hype and the popular press" to the real impact of quality management and examined the facts surrounding performance excellence. The research was based on about 600 recipients of various quality awards and similar recognition. The recognition provided to these organizations was based upon similar core values and concepts. Companies were mostly manufacturing firms (75 percent). All were publicly traded companies. Although they did not find that quality management turned "straw into gold," their research added significantly to the business case for using the criteria as a tool to enhance performance.

Hendricks and Singhal examined the following efficiency or growth measures to examine:

- Percent change in sales

- Stock price performance

- Percent change in total assets

- Percent change in number of employees

- Percent change in return on sales

- Percent change in return on assets

Implementation Costs Do Not Negatively Impact the Bottom Line

The research examined two five-year periods during the quality management implementation cycle. The first period can be called *beginning implementation*. This period started six years before and ended one year before the receipt of their first award. During this period, organizations are implementing quality

[2]This research is described in the following papers: K.B. Hendricks and V.R. Singhal, "Quality Awards and the Market Value of the Firm; An Empirical Investigation," *Management Science* 42:3 (1996): 415–436; K.B. Hendricks and V.R. Singhal, "Does Implementing an Effective TQM Program Actually Improve Operating Performance? Empirical Evidence From Firms that Have won Quality Awards," *Management Science* 43:9 (1997): 1258–1274; K.B. Hendricks and V.R. Singhal, "The Long-Run Stock Price Performance of Firms with Effective TQM Programs," working paper, Georgia Institute of Technology and The College of William and Mary, 1998.

management and incurring associated costs of implementation such as training, communications, and production and design changes. The researchers found no significant differences in financial measures between these companies (winners) and the control group of companies (nonwinners but similar in other respects) for this period. This is important because of the costs (both direct and indirect) associated with implementing quality management systems. The research suggests that the significant cost savings identified during this period of intensified focus on cycle time, time to market, and other factors pay for the implementation costs.

Improved Financial Results Can Be Expected With Successful Implementation

The study then examined results of companies from one year before winning the award to four years after the award was given. This period can be called *mature implementation* and it is in this period that one would expect the improved management to bear fruit. This was the case with this research. There were significant differences in financial performance between award winners and controls (nonwinners). For example, the growth in operating income averaged 91 percent for winners contrasted to 43 percent for non-award winners. Award-winning companies reported 69 percent growth in sales compared with 32 percent for the control group. The total assets of the winning companies increased 79 percent compared to 37 percent for the controls. Winners had significantly better results than the control group. The graphs on page 7 represent the study findings.

They found that award-winning companies outperformed control firms (non-award-winning companies) at least two-to-one, as Figure 1 indicates.

Hendricks and Singhal also found, prior to the period of implementation of these quality principles, that there was no significant difference between the companies. After implementation, performance of the award-winning firms was significantly better, suggesting the difference was due to the performance excellence systems that they installed.

In addition, Hendricks and Singhal found that small companies did significantly better than large companies in implementing the quality principles. Although large companies may have more resources with which to implement these systems, small companies may have an easier time deploying these sys-

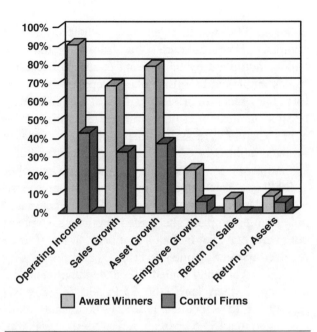

Figure 1 Comparison of Award-Winning and Control Firms.

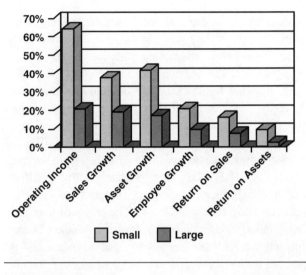

Figure 2 Comparison of Large and Small Award-Winning Companies.

tems fully throughout the organization and achieving maximum benefit.

• Although both small firms (less than $600m) and large firms benefit, small firms do even better

• Small winners outperformed the control counterparts by 63 percent, whereas large firms outperformed their controls by 22 percent

• A similar profile exists for low capital versus high capital-intensive award winners

Stock Price Performance of Winners is Significantly Better

Consistent with other efficiency and financial findings, the winners in the Hendricks and Singhal study all outperformed the S&P 500 Index by 115 percent to 80 percent. In actual dollars, the better performance would be worth $669 million for the average award winner. They also outperformed other benchmark composites from the New York, American, and NASDAQ stock exchanges. It is important to note here that most of the "winners" did not also win the Baldrige Award. Baldrige recipients performed two to three times better than the S&P 500 index (460 percent to 147 percent).

U.S. Department of Commerce Stock Price Study

For the past seven years, the Commerce Department's National Institute of Standards and Technology has compared winners of the Malcolm Baldrige National Quality Award to the Standard & Poor's 500. The Baldrige group consistently has outperformed the S&P 500. In the most recent study issued April 6, 2001, the Baldrige group beat the S&P 500 by 4.4 to 1. NIST has conducted the Baldrige Index study since 1995. That year it outperformed the S&P 500 by 6.5 to 1, and has beaten it each year since.

Methodology. A hypothetical sum was invested in each of the 1990–1999, publicly-traded Baldrige Award recipient's common stock, in the year they applied for the Award. The investment was tracked from the first business day of the month following the announcement of the Award recipients (or the date when they began public trading, if it is later), through December 1, 2000. One thousand dollars ($1000) was invested in each whole company, and for subsidiaries the sum invested was $1000 multiplied by the percent of the whole company's employee base the subunit represented at the time of its application. The same total dollar amount was invested in the Standard & Poor's (S&P) 500 on the same day. If a subunit was sold to another parent company, or if a company divested or merged, it was the subunit whose progress was followed, not the parent company's progress. The value of the original stock at the time of sale was determined and that dollar amount was reinvested in the new parent company.

Adjusting for stock splits, the value on December 1, 2000 was calculated. Information is reported two ways: all publicly-traded Award recipients and only whole company Baldrige Award recipients. The 24 publicly-traded Award recipients, as a group, outperformed the S&P 500 by approximately 4.2 to 1, achieving a 685.26 percent return compared to a 163.11 percent return for the S&P 500. The group of five, publicly traded, whole company Award recipients outperformed the S&P 500 by 4.4 to 1, achieving a 764.84 percent return compared to a 173.34 percent return for the S&P 500. A summary of the results follows.

1990–1999 Publicly Traded Award Recipients

	$ Investment	$ Value - 12/1/00	Change
1990–1999 All Award Recipients	7282.35	57,185.19	685.26%
S&P 500	7282.35	19,160.33	163.11%

1990–1999 Publicly Traded Whole Company Award Recipients

	$ Investment	$ Value - 12/1/00	Change
1990–1999 Whole Company Award Recipients	5000	43,241.93	764.84%
S&P 500	5000	13,667.22	173.34%

Results of 1990–1999 Baldrige Site Visited Applicants

10-Year Common Stock Comparison

Methodology. A hypothetical sum was invested in each 1990–1999 publicly traded, site visited applicant's common stock in the year they applied for the Award or in the year they became public. (In this study, the site visited applicant group includes Baldrige Award recipients.) The investment was tracked from the first business day of the month following the announcement of the Baldrige Award recipients (or the date when they began public trading, if it is later) through December 1, 2000. One thousand

dollars ($1000) was invested in each whole site visited company. For subsidiaries, the sum invested was $1000 multiplied by the percent of the parent company's employee base the subunit represented at the time they received a site visit or at the time they became public as a result of a merger or acquisition by a new parent. The same total dollar amount was invested in the S&P 500 index value on the same day.

Adjusting for stock splits, the value on December 1, 2000 was calculated. Information is reported two ways: all publicly traded site visited applicants and only whole company site visited applicants. (Note: a company may be included multiple times if they received more than one site visit.)

The 70 publicly traded site visited applicants, as a group, outperformed the S&P 500 by approximately 2.1 to 1, achieving a 321.80 percent return compared to a 153.54 percent return for the S&P 500. The group of 13 whole company site visited applicants outperformed the S&P 500 by almost 2 to 1, achieving a 312.39 percent return compared to a 158.12 percent return for the S&P 500. Names of Baldrige applicants are kept confidential. A summary of the results follows.

1990–1999 Publicly Traded Site Visited Award Applicants

	$ Investment	$ Value - 12/1/00	Change
1990–1999 Site Visit Applicants	23,537.43	99,280.06	321.80%
S&P 500	23,537.42	59,676.37	153.54%

1990–1999 Publicly Traded Whole Company Site Visited Award Applicants

	$ Investment	$ Value - 12/1/00	Change
1990–1999 Whole Company Site Visited Applicants	13,000	53,610.91	312.39%
S&P 500	13,000	33,555.82	158.12%

For a copy of the Baldrige Index stock study, see the World Wide Web at www.nist.gov/public_affairs/releases/stockstudy.htm or fax a request to 301-926-1630.

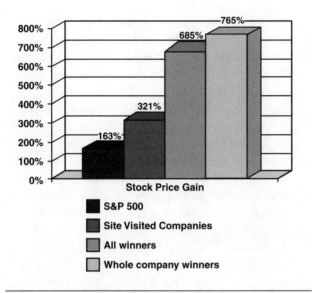

Figure 3 Baldrige Stock Study.

Quality Management is a Long-Term Solution
Companies that expect immediate gains from quality management systems are likely to be disappointed. It took years to create the culture you have today; it can take years to change it. Nevertheless, this research, combined with other results, makes a solid business case for using Baldrige-based management Criteria as the way to run the successful business of the future.

High-Performing Organizations

High-performing organizations outrun their competition by delivering value to stakeholders through an unwavering focus on customers and improved organizational capabilities. Examples of improved capabilities have occurred in all sectors of the economy, not just the private sector. These results range from time and cost savings to customer retention and loyalty.

Many examples of significant improvements are evident from using the Baldrige-based management system.

Consider the performance of the five winners of the 2001 Baldrige Award:

- Clarke American Checks, in San Antonio, Texas provides personalized checks, checkbooks, checking account and bill-paying accessories, and financial forms to financial services partners across the United States. Services include customer contact call centers and e-commerce and direct response marketing solutions on behalf of their partners. Since 1996, its market share increased 50 percent. In the same period, revenue increased both in actual dollars and percentage growth—from $300 million in 1995 to $462 million in 2000. Revenue growth has improved from 4.2 percent in 1996 to 16 percent in 2000, compared to the average industry growth of less than 1 percent. Revenue generated by customer service operations increased 279 percent from 1997 to 2000; revenue from e-commerce solutions has increased 1,077 percent since January 2000; and direct response marketing revenue has increased over 768 percent from 1995 to 2000.

Clarke American's overall associate satisfaction improved from 72 percent in 1994 to 84 percent in 2000, with over 96 percent responding. Customer satisfaction of business products reached 98 percent for September 2001, outperforming the banking industry average of 90 percent. Manufacturing Cycle Time (in-plant production time) improved by over 44 percent since 1995 and is under 18 hours for 2001 year-to-date. Check Manufacturing Units per Hour improved over 150 percent since 1991, increasing from 10 to 26. Levels of internal errors decreased 55 percent since 1995 and met Industry Week magazine's average for Best Plants. The S.T.A.R (Suggestions, Teams, Actions, Results) Program encourages associates to capture, implement, and share process improvements. Clarke American has implemented six S.T.A.R. ideas per associate for 2001 year-to-date, which exceeds the average level reported by the Employee Involvement Association. S.T.A.R. ideas implementation rates have increased from below 20 percent in 1995 to 70 percent, or over 20,000 ideas implemented for 2001 year-to-date. The company's Team Excellence program (an award program for high-performing teams) is responsible for over $15 million in cost reductions and $103 million in revenue growth from 1996–2000.

- The Chugach School District Office is based in Anchorage, Alaska. Chugach's 214 students are scattered throughout 22,000 square miles of south central Alaska. With 30 faculty and staff, CSD is the smallest organization to ever win a Baldrige Award. CSD delivers education instruction in the workplace, community, home, and school to students from preschool up to age 21. With heavy use of technology, education programs are provided 24-hours a day, seven days a week. Half of the students in the district are Alaska Natives. Results on the California Achievement Tests improved in all content areas from 1995 to 1999. Average national percentile scores increased in reading from 28th to 71st, in language arts from 26th to 72nd, in math from 54th to 78th, and in spelling from 22nd to 65th. In addition, the percent of students in the top quartile increased in reading from 17 to 56, in language arts from 25 to 33, and in math from 42 to 79. The percentage of CSD students who take college entrance exams has increased from 0 to 70 percent since 1998.

CSD's percentage of state funds that are used for instruction increased steadily from 51 percent in 1995 to 82 percent in 2001, surpassing the state's mandatory guideline of 70 percent. Every CSD student has an Individual Learning Plan (ILP) developed jointly with students, teachers, and parents to enable students to learn at their own pace. The district increased the number of computers from two per 27 students in 1994 to 21 per 27 students in 2001. Overall student use of the Internet increased from 5 percent in 1998 to 93 percent in 2001.

CSD reduced the faculty turnover rate from an average of 55 percent during 1975–1994 to an average of 12 percent during 1995–2000. Isolated working conditions contribute to faculty turnover despite high levels of satisfaction that range from 75 percent to 81 percent on a national satisfaction survey.

- The Pearl River School District (PRSD) located 20 miles north of New York City has three elementary schools, one middle school, and one high school. The district has about 330 employees and approximately 2460 students. Ninety-four percent of the students that begin their schooling in Pearl River complete their high

school education in the district. The percentage of students graduating with a Regents diploma increased from 63 percent in 1996 to 86 percent in 2001, while the percentage of students in schools with similar socio-economic profiles decreased to 58 percent. PRSD achieved a 90 percent passing rate in 2001. Helping students to prepare for college, PRSD improved Advanced Placement course performance from 34 percent of the students achieving a "3" or better in 1997 to 76 percent in 2001, while dramatically increasing the percentage of students taking the AP courses. The percentage of students taking the SAT I exam and the level of achievement increased over the past five years, approaching the highest reporting district in New York, and exceeds both the state and national averages. In addition, 75 percent of special education students take the SAT I exam (a rate that substantially exceeds the state and national averages of 3 and 2 percent respectively). While PRSD students and parents have a choice of more than 80 private and parochial schools in the district's service area, PRSD has increased its market share (percentage of all students eligible to attend PRSD who actually enroll in the district) from 71 percent in 1990 to 90 percent in 2000.

PRSD reduced non-instructional expenditures an average of 21 percent during the period 1994 to 2001. Instructional expenditures increased 43 percent during this same period. Student satisfaction, measured using a national survey, increased from 70 percent in 1998 to 92 percent in 2001 and surpasses the highest score in the survey's databank. Parent satisfaction, measured with the same survey instrument, increased from 62 percent in 1996 to 96 percent in 2001 and exceeds the highest score in the databank. Staff and faculty satisfaction, measured using a national survey, increased over the past four years from 89 percent to 98 percent for staff and 86 percent to 96 percent for faculty, which also exceeds the survey databank's highest reported score.

PRSD uses curriculum maps, developed by teams of teachers and senior leaders, to align its entire K–12 curriculum to state and national standards and align instruction within and across all grade levels. These maps, which detail the content area covered as well as the method of instruction and assessment techniques, are adjusted quarterly based on data analyses and through benchmarking the best practices of other school districts.

- The University of Wisconsin-Stout campus has about 1200 faculty and staff and about 7700 students. UW-Stout offers 27 undergraduate and 16 graduate degrees through three academic colleges: the College of Technology, Engineering, and Management; the College of Human Development; and the College of Arts and Sciences. In addition, UW-Stout also provides a variety of outreach programs and services to business, industry, and society. UW-Stout has developed an approach to leadership that has resulted in empowerment of faculty, staff, and students. High alumni satisfaction results exceed UW system and national averages. More than 90 percent of graduate program alumni and nearly 90 percent of undergraduate alumni say they would attend the university again. Employer ratings of graduates have consistently rated 99 to 100 percent of Stout graduates as "prepared for work."

  UW-Stout has developed partner relationship building processes to enhance the university's ability to deliver educational services and expand service to more students, locations, and programs. For over six years, this key educational delivery strategy has involved 27 partners, including technical colleges; K–12 systems; universities; professional and trade associations; Wisconsin, other U.S., and international organizations; and businesses. The percent of budget allocated to instruction has increased from 55 percent in 1997 to almost 60 percent in 2001, outperforming the UW system comprehensive university average.

- Pal's Sudden Service is a privately owned quick-service restaurant company with 17 locations in northeastern Tennessee and southwestern Virginia. Pal's has about 465 employees; 95 percent are in direct production and service

roles and 5 percent in management. Pal's competes directly with national fast food chains and offers a menu of hamburgers, hot dogs, chipped ham, chicken, french fries, and beverages as well as breakfast biscuits with country ham, sausage, and gravy. Even with substantially decreased sales and profits throughout the hospitality industry, Pal's sales continue to increase. Pal's 2001 market share of nearly 19 percent is up from 10 percent in 1994. Pal's profit leads the primary competitor by three percentage points. Pal's health inspection scores have been in the high 90-point range (out of 100) since 1996, while the scores of its best competitor have been in the low-to-mid 80-point range. In customer satisfaction, including quality, speed, and customer feedback, Pal's is outperforming its primary competitor. Customer satisfaction for quality in 2001 is 95.8 percent versus 84.1 percent for its best competitor's. Pal's order handout speed has improved by over 30 percent since 1995, decreasing from 31 seconds to 20 seconds, compared to its competitors' performance, which increased from 73 seconds to 76 seconds over the same period. Pal's level of customer complaints over the last seven years is less than one-fourth of the level of the best/primary competitor and is continuing to trend downward.

Pal's uses a variety of processes to learn about customer expectations. Owner/Operators participate regularly in "Marketing-By-Walking-Around" activities, interviewing current and potential customers to identify their wants and needs. Additionally, Pal's has established a Web site that provides customers with information about its food products, administers a Pal's contest with store coupons as prizes, and includes local entertainment information. The Web site also provides customers with opportunities for communication, all of which are answered personally by the company's president.

Pal's reduced front line employee turnover from 200 percent in 1995 to 127 percent in 2000, and it continues to decline in 2001. In comparison, the best competitor's turnover rate in 2000 is over 300 percent. On-the-job injury/accident claims have declined 75 percent since 1992.

The performance of earlier winners is just as strong:

- Dana Corporation-Spicer Driveshaft Division is North America's largest independent manufacturer and marketer of driveshafts for light, medium, heavy duty, and off-highway vehicles. From 1997 to 1999, sales increased by nearly 10 percent; economic value added increased from $15 million to $35 million. Internal defect rates decreased over 75 percent from 1996 to 2000. Spicer worked closely with its supplier base to reduce material costs by 10 percent and parts-per-million defects to less than one-fifth of the best-known competitor. Spicer's market share is two to three times greater than the best competitor. Product reliability is the best in the industry for all product categories, and warranty claims are approximately one-third of the industry average. Customer satisfaction rates are the best in the industry and complaints are less than three per million units shipped. Finally, employee satisfaction and turnover are better than the best competitor.

- KARLEE Company is a contract manufacturer of precision sheet metal and machined components for the telecommunications, semiconductor, and medical equipment industries. Founded in 1974 out of a garage, KARLEE is a woman-owned business located in Garland, Texas with 550 team members. For the past six years, sales growth rate has averaged more than 25 percent per year. In 2000, KARLEE went from an assembly lead-time of two to three weeks to less than two days. Overall customer satisfaction ratings have improved 32.2 percent, while production volumes have more than tripled. Team member satisfaction results since 1995 have been higher than its competitors.

- Los Alamos National Bank is an independent community bank that provides a full range of financial services to the consumer, commercial, and government markets in New Mexico. Because of streamlined procedures, LANB approves home equity loans in two days or fewer while its competitors take from one to six weeks. Eighty percent of the bank's customers are "very satisfied" with the service they received, considerably higher than the levels received by its primary

competitors (52 to 40 percent) and the national average for banks (55 percent). Customer loyalty is more than five times the national average. The bank's net income increased by more than 60 percent over the last five years; annual return on stock exceeded the S&P 500 by 50 percent; return on average assets exceeded the national average every year since 1995; earnings per share increased from $1.20 in 1995 to nearly $2.00 in 1999. Productivity is also high: assets per employee increased from $5 million in 1995 to $7 million in 2000—$1.2 million higher than the best competitor and nearly $4 million higher than the national average. Employee turnover has been cut from 34 percent to 17 percent with an employee profit sharing plan.

- Operations Management International (OMI) in Greenwood Village, Colorado operates and maintains wastewater and water treatment facilities in 29 states and worldwide. It is a private company, owned by its employees. Total revenue increased from about $80 million in 1996 to about $145 million in 2000, an average annual growth rate of 15 percent, while top competitor revenues dropped by 4.5 percent. When OMI took over management of water treatment facilities from other companies, it reduced operating costs between 21 and 23 percent. OMI has never failed to meet expectations and has exceeded expectations for 88 percent of its industrial clients. Accident rates among employees are half of the national average. OMI doubled its workforce over the past two years and reduced turnover by one-third.

- BI, a 1999 Baldrige recipient, is a training organization that helps the performance of people, thus it helps its customers achieve their business goals. BI designs and delivers performance improvement programs that integrate communications, training, measurement, and rewards. These programs benefit customers' distributors, employees, and consumers. BI designs training and helps customers with organizational change and strategic planning, customer loyalty programs, and sales incentive programs. During the five years prior to the award, BI's revenue grew 47 percent. Its successful strategy has been to target strategic accounts to create a much higher rate of customer satisfaction rather than target growth in overall market share. Its products and services have resulted in customer loyalty that outperforms its top two competitors. It has retained an average of 73 percent of customers and an average of 96.3 percent of revenue.

- STMicroelectronics, a 1999 winner, designs, develops, manufactures, and markets semiconductor-integrated circuits for consumer electronics and automotive, medical, telecommunications, and computer applications in the United States and around the world. ST performed better than key competitors in many financial and growth areas during a very volatile decade in its market. Its revenue grew from $493 million to $937 million from 1994–98, which exceeded the average of seven competitors. Its market share has increased from 1.88 percent (1991) to 2.36 percent (1998). Employee empowerment is widespread. Its employee satisfaction survey results exceeded the industry composite in 8 of 10 factors.

- The Ritz-Carlton Hotel Company, a 1999 winner, manages 36 luxury hotels worldwide. It is the only service company to receive a Baldrige Award twice. The Ritz-Carlton holds the top position in complete satisfaction with a score of 70 percent, compared to 56 percent for its closest competitor on a recent nationwide survey. Since 1995, pre-tax return on investment has nearly doubled. Training is key to employee retention and the company's customer-focused culture. First-year managers and employees receive 250 to 310 hours of training. It has developed an innovative customer database to record guests' preferences and customize services to meet these preferences.

- Sunny Fresh Foods, a 1999 winner, is the first food manufacturer to receive the Baldrige Award. It manufactures further-processed egg products, including pasteurized refrigerated and frozen egg products, fat-free products, peeled hard-cooked eggs and precooked egg products such as omelets, french toast, and frozen scrambled eggs. This company has increased market share in U.S. markets from 14th in 1988 to sec-

ond in 1999. It has received numerous awards from its customers. Its return on gross investment has tripled in the last several years. All of Sunny Fresh Foods' facilities score in the excellent range on sanitation. It has many innovative work system designs that create a safe facility and minimize injuries.

- Boeing Airlift and Tanker, a 1998 Baldrige winner, designs, develops, and produces military transport aircraft. They targeted 50 key processes for improvement and cut cycle time by over 80 percent. Return on net assets is seven times greater than the next-best competitor. Net asset turnover improved sevenfold since 1994 while the return on sales improved threefold. Empowered employee teams have produced a 60 percent improvement in productivity.

- Texas Nameplate Company, a 1998 winner, makes identification labels. Their market share in Texas increased from 69 to 93 percent and almost doubled nationally. A gain-sharing program augments wages by 11 percent and has helped double net profit as a percent of sales in the last four years. Gross profit as a percent of sales is 59 percent.

- ADAC Laboratories of California, a 1996 Baldrige Award winner, designs, manufactures, markets, and supports products for healthcare customers. Customer retention increased from 70 to 90 percent during the past five years. Since 1990, average cycle time declined from 56 hours to 17 hours and revenue tripled.

- Wainwright Industries, a 1994 Baldrige winner, cut the time for making one of its principal extruded products from 8.75 days to 15 minutes, and reduced defect rates tenfold.

- Cadillac, a 1990 winner, reduced the time for die changes in its stamping plant from eight hours to four minutes by redesigning the entire process.

- Corning Telecommunications Products Division, a 1995 Baldrige Award winner, has become the world market leader and the low-cost provider, and has earned the highest customer satisfaction ratings in the industry by far.

- In five years, Solectron Corporation, a 1991 and 1997 Baldrige winner, experienced a sales increase from $130 million to $3.7 billion, representing a 2800 percent improvement. Net profits soared more than 10-fold. Market share doubled since 1992. The stock price went up 60-fold since 1989.

- Globe Metallurgical, a 1988 Baldrige winner, experienced a 60 percent increase in revenues and a 40 percent increase in profits since 1992.

- Ames Rubber Corporation, a 1993 Baldrige winner, achieved a 99.9 percent quality and on-time delivery status through sharing quality techniques with suppliers.

- AT&T Transmission Sales Business Unit, a 1992 winner, achieved a 10-fold improvement in equipment quality and a 50 percent reduction in cycle time that saved $400 million over six years.

U.S. government organizations have also implemented the Baldrige Criteria and produced savings, improvements, and efficiency similar to that found in the private sector. Between 1990 and 2000, the U.S. Congress has adopted more than $136 billion in savings. Improved processes for government procurement have saved more than $12 million alone. More than 1200 work teams inside of various government agencies have improved work processes and reduced costs to save approximately $37 billion.

Similar improvements have also been found in other sectors of the economy including health care, although fewer examples are present since the sectors have only recently begun to use the Baldrige principles as a way of optimizing their performance.

Economic Impact of the Baldrige National Quality Program

In October 2001, Albert N. Link, Department of Economics, University of North Carolina at Greensboro and John T. Scott, Department of Economics at Dartmouth College reported on a study they completed which examined the economic impact of the Baldrige National Quality Program. Specifically, their study examined the net private benefits associated with the Baldrige National Quality Program to the U.S. private and public sector and the relationship between econo-

mywide net benefits and the social costs associated with operating the Program.

Based on information collected from a mail survey of the U.S. organizational members of the American Society for Quality (ASQ), the conservative estimate of the value (in constant 2000 dollars) of the net private benefits associated with the Baldrige National Quality Program is $2.17 billion. Conservatively, Link and Scott estimate the value (in constant 2000 dollars) of social benefits associated with the Baldrige National Quality Program to be $24.65 billion. Based on information provided by the Baldrige National Quality Program, the value (in constant 2000 dollars) of social costs associated with the Program to date is $119 million. Therefore, from an evaluation perspective for the economy as a whole, the benefit-to-cost ratio characterizing the Baldrige National Quality Program is conservatively 207-to-1.

The Worldwide Use of the Baldrige Criteria

As indicated, since the launch of the Baldrige Award in 1987, the performance of U.S. companies using the Baldrige principles has steadily increased. U.S. companies began to recapture market share lost to international competition. When the reason for the increased success of U.S. companies became apparent, other countries throughout the world began to create their own national quality awards based on the Baldrige Criteria. Although the U.S. Congress did not intend the criteria to benefit companies throughout the world, that is precisely what has happened. After all, the criteria are not secret. Millions of copies of the criteria are distributed freely through the World Wide Web. Many books have been written about the criteria and its impact on business performance.

According to the U.S. Department of Commerce, more than 50 countries throughout the world have adopted the criteria as a basis for their own quality awards in an effort to improve the competitiveness of businesses in their own countries. The map in Figure 4, provided by the U.S. Department of Commerce in March 2000, indicates the proliferation of Baldrige-based quality awards. The countries in black do not have programs, the countries in grey do. In fact, since this map was developed, several additional countries have developed their own Baldrige-based award programs to increase competitiveness.

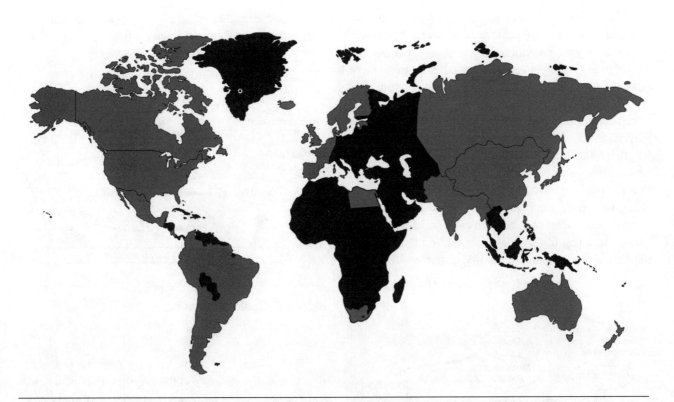

Figure 4 Key: Grey = countries with Baldrige-based quality award
Black = no award

THE INTEGRATED MANAGEMENT SYSTEM

Ingredients to Optimum Performance

Clearly, in today's highly competitive economy, past success means nothing. Desire, without disciplined and appropriate action, also means nothing. However, it is just as clear that implementing a disciplined approach to performance excellence based on the Baldrige Criteria produces winning levels of performance. The key to the success of the Baldrige Criteria has been the identification of the key drivers of high performance. The National Quality Award Office within the National Institute for Standards and Technology ensures that each element of the Baldrige Criteria is necessary, and together they are sufficient to achieve the highest levels of performance. Many management practices of the past have proven to be "necessary" ingredients of high performance. However, taken piecemeal, these practices by themselves have not been sufficient to achieve optimum performance.

Achieving winning levels of performance requires that each component of the organization's management system be optimized. In many ways, optimizing the performance of an organization's management system is like making an award-winning cake. Too much or too little of any key ingredient suboptimizes the system. For example, a cake may require eggs, flour, sugar, butter, and cocoa. A cake also requires a certain level of heat for a certain time in an oven. Too little or too much of any ingredient, including oven temperature, and the system (in this case the cake) fails to achieve desired results. The same principle is true in an organization. A successful organization requires a strong customer focus, skilled workers, efficient work processes, fact-based decision making, clear direction, and continuous improvement. Organizations that do not focus on all of these elements find that their performance suffers. Focusing on only a few of the required ingredients, such as reengineering to improve work processes or training to improve worker skills, are necessary but not sufficient by themselves to drive high levels of performance.

The following figures depict the elements necessary and sufficient to achieve high levels of performance in any organization or part of an organization. The elements apply to *any* managed enterprise, large or small, regardless of size, sector, product, or service.

Get Results, Produce Value. (Figure 5) In the first place, in order for an organization, a team, or an individual to stay in business (or keep a job) for any length of time, it must produce desired results. The work results must be valued. History has demonstrated that people, organizations, or even governments that failed to deliver value eventually went away or were overturned. Value can be measured in a variety of ways, including fitness for use, return on assets, profitability, reliability, and durability, to name a few.

Integrated Management System

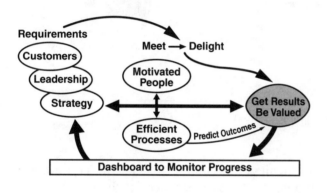

Figure 5 Get Results, Produce Value.

Customers. (Figure 6) Understand and meet their requirements. In addition, we have learned that it makes no difference if the producer of the goods or services believes they are valuable if the customer or user of the goods or services believes they are not. The customer is the only entity that can legitimately judge the value of the goods or services its suppliers produce. It is the customers who finally must decide whether the organization, team, or government continues to stay in business. Imagine you go to a restaurant, order seafood, and find that it tastes awful. Upon complaining about the bad tasting meal, it is not important to you that the chef claims that only the "finest ingredients were used." It also does not help if the chef claims that he likes the taste of the fish. It still tastes bad to you and unless the chef is willing to make an adjustment you are not going

to be satisfied and are unlikely to return. If enough customers find the food or service offensive and do not return, the restaurant goes out of business.

Integrated Management System

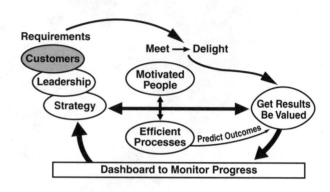

Figure 6 Customer requirements.

Accordingly, it is very important for the organization to clearly understand the requirements of its customers and obtain feedback from the customers after they have an opportunity to experience its products or services. The failure to understand the requirements of the customers may cause the organization to deliver the wrong thing, creating customer dissatisfaction, delay, or lower value. Every time our organizations fail to understand and meet customer requirements, value suffers. In order to consistently produce value, therefore, organizations must accurately determine the requirements of its customers and consistently meet or exceed those requirements. This creates the initial value chain that provides the competitive advantage for any organization or part of an organization.

To ensure that the customer is satisfied and likely to return (or recommend your service or product to others), it is important to determine if the customer received appropriate value. If the customer is dissatisfied, you have an opportunity to correct the problem and still maintain customer loyalty. In any case, it is important to remember that it is the customer and not the marketing department, engineering, manufacturing, or the service provider that ultimately judges value received and determines ultimate satisfaction.

Motivated People. (Figure 7) The next part of the management system to ensure optimum performance and value involves motivated people. In any organization or part of an organization, people do the work that produces customer value. As described above, if the work is not focused on customer requirements, customers may be dissatisfied. In order to satisfy customers, work may have to be redone, adding cost and suboptimizing value. In order to optimize output and value, people doing the work must have the willingness and desire to work. Disgruntled, disaffected, unwilling workers hurt productivity.

Integrated Management System

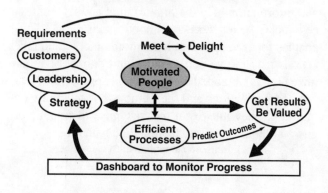

Figure 7 Motivated people.

However, "motivated people" means more than simply possessing the willingness to work. People must also possess the knowledge and skills to carry out their jobs effectively. In leading-edge technologies such as microelectronics engineering, the half-life of useful knowledge is 11 months. That means that one-half of the relevant knowledge of a microelectronics engineer becomes obsolete within 11 months. In 1989 the half-life was 18 months, approximately 50 percent greater. As new knowledge is created at an accelerating rate, it is more critical than ever to have effective training systems in place to ensure workers are up-to-date and can effectively apply the new knowledge.

In addition, in order to optimize output, people must be free from bureaucratic barriers and arbitrary restrictions that inhibit work. Every time work is delayed while waiting for an unnecessary approval adds cost but not value. Every time work has to be redone because of sloppy performance of a co-worker adds cost but not value. Every time that work has to be redone because of inadequate knowledge or ability adds cost but not value.

Remember that a single person cannot produce optimum levels of performance. However, a single person can prevent optimum levels of performance, and may not be aware that he or she is doing so. The question that should concern management is, "In your organization, how many people are disgruntled, discouraged, underskilled, or prevented from working effectively so that they suboptimize the organization's performance?"

Efficient Processes. (Figure 8) Even the most highly skilled, knowledgeable, and willing workers will fail to optimize value if asked to do stupid things. Over time, even the most efficient processes can become suboptimum and inefficient. Business process reengineering has been seen by some as a panacea for organizational optimization. Business process reengineering allows organizations to redesign and quickly eliminate much of the bureaucratic silliness and inefficiency that grows up over time. However, how long does it take for the newly reengineered process to lose efficiency? Even new processes must be evaluated periodically and improved or they eventually become suboptimal and obsolete. Ensuring that processes are optimal requires ongoing evaluation and refinement.

Integrated Management System

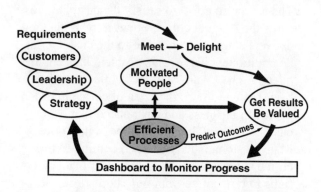

Figure 8 Efficient Process and predicting outcomes.

Every process in the organization has the potential for increasing or decreasing the value provided to customers. Obviously, core business processes are perhaps the most important. However, frequently the core processes of an organization are disrupted because of failed support processes. For example, production can come to a halt if key material from the procurement office is not available on time. Production can also be disrupted if key workers that were supposed to be provided by the personnel office are not available.

Any time an organization engages in rework, value for the customer is suboptimized. To make matters worse, if the need to engage in rework is not discovered until the product or service is complete, the cost of correction is higher, driving value lower. It is important, therefore, to uncover potential problems as early as possible, rather than wait for the end result to determine if the product or service is satisfactory. In order to uncover potential problems early we must be able to predict the outcomes of our work processes. This requires "in-process" measures. Through the use of these measures, organizations can determine if the product or service is likely to meet expectations. Consider the two examples that follow.

- Example one: A customer comes to the "Wait-And-See" coffee shop and orders a cup of coffee. The coffee is poured and delivered to the customer. The customer promptly takes a sip and informs the server that the coffee is too cold, too bitter, too weak, and has a harsh aroma. Furthermore, the customer complains that it took too long for the coffee to be served. The server, in effort to satisfy the customer, discards the original coffee, brews a fresh pot, and delivers a new cup of coffee to the customer at no additional charge. This problem happens frequently. The "Wait-And-See" coffee shop has been forced to raise the price of coffee in order to stay in business and has noticed that fewer customers are willing to pay the higher price. Many customers have stopped coming to this coffee shop entirely. The customers that continue to buy coffee from this shop are subsidizing the sloppy performance and poor quality.

- Example two: In order to increase the likelihood that its customers will like the coffee it serves, the "In-Process-Measure" coffee shop has asked its customers key questions about the quality of coffee and service that they expect. The "In-Process-Measure" coffee shop has determined through testing and surveys that its customers like coffee served hot (between 76 and 82 degrees Celsius); not too bitter or acidic (pH > 7.4); strong, but not too strong (75 grams of super-fine grind per liter of filtered water); with a fresh aroma (is served

within five minutes of brewing). By checking these measures, this coffee shop knows that nearly all customers will be satisfied with the quality and service it delivers. Since its customers like the coffee within the limits described above, no rework is required, no coffee is discarded, the price is lower, the value is higher, the store is profitable, and it is taking customers from the "Wait-And-See" coffee shop down the street.

Dashboard to Monitor Progress. (Figure 9) Data and information help the organization and its employees make better decisions about their work. This enables them to spot problems more quickly and take actions to improve performance and correct or minimize non-value-added costs. Without appropriate measures, organizations and their employees must rely on intuition. They must wait for customers to respond or guess at their likely satisfaction/dissatisfaction.

Integrated Management System

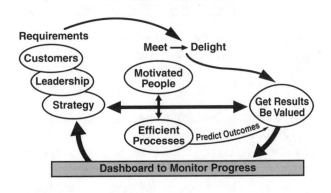

Figure 9 Information and data dashboard.

One of the problems in basing decisions on intuition or best guess is that it produces highly variable outcomes. The guess of one employee is not likely to be consistent with the guess of another. Appropriate data, therefore, are critical to increase decision making consistency and accuracy. In order for data to be used correctly to support decision making, organizations must develop a system to manage, collect, analyze, and display the results.

If the data that drive decision making are not accurate or reliable, effective decision making suffers. More mistakes are made, costs increase, and value is suboptimized. Furthermore, in the absence of relevant data and supporting analyses, leaders are generally unwilling to allow subordinates to substitute their intuition for that of the leader. As a result, decisions tend to get pulled to higher and higher levels in an organization, further suboptimizing the contribution of employees who are generally closest to and know the most about the work they do. Failure to fully utilize the talents of workers, as discussed above, further reduces efficiency, morale, and suboptimizes value production.

The system described in Figure 9, which includes customers, motivated people, efficient processes, and a dashboard to monitor progress leading to desired results and value, applies to any managed enterprise. It applies to whole corporations as well as departments, divisions, teams, and individual work. The system applies to schools, classrooms, government agencies, and health care organizations. In each case, in order to produce optimal value, the requirements of customers must be understood and met. People must be motivated, possess the skill and knowledge needed to do their work, and be free from distractions in order to optimize their performance. The organization must develop efficient work processes and monitor effectiveness of work to make adjustments in effort to maximize value.

Leadership. (Figure 10) What makes an organization unique is the direction that top leaders set for it. Leaders must understand the requirements of customers and the marketplace in deciding what direction is necessary to achieve success. However, it is not enough only to understand customer requirements. Leaders must also understand organizational capabilities and the needs and capabilities of employees, partners, and suppliers of critical goods and services.

Strategy. (Figure 11) Effective leaders use the process of strategy development to determine the most appropriate direction for the organization and identify the actions that must be taken to be successful in the future. Leaders use this strategy to identify the people and the processes that must be put in place to produce desired results and be valued by customers.

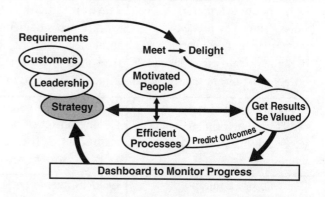

Integrated Management System

Figure 11 Stategy development and execution.

If leaders are not clear about the strategy and direction that must be taken to be successful, they force subordinates to substitute their own ideas about the proper direction and actions. This creates chaos within an organization. People come to work and want to be successful. Without direction from the top, they will still work hard but often at cross-purposes. Unless everyone is pulling in the same direction, processes, products, and services will not be optimized and value will be reduced.

Leaders cannot eliminate a single part of this management system and still expect to produce optimum value. Each part is necessary. Furthermore, studies repeatedly demonstrate that when these processes are integrated and used to run the business, they are sufficient to achieve high levels of performance. Imagine what might happen if one or more of the pieces of the integrated management system described above were missing. The following table provides some suggestions.

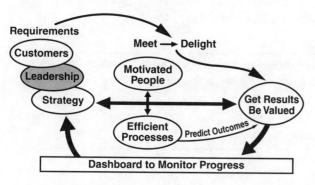

Integrated Management System

Figure 10 Leadership.

MISSING ELEMENT	ADVERSE CONSEQUENCE LEADING TO SUBOPTIMUM PERFORMANCE
Systems to understand customer requirements.	Designing, building, and delivering an unsatisfactory product or service. Adds delay. Increases cost due to rework.
Poor employee skills. Minimal initiative or self-direction.	Limited expansion opportunities. Unable to keep up with changing technology. Requires close monitoring. Difficulty in finding better ways to carry out work. Ultimately reduces morale, motivation, and performance.
Data about customer satisfaction, key process performance, and overall organizational performance do not exist or are incomplete.	Makes it difficult to engage employees in decision making about their work. Forces decisions to be made at higher levels on the basis of intuition or guesswork. Reduces decision accuracy and increases incorrect decisions. Makes it difficult to allocate resources appropriately or determine the best use of limited resources.
Leaders do not clearly set direction, performance expectations, vision, or values.	Causes subordinates to invent their own ideas and substitute them for a common set of performance expectations, vision, and values. Creates significant inefficiencies as people throughout the organization begin the work at cross-purposes, suboptimizing organizational performance.
Plans do not contain measurable objectives and a timeline for accomplishing each objective.	Leaders, managers, and employees do not know what level of performance is expected at any given time, making it difficult or impossible to effectively monitor progress. Accountability is not present.
Leaders do not make it clear that customers are the key to success.	If managers and employees do not focus on customers, then they become internally focused. Managers, engineering, or marketing drives the business, not customers. Customers and their requirements lose importance.
Top leaders do not encourage employees to develop and use their full potential.	Employee empowerment and well-being become optional. Some managers encourage employee participation, innovation, and creativity; most do not. The organization risks losing its best employees to competitors.
Customer comments and complaints are not encouraged. If a complaint is received it is not resolved promptly. The root cause of complaints is not identified.	Failure to capture customer comments and complaints, identify the root causes of the complaint, and work to prevent the problem from happening again, makes it difficult to learn about problems quickly and dooms the organization to repeat its failures. Failure to resolve complaints promptly increases customer dissatisfaction and reduces loyalty.
Poor two-way communication exists between leaders and the organization.	Unclear top-down communication makes it difficult to ensure alignment and focus throughout the organization, reducing teamwork and increasing bureaucratic stagnation. Poor upward communication maintains organizational fragmentation and prevents problems and barriers to effective work from being discussed and resolved.

THE CORE VALUES TO ACHIEVE PERFORMANCE EXCELLENCE

The criteria are built upon a set of interrelated Core Values and Concepts, which are embedded beliefs and behaviors found in high-performing organizations. They are the foundation for integrating key business requirements within a results-oriented framework that create a basis for action and feedback.

THE 2002 CORE VALUES AND CONCEPTS ARE:

Visionary Leadership

Every system, strategy, and method for achieving excellence must be guided by visionary leadership.

- Effective leaders convey a strong sense of urgency to counter the natural resistance to change that can prevent the organization from taking the steps that these Core Values for success demand.

- Such leaders serve as enthusiastic role models, reinforcing and communicating the Core Values by their words and actions. Words alone are not enough.

Visionary Leadership

An organization's senior leaders should set directions and create a customer focus, clear and visible values, and high expectations. The directions, values, and expectations should balance the needs of all your stakeholders. Your leaders should ensure the creation of strategies, systems, and methods for achieving excellence, stimulating innovation, and building knowledge and capabilities. The values and strategies should help guide all activities and decisions of your organization. Senior leaders should inspire and motivate your entire workforce and should encourage all employees to contribute, to develop and learn, to be innovative, and to be creative.

Senior leaders should serve as role models through their ethical behavior and their personal involvement in planning, communications, coaching, development of future leaders, review of organizational performance, and employee recognition. As role models, they can reinforce values and expectations while building leadership, commitment, and initiative throughout your organization.

Customer-Driven Excellence

This value demonstrates a passion for making the organization customer-driven. Without this, little else matters. Customers are the final judges of how well the organization did its job, and what they say counts. It is their perception of the service and product that will determine whether they remain loyal or constantly seek better providers.

- The organization must focus on systematically listening to customers and acting quickly on what they say.

- The organization must build positive relationships with its customers through focusing on accessibility and management of complaints.

- Dissatisfied customers must be heeded most closely, for they often deliver the most valuable information.

- If only satisfied and loyal customers (those who continue to do business with us no matter what) are paying attention, the organization will be led astray. The most successful organizations keep an eye on customers who are not satisfied and work to understand their preferences and meet their demands.

Customer-Driven Excellence

Quality and performance are judged by an organization's customers. Thus, your organization must take into account all product and service features and characteristics and all modes of customer access that contribute value to your customers and lead to customer acquisition, satisfaction, preference, referral, and loyalty, and to business expansion. Customer-driven excellence has both current and future components: understanding today's customer desires and anticipating future customer desires and marketplace offerings.

Value and satisfaction may be influenced by many factors throughout your customers' overall purchase, ownership, and service experiences. These factors include your organization's relationship with customers that helps build trust, confidence, and loyalty.

Customer-driven excellence means much more than reducing defects and errors, merely meeting specifications, or reducing complaints. Nevertheless, reducing defects and errors and eliminating causes of dissatisfaction contribute to your customers' view of your organization and thus also are important parts of customer-driven excellence. In addition, your organization's success in recovering from defects and mistakes ("making things right for your customer") is crucial to retaining customers and building customer relationships.

Customer-driven organizations address not only the product and service characteristics that meet basic customer requirements but also those features and characteristics that differentiate products and services from competing offerings. Such differentiation may be based upon new or modified offerings, combinations of product and service offerings, customization of offerings, multiple access mechanisms, rapid response, or special relationships.

Customer-driven excellence is thus a strategic concept. It is directed toward customer retention, market share gain, and growth. It demands constant sensitivity to changing and emerging customer and market requirements and to the factors that drive customer satisfaction and retention. It demands anticipating changes in the marketplace. Therefore, customer-driven excellence demands awareness of developments in technology and competitors' offerings, as well as rapid and flexible response to customer and market requirements.

Organizational and Personal Learning

The most potent value is organizational and personal learning. High-performing organizations are learning organizations—they evaluate and improve everything they do. They strive to get better at getting better.

- A culture of continuous improvement is essential to maintaining and sustaining true competitive advantage.

- Without systematic improvement and ongoing learning, organizations will ultimately face extinction.

- With systematic continuous improvement, time becomes a powerful ally. As time passes, the organization grows stronger and smarter.

- Leaders embed this value by linking rewards, recognition, and incentives for employees, supervisors, and managers at all levels to innovation, improvement, and learning. Otherwise, people do not think continuous change is important.

Organizational and Personal Learning

Achieving the highest levels of business performance requires a well-executed approach to organizational and personal learning. Organizational learning includes both continuous improvement of existing approaches and adaptation to change, leading to new goals and/or approaches. Learning needs to be embedded in the way your organization operates. This means that learning: (1) is a regular part of daily work; (2) is practiced at personal, work unit, and organizational levels; (3) results in solving problems at their source ("root cause"); (4) is focused on sharing knowledge throughout your organization; and (5) is driven by opportunities to effect significant change and to do better. Sources for learning include employees' ideas, research and development (R&D), customers' input, best-practice sharing, and benchmarking.

Organizational learning can result in: (1) enhancing value to customers through new and improved products and services; (2) developing new business opportunities; (3) reducing errors, defects, waste, and related costs; (4) improving responsiveness and cycle time performance; (5) increasing productivity and effectiveness in the use of all resources throughout your organization; and (6) enhancing your organization's performance in fulfilling its public responsibilities and service as a good citizen.

Employees' success depends increasingly on having opportunities for personal learning and practicing new skills. Organizations invest in employees' personal learning through education, training, and other opportunities for continuing growth. Such opportunities might include job rotation and increased pay for demonstrated knowledge and skills. On-the-job training offers a cost-effective way to train and to better link training to your organizational needs and priorities. Education and training programs may benefit from advanced technologies, such as computer- and Internet-based learning and satellite broadcasts.

Personal learning can result in: (1) more satisfied and versatile employees who stay with the organization; (2) organizational cross-functional learning; and (3) an improved environment for innovation.

Thus, learning is directed not only toward better products and services but also toward being more responsive, adaptive, and efficient—giving your organization marketplace sustainability and performance advantages.

Valuing Employees and Partners

Organizations must invest in their people to ensure they have the skills for today and to do what is necessary to succeed in the future. This core value has broadened from employee participation and development to valuing employees and partners. In high-performing organizations, the people who do the work of the organization should make most of the decisions about how the work is done. However, a significant barrier exists that limits employee decision making—access to data and poor data-based decision-making skills.

- As mentioned above, leaders are unwilling to let subordinates make decisions based on intuition—they reserve that type of decision for themselves.

- Therefore, access to data and developing skills to manage by fact is a prerequisite for optimizing employee contributions to the organization's success.

- Organizations cannot effectively push decision making down to the level where most of the work is done unless those doing the work have access to the necessary data and are skilled at making fact-based decisions.

Valuing Employees and Partners

An organization's success depends increasingly on the knowledge, skills, creativity, and motivation of its employees and partners.

Valuing employees means committing to their satisfaction, development, and well-being. Increasingly, this involves more flexible, high-performance work practices tailored to employees with diverse workplace and home life needs. Major challenges in the area of valuing employees include: (1) demonstrating your leaders' commitment to your employees' success; (2) recognition that goes beyond the regular compensation system; (3) development and progression within your organization; (4) sharing your organization's knowledge so your employees can better serve your customers and contribute to achieving your strategic objectives; and (5) creating an environment that encourages risk taking.

Organizations need to build internal and external partnerships to better accomplish overall goals. Internal partnerships might include labor-management cooperation, such as agreements with unions. Partnerships with employees might entail employee development, cross-training, or new work organizations, such as high-performance work teams. Internal partnerships also might involve creating network relationships among your work units to improve flexibility, responsiveness, and knowledge sharing.

External partnerships might be with customers, suppliers, and education organizations. Strategic partnerships or alliances are increasingly important kinds of external partnerships. Such partnerships might offer entry into new markets or a basis for new products or services. Also, partnerships might permit the blending of your organization's core competencies or leadership capabilities with the complementary strengths and capabilities of partners.

Successful internal and external partnerships develop longer-term objectives, thereby creating a basis for mutual investments and respect. Partners should address the key requirements for success, means for regular communication, approaches to evaluating progress, and means for adapting to changing conditions. In some cases, joint education and training could offer a cost-effective method for employee development.

Agility

Agility is a value usually driven by customer requirements and the desire to improve operating efficiency and lower costs.

- Except for a few pleasurable experiences, everyone wants things faster.

- Organizations that develop the capacity to respond faster by eliminating activities and tasks that do not add value find that productivity increases, costs go down, and customers are more loyal.

- Analyzing and improving work processes enables organizations to perform better, faster, and cheaper.

- To improve work processes, organizations need to focus on improving design quality and preventing problems. The cost of preventing problems and building quality into products and services is significantly less than the cost of taking corrective action later.

- It is critical to emphasize capturing learning from other design projects.

- Use information concerning customer preference, competitors' products, cost and pricing, marketplace profiles, and research and development (R&D) to optimize the process from the start, and avoid delay and rework.

- Public responsibility issues and factors, including environmental demands, must be included in the design stage.

Agility

Success in globally competitive markets demands agility—a capacity for rapid change and flexibility. All aspects of e-commerce require and enable more rapid, flexible, and customized responses. Businesses face ever-shorter cycles for the introduction of new/improved products and services, as well as for faster and more flexible response to customers. Major improvements in response time often require simplification of work units and processes and/or the ability for rapid changeover from one process to another. Cross-trained and empowered employees are vital assets in such a demanding environment.

A major success factor in meeting competitive challenges is the design-to-introduction (product/service initiation) cycle time. To meet the demands of rapidly changing global markets, organizations need to carry out stage-to-stage integration (such as concurrent engineering) of activities from research/concept to commercialization.

All aspects of time performance now are more critical, and cycle time has become a key process measure. Other important benefits can be derived from this focus on time; time improvements often drive simultaneous improvements in organization, quality, cost, and productivity.

Focus on the Future

To remain competitive, every organization must be guided by a common set of measurable goals and a focus on the future.

- These measurable goals, which emerge from the strategic planning process, serve to align the work of everyone in the organization.

- Measurable goals allow everyone to know where they are going and when they deviate from their path.

- Without measurable goals, everyone still works hard, but they tend to focus on the things they believe are important, not the direction set by top leaders. As a result, they can easily go in different directions—suboptimizing the success of the organization.

- Focusing on the future requires the organization's leaders to consider new, even revolutionary, ideas. Strategic objectives should reflect this future focus.

Focus on the Future

In today's competitive environment, a focus on the future requires understanding the short- and long-term factors that affect your business and marketplace. Pursuit of sustainable growth and market leadership requires a strong future orientation and a willingness to make long-term commitments to key stakeholders—your customers, employees, suppliers and partners, stockholders, the public, and your community. Your organization's planning should anticipate many factors, such as customers' expectations, new business and partnering opportunities, the increasingly global marketplace, technological developments, the evolving e-commerce environment, new customer and market segments, evolving regulatory requirements, community/societal expectations, and strategic moves by competitors. Strategic objectives and resource allocations need to accommodate these influences. A focus on the future includes developing employees and suppliers, creating opportunities for innovation, and anticipating public responsibilities.

Managing for Innovation

The accelerating speed of change today demands ever-increasing innovation. Such innovation cannot be random. It must be focused on factors that are essential to organizational success. To be focused, innovation must be managed. Innovation should focus on changing products, services, and processes to create more value for the organization's stakeholders, employees, and customers. The winners in the highly competitive race to innovate will be the organizations that uncover new paradigms of breakthrough performance. To begin to optimize this breakthrough capacity, everyone in the organization needs to be involved. The more brain power, the better. Requirements for innovation should be a part of every employee and managerial performance plan and appraisal. Just like continuous improvement, innovation must be imbedded in the culture and fabric of daily work. The best organizations are not satisfied to just "improve" or "innovate." The best organizations work hard at increasing the speed at which they improve and innovate. Anything less allows competitors to overtake them. Anything less allows customer expectations to exceed the speed of change, causing the customers to look elsewhere.

Managing for Innovation

Innovation means making meaningful change to improve an organization's products, services, and processes and to create new value for the organization's stakeholders. Innovation should lead your organization to new dimensions of performance. Innovation is no longer strictly the purview of research and development departments; innovation is important for all aspects of your business and all processes. Organizations should be led and managed so that innovation becomes part of the culture and is integrated into daily work.

Management by Fact

Management by fact is the cornerstone value for effective planning, operational decision making at all levels, employee involvement and empowerment, and leadership.

- People make decisions every day. However, without data, the basis for decision making is usually intuition—gut feel. Although intuition can be valuable at times, it introduces too much variation in the decision-making process. Intuition is not consistent person-to-person or time-to-time. It is also difficult to explain the rationale for decisions based on intuition. That makes communication more difficult within the organization. Finally, if the decision must be made on the basis of intuition, it is usually the boss' intuition that drives the decision. Because of this phenomenon, issues are pulled to ever higher levels for resolution. As a result, excessive reliance on intuition minimizes employee empowerment.

- Most drivers decide when to fill their fuel tanks based on data from the fuel gauge and get very uncomfortable if the gauge is broken. Yet people routinely make decisions of enormous consequence about customers, strategies, goals, and employees with little or no data. This is a recipe for disaster, not one designed to ensure optimization.

Management by Fact

Organizations depend on the measurement and analysis of performance. Such measurements should derive from business needs and strategy, and they should provide critical data and information about key processes, outputs, and results. Many types of data and information are needed for performance management. Performance measurement should include customer, product, and service performance; comparisons of operational, market, and competitive performance; and supplier, employee, and cost and financial performance.

Analysis refers to extracting larger meaning from data and information to support evaluation, decision making, and operational improvement. Analysis entails using data to determine trends, projections, and cause and effect that might not otherwise be evident. Analysis supports a variety of purposes, such as planning, reviewing your overall performance, improving operations, change management, and comparing your performance with competitors' or with "best practices" benchmarks.

A major consideration in performance improvement and change management involves the selection and use of performance measures or indicators. The measures or indicators you select should best represent the factors that lead to improved customer, operational, and financial performance. A comprehensive set of measures or indicators tied to customer and/or organizational performance requirements represents a clear basis for aligning all activities with your organization's goals. Through the analysis of data from your tracking processes, your measures or indicators themselves may be evaluated and changed to better support your goals.

Public Responsibility and Citizenship

Every high-performing organization practices good public responsibility and citizenship.

- Organizations must determine and anticipate any adverse effects to the public of their products, services, and operations. Failure to do so can undermine public trust and distract workers, and also adversely affect the bottom line. This is true of both private and public organizations.

  During the last few years we have seen several examples of companies that have been seriously hurt by failing to practice good citizenship or protect the interests of the public from risks they created. Even when unintended these issues can cripple companies. Consider Dow-Corning and the silicone breast implants, banks sued because of failing to provide adequate security for automatic teller machines (cash machines), or Exxon for the massive oil spill in the Pacific.

- Safety and legal requirements need to be met beyond mere compliance.

Public Responsibility and Citizenship

An organization's leaders should stress its responsibilities to the public and the need to practice good citizenship. These responsibilities refer to basic expectations of your organization related to business ethics and protection of public health, safety, and the environment. Protection of health, safety, and the environment includes your organization's operations, as well as the lifecycles of your products and services. Also, organizations should emphasize resource conservation and waste reduction at the source. Planning should anticipate adverse impacts from production, distribution, transportation, use, and disposal of your products. Effective planning should prevent problems, provide for a forthright response if problems occur, and make available information and support needed to maintain public awareness, safety, and confidence.

For many organizations, the product design stage is critical from the point of view of public responsibility. Design decisions impact your production processes and often the content of municipal and industrial wastes. Effective design strategies should anticipate growing environmental concerns and responsibilities.

Organizations should not only meet all local, state, and federal laws and regulatory requirements, but they should treat these and related requirements as opportunities for improvement "beyond mere compliance." This requires the use of appropriate measures in managing public responsibility.

Practicing good citizenship refers to leadership and support—within the limits of an organization's resources—of publicly important purposes. Such purposes might include improving education and health care in your community, environmental excellence, resource conservation, community service, improving industry and business practices, and sharing nonproprietary information. Leadership as a corporate citizen also entails influencing other organizations, private and public, to partner for these purposes. For example, your organization might lead or participate in efforts to help define the obligations of your industry to its communities.

Focus on Results and Creating Value

A results focus and an emphasis on creating value helps organizations communicate requirements, monitor actual performance, make adjustments in priorities, and reallocate resources. Without a results focus, organizations can become fixated on internal, self-directed processes and lose sight of the important factors for success—such as customers and their requirements.

Focus on Results and Creating Value

An organization's performance measurements need to focus on key results. Results should be used to create and balance value for your key stakeholders: customers, employees, stockholders, suppliers and partners, the public, and the community. By creating value for your key stakeholders, your organization builds loyalty and contributes to growing the economy. To meet the sometimes conflicting and changing aims that balancing value implies, organizational strategy should explicitly include key stakeholder requirements. This will help ensure that actions and plans meet differing stakeholder needs and avoid adverse impacts on any stakeholders. The use of a balanced composite of leading and lagging performance measures offers an effective means to communicate short-and long-term priorities, monitor actual performance, and provide a clear basis for improving results.

Systems Perspective

Taken together, the Baldrige Criteria promote a systems perspective and define the processes required to achieve optimum organizational performance. As with any system, no part can be ignored and still expect the whole to perform at peak levels. When part of a well-functioning system begins to underperform or work in a manner that is inconsistent with system requirements, the performance of the whole system suffers.

The same is true of a management system. If leaders are ambiguous, if plans are not clear, if work processes are not consistent, if people are not able to do the work they are asked to do, and if it is difficult to keep track of progress and make appropriate adjustments, it will be impossible for the organization to achieve maximum levels of performance. For most of the 20th century, a long list of "management gurus" has suggested a variety of quick and simple remedies to enhance organizational performance. By itself, each quick fix has failed. Hopefully we have learned that no single solution is sufficient to optimize performance in a complex system. Leaders that approach management from a systems perspective are more likely to optimize organizational performance than leaders who continue to take a piecemeal approach to organizational management. There is no magic potion for excellent management to achieve high performance.

There are always better ways to do things. The challenge is to find them, but we are not likely to find them alone. We must create an environment—a work climate where better ways will be sought out, recognized, and put in place by everyone.

Systems Perspective

The Baldrige Criteria provide a systems perspective for managing your organization to achieve performance excellence. The Core Values and the seven Baldrige Categories form the building blocks and the integrating mechanism for the system. However, successful management of overall performance requires organization-specific synthesis and alignment. Synthesis means looking at your organization as a whole and builds upon key business requirements, including your strategic objectives and action plans. Alignment means using the key linkages among requirements given in the Baldrige Categories, including the key measures/indicators.

Alignment is depicted in the Baldrige framework on page 68. Alignment includes your senior leaders' focus on strategic directions and on your customers. It means that your senior leaders monitor, respond to, and manage performance based on your business results. Alignment includes using your measures/indicators to link your key strategies with your key processes and align your resources to improve overall performance and satisfy customers.

Thus, a systems perspective means managing your whole organization, as well as its components, to achieve success.

PRACTICAL INSIGHTS

Connections and Linkages

A popular children's activity, connect the dots, helps them understand that, when properly connected, apparently random dots create a meaningful picture. In many ways, the 7 Categories, 18 Items, and 29 Areas to Address in the Baldrige Criteria are like the dots that must be connected to reveal a meaningful picture. With no tools to connect the dots, human resource development and use are not related to strategic planning; information and analysis are isolated from process management; and overall improvement efforts are disjointed, fragmented, and do not yield robust results. This book describes the linkages for and between each item. The exciting part about having them identified is that you can look for these linkages in your own organization and, if they don't exist, start building them.

Transition Strategies

Putting high-performance management systems in place is a major commitment that will not happen quickly. At the beginning, you will need a transition strategy to get you across the bridge from management by opinion or intuition to more data-driven management. The next part of this section describes one approach that has worked for many organizations in various sectors: creating a performance improvement council.

Performance Improvement Council

Identify a top-level executive leadership group of 6 to 10 members. Each member over that number will seem to double the complexity of issues and make decision making much more cumbersome. The executive leadership group could send a message to the entire organization by naming the group "the performance improvement council"—reinforcing the importance of continuous performance improvement to the future success of the organization.

The performance improvement council should be the primary policy-making body for the organization. It should spawn other performance improvement councils at lower levels to share practices and policies with every employee in the organization as well as to involve customers and suppliers. The structure permeates the organization as members of the performance improvement council become area leaders for major improvement efforts and sponsors for several process or continuous improvement task teams throughout the organization. The council structure, networked and cascaded fully, can effectively align the work and optimize performance at all levels and across all functions.

Council Membership

Selecting members for the performance improvement council should be done carefully. Each member should be essential for the success of the operation, and together they must be sufficient for success. The most important member is the senior leader of the organization or work unit. This person must participate actively, demonstrating the kind of leadership that all should emulate. Of particular importance is a commitment to consensus building as the modus operandi for the council. This tool, a core of performance improvement programs, is often overlooked by leadership. Other council members selected should have leadership responsibility for broad areas of the organization such as human resources, operations planning, customers, and data systems.

Performance Improvement Council Learning and Planning

The performance improvement council should be extremely knowledgeable about high-performance management systems. If not, as is often the case, performance improvement council members should be among the first in the organization to learn about continuous improvement tools and processes.

To be effective, every member of the council (and every member in the organization) must understand the Baldrige Criteria, because the Criteria describe the components of the entire management system. Participation in examiner training has proved to be the very best way to understand the complexities of the system needed to achieve performance excellence. Any additional training beyond this should be carried out in the context of planning—that is, learn tools and use them to plan the performance improvement implementation, practices, and policies.

The performance improvement council should:

- Develop an integrated, continuous improvement strategic performance improvement and business plan.

- Create the web (communication plan and infrastructure) to transmit performance improvement policies throughout the organization.

- Define the roles of employees, including new recognition and reward structures, to cause needed behavioral changes.

- Develop a master training and development plan. Involve team representatives in planning so they can learn skills close to when they are needed. Define what is provided to whom, and when and how success will be measured.

- Launch improvement projects that will produce both short- and long-term successes. Improvement projects should be clearly defined by the performance improvement council and driven by the strategic plan. Typical improvement projects include important human resource processes such as career development, performance measurement, and diversity, as well as improving operational products and services in the line areas.

- Develop a plan to communicate the progress and successes of the organization. Through this approach, the need for performance improvement processes is consistently communicated to all employees. Barriers to optimum performance are weakened and eliminated.

- Create champions to promote performance excellence through the Categories of the Baldrige Criteria.

Category Champions

This section describes the responsibilities of category champions. The people in the administrative or leadership cabinet should each be the champion of a category.

Organizational Leadership Champion

The Organizational Leadership Champion is a senior executive who, in addition to other executive duties, works to coordinate and enhance leadership effectiveness and alignment throughout the organization. It is both a strategic and an operational activity.

From the strategic side, the champion should focus on ensuring that all senior leaders:

- Understand what is expected of them as leaders of organizational change

- Agree to achieve consensus, and subsequently act consistently and speak with one voice as a senior leadership team

- Serve as role models of performance excellence for managers and employees at all levels of the organization

- Set clear strategy and directions to enhance future opportunities for the organization

- Develop future leaders (succession planning) throughout the organization

- Create measurable performance expectations and monitor performance to achieve the key improvements and strategic objectives of the organization. This means that necessary data and analyses must be coordinated to ensure appropriate information is available for the champion and the entire senior leadership team

From the operational side, the champion should work to identify and eliminate both individual and system deficiencies, territorial conflicts, and knowledge shortfalls that limit a leader's ability to meet expectations and goals consistently.

The champion should be the focal point in the organization to ensure all parts of the organization have systematic processes in place so they fully understand leadership and management requirements.

A process should exist to monitor ongoing initiatives to ensure leaders effectively set and communicate organizational values to employees.

- They must demonstrate that they focus on delivering value to customers and other stakeholders.

- They must aggressively reinforce an environment that promotes empowerment and innovation throughout the workforce. This may involve reviewing policies, systems, work processes, and the use of resources—ensuring sufficient data are available to assist in manager and employee decision making.

The champion should coordinate the activities involving the review of organizational performance and capabilities.

- Key performance measures should be defined.

- Systems to review organizational success, performance, and progress relative to goals should be in place.

- Performance review findings should be communicated widely throughout the organization and, as appropriate, to key suppliers and customers to help ensure organizational alignment.

- Performance review findings should be translated into priorities for improvement and innovation at different levels throughout the organization.

- Performance review findings, together with employee feedback, should be used systematically to assess and improve senior leadership effectiveness and the effectiveness of managers throughout the organization.

Finally, the champion must work as part of the senior leadership team to help coordinate all facets of the management system to drive high performance. This involves teaching the team about the requirements of effective and consistent leadership at all levels and its impact on organizational performance. The senior leader of the organization usually serves as the Organizational Leadership Champion and leads this council.

Strategic Planning Champion

The Strategic Planning Champion is a senior executive who, in addition to other executive duties, works to coordinate and enhance strategic planning and action plan alignment throughout the organization. It is both a strategic and an operational activity.

From the strategic side, the champion should ensure that the focus of strategy development is on sustained competitive leadership, which usually depends on achieving revenue growth, as well as consistently improving operational effectiveness. The Strategic Planning Champion should help the senior leadership team acquire a view of the future and provide clear strategic guidance to the organization through goals, objectives, action plans, and measures.

From the operational side, the champion should work to ensure sufficient data are available regarding:

- The organization's operational and human resource capabilities

- Internal and external risks

- The competitive environment and other challenges that might affect future direction

The champion should be the focal point in the organization to ensure all parts of the organization have systematic processes in place so they fully understand the implications of strategy on their daily work.

The champion should ensure that strategy is customer and market focused and is actually used to guide ongoing decision making and resource allocation at all levels of the organization.

- A process should exist to convert strategy into actions at each level of the organization, which are aligned to achieve goals necessary for business success

- Every employee should understand his or her role in carrying out actions to achieve the organization's goals

The champion should coordinate the activities involving strategy development and deployment to:

- Acquire and use various types of forecasts, projections, scenarios, or other techniques to understand the plausible range of future options.

- Determine how the projected performance of competitors is likely to compare with the projected performance of the organization in the same time frame in order to set goals to insure competitive advantage.

- Determine what capabilities must be developed within the organization to achieve strategic goals and coordinate with other members of the senior leadership team and category champions to ensure those capabilities are in place.

- Determine what changes in services or products might be needed as a part of strategic positioning and direction.

- Ensure a system is in place to develop action plans that address strategic goals and objectives. Ensure those action plans are understood throughout the organization, as appropriate.

- Ensure a system is in place to identify the human resource requirements necessary to achieve strategic goals and objectives. This may include training, support services for employees, reorganization, and new recruitment, to name a few.

- Ensure a system is in place to allocate resources throughout the organization sufficient to accomplish the action plans.

- Define the expected path along which growth and performance are likely to take each strategic objective. Identify timelines that permit effective, fact-based monitoring.

- Coordinate with the leadership system of performance review to help ensure priorities for improvement and innovation at different levels throughout the organization are aligned with strategy and action plans.

- Ensure the process for strategic planning, plan deployment, the development of action plans, and the alignment of resources to support actions is systematically evaluated and improved each cycle. Also evaluate and improve the effectiveness of determining the projected performance of competitors for use in goal setting.

Finally, the champion must work as contributing member of the senior leadership team to help coordinate all facets of the management system to drive high performance. This involves teaching the team about the requirements of strategic planning and its impact on organizational performance.

Customer Value Champion

The Customer Value Champion is a senior executive who, in addition to other executive duties, will coordinate and enhance customer satisfaction, relations, and loyalty throughout the organization. It is both a strategic and an operational activity.

From the strategic side, the champion should focus on ensuring that the drivers of customer satisfaction, customer retention, and related market share (which are key factors in competitiveness, profitability, and business success) are considered fully in the strategic planning process. This means that necessary data and analyses must be coordinated to ensure appropriate information is available for the executive planning councils.

From the operational side, the champion should work to identify and eliminate system deficiencies, territorial conflicts, and knowledge shortfalls that limit the organization's ability to meet customer satisfaction, retention, and loyalty goals consistently.

The champion should be the focal point in the organization to ensure all parts of the organization have systematic processes in place so they fully understand key customer, market, and operational requirements as input to customer satisfaction and market goals.

A process should exist to monitor ongoing initiatives to ensure they are aligned with the customer aspects of the strategic direction. This may involve:

- Reviewing policies, systems, work processes, the use of resources, and the availability of employees who are knowledgeable and focus on customer relations and loyalty

- Ensuring sufficient data are available to assist in decision making about customer issues

- Ensuring that strategies and actions relating to customer issues are aligned at all levels of reorganization from the executives to the work unit or individual job level

The champion should coordinate the activities involving understanding customer requirements as well as managing the interaction with customers, including how the organization determines customer satisfaction and satisfaction relative to competitors. (Satisfaction relative to competitors and the factors that lead to customer preference are of increasing importance to managing in a competitive environment.)

- The champion should also examine the means by which customers have access to seek information, assistance, or comment and complain.

- The champion should coordinate the definition of customer contact requirements and the deployment of those requirements to all points in the organization that have contact with customers.

- The champion should ensure that systems exist to respond quickly and resolve complaints promptly to recover customer confidence that might be otherwise lost.

- The champion should ensure that employees responsible for the design and delivery of products and services receive information about customer complaints so they may eliminate the causes of these complaints.

- The champion should work with appropriate line managers to help set priorities for improvement projects based on the potential impact of the cost of complaints and the impact of customer dissatisfaction and attrition on the organization.

- The champion should be charged with coordinating activities to build loyalty and positive referral as well as evaluating and improving customer relationship-building processes throughout the organization.

Finally, the champion must work as contributing member of the senior leadership team to help coordinate all facets of the management system to drive high performance. This involves teaching the team about the requirements of customer and market focus and its impact on organizational performance.

Information and Analysis Champion

The Information and Analysis Champion is an executive-level person who, in addition to other executive duties, will coordinate and enhance information and analysis systems throughout the organization to ensure that they meet the decision-making needs of managers, employees, customers, and suppliers. It is both a strategic and an operational activity.

From the strategic side, information and data can provide a competitive advantage. The champion should focus on ensuring, to the extent possible, that timely and accurate information and data are available to enhance the delivery of new and existing products and services to meet emerging market needs.

From the operational side, the champion should work to ensure that information and data are available throughout the organization to aid in decision making at all levels. This means coordinating with all other champions to ensure data are available for day-to-day review and decision making at all levels for their areas of responsibility.

The Information and Analysis Champion has responsibility for both information infrastructure as well as ensuring the appropriate use of data for decision making. The champion should coordinate activities throughout the organization involving data collection, accuracy, analysis, retrieval, and use for decision making. The champion should ensure:

- Complete data are available and aligned to strategic goals, objectives, and action plans to ensure performance against these goals, objectives, and action plans can be effectively monitored

- Systems are in place to collect and use comparative data and information to support strategy development, goal setting, and performance improvement

- Data and information throughout the organization are accurate and reliable to enhance fact-based decision making

- Data and information are used to support a better understanding of the cost and financial impact of various improvement options

- Appropriate correlations and performance projections are available to support planning

- The performance measurement system is evaluated and improved to ensure it meets business needs

- Data analysis supports the senior executives' organizational performance review and organizational planning

- Data analysis addresses the overall health of the organization

- The results of organization-level analysis are available to workgroup and functional-level operations to support decision making at those levels

- Data analysis supports daily decisions regarding operations throughout the organization to ensure actions align with plans

Finally, the champion must work as part of an organizationwide council to help coordinate all facets of the management system to drive high performance.

Human Resource Focus Champion

The Human Resource Focus Champion is an executive-level person who, in addition to other executive duties, will coordinate and enhance systems to enable employees to develop and utilize their full potential, consistent with the organization's strategic objectives. This includes building and maintaining a work environment conducive to full employee participation and growth. It is both a strategic and an operational activity.

From the strategic side, the human resource constraints of the organization must be considered in the development of strategy, and subsequently eliminated to ensure the workforce is capable of achieving the strategies necessary for business success.

From the operational side, the champion should ensure that the work climate enhances employee satisfaction and well-being and that work is organized and jobs are designed to enable employees to achieve higher levels of performance.

The Human Resource Focus Champion has responsibility for ensuring that employees (including managers and supervisors at all levels; permanent, temporary, and part-time personnel; and contract employees supervised by the organization) receive the same kind of focus and attention as customers, so that their needs are met to enable them to contribute fully to the organization's goals and objectives. The champion should ensure:

- Work and jobs are structured to promote cooperation, collaboration, individual initiative, innovation, and flexibility.

- Managers and supervisors encourage and motivate employees to develop and use their full potential.

- An effective system exists to provide accurate feedback about employee performance and to enhance their performance. This includes systems to identify skill gaps and recruit or reassign employees to close those gaps, as well as ensuring that fair work practices are followed within the organization. This may also include evaluating managers and enhancing their ability to provide accurate feedback and effective coaching to improve employee performance.

- Compensation, recognition, and rewards are aligned to support high-performance objectives of the organization (contained in strategic plans and reported in the balanced scorecard or business results report card).

- Education and training support business objectives and build employee knowledge, skills, and capabilities to enhance employee performance. This includes ensuring employees understand tools and techniques of performance measurement, performance improvement, quality control methods, and benchmarking. This also includes ensuring that managers and supervisors reinforce knowledge and skills on the job.

- The work environment is safe, with measurable performance measures and targets for each key factor affecting employee safety.

- Factors that affect employee well-being, satisfaction, and motivation are routinely measured and actions are taken promptly to improve conditions that adversely affect morale, motivation, productivity, and other key business results.

Finally, the champion must work as part of an organizationwide council to help coordinate all facets of the management system to drive high performance.

Process Management Champion

The Process Management Champion is an executive-level person who, in addition to other executive duties, will coordinate and enhance all aspects of the organization's systems to manage and improve work processes to meet the organization's strategic objectives. This includes customer-focused design, product and service delivery, internal support services, and supplier and partner systems. It is both a strategic and operational activity.

From the strategic side, rapid and accurate design, development, and delivery of products and services creates a competitive advantage in the marketplace.

From the operational side, the champion should work to ensure all key work processes are examined and optimized to achieve higher levels of performance, reduce cycle time and costs, and subsequently add to organizational profitability.

The Process Management Champion has responsibility for creating a process management orientation within the organization. Since all work is a process, the Process Management Champion must ensure that the process owners (including processes owned by other champions) systematically examine, improve, and execute their processes consistently. The champion should ensure:

- Systematic continuous improvement activities are embedded in all processes, which lead to ongoing refinements.

- Initial and ongoing customer requirements are incorporated into all product and service designs, production and delivery systems, and processes. This includes core production processes as well as key business (such as research and development, asset management, technology acquisition, and supply chain management) and internal support processes (such as finance and accounting, facilities management, administration, procurement, and personnel).

- Design, production, and delivery processes are structured and analyzed to reduce cycle time; increase the use of learning from past projects or other parts of the organization; reduce costs; increase the use of new technology and other effectiveness or efficiency factors; and ensure all products and services meet performance requirements.

Finally, the champion must work as part of an organizationwide council to help coordinate all facets of the management system to drive high performance.

Business Results Champion

The Business Results Champion is an executive-level person who, in addition to other executive duties, will coordinate the display of the organization's business results. This champion has substantially different work than the champions for Categories 1 through 6. No actions leading to or resulting from the performance outcome data are championed by the Business Results Champion. Those actions are driven by the Category 1 through 6 champions because they have responsibility for taking action to implement and deploy procedures necessary to produce the business results. For example, the Information and Analysis Champion (Category 4) is responsible for collecting data that reflect all areas of strategic importance leading to business results. The Category 4 champion is also responsible for ensuring data accuracy and reliability.

The Business Results Champion is responsible, however, for ensuring that the organization is able to display all business results required by Category 7 to provide evidence of the organization's performance and improvement in key business areas and facilitate monitoring by leaders. These include customer satisfaction, product and service performance, financial and marketplace performance, human resource results, and operational performance.

Results must be displayed by appropriate segment and group, such as different customer groups, market segments, employee groups, or supplier groups. Appropriate comparison data must be included in the business results display to judge the relative "goodness" or "strength" of the results achieved.

Finally, the champion must work as part of an organizationwide council to help coordinate all facets of the management system to drive high performance. For example, if the organization is not collecting data necessary for inclusion in the business results report card, the Business Results Champion coordinates work with the other champions on the council to ensure those data are available.

The Critical Skills

A uniform message, set of skills or core competencies, and constancy of purpose are critical to success. Core training should provide all employees with the knowledge and skills on which to build a learning organization that continually gets better. Such training typically includes team building, leadership skills, consensus building, communications, and effective meeting management. These are necessary for effective teams to become involved in solving critical problems.

Another important core skill involves using a common process to define customer requirements accurately, determining the ability to meet those requirements, measure success, and determine the extent to which customers—internal and external—are satisfied. When a problem arises, employees must be able to define the problem correctly, isolate the root causes, generate and select the best solution to eliminate the root causes, and implement the best solution.

It is also important to be able to understand data and make decisions based on facts, not merely intuition or feelings. Therefore, familiarity with tools to analyze work processes and performance data is important. With these tools, work processes can be analyzed and vastly improved. Reducing unnecessary steps in work processes, increasing process consistency, reducing variability, and reducing cycle time are powerful ways to improve quality and reduce cost simultaneously.

Courses in techniques to acquire comparison and benchmarking data, work process improvement and reengineering, supplier partnerships and certification, role modeling for leaders' strategic planning, and customer satisfaction and loyalty will help managers and employees expand their optimization and high-performance thrust across the entire organization.

LESSONS LEARNED

Twenty years ago the fierce global competition that inspired the quality movement in the United States was felt primarily by major manufacturers. Today, all sectors are under intense pressure to "be the best or be history." The demand for performance excellence reaches all corners of the economy, from manufacturing and service industries to professional services, education, health care, public utilities, and government. All of these segments have contributed valuable lessons to the quality movement and have played an important part in our recovery from the economic slump caused by poor service and products of the 1970s. Relying on the Baldrige model, we will share some of the insights and lessons learned from leaders of high-performing organizations.

Desire and History Are Not Enough

It is important to point out a fact that is perhaps obvious to all: In order to optimize organizational performance, organizations must actually use the principles contained in the Baldrige Criteria. It is not enough to think about them. It is not enough to have used them in the past and no longer continue to do so. It is not enough to use a part but not all of the criteria. To leave out any part suboptimizes the performance of the organization.

The recent experience of Xerox provides a useful example. Xerox won the Baldrige Award in 1989. They demonstrated significant performance improvement through the 1980s and continued to grow substantially through the 1990s. They used the Baldrige Criteria as the way they ran their business, not just a list of additional activities they would do if they felt like it. They were absolutely customer focused. They made decisions based on data and fully engaged and involved their entire workforce. They continuously evaluated and improved their effectiveness in every aspect of their work. In fact, one business unit, Xerox Business Services (XBS), which makes copies of and manages documents, won the Baldrige Award again in 1997. The performance of XBS was similar to Xerox as a whole. In 1989, XBS, with a few hundred employees, generated approximately $300 million in annual revenue. They worked so efficiently and satisfied customers so well that their market grew from

$300 million in 1989 to approximately $2 billion in 1997 and to approximately $4 billion in 2000.

However, the new CEO, Richard Thoman (a transplant from IBM), was not able to provide the leadership needed to maintain the customer focus and bring the company into the emerging digital market. Xerox performance began to suffer. Its stock price plummeted, losing approximately 80 percent of its value. The Xerox Board of Directors, after firing Thoman and rehiring the previous CEO, Paul Allaire (who had retired from that position), is struggling to rebuild the processes and systems that led Xerox to high levels of performance excellence in the past. However, it may take the company years to recover.

The Xerox story points out an important lesson. While using the Baldrige Criteria can help an organization reach high levels of performance, organizations cannot expect to sustain those levels of performance without continuing to use the criteria as the way they run the business. High-performance athletes of all types know this lesson very well. In order to continue to win, they cannot rest on the success of the past. To continue to win, world-class athletes must continue to follow the discipline of training, diet, effective coaching, and take advantage of technological advances in equipment. The same is true in any competitive environment.

A Tale of Two Leaders

It was a time of turbulence; it was a time of peace. It was a time of growth and streamlining. It was the happiest of times; it was also the most painful of times. Most of all it was a time that demanded change—although it was more comfortable to consider it a time for the status quo.

The following tales are of two leaders. One is consistent and persistent in communicating the direction and message that will bring about excellent results and high performance. Another is uncertain and vague. He does not wish to push his people into anything, let alone the difficult commitment related to using the Baldrige Criteria as the way to run the business. After all, they are still profitable and healthy. Why rock the boat? You may know these people or someone who reminds you of them. If so, you will understand the reason for this section.

There is no lonelier, more challenging, yet critical and rewarding job than that of the leader. I work with many, many leaders who listen to advice carefully. They really want to know the best approaches to optimize their organizations. Yet what they do with the advice and counsel is always interesting and unpredictable. This section is intended to help those leaders go resolutely down the right path.

Neither leader exists in real life, but both leader profiles are based on actual events and observations of different people in leadership positions.

The Tales

Background Tale One

John was the CEO of a Fortune 500 manufacturing company that was slowly but surely losing market share. Shareholders and employees were happy because profits and growth, although slower, were still hearty. However, their business that once enjoyed a near monopoly position was rapidly facing more and more competition. Customers that had to beg and plead for limited products and service over the years were happily turning to competitors who were trying in earnest to meet their needs and even delight them. In such an environment, aggressive, customer-focused companies were winning the hearts, minds, and pocketbooks of John's customers. John decided, after working with a consulting firm or two and studying the work of Deming, that performance excellence was urgently needed to keep the company in business more than five years.

The First Message to the Leadership Team

John called an urgent meeting of his senior team. Many members of this team had been there since the company began its 20-year growth spurt and had been good soldiers in times of runaway growth and profit. John was wondering how many of the senior staff would welcome the message he was about to send. The meeting was scheduled the next week for five days at the corporate headquarters. Short of an emergency illness, attendance was required.

During the next few days, John received 20 phone calls from secretaries that informed John their bosses could not attend because of other priority commitments. Priorities were quickly realigned when they were informed that attendance was not optional.

The week-long meeting began with training—the kind of training where the group was required to participate, listen, and discuss the content. The training was presented by an outside firm with frequent discussions of companywide application and emphasis presented by John. At the end of three days, John took over the meeting and asked for input on how best to apply these principles to the organization at all levels. The leadership group voiced resistance to change, some more than others. They basically voiced concern that "this performance excellence stuff with all of its requirements for empowerment and data" would get in the way of their doing business and was not needed.

John clarified the objectives of the group by walking to the white board and writing: "This new program, performance excellence, will be in the way of doing business effectively." The senior staff pretty much agreed.

John responded by placing a large "X" through the word "in." The statement now read, "Performance excellence will be the way of doing business effectively." John notified the attendees, "I will negotiate an exit package with anyone who does not understand the implications of this message, and who does not want to be part of this new way of doing business." John learned that day that to institute meaningful change, it may be necessary to fire someone he liked. However, he also realized that to ignore the challenges and lack of commitment would be seen by everyone as tacit approval and send the message that the new way of doing business was "optional."

The Next Steps

John focused on two next steps: (1) making sure his top team role-modeled behavior that would facilitate the needed changes; and (2) planning and implementing a companywide training requirement to communicate the new skills and performance expectations. John started to change his behavior and the behavior of his top staff, feeling that "walking the talk" would signal the importance of new behaviors more than any speech or videotaped presentation. The next top staff meeting was called within a week to plan the design and rollout of training corporatewide, including all foreign and domestic sites. The top staff had very little interest in training, feeling largely that this was a human resource function and should be delegated to that department. Based on the advice of external advisors, John informed the staff that it was now their job to plan, design, and execute this training. A "core design team" was formed with senior leaders and expert content and course design specialists to design the training within one month and present it to the senior corporate leaders.

In spite of prior agreements to manage their meetings effectively, to be on time, not interrupt, and follow the agenda, most continued to ignore the rules. Behaviors of the top leadership group at this meeting included the usual set of interruptions, "I told you so's," and everyone talking at the same time. John, whose goal was to create a listening and learning environment, challenged the group to "ante up." He asked that all top leaders bring fifty $20 bills to the meeting. John introduced new meeting ground rules. They were simple. Interruptions, put downs, blocking behaviors, and talking while someone else was, were violations of meeting ground rules. On the other hand, building on ideas, clarifying ideas, supporting, and disagreeing respectfully were good meeting behaviors. Every violation was worth a $20 bill. Good meeting behaviors were rewarded, although they did not materialize until several meetings had been completed.

At first, it seemed that the pot would win big time—no one took John seriously. After about the third meeting, with penalties piling up, their behavior actually changed. Other meeting management skills were slowly introduced, such as time frame limits and action planning. Then John was confident his team could role model this behavior to others. He ordered that, "This is the way we treat each other at all meetings including staff meetings, communication forums, and all company business meetings." A core value and new behavior of courtesy and professionalism became deployed companywide through the senior management team.

Training and the Change Process
Each five-day, high-performance management course was identical, ensuring that a uniform message and set of skills were communicated. Each course was eventually taught by two instructors, a shop supervisor and a manager, so that management and the workforce would both be involved. John personally taught the top-leadership team the entire five-day course, assisted by a member of the design team, and this tale spread across the organization like wildfire. It was the thing to be invited to take part in this instruction because their leader had done it. The core skills became part of the fabric of the organization—the way to conduct business. They included fact-based decisions, a focus on customers, and using and

improving processes. Also included was a way to solve problems continually with a well-defined process at the level the problem was occurring.

The focus had shifted from *status quo* to a thirst for improvement. Improvement began to bring rewards whereas the *status quo* was disdained. A comprehensive business evaluation was conducted and improvement targets were identified. Clear assignments with reasonable but aggressive goals were cascaded to all levels of the organization. Performance planning, goals, compensation, and recognition were aligned to support the overall business strategy, especially the need to focus better on satisfying internal and external customers. Managers who did not work to meet these new goals, who did not role model the behaviors necessary to achieve high performance, were reassigned to jobs that did not require their management skills. New role models emerged to lead the organization at all levels. Within three years the company regained market share, improved profitability, expanded its employee base, and became, once again, one of the world's most admired companies.

Background Tale Two
Victor was the CEO of a West coast manufacturing company that also was a proud member of the Fortune 500. Company performance had been uneven over the past few years. Profits were low this year relative to previous years but the company still met financial targets. Product demands were high and the outlook was fairly good for the next quarter. The industry as a whole was fairly evenly matched as far as management problems. Trends for return on investment were also uneven, and other indicators such as sales volume and net profit were up and down. Investors were not happy, especially when other companies consistently outperformed them. Victor thought that it was time to do something different. Victor consulted several valuable and trusted advisors and then decided that high performance excellence might be worth considering.

The First Message to the Leadership Team
Victor scheduled a series of weekly dinner meetings over the next month (January) and engaged several different top consultants to talk to the group about the business case for using high-performance management. He invited 50 top-level managers from across the country to attend. Most top leaders attended the meetings, enjoyed the dinners, and Victor attended most but not all of them.

The sessions were interesting—the top leaders found the meetings were a great forum for politicking, posturing, wining and dining, and trying to sharpshoot the consultant. Victor asked his top leaders to come together for a half day in the spring to discuss the content and direction of the high-performance initiative, being convinced intellectually by the dinner discussions that this was the right direction for the company. At the half-day meeting, it was obvious that about half of the group agreed with the CEO and about half were uncertain or downright resistant, particularly one very senior vice president. Victor left the team with this message, "Let me take your comments under advisement and think about them as we go forward." Later, at the consultant's suggestion, he conducted an organizational assessment to identify problems that might be contributory to the uneven, up-and-down performance. The assessment uncovered several serious problems that required change, yet the senior leaders continued to resist.

The Next Steps

Victor finally hired one of the external advisors who withstood the test of several dinner meetings and the challenges of his threatened senior management team. Victor asked the advisor to speak to the top leaders of the entire company about what a great group they were and how important the performance excellence initiative was going to be for the company. The advisor closed by telling them that only the best go after high performance; if they did not, their competitors would. During the following discussion sessions, Victor's chief operating officer announced to the group that he was far from convinced and stated he was not going to change the way he did business. That comment went unchallenged by Victor or anyone else in the company. Frustration continued to build.

In an effort to regain momentum, Victor wanted to create a change team. He asked each division to send a person to "facilitate" the initiative and receive appropriate training in managing change. The people selected were far from the best each division could offer since no selection criteria were provided and many thought this was a waste of time and talent. The division leaders supplied people that were expendable. The people who formed the facilitator group, for their part, were very enthusiastic but not particularly respected or credible. They were given absolutely no relief from any regular duties so they were stretched very thin. Also, the division heads were not supportive

in any way of their participation so they were almost punished for participating on this team. As the facilitators worked to please the demands of the CEO, there was no clear charter or mission as to what they were actually supposed to accomplish—no way to assess their performance or keep track of progress.

The power struggle intensified between the COO (who thought this was not the way to go and would have none of it) and the CEO. The CEO and the top management team arranged to travel to a leadership conference where they could hear presentations from high-performance organizations that had used the performance excellence techniques successfully. The CEO made it a priority to plan only morning presentations so everyone could play tennis or golf together each afternoon. Tennis and golf, not the need for better management systems, was the main topic of discussion at the evening dinners. A good time was had by all, but no consensus around change developed or was even discussed.

Training and the Change Process

Still, Victor wanted the facilitators to continue their work to assist change. The internal facilitators were placed in charge of conducting training for the entire organization. After the initial training was designed, a date was set to present a half-day version to the senior staff. Although the training designed for employees and lower level managers was a four-day course, the senior staff did not feel they needed the same intense training or skills as the workforce. However, Victor made it a high priority for his direct reports to attend. At the last minute, Victor had to attend a function related to the Board of Directors and did not attend.

The training was, to put it mildly, a disaster. The executives, prompted by the snide comments of the COO, never gave it a chance. They concluded that the training was not effective and should not be rolled out to the employees. In the face of compelling opposition, Victor quietly diverted his attention elsewhere.

Leadership Style Summary

It is probably obvious what the current state is of John's high-performance "way to run the business" versus the high-performance "initiative" at Victor's company. Perhaps you could spot some of the problems each type of leader addressed and solutions they supported.

Using symbols and language to manage the change to high performance is tricky and usually demands that some external person is involved who can provide good sound advice, based on experience and expertise, to the CEO. Using power constructively is absolutely critical, since failure of the top leader to use all forms of power and influence available will intensify conflict and power struggles that act as a de facto barrier to change.

Motivating people to act constructively, and not feel threatened, is another challenge. Providing a clear focus on the future state while rewarding behavior that facilitates the transition will work to ensure the change actually happens. Victor's vision was unclear. He did not act as a leader. He ensured his facilitators would never succeed by never championing their work in any way. The next time Victor gets a new idea, these people (if they are still employees) will take a nosedive rather than be at the forefront of the initiative.

John never lost his vision or influence as CEO. He ensured his management team was supportive by first defining and clarifying organizational values, direction, and expectations; encouraging them to climb on board; and ensuring they acquired the skills and support to spread the approaches throughout the company.

LEADERSHIP

Based on the CEO research cited earlier, coupled with the relentless pace of change in all sectors and increasingly global competition, there are several strong messages leaders need to understand. Then they must be willing to take the necessary steps to change. This will require an assessment of current management systems and a willingness to drive the necessary adjustment. Once the assessment is complete and priorities are agreed upon, line up plans and resources and support the change wholeheartedly. Focus on the marketplace for your cues to change. Ask, for example:

* Is your competition growing weaker?

* Is the economy more stable and secure?

* Are the demands of all of your customers declining?

* Do you have all of the resources you need to meet your future goals?

* Do you believe your employees will be willing or able to continue working at the pace you have set for them? Will they do more?

If the answer is NO to any of these questions, read on.

Assess management systems and launch improvements. This will require your organization to assess their management against the Baldrige Criteria. After the assessment is complete, identify the vital few next steps, assign responsibility, make improvements, and reevaluate.

Great Leaders Are Great Communicators Who Lead by Example

One characteristic of a high-performance organization is outstanding performance results. How does an organization achieve such results? How does it become world-class? We have found unanimous agreement on the critical and fundamental role of leadership. There is not one example of an organization or unit within an organization that achieves superior levels of performance without the personal and active involvement of its top leadership. Top leaders in these organizations create a powerful vision that focuses and energizes the workforce. Everyone is pulling together toward the same goals. Frequently, an inspired vision, combined with appropriately aligned recognition and reward, is the catalyst that builds trust and launches initiatives to overcome the organizational status quo.

Great leaders communicate clear objectives. They assign accountability, ensure that employees have the tools and skills required, and create a work climate where individual initiative and the transfer of learning thrives. They reward teamwork and data-driven improvement. While practicing what they preach they serve as role models for continuous improvement, consensus building, and fact-based decision making; they push authority and accountability to the lowest possible levels.

One lesson from great leaders is to refrain from the use of the word "quality." Too often, when skilled, hard-working, dedicated employees are told by leaders, "We must improve quality," they conclude that their leaders believe they have not been working hard enough. The workforce hears an unintended message, "We have to do this because we are not good." They frequently retort with, "We already do quality work!" Registered professionals (engineers, chemists, psychologists, physicians, teachers, to name a few) often exacerbate the communication problem by arguing that they, not customers, are the best ones in a position to know and define "quality." These messages confuse the workforce. Unfortunately, the use of the word quality can create an unintended barrier of mistrust and negativism that leaders must overcome before even starting on the road to performance excellence.

Instead, we advise leaders to create a work climate that enables employees to develop and use their full potential, to improve continually the way they work—to seek higher performance levels and reduce activities that do not add value or optimize performance. Most employees readily agree that there is always room for improvement—all have seen work that does not add value.

The use of the word quality can also open leadership to challenges as to what definition of quality the organization should use. This leads to our second lesson learned. Leaders will have to overcome two organizational tendencies—to reject any management model or approach "not invented here" and to think that there are many equally valid models. Quality differs from a decision tree or problem-solving model where there are many acceptable alternatives. The Baldrige model—and the many national, state, and organization assessment systems based on it—is accepted as the standard for defining performance excellence in organizations worldwide. Its criteria provide validated, leading-edge practices for managing an organization to achieve peak performance.

A decade of extraordinary business results shown by Baldrige Award winners and numerous state-level, Baldrige Award-based winners have helped convince those willing to learn and listen.

To be effective, leaders must understand the Baldrige model and communicate to the workforce and leadership system their intention to use that model for assessment and improvement. Without clear leadership commitment to achieving the requirements of the comprehensive Baldrige model, resources may be spent chasing fads, special projects, and isolated strategies such as activity-based costing, management by objective, reengineering, project management, quality circles, and ISO 9000 certification, to name a few. Without clear leadership there will be many "hikers" walking around but no marked trails for them to follow. Once leaders understand the system and realize that it is their responsibility to share the knowledge and mark the trails clearly, performance optimization is attainable. This brings us to our third leadership lesson learned.

A significant portion of senior leaders' time—as much as 60 percent to 80 percent—should be spent in visible Baldrige-related leadership activities such as goal setting, planning, reviewing performance, recognizing and rewarding high performance, and spending time understanding and communicating with customers and suppliers, not micromanaging subordinates' work. The senior leaders' perspective in goal setting, planning, and reviewing performance must look at the inside from the outside. Looking at the organization through the critical eyes of external customers, suppliers, and other stakeholders is a vital perspective.

The primary role of the effective senior leader is to focus the organization on satisfying customers through an effective leadership system. Leaders must role model the tools of consensus building and decision making as the organization focuses on its vision, mission, and strategic direction to keep customers loyal.

Falling back on command-and-control behavior is likely to be self-defeating. The leadership system will suffer from crossed wires and mixed messages. Proclamations such as, "I want this mission rolled out by the end of the second quarter" fall into the self-defeating, major mistake category. Leaders must be clear and resolute as well as encouraging and nurturing.

Using the consensus approach to focus the organization on its mission and vision will take longer. This is similar to taking more time during the product design phase to ensure that problems are prevented later. The additional time is necessary for organizational learning, support, and buy-in, particularly around two areas—integrating global marketplace realities and better understanding the competitive environment. The resulting vision will have more depth and focus. The leadership system will be stronger as more leaders and managers understand and agree on the course of action. Ultimately, the deployment of the vision and focus will take less time because of the greater buy-in and support created during the process.

Listen

Successful leaders know the power in listening to their people—those they rely on to achieve their goals. One vital link to the pulse of the organization is employee feedback. To determine whether what you have said has been understood, ask for feedback and then listen carefully. To know whether what you have outlined as a plan makes sense or has gaping faults, ask for feedback and then listen. Your leadership system cannot improve without your listening and acting on employee feedback, and your goals and action plans cannot be improved without it. In fact, the 2002 Baldrige Criteria [Item 1.1b(3), Note 3] indicate that leaders should use employee feedback in assessing and improving their leadership effectiveness and the effectiveness of managers at all levels.

Manage and Drive Change

Business leaders can count on relentless, rapid change being part of the business world. The rate of change confronting business today is far faster than that driven by the Industrial Revolution. Skills driven by the Industrial Revolution carried our parents through a 40-year work life. Human knowledge now doubles every five to seven years, instead of the 40 years it took in the 1930s. Today, our children are told to expect five career (not job) changes during their work life.

There are several lessons for leaders today. Change may not occur on the schedule they set for it. It is often faster or too uneven to predict at all. Also, change driven by leaders is often resisted by those most successful—they have difficulty seeing the need to change. Take, for example, a school district that scheduled a quality improvement workshop for its middle school faculty. The day before the training, the district leadership received a letter protesting the workshop on the grounds it was not needed. The letter was signed by the 20 best teachers in the school. To the credit of the school district leadership, they held the workshop anyway, and the truly outstanding teachers saw the value in continuous improvement once they began to listen.

Leaders who hold the values of high performance will need to drive change to make the necessary improvements. Change will not happen naturally. It is rarely driven by those at the bottom (except for revolutionaries). Embracing the concepts of organizational learning (not just individual) will facilitate change in the organization. Leaders will need organizational learning as an ally as they manage change and drive it through the organization.

STRATEGIC PLANNING

Deploy Through People Not Paper

Strategic planning helps identify the things an organization must consider as it plans its future. The resulting strategic plan may also include elements of a quality plan; business plan; tactical plan; operational plan; financial plan; facilities plan; environmental, health, and safety plan; and human resources plan, to name a few. Each subplan seeks to identify the specific things to do in order to be successful in the future and achieve the overall strategy. Easily enough said, but trying to get agreement on exactly what strategic planning is will result in an interesting variety of ideas. Therefore, the planning process should begin by ensuring that all contributors agree on terminology. Otherwise the strategic plan may be incomplete—a marketing plan, a budget plan, or a financial business plan, depending on who is leading the team.

Developing separate plans for each aspect of business success is counterproductive. This approach almost guarantees a nonintegrated and short-lived systematic performance improvement effort. Therefore, leaders should concentrate on the few critical improvement goals in the strategic plan necessary for organizational success, such as improving customer loyalty and reducing errors or cycle time. The well-developed strategic plan also:

- Documents the financial impact of achieving these few goals

- Details actions to support the goals

- Discusses the competitive environment that drives the goals

The most critical lesson learned when it comes to strategic plans is that there can be no rest until it is certain every person in the organization understands his or her role in the plan and how their contribution will be measured. One highly successful organization simplified this document to a single electronic page, to which senior leaders referred each month by computer during performance results reviews. Everyone at all levels used their own one-page document to deploy the plan and define actions needed.

CUSTOMER AND MARKET FOCUS

Customers Expect Solutions to Problems They Don't Know They Have

The high-performing organization systematically determines its customers' short- and long-term service and product requirements. It does this based on information from former as well as current and potential customers. It builds relationships with customers and continuously obtains information, using it to improve its service and products and understand better customer preferences. The smart organization prioritizes the drivers of satisfaction and loyalty of its customers, compares itself to its competitors, and continuously strives to improve its satisfaction and loyalty levels.

As the organization becomes more and more systematic and effective in determining customer needs, it learns that there is high variation in customer needs. The more sophisticated the measurement system, the more variation will become apparent. It is particularly important that organizations focus on this vital process and make it a top priority that their customers have access to people to make known their requirements and their preferences. How else can modern organizations ensure they are building relationships with their customers? After all, few of us have storefront windows on Main Street where our customers come and chat regularly.

One specific lesson learned comes from voice-mail—a big step forward in convenience and efficiency can be a big step backward in customer relationship building if used poorly. For example, a major international financial institution put their highest priority customers on a new voicemail system. Customers were never informed about the system and one day called their special line to find rock music and a three-tiered voicemail system instead of their personal financial account manager. This is a good example of a step in the wrong direction—customers were never asked about their requirements and preferences and the organization heard about it quickly in the form of lost accounts and angry, frustrated customers.

Another important first lesson is to segment customers according to their needs and preferences and do what is necessary to build strong, positive relationships with them. More and more customers are looking for service providers to define their unique needs for them and respond to those unique needs. In short, customers are expecting solutions to problems that they, the customers, have not yet realized.

Organizations that make it easy for customers to complain are in a good position to hear about problems early so that they can fix them and plan ahead to prevent them. If organizations handle customer complaints effectively at the first point of contact, customer loyalty and satisfaction will increase. When organizations do not make it easy for customers to complain, when finally given the chance to provide feedback, they will not bother to complain; they simply will no longer do business with these organizations.

As the customer-focused organization matures, it will likely evolve around customer types. This evolution leads to restructuring that is guided by shared organizational values. The speed with which this restructuring occurs varies according to marketplace conditions and the organization's ability to change. Today we see more restructuring that eliminates parochial, regional centers in favor of creating customer service groups that meet customer requirements around the world using up-to-date technologies.

The next lesson has to do with educating the organization's leadership in the fundamentals of customer loyalty and customer satisfaction research models before beginning to collect customer satisfaction data. Failure to do this may affect the usefulness of the data as a strategic tool. At the very least, it will make the development of data collection instruments a long, misunderstood effort, creating rework and unnecessary cost.

Do not expect everyone to welcome customer feedback—many fear accountability. Time and time again, the organizations most resistant to surveying customers, conducting focus groups, and making it easy for customers to complain are the same organizations that do not have everyday contact handling systems, response time standards, or trained and empowered frontline employees to serve customers and deal with their concerns promptly. Frontline employees who are not ready to acknowledge customer concerns are not capable of assuming responsibility to solve customer problems.

No single feedback tool is intended to stand alone. A mail-based survey does not take the place of personal interviews. Focus groups do not replace surveys. The high-performance organization uses multiple listening posts and trains frontline employees to collect customer feedback and improve those listening posts. In the high-performance organization, for example, even an accounts receivable system is viewed as a listening post.

Do not lose sight of the fact that the best customer feedback method, whether it be a survey, focus group, or one-on-one interview, is only a tool.

- Make sure the data gathered are actionable
- Aggregate the data from all sources to permit complete analyses
- Use the data to improve strategic planning and operating processes

Finally, be aware that customers are not interested in your problems. They merely want products or services delivered as promised. They become loyal when consistent value is provided that sets you above all others. Merely meeting their basic expectations brands you as marginal. To be valued you must consistently delight and exceed the customers' expectations.

Information and Analysis

Data-Driven Management and Avoiding Contephobia

The high-performance organization collects, manages, and analyzes data and information to drive excellence and improve its overall performance. Said another way, information is used to drive actions. Using data and information as strategic weapons, effective leaders compare their organization constantly to competitors, similar service providers, and world-class organizations.

While people tend to think of data and measurement as objective and hard, there is often a softer by-product of measurement. That by-product is the basic human emotion of fear. This perspective on data and measurement leads to the first lesson learned about information and analysis. Human fear must be recognized and managed in order to practice data-driven management.

This fear can be found in two types of people. The first are those who have a simple fear of numbers—those who hated mathematics in school and probably stretch their quantitative capabilities to balance their checkbook. These individuals are lost in numerical data discussions. When asked to measure or when presented with data, they can become fearful, angry, and resistant. Their reactions can actually undermine improvement efforts.

The second type of individual, who understands numbers, realizes that numbers can impose higher levels of accountability. The fear of accountability, contephobia (from fourteenth-century Latin "to count," modified by the French "to account"), is based on the fear of real performance failure that numbers might reveal or, more often, an overall fear of the unknown that will drive important decisions. Power structures can and do shift when decisions are data-driven.

Fearful individuals can undermine effective data-driven management systems. In managing this fear, leaders must believe and communicate through their behavior that a number is not inherently right or wrong. It is important for leaders at all levels to demonstrate that system and process improvement, not individuals, are the focus of performance improvement.

A mature, high-performance organization will collect data on competitors and similar providers and benchmark itself against world-class leaders. Some individuals may not be capable of seeing the benefit of using this process performance information. This type of data is known as benchmarking data. The focus is on identifying, learning from, and adopting best practices or methods from similar processes, regardless of industry or product similarity. Adopting the best practices of other organizations has driven quantum leap improvements and provided great opportunities for breakthrough improvements.

Lesson number two, therefore, is that an organization that has difficulty comparing itself with dissimilar organizations is not ready to benchmark and is not likely to be able to optimize its own performance as a result.

The third lesson in this area relates to not being a DRIP. This refers to a tendency to collect so much data (which contributes to contephobia) that the organization becomes data rich and information poor. This is wrong. Avoid wasting capital resources and stretch the resources available for managing improvement by asking this question: "Will these data help make improvements for our customers, key financials, employees, or top result areas?" If the answer is no, do not waste time collecting, analyzing, and trying to use the data.

Human Resource Focus

Human Resources (Not just the Department)

Personnel departments have been renamed in many organizations, often to "human resources." This name change is intended to draw attention to the fact that people are valuable resources of the organization, not just dispensable commodities to be hired, fired, and commanded. Now, however, the leap made by successful organizations is that human resources need to be part of every strategic and operational decision of the organization. This focus goes far beyond the department of human resources. In high-performing organizations, employees are treated like any valuable asset of the organization—investment and development are critical to optimize the asset. People should be perceived as internal customers, and a vital part of the chain that eventually serves an external customer.

One of the valuable lessons learned in this regard is not to let an out-of-date or territorial "personnel or human resources department" use archaic rules to stop your performance improvement program. Although many human resources professionals are among the brave pioneers in high-performance organizations, others have tried to keep compensation and promotions tied to "seat time" and tenure rather than performance. This outdated approach will definitely stop progress in its tracks or slow it significantly.

The Big Challenge is Trust

The high-performing organization values its employees and demonstrates this by enabling people to develop and realize their full potential while providing them incentives to do so. The organization that is focused on human resource excellence maintains a climate that builds trust. Trust is essential for employee participation, engagement, personal and professional growth, and high organizational performance.

The first human resource lesson is perhaps the most critical one. That is, revise—overhaul, if necessary—recognition, compensation, promotion, and feedback systems to support high-performance work systems. If leaders personally demonstrate all the correct leadership behaviors, yet continue to recognize and reward "fire fighting" performance, offer pay and bonuses tied only to traditional bottom line results, and promote individuals who do not represent high-performance role models—those leaders will find their improvement effort is short-lived. The leadership system with all its webs and intricate circuits will short out due to mixed signals.

Promotion, compensation, recognition, and reward must be tied to the achievement of key high-performance results, including customer satisfaction, innovation, performance improvement, and other business results. The promotion/compensation/recognition tool is a powerful tool to assist in aligning, or misaligning, the work of the organization.

A second human resource lesson learned relates to training and development. Training is not a panacea or a goal in itself. The organization's direction and goals must support training, and training must support organization priorities. Its human resources are the competitive edge of a high-performing organization. Training must be part of an overall business strategy. If not, money and resources are probably better spent on a memorable holiday party.

Timing is critical. Broad-based workforce skill training should not come first. Many organizations rush out and train their entire workforce only to find themselves having to retrain months or years later. Key participants should be involved in planning skill training so that important skills are delivered just in time for them to use in their assignments.

Continuous skill development requires management support to reinforce and strengthen skills on the job. Leadership development at all levels of the organization needs to be built into employee development. New technology has increased training flexibility so that all knowledge does not have to be transferred in a classroom setting. Consider many options when planning how best to update skills. After initial skill building occurs, high-performing organizations emphasize organizational learning where employees take charge of their own learning, using training courses as only one avenue for skill upgrading. Transferring learning to other parts of the organization or projects is a valuable organizational learning strategy and reinforcement technique. Training must be offered when an application exists to use and reinforce the skill. Otherwise, most of what is learned will be forgotten. The effectiveness of training must be assessed based on the impact on the job, not merely the likeability of the instructor or the clarity of course materials.

Employee surveys are often used to measure and improve employee satisfaction. Surveys are especially useful to identify key issues that should be discussed in open employee forums. Such forums are truly useful if they clarify perceptions, provide more in-depth understanding of employee concerns, and open the communication channels with leaders. Organizations have success in improving employee satisfaction by conducting routine employee satisfaction surveys, meeting with employees to plan improvements, and tying improvements in satisfaction ratings to managers' compensation.

Two final human resource excellence lessons have to do with engaging and involving employees in decisions about their work. Involving employees in decision making without the right skills or a sense of direction produces chaos, not high performance.

- First, leaders who empower employees before communicating and testing that a sense of direction has been fully understood will find that they are managing chaos.

- Second, not everyone wants to be empowered, and to do so may represent a barrier to high performance. While there may be individuals who truly seek to avoid responsibility for making improvements, claiming "that's management's job," these individuals do not last long in a high-performing organization. They begin to stick out like a lone bird in the winter. Team members who want the organization to thrive and survive do not permit such people to influence (or even remain on) their team.

The bigger reason for individuals failing to "take the empowerment and run with it" is management's mixed messages. In short, management must convince employees that they (managers) really believe that employees know their own processes best and can improve them. Consistent leadership is required to help employees overcome legitimate, long-standing fear of traditional management practices used so often in the past to control and punish.

Remember, aligning compensation and reward systems to reinforce performance plans and core values is one of the most critical things to enhance organizational performance; however, getting employees to believe their leaders really trust them to improve their own processes is difficult.

Process Management

Listen to Process Owners and Keep Them Involved

Process management involves the continuous improvement of processes required to meet customer requirements and deliver quality products and services. Virtually every high-performance organization identifies key processes and manages them to ensure that customer requirements are met consistently and performance is continuously improved.

The first lesson learned has to do with the visibility of processes. Many processes are highly visible, such as serving a meal or purchasing. However, when a process is hard to observe, such as service design or customer response, as so many are in the service sector, it cannot be assumed that everyone will see the organization as a collection of processes. The simple exercise of drawing a process flow diagram with people involved in an invisible process can be a struggle, but also a valuable revelation. With no vantage point from which to see work as a process, many people never think of themselves as engaged in a process. Some even deny it. The fact that all work—visible and invisible—is part of a process must be understood throughout the organization before employees can begin to consistently execute and improve key processes.

Once this is understood, a second process management lesson comes to light. Process owners are the best ones, but not the only ones, to improve their processes. They must be part of process improvement teams. These teams are often made up of carefully selected cross-discipline, cross-functional, multilevel people who bring fresh insight to the examination of a process. Do not lose sight of the process owner— the person with expert knowledge of the process who should be accountable for long-term improvement to it. In a misguided effort to ensure that all of its process improvement teams were cross-functional and multilevel, one organization enlisted volunteers to join process improvement teams. Using this democratic process, a marketing process improvement team ended up with no credible marketing expertise among its members. Instead, a group of frustrated support and technical staff members, who knew nothing about marketing, wasted time and money mapping and redesigning a process doomed to fail.

The third process management lesson learned involves an issue mentioned earlier. When focusing too closely on internal process data, there is a tendency to lose sight of external requirements. Organizations often succeed at making their processes better, faster, and (maybe) cheaper for them, but not necessarily to the benefit of their customers. When analyzing internal process data, someone must stubbornly play the role of advocate for the customers' perspective. Ensure that the data will help make improvements for customers, key financials, employees, or top result areas. Avoid wasting resources on process improvements that do not benefit customers, employees, or the key performance objectives of your organization.

A fourth lesson involves design processes, an important but often neglected part of process management. The best organizations have learned that improvements made early in the process, beginning with design, save more time and resources than those made farther "downstream." To identify how design processes can be improved it is necessary to include ongoing evaluation and improvement cycles.

Business Results

Encourage Activities That Lead to Desired Business Results

Results fall into four broad categories.

1. Customer-focused, such as customer satisfaction and product and service quality

2. Financial and market

3. Human resource

4. Organizational effectiveness, such as key design, production, delivery and support performance, regulatory/legal compliance, and the extent that strategic objectives were achieved

Customer-focused is a critical and ongoing result that every successful organization or work unit within an organization must achieve. Systems must exist to make sure that the data from customer satisfaction and dissatisfaction are used at all levels to plan and make improvements. Remember that when customers are asked their opinion, an expectation is created in their minds that the information will be used to make improvements that benefit them.

Some organizations have found it beneficial to have their customers analyze some of their business results with the idea of learning from them as well as building and strengthening relationships. This may or may not be appropriate for your organization, but many successful ones have shared results with key customer groups at a level appropriate for their specific organization.

Product and service quality results provide useful information on key measures of the product or service itself. This information allows an organization to predict whether customers are likely to be satisfied—usually without asking them. For example, one of the nation's most successful and fastest-growing coffee shops knows from its customers that a good cup of coffee is hot, has a good taste, is not too bitter, and has a rich aroma. The measures for these product characteristics are temperature, pH (acidity), and the time lapsed between brewing and serving. With these measures, they can predict whether their customers are likely to be satisfied with the coffee before they serve it. One important lesson in this area is to select measures that correlate with, and predict, customer preference, satisfaction, and loyalty.

Financial and market performance is a key to survival. Organizations that make improvements that do not ultimately improve financial performance are wasting resources and growing weaker financially. This is true for both private sector (for profit) and public sector (not-for-profit, education, government) organizations. It is important to avoid over-reliance on financial results. Financial results are the lagging indicators of organization performance. Leaders who focus primarily on financials often overlook or cannot respond quickly to changing business needs. Focusing on finances to run the business—to the exclusion of leading indicators such as operational performance and employee satisfaction—is like driving your car by looking only in the rear view mirror. You cannot avoid pot holes and turns in the road.

Human resource performance results provide early alert to problems that may threaten success. Absenteeism, turnover, accidents, low morale, grievances, and poor skills or ineffective training suboptimize organizational effectiveness. By monitoring performance in these areas, leaders can adjust quickly and prevent little problems from overwhelming the organization.

Organizational effectiveness and operational and service results pertain to measures of internal effectiveness that may not be of immediate interest to customers, such as cycle time (how long it takes to brew a pot of coffee), waste (how many pots you have to pour out because the coffee sat too long), and payroll accuracy (which may upset the affected workers). Ultimately, improving internal work process efficiency can result in reduced cost, rework, waste, scrap, and other factors that affect the bottom line, whether profit-driven or budget-driven. As a result, customers are indirectly affected. To stay in business, to remain competitive, or to meet increased performance demands with fewer resources, the organization will be required to improve processes that enhance operational and support service results. The results also need to address the organization performance regarding regulatory, legal compliance and citizenship. Results relating to accomplishment of organizational strategy are also to be addressed.

LEADERSHIP SUMMARY: SEVEN MUST-DO PRACTICES

Keys to Optimizing Performance

There is no evidence of an organization optimizing performance and achieving Baldrige recognition without enhancing the entire management system, from leadership and planning to customers, people, and processes. Although all of these processes are critical in the long term, it is the responsibility of top leaders to set the direction, values, and expectations that drive change and create a sense of urgency. Leader actions absolutely determine the speed and success of the effort to optimize organizational performance. If leaders fail to take the following actions, the transformation to a high-performing organization will be seriously delayed and most likely not take place.

1. Role Model Effective Leadership Practices. Like it or not, your actions drive the actions of others far better than your words. Rhetoric without appropriate action is virtually worthless. Do not expect anyone else to do the things you will not.

- If you do not aggressively drive performance excellence in word and deed, others will think it is optional.

- If you do not have time to innovate, no one else will think innovation is important.

- If you do not empower the employees with whom you work, other managers will follow your lead (and fail to empower and engage their employees).

- If you do not hold managers accountable for empowering their subordinates, they will believe empowerment is optional.

- If you do not seek data to help make better decisions, others will emulate you.

- If you do not learn new things, you may not keep up with important changes affecting your business and others will not see the value in learning.

Develop a list of attributes you want to role model. Check how you are perceived on these leadership attributes from peer, subordinate, and employee feedback. Change the areas where you are role modeling the wrong things.

2. Favor Actions Based on Fact Rather than Intuition. The lack of facts and data force leaders to default to intuition as the basis for decision making. Many great leaders have relied on intuition when facts were unavailable. However, no great leader relied only on intuition, or even mostly on intuition. The best leaders make consistently good decisions, which require reliable facts and data.

We rarely have access to all of the information we want prior to making decisions. However, we will surely not have enough fact-based information unless we prepare in advance. To make consistently better decisions, the best leaders drive fact-based diagnosis of organizational performance that focuses on closing the gaps in areas critical to success. This information is readily available and easy to understand.

3. Learn Constantly. Great leaders recognize that current knowledge limits their capabilities and success. You may think you have all of the knowledge and skills you need but how do you know what you do not know? Do not expect your subordinates to learn for you because they suffer from the same limits. Considering the pace of change and the speed with which human knowledge is doubling, unless you aggressively pursue new knowledge, you will most certainly become obsolete and less effective faster.

Identify and list the things you must learn to become a better leader. Ask your subordinates to give you feedback to help you complete the list. Set learning goals and timelines to monitor the pace of new learning.

4. Share Knowledge. Enhance the impact of your new knowledge by sharing it with others. By teaching others and answering their questions, your grasp of the knowledge becomes stronger and you can apply it faster and easier. It is also a good way to role model the value of learning.

Set a schedule to teach others about performance excellence systems and processes at least two to four times each year and stick to it.

5. Require Other Leaders in Your Organization to Do the Same. The performance of individuals drives the performance of the organization. If your performance is suboptimal because you lack certain knowledge, skills, and abilities, the same is certainly true for your subordinates and their employees. After they see the value you place in role modeling effective practices, learning, and coaching, make it clear you expect them to do the same. It is critical to clearly set this expectation for learning, as well as setting clear, measurable expectations for work after they complete the training.

Discuss your concerns, expectations, and answer their questions. You will have to do this very often at first. Be consistent. Those who resist change look for loopholes and ways to avoid change. Do not create loopholes for them. Permit no excuses for those who refuse to learn. Champion the requirements leading to optimum organizational performance.

6. Align Expectations, Measures, Rewards, and Recognition. *The system you have put in place is perfectly suited to produce the results you are currently getting.* If you want to change the outcomes you must change the people and processes that produce them. Training is only a part of the change process.

- Express all new expectations for both individual and group performance in measurable terms.

- Measure progress regularly and give prompt feedback.

- Visibly reward and recognize the desired behavior.

- Find other work for those who cannot or will not do the things needed for driving high performance. By rewarding those who achieve desired results and removing those who do not, you make it clear that performance excellence is crucial to success—it is not optional. If you keep a manager in place who has not taken the necessary steps to improve, you must realize that the subordinates of that manager conclude that his performance must be OK.

To enhance desired business results, ensure that goals, strategic objectives, actions, measures, analysis, and reward and recognition are completely aligned. Remember, "What gets measured, gets done. What gets rewarded gets done first." If our strategic objectives are truly critical to our future success, be sure to assign actions, measure progress, and reward desired behavior and outcomes.

7. Use Training as a Tool to Develop Skills and Inform—Not as a Substitute for Personal Leadership Action. Employees desire and expect important information to come from their leaders.

- Do not simply tell employees to do something new and different and expect it will be done. You must check understanding, measure and monitor progress, and provide appropriate incentives to actually get the desired behavior.

- Sending subordinate managers and employees to training and expecting the trainer to give the new management directions will rarely produce the desired results. It usually produces high skepticism, hostility, and reinforces the idea that leaders are not serious and committed to the new program or change—otherwise they would introduce it themselves. It also makes the trainer and the curriculum the target of criticism and blame:

  – "This class is a waste of time."

  – "The trainer should tell us what to do when we get back to the office."

  – "I do not know why I am here."

  – "Just how serious is management about these changes/programs? Have they taken this training?"

  – "What resources is management going to commit to this effort?"

- Before sending anyone to training, participants need to understand and be able to describe why they are there and what they are expected to get out of the training. These expectations should be set by the leaders that send the participants, not the trainers. Leaders could ask trainers to "pretest" the class to determine the extent to which participants understand why they are there. Those who are not prepared should be sent back. It should be the job of the sending manager to provide the proper foundation and preparation for his or her subordinate employees prior to training.

If you do not do the seven activities listed above, you are by your actions telling your employees and subordinate managers that performance excellence is optional—something to do when they have nothing else to do. In that event, you and your organization will most certainly fail to achieve the desired change and improvement.

LEADING THE CHANGE TO HIGH PERFORMANCE

To effectively lead an organization to improve the culture usually requires refreshing. Changing culture is not easy and requires dedicated and unwavering consistency in support of the "new way" or "desired way" of behaving and believing. The following actions are usually critical to change culture in an organization.

- **Establish clear goals and a clear direction.** Explain clearly what will be required and how the new requirements are different from the old. If you do not know what new behaviors are required, find out. Talk to those leaders who have successfully engineered this kind of improvement in the past. Leaders who are not clear invite confusion and inaction.

- **Show unwavering commitment.** Leaders are pivotal to the success of the enterprise—employees watch them closely. Don't blink in the face of setbacks—quitting is easy and doing so will make employees more cynical and demoralized. When leadership commitment and support is seen as tentative, employees and other subordinates will perceive the changes as "optional," take-or-leave suggestions. Considering the profound ability most people have to resist change, this creates more support for doing nothing.

- **Prove you will change.** If leaders do not "walk the talk," and demonstrate their eagerness to operate differently, others once again conclude that the leaders are not serious and the new requirements are optional.

- **Keep the energy level high and focused on both process improvements and better performance outcomes**. Select improvements that are easy as well as difficult. Small successes are needed to keep the energy and support for performance excellence high. Larger improvement projects take longer to carry out but usually bring greater benefit. Celebrate process improvements as well as better performance outcomes.

- **Encourage people to challenge the status quo when doing so is consistent with enhancing customer value and organizational goals.** Do not tolerate system craziness—break old bureaucratic rules and policies that prevent or inhibit work toward goals. Free your people from bureaucratic silliness and you will find great energy and support from employees.

- **Change rewards to make them consistent with goals and objectives.** Make following the new culture and achieving goals worthwhile by rewarding desired behaviors and making the continued use of the old ones unpleasant. All employees must understand that the rewards are issued for behaving in a certain way and for achieving desired results. Rewards, including compensation and incentives, should not be considered an entitlement of employment. It is important to test the effectiveness of rewards and recognition. Remember, just because you value a reward does not mean that employees will do the same.

- **Measure progress.** What gets measured gets done. When leaders use measurements to track progress, people think they are serious about tracking and improving. If you do not bother measuring, employee productivity is usually lower. In addition, measurements help identify those who should be rewarded, and those who should not. Finally, keep measurements simple and efficient. Do not allow the process of measurement to divert energy and focus. Stop collecting data that no longer supports effective decisionmaking.

- **Communicate, communicate, communicate.** Communication cannot replace an inspiring vision and sound goals, but poor communication can scuttle them. People must understand the logic and rationale behind the vision and goals. Leaders must tell them what's coming, how they will be affected, and what's expected of them. Remember to take every opportunity to communicate your desires—once is not enough. The opponents of change will work nonstop to undermine the new goal, vision, and culture—communicate consistently to overcome this resistance. Also remember that even motivated and supportive people forget—remind them often of the vision and new expectations. Leaders that do not communicate effectively invite the rumor mill to fill in the blank spaces. Bad news, bad rumors, and outright lies frequently fill the communication gap leaders might inadvertently leave.

- **Involve everyone.** People who do not actively support change oppose it, perhaps inadvertently. Insist on full involvement and define a role for everyone. Find ways to make everyone accountable for transforming the culture and improving performance. Remember that if a manager fails to support the changes needed to improve performance, it is probably a good idea to encourage that person to find other work—preferably with a competitor.

- **Start fast, then go faster.** Slow progress, which the opponents of change like to see, creates a self-fulfilling prophecy—that the proposed changes will not be effective. However, speed creates a sense of urgency that helps overcome organizational inertia, achieve stunning results, and defeat the gloom and pessimism of naysayers.

Remember to remain steadfast in support, walk the talk, involve everyone, communicate, achieve quick results, measure, and reward progress.

Improve Performance, Efficiency, and Timeliness

What does it mean?

- Includes but is not limited to process identification, analysis, and improvement. We must define and measure process cycle time and defects and reduce them.

What is the manager's responsibility?

- Set an example—ask for data/measurements on cycle time and defects
- Make time available
- Make training available
- Ensure that records discipline exists
- Charter teams
- Set low goals, get low performance
- If you do not tell employees what you expect, do not be surprised if they do not get where you want them to go

Create a Participative, Cooperative Workplace

What does it mean?

- Includes but is not limited to setting boundary conditions and relevant goals, then moving decisions to the lowest possible level, using work teams for planning and process improvement, and creating a "family-friendly" work environment. Leaders motivate people; provide training for managers and employees; encourage the development of self-directed work teams; delegate authority and decision making downward; empower people to focus on achieving mission and vision; value diversity; provide open communication in all directions; and measure and improve employee well-being, motivation, and satisfaction.

What is the manager's responsibility?

- Coach and counsel, rather than control
- Encourage participation with the goal of achieving better decision quality—make better use of human resources
- Create and build a highly motivated and satisfied workforce

Planning Action

- Based on vision and results from the previous year, every organization clarifies direction through planning and the deployment of the plan to guide daily action

- Leaders are responsible for:

  – Identifying improvement opportunities in their units and identifying the key actions needed to achieve the improvements

  – Identifying who will lead the improvements and chartering teams to do so

- All managers have responsibility for identifying unit and individual performance objectives to achieve desired performance levels and targets at all levels of the organization

Taking Action

- All leaders have a responsibility for communicating the mission, vision, goals, and improvement targets to all employees.

- It is very important that leaders and employees understand and agree fully with the planned objectives. The plan deployment process cascades from top management to all locations and levels of the organization. Top managers do not micromanage the process. This means that the top leaders determine the objective or target and an action officer determines the means. This then sets the target for the next level to determine means. Figure 12 provides one example of this effect.

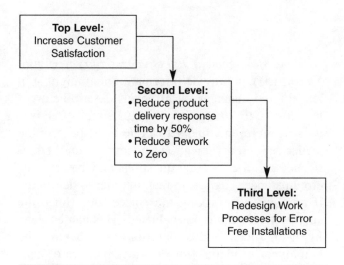

Figure 12 Deploying strategic objectives.

Personal Management Effectiveness—The Use of Upward Evaluations

Formal upward evaluations have been used for over 50 years to help assess job satisfaction. As organizations become committed to improving labor relations and manager effectiveness, upward evaluation has become a widely used tool that more and more leaders value.

Three reasons why upward feedback is beneficial include:

1. Validity—Subordinates interact regularly with their managers and have a unique vantage from which to assess manager style.

2. Reliability—Numerous subordinates provide the best chance for reliable data.

3. Involvement and Morale—Asking people to comment on the effectiveness and style of their managers boosts morale and sends a clear message that the organization is serious about increasing employee involvement.

Before managers can effectively change the way they manage, they should gather facts about their current style. They need to know what aspects of their style are considered strong and should not be changed. The starting point for improving management style, therefore, is an honest assessment of the manager's current behavior by his or her subordinates, peers, and supervisors.

The Feedback Process

1. Leaders solicit feedback on how they perform against specific behaviors that are characteristic of an effective manager.

2. They use this information to plan personal improvement strategies.

3. They share the results of the survey with their employees and discuss improvement actions.

4. They make improvements as planned and start the process again next year.

Figure 13 maps the process.

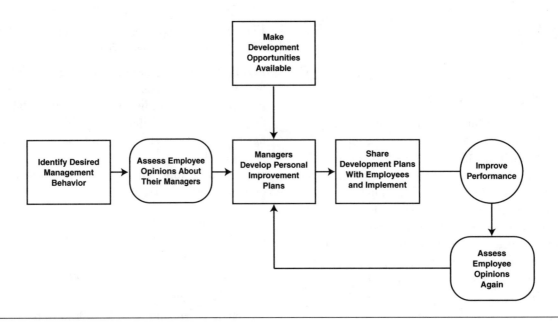

Figure 13   Improving leadership effectiveness.

This process enables employees to help their manager understand how he or she is perceived, as well as identify areas of strength on which the manager can build. However, some important procedures should be in place to prevent improper use of the tool.

- Feedback should always be used and interpreted in the spirit of continuous personal improvement. Personally identifiable results should go only to the manager who was rated and should not be used as a basis for performance ratings, promotion, assignments, or pay adjustments (unless, of course, the manager refuses to work to improve).

- Anonymity for those completing questionnaires should be carefully protected. No one other than the employee should see the actual completed questionnaire. To further protect anonymity, questionnaires should not be summarized and reported to the manager in cases where fewer than three to five employees completed the questionnaire.

- Personally identifiable results should be provided only to the manager named on the questionnaire. When the managers receive the results, they review their own ratings to determine their strengths and opportunities for improvement. Then they take steps to improve.

The *Management Effectiveness Survey* (figure 14 and 15) can provide information that might help leaders and managers at all levels determine areas to address to strengthen their personal effectiveness. It represents one set of questions to examine leadership communication, openness, and effectiveness. Certainly other questions may be asked as circumstances change. In fact, in order to determine if any survey is asking the correct questions, the survey itself should be evaluated. This can be done by using open ended questions and asking the employees to identify other issues that are of concern to them and should be included in the survey. Also ask if some of the questions are not relevant or important and should be eliminated. Then adjust the survey accordingly.

In addition to aggregating scores from employees, it is also useful to compare the perceptions of managers with the perception of the leader or manager who is the target of the assessment. Many times, employees identify a specific weakness that the leader believes is much stronger. These differences, together with key areas where both parties agree that a weakness exists, could be targeted for specific improvement. By aggregating the assessment data for all managers and making the overall results available to individuals, they can determine how their stage of development compares with other managers in the office.

Management Effectiveness Survey

The following questionnaire lists some key indicators to help you assess your manager's style in several key areas. Enter 1 for strongly disagree, 2 for disagree, 3 for agree, and 4 for strongly agree. If you cannot answer a question leave it blank.

General

1. My manager keeps me well informed about what's going on in the office.   1 2 3 4
2. My manager clearly and accurately explains the reasons for decisions that affect my work.   1 2 3 4
3. I am satisfied with my involvement in decisions that affect my work.   1 2 3 4
4. My manager delegates the right amount of responsibility to me and does not micromanage.   1 2 3 4
5. My manager gives me honest feedback on my performance.   1 2 3 4
6. I have confidence in my manager's decisions.   1 2 3 4
7. My manager has the knowledge he/she needs to be effective.   1 2 3 4
8. I can depend on my manager to honor the commitments he/she makes to me.   1 2 3 4
9. My manager treats people fairly and with dignity and respect.   1 2 3 4
10. My manager is straightforward and honest with me.   1 2 3 4
11. My manager is committed to resolving the concerns that may be identified in this survey and had made improvements based on past surveys (if applicable).   1 2 3 4
12. My manager strongly supports doing the right thing for the customer.   1 2 3 4
13. The communication process in my unit is effective. I always understand what is being communicated. (Unit refers to the level in the office your manager heads.)   1 2 3 4
14. In my unit, there is an environment of openness and trust.   1 2 3 4
15. I feel free to speak up when I disagree with a decision.   1 2 3 4
16. I feel I can elevate issues to higher-level managers without fear of reprisal.   1 2 3 4
17. The people I work with cooperate to get the job done.   1 2 3 4
18. In my unit, we are simplifying the way we do our work.   1 2 3 4
19. We have an effective process for preparing people to fill open positions.   1 2 3 4
20. All employees have fair advancement opportunities based on skills and abilities. Diversity of ideas is valued.   1 2 3 4

Effective Management Practices

My manager frequently. . .

21. provides me with honest feedback on my performance.   1 2 3 4
22. encourages me to monitor my own efforts.   1 2 3 4
23. encourages me to make suggestions to improve work processes.   1 2 3 4
24. ensures I have the information I need to do my job.   1 2 3 4
25. defines his/her requirements of me in clear, measurable terms.   1 2 3 4
26. acts as a positive role model for performance excellence.   1 2 3 4
27. ensures that organizational goals and objectives are understood at all levels.   1 2 3 4
28. favors facts before making decisions affecting our customers, employees, and organization.   1 2 3 4
29. identifies and removes barriers to alleviate work-related problems.   1 2 3 4
30. encourages people in our unit to work as a team.   1 2 3 4
31. informs us regularly about the state of the business.   1 2 3 4
32. encourages me to ask questions and creates an environment of openness and trust.   1 2 3 4
33. behaves in ways which demonstrate respect for others.   1 2 3 4
34. ensures regularly scheduled reviews of progress toward goals.   1 2 3 4
35. monitors my progress and compares against benchmarks.   1 2 3 4
36. ensures that rewards and recognition is fairly applied and closely tied to strategic goals, objectives, and required actions plans.   1 2 3 4
37. sets objectives based on strategic objectives and customer requirements.   1 2 3 4
38. runs effective meetings.   1 2 3 4
39. uses a disciplined, fact-based process to solve problems.   1 2 3 4
40. treats performance excellence as a basic operating principle.   1 2 3 4

Please list on the back of this form additional questions that the survey should ask about your manager. Also tell us which questions already on the survey are not very important and should be removed. In this way we can improve the effectiveness of the survey and better identify areas most needing improvement.

Figure 14 Sample Management Effectiveness Survey.

Sample Scored Survey

10 Employees completed the instrument

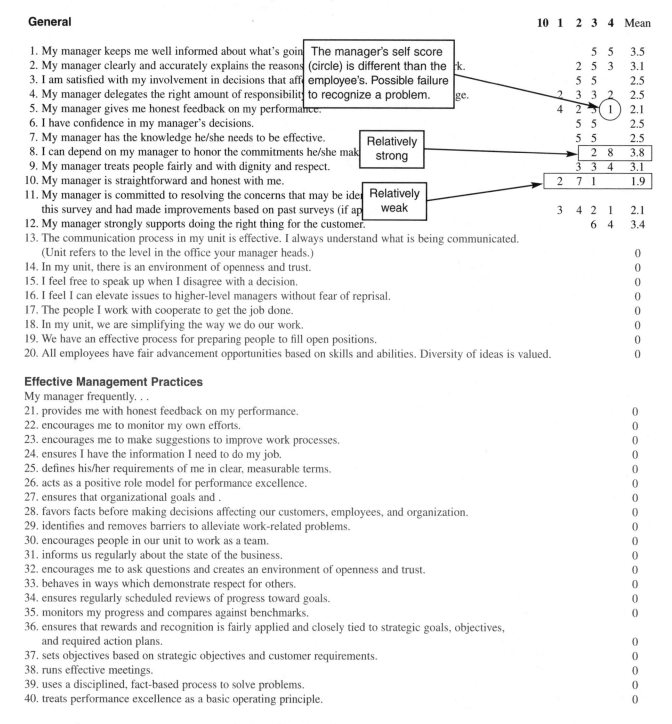

General

	10	1	2	3	4	Mean

1. My manager keeps me well informed about what's goin[g] | The manager's self score (circle) is different than the employee's. Possible failure to recognize a problem. | | | | 5 | 5 | 3.5
2. My manager clearly and accurately explains the reasons [...] k. | | | 2 | 5 | 3 | 3.1
3. I am satisfied with my involvement in decisions that aff[ect] | | | 5 | 5 | | 2.5
4. My manager delegates the right amount of responsibilit[y ...] ge. | 2 | 3 | 3 | 2 | 2.5
5. My manager gives me honest feedback on my performance. | 4 | 2 | 3 | (1) | 2.1
6. I have confidence in my manager's decisions. | | | 5 | 5 | | 2.5
7. My manager has the knowledge he/she needs to be effective. | | | 5 | 5 | | 2.5

Relatively strong

8. I can depend on my manager to honor the commitments he/she mak[es] | | | 2 | 8 | 3.8
9. My manager treats people fairly and with dignity and respect. | | | 3 | 3 | 4 | 3.1
10. My manager is straightforward and honest with me. | 2 | 7 | 1 | | 1.9

Relatively weak

11. My manager is committed to resolving the concerns that may be iden[tified ...] this survey and had made improvements based on past surveys (if ap[plicable]) | 3 | 4 | 2 | 1 | 2.1
12. My manager strongly supports doing the right thing for the customer. | | 6 | 4 | | 3.4
13. The communication process in my unit is effective. I always understand what is being communicated. (Unit refers to the level in the office your manager heads.) | 0
14. In my unit, there is an environment of openness and trust. | 0
15. I feel free to speak up when I disagree with a decision. | 0
16. I feel I can elevate issues to higher-level managers without fear of reprisal. | 0
17. The people I work with cooperate to get the job done. | 0
18. In my unit, we are simplifying the way we do our work. | 0
19. We have an effective process for preparing people to fill open positions. | 0
20. All employees have fair advancement opportunities based on skills and abilities. Diversity of ideas is valued. | 0

Effective Management Practices

My manager frequently. . .

21. provides me with honest feedback on my performance. | 0
22. encourages me to monitor my own efforts. | 0
23. encourages me to make suggestions to improve work processes. | 0
24. ensures I have the information I need to do my job. | 0
25. defines his/her requirements of me in clear, measurable terms. | 0
26. acts as a positive role model for performance excellence. | 0
27. ensures that organizational goals and . | 0
28. favors facts before making decisions affecting our customers, employees, and organization. | 0
29. identifies and removes barriers to alleviate work-related problems. | 0
30. encourages people in our unit to work as a team. | 0
31. informs us regularly about the state of the business. | 0
32. encourages me to ask questions and creates an environment of openness and trust. | 0
33. behaves in ways which demonstrate respect for others. | 0
34. ensures regularly scheduled reviews of progress toward goals. | 0
35. monitors my progress and compares against benchmarks. | 0
36. ensures that rewards and recognition is fairly applied and closely tied to strategic goals, objectives, and required action plans. | 0
37. sets objectives based on strategic objectives and customer requirements. | 0
38. runs effective meetings. | 0
39. uses a disciplined, fact-based process to solve problems. | 0
40. treats performance excellence as a basic operating principle. | 0

Figure 15   Sample Management Effectiveness Survey scored.

Create Performance Excellence Standards for Managers— A Key Job Element

Virtually every organization has the ability to determine what performance requirements are critical for the success of employees and managers. These critical performance requirements are usually included as a key requirement in performance plans and appraisals. By declaring that performance excellence is critical to the success of the organization, a specific key performance requirement can be included in the performance plan (sometimes these are called personal commitment plans, personal improvement plans, or personal management objectives, to name a few) and evaluation of managers and leaders. Using this approach, every manager and supervisor begins to take performance excellence more seriously.

- Using the following performance standards as an example, in order for a manager to receive a rating at a particular level, that manager must have accomplished all of the activities described for that rating level. If all are not met, the rating goes to the lowest level at which all are met.

- The writer of the performance appraisal must cite measurable examples in the performance appraisal for actions listed under the rating level.

- Supervising reviewers must verify that these actions have indeed been taken. Under this system, managers are strongly encouraged to keep accurate records of activities which might exemplify compliance with these standards.

Overall Performance Standard for Leadership

The individual visibly demonstrates adherence to the high personal standards and characteristics of leaders in a high-performing organization.
The individual:

- Understands the business processes of the unit.

- Is customer focused and customer driven. Demonstrates a firm commitment to the principles of customer satisfaction. Understands their requirements and consistently works to meet and exceed them.

- Understands and personally uses performance excellence principles and tools for decision making and planning.

  - Favors the use of data and facts to drive decisions and ensures that employees and subordinate managers do the same.

  - Ensures that organizational goals are converted to appropriate actions to align work within his or her organizational unit.

  - Measures and monitors progress toward achieving the goals within his or her organizational unit.

- Demonstrates a firm commitment to the principles of employee empowerment, well-being, and satisfaction.

  - Promotes flexibility and individual initiative.

  - Encourages and supports the personal and professional development of self and employees.

  - Supports effective training and reinforces the use of new skills on the job.

  - Ensures compensation is aligned to support business strategies and actions.

  - Rewards and recognizes employees who incorporate the principles of performance excellence in their day-to-day work.

- Fosters an atmosphere of open, honest communication and knowledge sharing among employees and business units throughout the organization.

- Rigorously drives the systematic, continuous improvement of all work processes, including his or her personal effectiveness as a leader.

- Achieves consistently improving performance outcomes in customer satisfaction; employee well-being, motivation, and satisfaction; operational excellence; and financial (cost/budget) performance.

Rating Number 1: Performance is unsatisfactory. The individual frequently fails to meet the performance standard for leadership.

- Does not fully understand the business processes of the unit.

- Consistently disregards the needs of customers.

- Does not understand and has not taken steps to implement performance excellence (may even work against the changes needed).

  - Intuition tends to dominate decision making, not data or facts.

  - Organizational goals and actions are not aligned to actions within his or her unit.

  - May measure and monitor some performance outcomes (such as budget tracking) but most measures are not aligned to organizational goals.

- Does not effectively promote employee well-being, motivation, and morale.

  - Tends to micromanage—does not delegate decision-making authority to the lower levels except as directly instructed to do so.

  - Rarely listens to employees or cares what they think.

  - Does not consistently promote flexibility and individual initiative.

  - Does not consistently encourage and support the personal and professional development of self and employees.

  - May send employees to training but does not consistently reinforce the use of new skills on the job.

  - Has not taken effective steps to ensure compensation and other rewards or recognition are aligned to support business strategies and actions.

  - Reward and recognition is not aligned to support organizational goals or the principles of performance excellence or customer satisfaction.

- Does not communicate effectively or foster an atmosphere of knowledge sharing among employees and business units.

- Does not regularly assess or improve work processes, including his or her personal effectiveness as a leader.

- Does not achieve consistently improving performance outcomes in customer satisfaction; employee well-being, motivation, and satisfaction; operational excellence; and financial (cost/budget) performance.

Rating Number 2: Performance is minimally acceptable. Individual occasionally fails to meet the performance standard for leadership. Performs higher than indicated by level one but less than level three.

Rating Number 3: Performance is acceptable. Individual basically meets the performance standard for leadership.

- Is considered to be a capable leader.

- Understands the key business processes of the unit.

- Is customer driven and promotes customer-focused values throughout his or her unit.

  - Demonstrates a commitment to the principles of customer satisfaction.

  - Develops systems to understand customer requirements, strengthen customer relationships, resolve customer problems and prevent them from happening again, and obtain information about customer satisfaction and dissatisfaction.

- Personally uses many performance excellence principles and tools for decision making and planning.

  - Visibly supports performance excellence within the organization. Usually uses data and facts to drive decisions and ensure that many employees and subordinate managers do the same.

  - Ensures that key organizational goals are converted to appropriate actions to align most work within his or her organizational unit. Most goals and actions have defined measures of progress and timelines for achieving desired results.

- Demonstrates some commitment to the principles of employee empowerment, well-being, and satisfaction. Is well-regarded by employees for:

  - Involving the workforce in identifying improvement opportunities and developing improvement plans.

  - Valuing employee input on work-related matters.

  - Promoting flexibility and individual initiative and ensuring that many subordinate managers do the same.

  - Encouraging and supporting the personal and professional development of self and employees.

  - Supporting effective training and reinforcing the use of new skills on the job.

  - Ensuring compensation is aligned to support business strategies and actions.

  - Rewarding and recognizing employees who incorporate the principles of performance excellence in their day-to-day work.

- Fosters an atmosphere of open, honest communication and knowledge sharing among employees and business units throughout the organization.

- Visibly drives continuous improvement of many work processes, including his or her personal effectiveness as a leader.

- Achieves consistently improving performance outcomes in customer satisfaction; employee well-being, motivation, and satisfaction; operational excellence; and financial (cost/budget) performance.

- The levels of performance outcomes are better than average when compared with organizations providing similar programs, products, or services

Rating Number 4: Individual occasionally exceeds the performance standard for leadership. Performs higher than indicated by level three but less than level five. Performance is very good.

Rating Number 5: Individual consistently exceeds the performance standard for leadership. Is considered a role model for leadership. Performance is superior.

- Understands the business processes of the unit in great detail.

- Is customer driven and actively promotes customer-focused values throughout his or her unit.

- Demonstrates a firm commitment to the principles of customer satisfaction.

- Develops effective systems to understand customer requirements, strengthen loyalty and customer relationships, resolve customer problems immediately and prevent them from happening again, and obtain timely information about customer satisfaction and dissatisfaction.

- Advocates the needs of customers through the collection and use of information on customer satisfaction, dissatisfaction, and product performance.

- Personally uses performance excellence principles and tools for decision making and planning.

  - Serves as a performance excellence champion within the organization and as a resource within the work unit, providing guidance, counsel, and instruction in performance excellence tools, processes, and principles.

  - Is a role model for using data and facts to drive decisions and ensures that employees and subordinate managers do the same.

  - Ensures that all organizational goals are converted to appropriate actions to align work within his or her organizational unit.

  - Each goal and action has defined measures of progress and timelines for achieving desired results.

- Demonstrates a firm commitment to the principles of employee empowerment, well-being, and satisfaction. Is highly regarded by employees for:

  - Involving the workforce in setting standards of performance, identifying improvement opportunities, and developing improvement plans.

  - Seeking and valuing employee input on work-related matters.

  - Promoting flexibility and individual initiative and ensuring that subordinate managers do the same.

  - Encouraging and supporting the personal and professional development of self and employees.

  - Supporting effective training and reinforcing the use of new skills on the job.

– Ensuring compensation is aligned to support business strategies and actions.

– Rewarding and recognizing employees who incorporate the principles of performance excellence in their day-to-day work.

- Fosters an atmosphere of open, honest communication and knowledge sharing among employees and business units throughout the organization.

  – Checks the effectiveness of nearly all communication and makes changes to improve.

- Rigorously drives the systematic, continuous improvement of all work processes, including his or her personal effectiveness as a leader.

  – Develops personal action plan and always incorporates results of 360-degree feedback to continuously improve his/her leadership effectiveness and ensures subordinate managers do the same.

- Achieves consistently improving performance outcomes in customer satisfaction; employee well-being, motivation, and satisfaction; operational excellence; and financial (cost/budget) performance.

  – The levels of performance outcomes are among the highest in the organization and are also high when compared with organizations providing similar programs, products, or services.

Performance Excellence Standards Table

Level 1	Level 2	Level 3	Level 4	Level 5
Performance is unsatisfactory: Individual frequently fails to meet the performance standard for leadership. Is considered a poor leader.	**Better than level 1 and some of level 3.**	**Performance is acceptable: Individual basically meets the performance standard for leadership. Is considered to be a capable leader.**	**All of level 3 and some of level 5.**	**Performance is superior: Individual consistently exceeds the performance standard for leadership. Is considered a role model for leadership.**
• Does not fully understand the key business processes of the unit.		• Understands the key business processes of the unit.		• Understands the business processes of the unit in great detail.

• Consistently disregards the needs of customers.		• Is customer driven and promotes customer-focused values throughout his or her unit.
		  • Demonstrates a commitment to the principles of customer satisfaction.
		  • Develops systems to understand customer requirements, strengthen customer relationships, resolve customer problems and prevent them from happening again, and obtain information about customer satisfaction and dissatisfaction.
				• Is customer driven and actively promotes customer-focused values throughout his or her unit.
				  • Demonstrates a firm commitment to the principles of customer satisfaction.
				  • Develops effective systems to understand customer requirements, strengthen loyalty and customer relationships, resolve customer problems immediately and prevent them from happening again, and obtain timely information about customer satisfaction and dissatisfaction.
				  • Advocates the needs of customers through the collection and use of information on customer satisfaction, dissatisfaction, and product performance.

Performance Excellence Standards Table

Level 1	Level 2	Level 3	Level 4	Level 5
Performance is unsatisfactory: Individual frequently fails to meet the performance standard for leadership. Is considered a poor leader.	**Better than level 1 and some of level 3.**	**Performance is acceptable: Individual basically meets the performance standard for leadership. Is considered to be a capable leader.**	**All of level 3 and some of level 5.**	**Performance is superior: Individual consistently exceeds the performance standard for leadership. Is considered a role model for leadership.**

• Does not understand and has not taken steps to implement performance excellence (may even work against the changes needed).
  • Intuition tends to dominate decision making, not data or facts.
  • Organizational goals and actions are not aligned to actions within his or her unit.
  • May measure and monitor some performance outcomes (such as budget tracking) but most measures are not aligned to organizational goals.
• Does not understand and has not taken steps to implement performance excellence (may even work against the changes needed).
		• Personally uses many performance excellence principles and tools for decision making and planning.
		  • Visibly supports performance excellence within the organization.
		  • Usually uses data and facts to drive decisions and ensure that many employees and subordinate managers do the same.
		  • Ensures that key organizational goals are converted to appropriate actions to align most work within his or her organizational unit.
		  • Most goals and actions have defined measures of progress and timelines for achieving desired results.
				• Personally uses nearly all performance excellence principles and tools for decision making and planning.
				  • Serves as a performance excellence champion within the organization and as a resource within the work unit, providing guidance, counsel, and instruction in performance excellence tools, processes, and principles.
				  • Is a role model for using data and facts to drive decisions and ensures that employees and subordinate managers do the same.
				  • Ensures that all organizational goals are converted to appropriate actions to align nearly all work within his or her organizational unit.
				  • Each goal and action has defined measures of progress and timelines for achieving desired results.

Performance Excellence Standards Table

Level 1	Level 2	Level 3	Level 4	Level 5
Performance is unsatisfactory: Individual frequently fails to meet the performance standard for leadership. Is considered a poor leader.	**Better than level 1 and some of level 3.**	**Performance is acceptable: Individual basically meets the performance standard for leadership. Is considered to be a capable leader.**	**All of level 3 and some of level 5.**	**Performance is superior: Individual consistently exceeds the performance standard for leadership. Is considered a role model for leadership.**
• Does not effectively promote employee well-being, motivation, and morale. • Tends to micromanage; does not delegate decision-making authority to the lower levels except as directly instructed to do so. • Rarely listens to employees or cares what they think. • Does not consistently promote flexibility and individual initiative. • Does not consistently encourage and support the personal and professional development of self and employees. • May send employees to training but does not consistently reinforce the use of new skills on the job. • Has not taken effective steps to ensure compensation and other rewards or recognition are aligned to support business strategies and actions. • Reward and recognition is not aligned to support organizational goals or the principles of performance excellence or customer satisfaction.		• Demonstrates some commitment to the principles of employee empowerment, well-being, and satisfaction. Is well regarded by employees for: • Involving the workforce in identifying improvement opportunities and developing improvement plans. • Valuing employee input on work-related matters. • Promoting flexibility and individual initiative and ensuring that many subordinate managers do the same. • Encouraging and supporting the personal and professional development of self and employees. • Supporting effective training and reinforcing the use of new skills on the job. • Ensuring compensation is aligned to support business strategies and actions. • Rewarding and recognizing employees who incorporate the principles of performance excellence in their day-to-day work.		• Demonstrates a firm commitment to the principles of employee empowerment, well-being, and satisfaction. Is highly regarded by employees for: • Involving the workforce in setting standards of performance, identifying improvement opportunities, and developing improvement plans. • Seeking and valuing employee input on work-related matters. • Promoting flexibility and individual initiative and ensuring that nearly all subordinate managers do the same. • Encouraging and supporting the personal and professional development of self and employees. • Supporting effective training and reinforcing the use of new skills on the job. • Ensuring compensation is aligned to support business strategies and actions. • Rewarding and recognizing employees who incorporate the principles of performance excellence in their day-to-day work.

Performance Excellence Standards Table

Level 1	Level 2	Level 3	Level 4	Level 5
Performance is unsatisfactory: Individual frequently fails to meet the performance standard for leadership. Is considered a poor leader.	**Better than level 1 and some of level 3.**	**Performance is acceptable: Individual basically meets the performance standard for leadership. Is considered to be a capable leader.**	**All of level 3 and some of level 5.**	**Performance is superior: Individual consistently exceeds the performance standard for leadership. Is considered a role model for leadership.**
• Does not communicate effectively or foster an atmosphere of knowledge sharing among employees and business units.		• Fosters an atmosphere of open, honest communication and knowledge sharing among employees and business units throughout the organization.		• Fosters an atmosphere of open, honest communication and knowledge sharing among employees and business units throughout the organization. • Checks the effectiveness of nearly all communication and makes changes to improve.
• Does not regularly assess or improve work processes, including his or her personal effectiveness as a leader.		• Visibly drives continuous improvement of many work processes, including his or her personal effectiveness as a leader.		• Rigorously drives the systematic, continuous improvement of all work processes, including his or her personal effectiveness as a leader. • Develops personal action plan and always incorporates results of 360 degree feedback to continuously improve his/her leadership effectiveness and ensures subordinate managers do the same.
• Does not achieve consistently improving performance outcomes in customer satisfaction; employee well-being, motivation, and satisfaction; operational excellence; and financial (cost/budget) performance.		• Achieves consistently improving performance outcomes in customer satisfaction; employee well-being, motivation, and satisfaction; operational excellence; and financial (cost/budget) performance. • The levels of performance outcomes are better than average when compared with organizations providing similar programs, products, or services.		• Achieves consistently improving performance outcomes in customer satisfaction; employee well-being, motivation, and satisfaction; operational excellence; and financial (cost/budget) performance. • The levels of performance outcomes are among the highest in the organization and are also high when compared with organizations providing similar programs, products, or services.

Definitions

Performance Excellence Tools: Problem-solving process, performance improvement process, benchmarking, and statistical methods to aid decision making.

Performance Excellence Champion: One who consistently and emphatically advocates the principles of performance excellence in the workplace and whose actions are totally consistent with his/her words.

Lessons Learned Conclusions

Successful leaders will create a customer focus and a context for action at all levels of the organization. Effective leaders will distribute authority and decision making to all levels of the organization. Nearly instantaneous, two-way communication will permit clear strategies, measurable objectives, and priorities to be identified and deployed organizationwide. Problems will be identified and resolved with similar speed. Success in this environment will demand different skills of employees and managers. Unless all managers and employees understand where the organization is going and what must be done to beat the competition, it will be difficult for them to make effective decisions consistent with overall direction and strategy. If employees at all levels are not involved in decision making, organizational effectiveness is reduced—making it more difficult to win in a highly competitive market.

In closing this section, I would like to suggest that the scenario previously described is already happening today among the world's best-performing organizations.

- These organizations have effective leadership at all levels, with a clear strategy focused on maximizing customer value. Middle-level managers support, rather than block, the values and direction of the top leaders.

- They have developed ways to challenge themselves and improve their own processes when doing so promotes customer value and improves operating effectiveness.

- They engage workers fully and promote organizational and personal learning at all levels. They ensure that knowledge is shared within the organization to avoid duplication of effort.

- They have created effective data systems to enhance decision making at all levels.

- They have developed and aligned reward, recognition, compensation, and incentives to support the desired customer-focused behavior among all leaders, managers, and employees.

- They have found ways to design effective work processes and ensure that those processes are improved continuously.

- They closely monitor their performance and the performance of their principal competitors. They use this information to adjust their work and continue to improve.

These organizations are among the best in the world at what they do and they will continue to win, as long as they continue to apply the current principles of performance excellence.

AWARD CRITERIA FRAMEWORK

Organizations must position themselves to respond well to the environment within which they compete. They must understand and manage threats and vulnerabilities as well as capitalize on their strengths and opportunities, including the vulnerabilities of competitors. These factors guide strategy development, support operational decisions, and align measures and actions—all of which must be done well for the organization to succeed. Consistent with this overarching purpose, the award Criteria contain the following basic elements: Driver Triad, Work Core, Brain Center, and Business Outcomes (Figure 16).

Figure 17   Driver Triad.

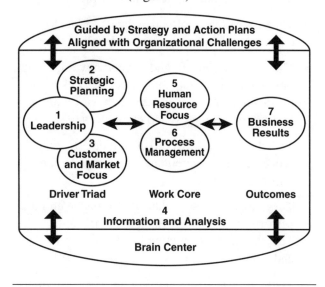

Figure 16   Performance Excellence Framework.

The Driver Triad

The Driver Triad (Figure 17) consists of the categories of Leadership, Strategic Planning, and Customer and Market Focus. Leaders use these processes to set direction and goals, monitor progress, make resource decisions, and take corrective action when progress does not proceed according to plan. The processes that make up the Driver Triad require leaders to set direction and expectations for the organization to meet customer and market requirements, and fully empower employees (Category 1), provide the vehicle for determining the short- and long-term strategies for success as well as communicating and aligning the organization's work (Category 2), and produce information about critical customer requirements and levels of satisfaction, and strengthen customer relations and loyalty (Category 3).

The Work Core

The Work Core (Figure 18) describes the processes through which the primary work of the organization takes place and consists of Human Resource Focus (Category 5) and Process Management (Category 6). These Categories recognize that the people of an organization are responsible for doing the work. To achieve peak performance, these people must possess the right skills and must be allowed to work in an environment that promotes initiative and self-direction. The work processes provide the structure for continuous learning and improvement to optimize performance.

Figure 18   Work Core.

Business Results

The processes defined by the Driver Triad, Work Core, and Brain Center produce the Business Results (Category 7). Business results (Figure 19) reflect the organization's actual performance and serve as the basis for leaders to monitor progress against goals and make adjustments to increase performance. These Business Results include customer focus, financial and market performance, human resource performance, and internal operating effectiveness.

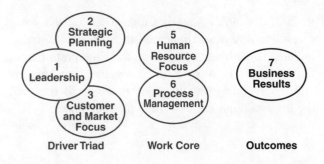

Figure 19   Outcomes.

Brain Center

The foundation for the entire management system is Information and Analysis (Category 4). Information and Analysis processes capture, store, analyze, and retrieve information and data critical to the effective management of the organization and to a fact-based system for improving organization performance and competitiveness. Rapid access and reliable data and information systems are especially critical to enhance effective decision making in an increasingly complex, fast-paced, global competitive environment.

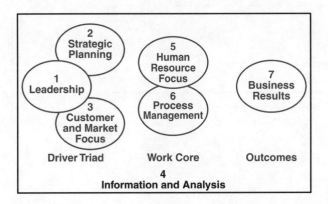

Figure 20

Information and Analysis is also called the Brain Center of an effective management system (Figure 21).

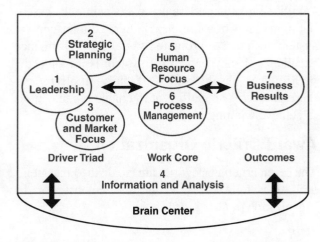

Figure 21

Organizations develop effective strategic plans to help set the direction necessary to achieve future success. Unfortunately, these plans are not always communicated and used to drive actions. The planning process and the resulting strategy are virtually worthless if the organization does not use the plan and strategy to guide decision making at all levels of the organization (Figure 22). When decisions are not guided by strategy, managers and other employees tend to substitute their own ideas for the correct direction. This frequently causes teams, individuals, and whole business units to work at cross-purposes,

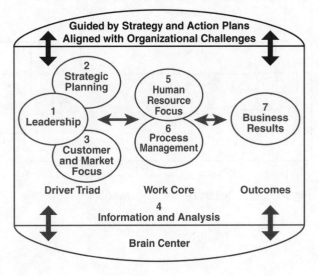

Figure 22

suboptimizing performance and making it more difficult for the organization to achieve desired results.

Taken together, these processes define the essential ingredients of a complex, integrated management system designed to promote and deliver performance excellence. If any part of the system is missing, the performance results suffer. If fully implemented, these processes are sufficient to enable organizations to achieve winning performance.

Award Criteria Organization

The seven criteria categories are subdivided into Items and Areas to Address. Figure 23 demonstrates the organization of Category 1.

Items
There are 18 items, each focusing on a major requirement. Item titles and point values are on page 71.

Areas to Address
Items consist of one or more Areas to Address (Areas). Information is submitted by applicants in response to the specific requirements of these Areas. There are 29 Areas to Aaddress.

Subparts
There are 85 subparts in the 2002 Criteria. Areas consist of one or more subparts, where numbers are shown in parentheses. A response should be made to each subpart.

Notes
In 2002 the notes have not changed.Read the notes carefully. If a note indicates the process "should" include something, examiners will interpret it as a requirement. If a note indicates that the process "might" include something, examiners will not treat the list as a requirement—only as an example.

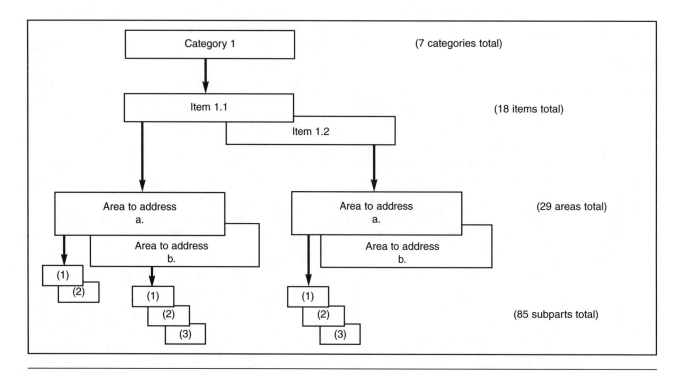

Figure 23   Organizations of Category 1.

BALDRIGE AWARD CATEGORIES AND POINT VALUES

Examination Categories/Items	Maximum Points
Preface Organizational Profile	
P.1 Organizational Description	
P.2 Organizational Challenges	
1 Leadership (120 points)	
1.1 Organizational Leadership	80
1.2 Public Responsibility and Citizenship	40
2 Strategic Planning (85 points)	
2.1 Strategy Development	40
2.2 Strategy Deployment	45
3 Customer and Market Focus (85 points)	
3.1 Customer and Market Knowledge	40
3.2 Customer Relationships and Satisfaction	45
4 Information and Analysis (90 points)	
4.1 Measurement and Analysis of Organizational Performance	50
4.2 Information Management	40
5 Human Resource Focus (85 points)	
5.1 Work Systems	35
5.2 Employee Education, Training, and Development	25
5.3 Employee Well-Being and Satisfaction	25
6 Process Management (85 points)	
6.1 Product and Service Processes	45
6.2 Business Processes	25
6.3 Support Processes	15
7 Business Results (450 points)	
7.1 Customer-Focused Results	125
7.2 Financial and Market Results	125
7.3 Human Resource Results	80
7.4 Organizational Effectiveness Results	120
Total Points	**1000**

KEY CHARACTERISTICS—2002 PERFORMANCE EXCELLENCE CRITERIA

The criteria focus on business results and the processes required to achieve them. Business results are a composite of the following:

- Customer satisfaction and retention

- Financial and marketplace performance

- Product and service performance

- Productivity, operational effectiveness, and responsiveness

- Human resource performance and development

- Supplier performance and development

- Public responsibility and good citizenship

These results areas cover overall organization performance, including financial performance. The results areas also recognize the importance of suppliers and of community and national well-being. The use of a composite of indicators helps to ensure that strategies are balanced—that they do not inappropriately trade off among important stakeholders or objectives or between short- and long-term goals.

The criteria encourage wide latitude in how requirements are met. Accordingly, the criteria do not prescribe:

- Specific tools, techniques, technologies, systems, measures, or starting points

- That organizations should or should not have departments for quality, planning, or other functions

- That different units of the organization should be managed in the same way

- How the organization or business units within the organization should be organized

Processes to achieve performance excellence are very likely to change as the work climate, organizational needs and strategies, and the nature of customer expectations and competition evolve. Hence, the criteria themselves are refined as part of annual performance

reviews to ensure that they continue to distinguish high-performing organizations from all others.

The criteria do not prescribe specific approaches or methods, because:

- The focus is on results, not on procedures, tools, or organizational structure. Organizations are encouraged to develop and demonstrate creative, adaptive, and flexible approaches for meeting basic requirements. The criteria do not encourage complacency. Nonprescriptive requirements are intended to foster both incremental and major (breakthrough) improvement as well as basic change

- Selection of tools, techniques, systems, and organizations usually depends on many factors such as business size, business type, the organization's stage of development, and employee capabilities and responsibilities

- Focusing on common requirements within an organization, rather than on common procedures, fosters better understanding, communication, sharing, and alignment, while supporting creativity and diversity in approaches

The criteria support a systems approach to organizationwide goal alignment. The systems approach to goal alignment is embedded in the integrated structure of the criteria and the results-oriented, cause-effect linkages among the criteria parts.

The measures in the criteria tie directly to customer value and to overall performance that relate to key internal and external requirements of the organization. Measures serve both as a communications tool and a basis for deploying performance requirements. Such alignment ensures consistency of purpose while at the same time supports speed, innovation, and decentralized decision making.

Learning Cycles and Continuous Improvement

In high-performing organizations, action-oriented learning takes place through feedback between processes and results facilitated by learning or continuous improvement cycles. The learning cycles have four, clearly defined and well-established stages (Figure 24).

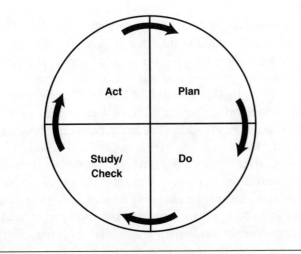

Figure 24 Continuous improvement cycle.

1. Plan—planning, including design of processes, selection of measures, and deployment of requirements

2. Do—execute plans

3. Study/check—assess progress, taking into account internal and external results

4. Act—revise plans based on assessment findings, learning, new inputs, and new requirements

Goal-Based Diagnosis

The Criteria and the scoring guidelines make up the diagnostic assessment system. The Criteria, as discussed previously, are a set of 18 items. The scoring guidelines spell out the assessment dimensions—approach, deployment, and results—and the key factors used to assess against each dimension. An assessment provides a profile of strengths and opportunities for improvement to help organizations identify areas that, if addressed, will move the organization ahead and help optimize its performance and business outcomes. As a result, the Baldrige-based diagnostic assessment system is a powerful management tool that goes beyond minimal certification or compliance reviews such as those required by ISO 9000.

Changes from the 2001 Criteria

The Criteria for Performance Excellence have evolved significantly over time to help businesses address a dynamic marketplace, focus on strategy-driven performance, and manage for results that balance the needs of all stakeholders. The Criteria have continually progressed toward a systems perspective of overall organizational performance management.

To help stabilize the management environment, the Baldrige Criteria for Performance Excellence *usually* undergo substantive changes during the odd-numbered years (1999, 2001, and so on). The even-numbered years are reserved for clarifying changes. In 2002 some changes have been made in the definitions only. There have been no changes in the 2001 Award Criteria.

Each year, decisions regarding what elements in the Criteria to revise must balance the need to ensure the Criteria are at the leading edge of validated management practice (to help users address the increasingly complex challenges they face) versus the desire to stabilize the Criteria (to allow users to have continuity in the application of the Criteria). Recognizing the significant challenges associated with the changes in Categories 4 (Information and Analysis) and 6 (Process Management) made in the 2001 Criteria and the challenging systems perspective provided by linkage to the new Organizational Profile, the decision was made to make no revisions to the Criteria for 2002. In addition, no revisions were made to the Item Notes or Category and Item Descriptions.

The most significant changes in the Criteria for 2002 involve the Glossary of Key Terms, which has been almost doubled in size to include the following 19 new terms.

- To help clarify the scoring guidelines: basic requirements, overall requirements, multiple requirements, levels, trends, effective, anecdotal, and integration

- To help clarify the Organizational Profile: purpose, vision, mission, values, goals, and strategic challenges

- To help clarify general terms in the Criteria: performance projections, performance excellence, leadership system, and work systems.

The Criteria for Performance Excellence are based on the validated practices that drive leading edge performance. Emerging "theories" that purport to offer better performance are not accepted without validation. Thus, the Criteria offer serious business leaders some protection against the "Pied Pipers of Today's Management Fads," keeping them out of harms way.

The Criteria continue to enhance strategy-driven performance, address the needs of all stakeholders, and accommodate important changes in business needs and practices. For example, the increasing importance of e-commerce, the use of Internet-based interactions, and the alignment of all aspects of the performance management system receive attention in the 2002 Criteria. In addition, the Criteria continue to emphasize the roles of data, information, and information and knowledge management and their use in business.

The Organizational Profile, the Criteria Items, and the Scoring Guidelines have been aligned so that the assessment addresses both changing business needs/directions and ongoing evaluation/improvement of key processes. Both are important because prioritized process improvement ("doing things better") and addressing changing needs ("doing the right business things") are critical to success in an increasingly competitive environment, and they frequently compete for the same resources.

Organizational Profile

The Organizational Profile is a snapshot of your organization, the key influences on how you operate, and the key challenges you face.

IMPORTANCE OF THE ORGANIZATIONAL PROFILE

The Organizational Profile is critically important because:

- It is the most appropriate starting point for self-assessment and for writing an application

- It helps you identify potential gaps in key information and focus on key performance requirements and business results

- It is used by the Examiners and Judges in all stages of application review, including the site visit, to understand your organization and what you consider important. it set the context for the assessment.

- It may be used by itself for an initial self-assessment. If you identify topics for which conflicting, little, or no information is available, it is possible that your assessment need go no further and you can use these topics for action planning

Page Limit

For Baldrige Award applicants, the Organizational Profile is limited to five pages. These are not counted in the overall application page limit. Typing and format instructions for the Organizational Profile are the same as for the application. These instructions are given in the Baldrige Award Application Forms booklet.

P.1 Organizational Description Item Linkages

Describe your organization's business environment and your key relationships with customers, suppliers, and other partners.

Within your response, include answers to the following questions:

a. Organizational Environment

   (1) What are your organization's main products and/or services? Include a description of how they are delivered to customers.

   (2) What is your organizational context/culture? Include your purpose, vision, mission, and values, as appropriate.

   (3) What is your employee profile? Include educational levels, workforce and job diversity, bargaining units, use of contract employees, and special safety requirements, as appropriate.

   (4) What are your major technologies, equipment, and facilities?

   (5) What is the regulatory environment under which your organization operates? Include occupational health and safety regulations; accreditation requirements; and environmental, financial, and product regulations.

b. Organizational Relationships

   (1) What are your key customer groups and/or market segments? What are their key requirements for your products and services? Include how these requirements differ among customer groups and/or market segments, as appropriate.

   (2) What are your most important types of suppliers and dealers and your most important supply chain requirements? What are your key supplier and customer partnering relationships and communication mechanisms?

Notes:

N1. Customer group and market segment requirements [P.1b (1)] might include on-time delivery, low defect levels, price reductions, electronic communication, and after-sales service.

N2. Communication mechanisms [P.1b (2)] should be two-way and might be in person, electronic, by telephone, and/or written. For many organizations, these mechanisms might be changing.

P.1 Organizational Description Item Linkages

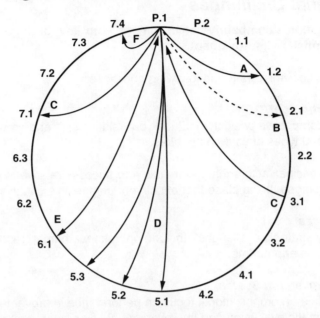

NATURE OF RELATIONSHIP	
A	The regulatory environment described in P.1a(5) sets the context for the review of the management systems for public responsibility citizenship [1.2a(1)].
B	Employee educational levels, diversity, and other characteristics [P.1a(3)] may affect the determination of human resource strengths and weaknesses as a part of the strategic planning process [2.1a(2)].
C	The customer and market groups reported in P.1b(1) were determined using the processes described in 3.1a(1 and 2). The information in P.1b(1) helps examiners identify the kind of results, broken out by customer and market segment, that should be reported in Item 7.1.
D	Employee characteristics such as educational levels, workforce and job diversity, the existence of bargaining units, the use of contract employees, and other special requirements help set the context for determining the requirements for knowledge and skill sharing across work units, jobs, and locations [5.1a(1)], determining appropriate training needs by employee segment [5.2a(1)], and tailoring benefits, services, and satisfaction assessment methods for employees according to various types and categories [5.3b(1, 2, and 3)].
E	The information in P.1a(1) derives from the delivery processes described in 6.1a and helps set the context for the examiner review of those processes [6.1b(1)].
F	The regulatory requirements described in P.1a(5), and the key suppliers and dealers listed in P.1b(2) create an expectation that related performance results will be reported in 7.4b and 7.4a respectively.

P.2 Organizational Challenges

Describe your organization's competitive environment, your key strategic challenges, and your system for performance improvement.

Within your response, include answers to the following questions:

a. Competitive Environment

(1) What is your competitive position? Include your relative size and growth in your industry and the numbers and types of your competitors.

(2) What are the principal factors that determine your success relative to your competitors? Include any changes taking place that affect your competitive situation.

b. Strategic Challenges

What are your key strategic challenges? Include operational, human resource, business, and global challenges, as appropriate.

c. Performance Improvement System

How do you maintain an organizational focus on performance improvement? Include your approach to systematic evaluation and improvement of key processes and to fostering organizational learning and knowledge sharing.

Notes:

N1. Factors (P.2a [2]) might include differentiators such as price leadership, design services, e-services, geographic proximity, and warranty and product options.

N2. Challenges (P.2b) might include electronic communication with businesses and end-use consumers, reduced product introduction cycle times, mergers and acquisitions, global marketing and competition, customer retention, staff retention, and value-chain integration.

N3. Performance improvement (P.2c) is an assessment dimension used in the Scoring System to evaluate the maturity of organizational approaches and deployment (see pages 241-249). This question is intended to help you and the Baldrige Examiners set a context for your approach to performance improvement.

P.2 Organizational Challenges Item Linkages

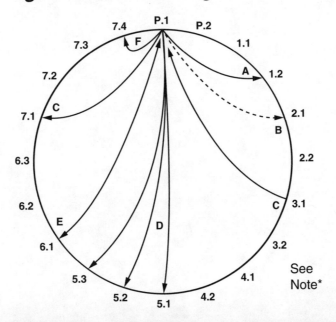

NATURE OF RELATIONSHIP	
A	Leaders [1.1a(2)] are responsible for creating an environment that drives organizational learning, which in turn contributes to the overall focus on performance improvement [P.2c]. The overall approaches to systematic evaluation and improvement, organizational learning, and knowledge sharing identified in P.2c should be consistent with overall requirements for improvement specifically required in Items 1.1b(3) leadership effectiveness; 3.1a(3) customer requirements definition; 3.2a(4) building customer relationships and providing easy customer access; 3.2b(4) determining customer satisfaction; 4.1a(4) and 4.1b(3) producing analyses to support continuous and breakthrough performance improvements; 4.2a(3) keeping data availability current, especially in a volatile work environment; 4.2b(2) keeping software and hardware current; 5.2a(4) training and education effectiveness; 5.3a improving workforce health, safety, and well-being; 6.1a(6) test and coordinate designs to improve effectiveness; 6.1b(5) improve production and delivery processes; 6.2b(6) improve nonproduct and nonservice business systems; and 6.3b(7) improve support services.
B	The competitive environment defined in P.2a should be examined as part of the strategy development process [2.1a(2)].
C	Information about competitors, which is needed to create the description for P.2a, use processes discussed in Items 3.1a(1), 3.2b(3), and 4.1a(3).
D	Progress in achieving strategic challenges, as described in P.2b, should be reported in Item 7.4a(2). In addition, the strategic challenges identified in P.2b should be consistent with the strategic objectives in 2.1b(1).

*Note: Evaluation and improvement is pervasive, linking most of the Items in Categories 1 through 6 with P.2 and will not be repeated on all the Item maps in Categories 1 through 6.

1 Leadership—120 Points

The Leadership Category examines how your organization's senior leaders address values, directions, and performance expectations, as well as a focus on customers and other stakeholders, empowerment, innovation, and learning. Also examined is how your organization addresses its responsibilities to the public and supports its key communities.

The leadership system must promote organizational core values, set high-performance expectations, and promote an organizationwide focus on customers, employee empowerment, learning, and innovation. The Leadership Category looks at how senior leaders guide the organization in setting directions and seeking future opportunities. Senior leaders must communicate clear values and high-performance expectations that address the needs of all stakeholders. The category also looks at the how the organization meets its responsibilities to the public and how it practices good citizenship.

The category contains two Items:

Organizational Leadership

- Communicating and reinforcing clear values, performance expectations, and a focus on creating value for customers and other stakeholders.

- Reinforcing an environment for empowerment and innovation and employee and organizational learning.

- Reviewing organizational performance and capabilities, competitiveness, and progress relative to goals, and setting priorities for improvement.

- Evaluating and improving the effectiveness of senior leadership and management throughout the organization, including employee input in the process.

Public Responsibility and Citizenship

- For regulatory and other legal requirements in areas such as safety, environmental protection, and waste management; anticipating public concerns and addressing risks to the public; and ensuring ethical business practices.

- For strengthening and supporting key communities.

1.1 Organizational Leadership (80 Points)
Approach/Deployment Scoring

Describe how senior leaders guide your organization, including how they review organizational performance.

Within your response, include answers to the following questions:

a. Senior Leadership Direction
(1) How do senior leaders set and deploy organizational values, short- and longer-term directions, and performance expectations, including a focus on creating and balancing value for customers and other stakeholders? Include how senior leaders communicate values, directions, and expectations through your leadership system and to all employees.

(2) How do senior leaders create an environment for empowerment, innovation, organizational agility, and organizational and employee learning?

b. Organizational Performance Review
(1) How do senior leaders review organizational performance and capabilities to assess organizational success, competitive performance, progress relative to short- and longer-term goals, and the ability to address changing organizational needs? Include the key performance measures regularly reviewed by your senior leaders. Also, include your key recent performance review findings.

(2) How are organizational performance review findings translated into priorities for improvement and opportunities for innovation? How are they deployed throughout your organization and, as appropriate, to your suppliers/partners to ensure organizational alignment?

(3) How do senior leaders use organizational performance review findings to improve both their own leadership effectiveness and your leadership system?

Notes:
N1. Organizational directions [1.1a (1)] relate to strategic objectives and action plans described in Items 2.1 and 2.2.

N2. Senior leaders' organizational performance reviews (1.1b) should be informed by organizational performance analyses described in 4.1b and strategic objectives and action plans described in Items 2.1 and 2.2.

N3. Leadership effectiveness improvement [1.1b (3)] should be supported by formal and/or informal employee feedback/surveys.

N4. Your organizational performance results should be reported in Items 7.1, 7.2, 7.3, and 7.4.

Interpretation

There are two distinctly different aspects to the requirements of this Item [1.1]. The first part [1.1a] describes "sending" or outgoing actions of leaders. Through their outward focus they push values, create expectations, and align the work of the organization. The second part [1.1b] requires leaders to receive, rather than send, information. Here they must monitor progress and use this incoming data to determine where resources and priorities must be aligned to ensure appropriate progress is achieved.

The "sending" part of this Item [1.1a] looks at how senior leaders create and sustain values that promote high performance throughout the organization. In promoting high performance, senior leaders set and deploy values, short- and longer-term directions, and performance expectations and balance the expectations of customers and other stakeholders. Leaders develop and implement systems to ensure values are understood and consistently followed. An organization's failure to achieve high levels of performance can almost always be traced to a failure in leadership.

- To consistently promote high performance, leaders must clearly set direction and make sure everyone in the organization understands his or her responsibilities. Success requires a strong future orientation and a commitment to improvement, innovation, and the disciplined change that is needed to carry it out. This requires creating an environment for empowerment, learning, innovation, and organizational agility, as well as the means for rapid and effective application of knowledge.

- Leaders also ensure that organizational values actually guide the behavior of managers and employees throughout the organization or the values are meaningless. To enhance performance excellence the "right" values must be adopted. These values must include a focus on customers and other stakeholders. Since various customer and stakeholder groups often have conflicting interests, leaders must strike a balance that optimizes the interests of all groups. The failure to ensure a customer focus usually causes the organization and its employees to focus internally. The lack of a customer focus forces workers to default to their own ideas of what customers really "need." This increases the risk of becoming

arrogant and not caring about the requirements of customers. It also increases the potential for creating and delivering products and services that no customer wants or values. That, in turn, increases rework, scrap, waste, and added cost/lower value.

- Leaders must create an environment for empowerment and agility, as well as the means for rapid and effective application of knowledge.

The "receiving" part of this Item [1.1b] looks at how senior leaders review organizational performance in a disciplined, fact-based manner, what key performance measures they regularly review, and how review findings are used to drive improvement and innovation. This organizational review should cover all areas of performance, and provide a complete and accurate picture of the "state of health" of the organization. This includes not only how well the organization is currently performing, but also how well it is moving to secure future success.

- Key performance measures should focus on and reflect the key drivers of success leaders regularly review. These measures should relate to the strategic objectives necessary for success.

- Leaders should use these reviews to drive improvement and change. These reviews should provide a reliable means to guide the improvement and change needed to achieve the organization's key objectives, success factors, and measures.

- Leaders must create a consistent process to translate the review findings into an action agenda, sufficiently specific for deployment throughout the organization and to suppliers/partners and key customers as appropriate.

- In addition, leaders and managers at all levels must evaluate their personal effectiveness. To ensure the evaluation is accurate, employees must provide feedback to the leaders and managers at all levels.

- Finally, leaders and managers at all levels should take action, based on the feedback, to improve their effectiveness. It is critical that leaders, managers, and supervisors at all levels and in all parts of the organization effectively drive and reinforce the principles of performance excellence through words and actions. Remember, nearly every failure to achieve and sustain excellence can be traced to a failure on a part of leaders and managers. Jack Welch, CEO of General Electric in his last letter to stockholders, emphasized the importance of rewarding and nurturing the top 20 percent of employees, and getting rid of the bottom 10 percent. The same is true of managers who do not or will not aggressively and effectively lead the effort to enhance performance excellence.

How it Fits Together

1.1 Organizational Leadership

How senior leaders guide the organization in setting direction and developing and sustaining an effective leadership system throughout the organization

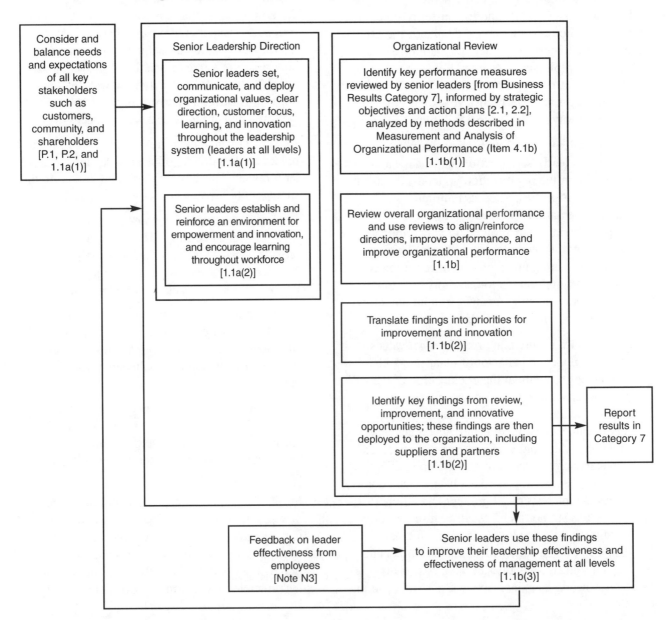

1.1 Organizational Leadership Item Linkages

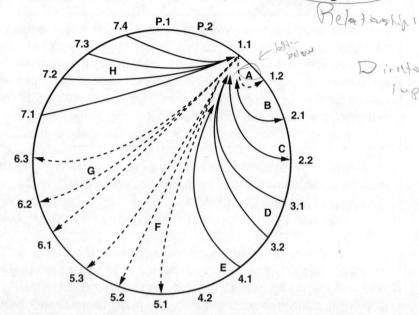

Relationship

Direction of Arrows is important

NOTE: See page xv for a key to the meaning of the arrows.

NATURE OF RELATIONSHIP	
A	Leaders [1.1], in support of organizational values, role model and support corporate responsibility [1.2a] and practice good citizenship [1.2b].
B	To effectively set organizational direction and expectations, leaders [1.1a(1)] participate in the strategic planning process [2.1]. As a part of this effort, leaders [1.1a(1)] ensure that strategic objectives balance the needs of key stakeholders [2.1b(2)]. Leaders also use the time lines for achieving strategic objectives [2.1b(1)] as a basis for defining and monitoring expected progress closely [1.1b(1)].
C	Leaders [(1.1a(1)] ensure that plans are clearly communicated and understood (deployed) at all levels throughout the organization and used to align work [2.2a(1)]. Leaders [1.1a] also approve the overall goals set forth in the plan based, in part, on information about the expected levels of competitor performance [2.2b].
D	Leaders [1.1a(1)] use information from customers about requirements and preferences [3.1a] and satisfaction/dissatisfaction [3.2] to set direction and create opportunity for the organization. Leaders [1.1] also have a responsibility for personally building relationships with key customers [3.2a] (creating a bidirectional relationship).
E	Leaders [1.1b(1)] use analyses of data [4.1b(1, 3)] to monitor organizational performance and understand relationships among performance, employee satisfaction, customers, markets, and financial success. These analyses are also used for decision making at all levels to set priorities for action and allocate resources for maximum advantage [1.1b(2)]. They are also responsible for using comparative data [from 4.1a(3)] to set meaningful goals to achieve organizational success.

Continued

NATURE OF RELATIONSHIP	*continued*
F	Leaders [1.1a(2)] create an environment for employee empowerment, innovation, and learning throughout the entire organization through the design of work and jobs [5.1a(1)]. They ensure that the compensation and recognition system [5.1a(3)] encourages employees at all levels to achieve performance excellence in areas most critical to the organization. Leaders [1.1a(2)] are also responsible for supporting appropriate skill development of all employees through training and development systems and reinforcing learning on the job [5.2a], as well as creating effective systems to enhance employee satisfaction, well-being, and motivation [5.3].
G	Leaders [1.1] are responsible for creating an environment that supports high performance, including monitoring processes for design and delivery [6.1], business [6.2], and support services [6.3] processes. Leaders must ensure that design, production/delivery, support, and supplier performance processes are aligned and consistently evaluated and refined.
H	Senior leaders [1.1b] use performance results data [from Category 7] for many activities, including monitoring organizational performance [1.1b(1)]; deploying review findings to focus work and ensure alignment [1.1b(2)]; strategic planning [2.1a]; setting goals and priorities [2.1b(1)]; reinforcing or rewarding employee performance [5.1a(3)]; and for improving their effectiveness and the effectiveness of leaders at all levels [1.1b(3)].

↗ New   *Don't Use Adis for "So What Into's" Cookie Cutter*

IF YOU DON'T DO WHAT THE CRITERIA REQUIRE...	
Item Reference	**Possible Adverse Consequences**
1.1a(1)	If senior leaders fail to make performance expectations clear (especially defining them in measurable terms), it may create uncertainty among managers and employees throughout the organization about what they must accomplish. This may cause managers to substitute their own ideas and objectives, which may not be in alignment with those of top leadership. The lack of alignment may also contribute to redundancy. As a consequence, some parts of the organization can end up working at cross-purposes with other parts of the organization.
1.1a(1)	If senior leaders do not create an environment that focuses on creating value for customers and other stakeholders, employees and managers within the organization may become internally focused and risk negatively impacting the customer value on which the organization was built. An internal focus may contribute to a climate where employees are not primarily interested in listening to customer requirements or concerns. This may produce a high level of organizational arrogance where employees believe they know what the customers want better than the customer. This type of behavior can antagonize customers and produce high levels of customer dissatisfaction.
1.1a(2)	If senior leaders do not create an environment that promotes employee empowerment, they risk not leveraging the brain power of a formidable asset—their people. As a consequence, leaders may be effectively sending a message that employees do not have the skills or ability to make decisions on their own—that micromanagement is the preferred approach within the organization. This kind of an environment tends to migrate decision making to higher and higher levels in the organization, creating excessive delay and working against organizational agility. Unnecessary levels of review and approval may also tend to minimize innovation and creativity throughout the organization. Taken together, these problems are likely to add cost but not value—making it increasingly difficult to be successful in a highly competitive industry.
1.1b(1)	If senior leaders do not have a systematic, fact-based process in place that enables them to review organizational performance and assess progress toward goals, it may send a message throughout the organization that performance outcomes are really not that important. If results are not important to top leaders, they may not be considered important to lower levels within the organization and employees at all levels may not contribute optimum effort to achieve these (unimportant) results. Furthermore, if organizational performance reviews are not aligned with strategic objectives [Item 2.1b(1)] and related actions [Item 2.2a(1)] people in the organization may not be focusing their work in areas essential to organizational success, further suboptimizing organizational performance and value to the customer.
1.1b(2)	Even if senior leaders have an effective process to review organizational performance [Item 1.1b(1)] but do not effectively use these review findings to identify priorities for improvement and areas that should be targets of innovation, they may not be providing appropriate focus and alignment throughout the organization. This may make it difficult for workers and managers throughout the organization to determine if resources are being used

Continued

IF YOU DON'T DO WHAT THE CRITERIA REQUIRE... *continued*

	appropriately or if they should be reallocated. The long-standing failure to identify priorities for improvement or targets of innovation may contribute to the perception that the *status quo* is acceptable and continuous improvement is not important. This may further contribute to organizational stagnation and may make it difficult to keep pace with competitors and increasing customer requirements.
1.1b(3)	Even a new employee can tell the difference between an effective leader and an incompetent one. Unfortunately, an incompetent leader is frequently blind to this fact. *(Where do you think Scott Adams gets his material for the Dilbert cartoon?)* The combination of organizational performance outcomes and employee (subordinate) feedback can provide critical information to help leaders throughout the leadership system identify personal strengths and opportunities for improvement. Without this information leaders may not be able to focus effectively on key areas where improvement would be essential not only to personal growth and development but to better organizational results. Leaders that do not have accurate feedback about their strengths and weaknesses may not be able to keep pace with changing business needs and directions as they are challenged to work smarter by customers, competitors, and the demands of stockholders and other stakeholders. They may not be able to lead their organization to winning levels of performance excellence.

1.1 ORGANIZATIONAL LEADERSHIP—SAMPLE EFFECTIVE PRACTICES

Perhaps most critical is that senior leaders demonstrate absolute, unwavering commitment to performance excellence—even aligning reward and recognition to provide incentives and disincentives. The best senior leaders do not tolerate a lack of aggressive commitment and urgent action from subordinate managers at any level. They must send a clear message to employees that the effort is serious.

A. Senior Leadership Direction

- All senior leaders are personally involved in performance improvement.

- Senior leaders spend a significant portion of their time on performance improvement activities.

- Senior leaders carry out many visible activities (for example, goal setting, planning, and recognition and reward of performance and process improvement).

- Senior leaders regularly communicate performance excellence values to managers and ensure that managers demonstrate those values in their work.

- Senior leaders participate on performance improvement teams and use quality tools and practices.

- Senior leaders spend time with suppliers, partners, and customers.

- Senior leaders mentor managers and ensure that promotion criteria reflect organizational values.

- Senior leaders study and learn about the improvement practices of other organizations.

- Senior leaders clearly and consistently articulate values (customer focus, customer satisfaction, role model leadership, continuous improvement, workforce involvement, and performance optimization) throughout the organization.

- Senior leaders ensure that organizational values are used to provide direction to all employees in the organization to help achieve the mission, vision, and performance goals.

- Senior leaders use effective and innovative approaches to reach out to all employees to spread the organization's values and align its work to support organizational goals.

- Senior leaders effectively surface problems and encourage employee risk-taking.

- Roles and responsibilities of managers are clearly defined, understood by them, and used to judge their performance.

- Managers walk the talk (serve as role models) in leading quality and systematic performance improvement.

- Job definitions with quality indices are clearly delineated for each level of the organization, objectively measured, and presented in a logical and organized structure.

- Many different communication strategies are used to reinforce quality values.

- Leader behavior (not merely words) clearly communicates what is expected of the organization and its employees.

- Systems and procedures are deployed that encourage cooperation and a cross-functional approach to management, team activities, and problem solving.

- Leaders monitor employee acceptance and adoption of vision and values using annual surveys, employee focus groups, and e-mail questions.

- A systematic process is in place for evaluating and improving the integration or alignment of quality values throughout the organization.

B.   Organizational Performance Review

- Reviews against measurable performance standards are held frequently.

- Actions are taken to assist units that are not meeting goals or performing to plan.

- Senior leaders systematically and routinely check the effectiveness of their leadership activities (for example, seeking feedback at least annually from employees and peers using an upward or 360-degree evaluation), and take steps to improve.

- Leaders at all levels determine how well they carried out their activities (what went right or wrong and how they could be done better).

- There is evidence of adopting changes to improve leader effectiveness.

- Priorities for organizational improvement and innovation are driven by customer, performance, and financial data.

- Senior leaders base their business decisions on reliable data and facts pertaining to customers, operational processes, and employee performance and satisfaction.

- Senior leaders hold regular meetings to review performance data and communicate problems, successes, and effective approaches to improve work.

- Senior leaders conduct monthly reviews of organizational performance. This requires that subordinates conduct biweekly reviews and that workers and work teams provide daily performance updates. Corrective actions are developed to improve performance that deviates from planned performance.

1.2 Public Responsibility and Citizenship (40 Points)
Approach/Deployment Scoring

Describe how your organization addresses its responsibilities to the public and practices good citizenship.

Within your response, include answers to the following questions:

a. **Responsibilities to the Public**

    (1) How do you address the impacts on society of your products, services, and operations? Include your key processes, measures, and targets for regulatory and legal requirements and for addressing risks associated with your products, services, and operations.

    (2) How do you anticipate public concerns with current and future products, services, and operations? How do you prepare for these concerns in a proactive manner?

    (3) How do you accomplish ethical business practices in all stakeholder transactions and interactions?

b. **Support of Key Communities**

How do your organization, your senior leaders, and your employees actively support and strengthen your key communities? Include how you identify key communities and determine areas of emphasis for organizational involvement and support.

Notes:

N1. Public responsibilities in areas critical to your business also should be addressed in Strategy Development (Item 2.1) and/or in Process Management (Category 6). Key results, such as results of regulatory/legal compliance or environmental improvements through use of "green" technology or other means, should be reported as Organizational Effectiveness Results (Item 7.4).

N2. Areas of community support appropriate for inclusion in 1.2b might include your efforts to strengthen local community services, education, and health; the environment; and practices of trade, business, or professional associations.

N3. The health and safety of employees are not addressed in Item 1.2; you should address these employee factors in Item 5.3.

This Item [1.2] looks at how the organization fulfills its public responsibilities and encourages, supports, and practices good citizenship.

The first part of this Item [1.2a] looks at how the organization addresses current and future impacts on society in a proactive manner and how it ensures ethical business practices in all stakeholder interactions. The impacts and practices are expected to cover all relevant and important areas—products, services, and operations.

- An integral part of performance management and improvement is proactively addressing legal and regulatory requirements and risk factors. Addressing these areas requires establishing appropriate measures and/or indicators that senior leaders track in their overall performance review. The organization should be sensitive to issues of public concern, whether or not these issues are currently embodied in law. The failure to address these areas can expose the organization to future problems when it least expects them. Problems can range from a sudden decline in consumer confidence to extensive and costly litigation. In this regard, it is important to anticipate potential problems the public may have with both current and future products. Sometimes a well-intended product or service could create adverse public consequences.

- For example, consider the use of automatic teller machines (ATMs) or cash machines as they are called today. When these machines were first introduced, many in the industry believed that the public would never accept the machines as a surrogate for a human being. For the most part, these machines were considered an eyesore and were installed in out-of-the-way places, usually at the back of the bank building. However, the extraordinary success of these devices resulted in hundreds of millions of people conducting cash transactions outside the relative safety of the bank building. This gave rise to more robberies, abductions, and even murder. By failing to consider the potential adverse consequence of these cash machines located in out-of-the-way places, banks were exposed to increased litigation and costs associated with

relocating or providing appropriate security enclosures in an effort to reduce public risk.

- Good public responsibility implies going beyond minimum compliance with laws and regulations. Top-performing organizations frequently serve as role models of responsibility and provide leadership in areas key to business success. For example, a manufacturing company might go beyond the requirements of the environmental protection regulations and develop innovative and award-winning systems to protect the environment and reduce pollution. This has a double benefit. Not only do they develop good relations with regulators (and occasionally receive the "benefit-of-the-doubt"), but when regulators increase requirements, the high-performing organizations are already in compliance, usually way ahead of competitors who only met minimum requirements.

- Good citizenship opportunities are available to organizations of all sizes. These opportunities include encouraging and supporting employees' community service.

- Ensuring ethical business practices are followed by all employees lessens the organization's risk of adverse public reaction as well as criminal prosecution. Programs to ensure ethical business practices typically seek to prevent activities that might be perceived as criminal or near criminal. Examples of unethical business practices might include falsifying expense reports or quality-control data, accepting lavish gifts from a contractor, or seeking kickbacks.

The second part of this Item [1.2b] looks at how the organization, its senior leaders, and its employees identify, support, and strengthen key communities as part of good citizenship practices.

- Good citizenship practices typically vary according to the size, complexity, and location of the organization. Larger organizations are generally expected to have a more comprehensive approach to citizenship than small organizations.

- Examples of organizational community involvement include: influencing the adoption of higher standards in education by communicating employability requirements to schools and school boards; partnering with other businesses and health care providers to improve health in the local community by providing education and volunteer services to address public health issues; and partnering to influence trade and business associations to engage in beneficial, cooperative activities, such as sharing best practices to improve overall U.S.-global competitiveness and the environment.

• In addition to activities directly carried out by the organization, opportunities to practice good citizenship include employee community service that is encouraged and supported by the organization. Frequently, the organization's leaders actively participate on community boards and actively support their work. Usually, organizations—like people—support causes and issues that they value. Top-performing organizations are not content to simply donate money, people, and products/services to these causes without examining the impact of this support. Like other parts of their business, they evaluate and refine the effectiveness of community support, consistent with business strategies and objectives.

1.2 Public Responsibility and Citizenship

How the organization addresses public responsibilities and practices good citizenship

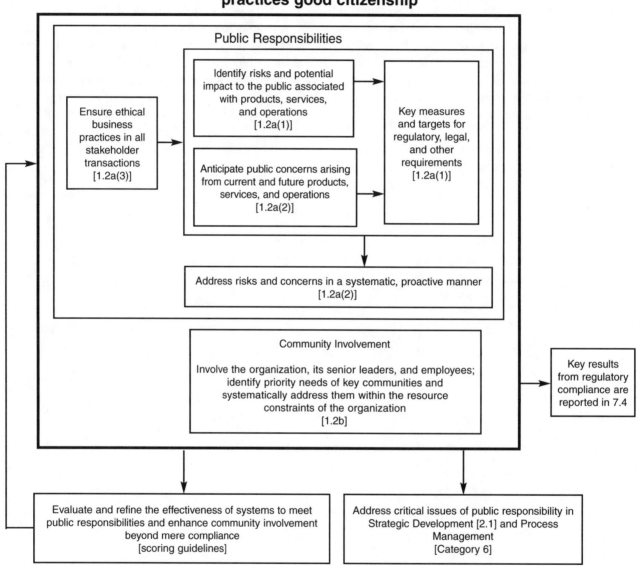

1.2 Public Responsibility and Citizenship Item Linkages

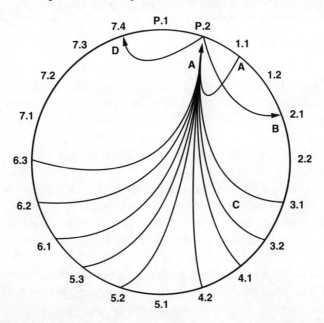

NATURE OF RELATIONSHIP	
A	Leaders, in support of organizational values [1.1a], have a responsibility for setting policies and ensuring that practices and products of the organization and its employees do not adversely impact society or violate ethical standards, regulations, or law [1.2a]. They are also responsible to be personally involved and to ensure that the organization and its employees strengthen key communities in areas such as local community services, education, the environment, business and professional associations, and health and welfare [1.2b].
B	Public health and safety concerns, environmental protection, and waste management issues [1.2a] are important factors to consider in strategy development [2.1a(2)].
C	Training [5.2] is provided to ensure all employees understand organization ethical business practices [1.2a(3)] as well as the importance of strengthening key communities [1.2b]. In addition, recruitment and hiring and the design of work systems should capitalize on the ideas, culture, and thinking of key communities and their impact on the organization [5.1a(5)].
D	Managers at all levels have responsibility for ensuring that work practices of the organization [6.1, 6.2 and 6.3] are consistent with the organization's standards of ethics and public responsibility [1.2].
E	Key results, such as results of regulatory compliance, environmental improvements, and support to key communities, are reported in Organization-Effectiveness Results [7.4b]. In addition, these results are monitored to determine if process changes are needed. (Compliance results in areas of employee safety are reported in 7.3, based on processes described in Item 5.3, Employee Well-Being and Satisfaction, and are not a part of the requirements in 1.2.)
F	The regulatory environment described in P.1a(5) sets the context for the review of the management systems for public responsibility citizenship [1.2a (1)].

IF YOU DON'T DO WHAT THE CRITERIA REQUIRE...

Item Reference	Possible Adverse Consequences
1.2a(1)	Organizations that fail to consider the impact on the public of their products, services, and operations may be seriously impaired in the future if it is determined that these products or services caused harm. (The problem may be so serious that it could cause the organization to go out of business relatively quickly, as in the case of Dow-Corning and the silicone breast implants.) In the short-term, organizations that fail to comply with regulatory and legal requirements may find themselves facing costly sanctions or be inhibited from conducting business. The failure to consider risks associated with products, services, and operations may contribute to costly corrective action or litigation. For example, banks throughout the world have been forced to pay damages to users of automatic teller machines (ATMs) because of the failure to provide adequate security, which resulted in abductions, robbery, and murders.
1.2a(2)	Organizations that fail to anticipate and consider potential concerns that the public may have with current and future products, services, and operations may be faced with costly redesign or redirection. When an organization appears to treat the public and the community within which it works with impunity and disregards their concerns, it becomes extremely difficult to recover trust and confidence. When the organization finds it needs public support to carry out its work or expand its operations it may find it difficult to secure that support from the public.
1.2a(3)	Organizations that do not ensure ethical business practices in all transactions and interactions with stakeholders (public, customers, stockholders, employees, suppliers, and so on) run the risk of violating the public trust. Accordingly, these organizations may face serious adverse consequences when their misdeeds are discovered. (One only needs to consider the difference between Enron and Tylenol. Both companies faced disasters that threatened their existence. Tylenol responded ethically and is still thriving.) Moreover, if the unethical practices of leaders are considered an acceptable business standard in the organization and repeated by others, it can contribute to numerous unpredictable problems that divert human and financial resources to correct.
1.2b	Organizations that fail to act as good corporate citizens and support the local community may find it difficult to get support in return, especially for projects or initiatives that require local approval. For example, local communities typically provide the bulk of support for services as well as new workers. Organizations that fail to support local education, or trade and professional associations may find themselves faced with a shortage of skilled workers in key areas and important services they need to conduct business.

1.2 PUBLIC RESPONSIBILITY AND CITIZENSHIP—SAMPLE EFFECTIVE PRACTICES

A. Responsibilities to the Public

- The organization's principal business activities include systems to analyze, anticipate, and minimize public hazards or risk.

- Indicators for risk areas are identified and monitored.

- Improvement strategies are used consistently, target performance levels are set, and progress is reviewed regularly and tied to recognition and reward.

- The organization considers the impact that its operations, products, and services might have on society and considers those impacts in planning.

- The effectiveness of systems to meet or exceed regulatory or legal requirements is systematically evaluated and improved.

B. Support of Key Communities

- Senior leaders and employees at various levels in the organization are involved in professional organizations, committees, task forces, or other community activities.

- Organizational resources are allocated to support involvement in community activities outside the organization. The effectiveness of these allocations is examined to determine if expectations are met and resources are used wisely.

- Employees participate in local, state, or national quality award programs and receive recognition from the organization.

- Employees participate in a variety of professional quality and business improvement associations.

- The effectiveness of processes to support and strengthen key communities is systematically measured, evaluated, and improved.

2   Strategic Planning—85 Points

> The Strategic Planning Category examines how your organization develops strategic objectives and action plans. Also examined are how your chosen strategic objectives and action plans are deployed and how progress is measured.

The Strategic Planning Category looks at the organization's process for strategic and action planning, and deployment of plans to make sure everyone is working to achieve those plans. Customer-driven quality and operational performance excellence are key strategic issues that need to be integral parts of the organization's overall planning.

- Customer-driven quality is a strategic view of quality. The focus is on the drivers of customer satisfaction, customer retention, new markets, and market share—key factors in competitiveness, profitability, and business success.

- Operational performance improvement contributes to short- and longer-term productivity growth and cost/price competitiveness. Building operational capability—including speed, responsiveness, and flexibility—represents an investment in strengthening the organization's competitive position now and into the future.

Over the years, much debate and discussion have taken place around planning. Professors in our colleges and universities spend a great deal of time trying to differentiate strategic planning, long-term planning, short-term planning, tactical planning, operational planning, quality planning, business planning, and human resource planning, to name a few. However, a much simpler view might serve us better. For our purposes, the following captures the essence of planning:

- Strategic planning is simply an effort to identify the things we must do to be successful in the future

- Once we have determined what we must do to be successful (the plan), we must take steps to execute that plan (the actions)

Accordingly, the key role of strategic planning is to provide a basis for aligning the organization's work processes with its strategic directions, thereby ensuring people and processes in different parts of the organization are not working at cross-purposes. To the extent that alignment does not occur, the organization's effectiveness and competitiveness is reduced.

The Strategic Planning Category looks at how the organization:

- Understands the key customer, market, and operational requirements as input to setting strategic directions. This helps to ensure that ongoing process improvements are aligned with the organization's strategic directions.

- Optimizes the use of resources and ensures bridging between short- and longer-term requirements that may entail capital expenditures, supplier development, new human resource recruitment strategies, reengineering key processes, and other factors affecting business success.

- Ensures that deployment will be effective—that there are mechanisms to transmit requirements and achieve alignment on three basic levels: (1) the organization/executive level; (2) the key process level; and (3) the work-unit/individual-job level.

The requirements for the Strategic Planning Category are intended to encourage strategic thinking and acting—to develop a basis for achieving and maintaining a competitive position. These requirements do not demand formalized plans, planning systems, departments, or specific planning cycles. They also do not imply that all improvements could or should be planned in advance. They do, however, require plans and the alignment of actions to those plans at all levels of the organization. An effective improvement system combines improvements of many types and degrees of involvement. An effective system to improve performance and competitive advantage requires fact-based strategic guidance, particularly when improvement alternatives compete for limited resources. In most cases, priority setting depends heavily upon a cost rationale. However, an organization might also have to deal with critical requirements, such as public responsibilities, that are not driven by cost considerations alone.

Strategic planning consists of the planning process, the identification of goals and actions necessary to achieve success, and the deployment of those actions to align the work of the organization.

Strategy Development

- Customers: market requirements and evolving expectations

- Competitive environment: industry, market, and technology

- Financial and societal risks

- Human resource capabilities and needs

- Operational capabilities and needs, including resource availability

- Supplier capabilities and needs

- Clear strategic objectives with timetables

Strategy Deployment

- Translate strategy into action plans and related human resource plans

- Align and deploy action plan requirements, performance measures, and resources throughout the organization

- Project expected performance results, including assumptions of competitor performance increases

2.1 Strategy Development (40 points)
Approach/Deployment Scoring

Describe how your organization establishes its strategic objectives, including enhancing its competitive position and overall performance.

Within your response, include answers to the following questions:

a. Strategy Development Process

(1) What is your overall strategic planning process? Include key steps, key participants, and your short- and longer-term planning time horizons.

(2) How do you ensure that planning addresses the following key factors? Briefly outline how relevant data and information are gathered and analyzed to address these factors:
- Customer and market needs/expectations/opportunities
- Your competitive environment and your capabilities relative to competitors
- Technological and other key changes that might affect your products/services and/or how you operate
- Your strengths and weaknesses, including human and other resources
- Your supplier/partner strengths and weaknesses
- Financial, societal, and other potential risks

b. Strategic Objectives

(1) What are your key strategic objectives and your timetable for accomplishing them? Include key goals/targets, as appropriate.

(2) How do your strategic objectives address the challenges identified in response to P.2 in your Organizational Profile? How do you ensure that your strategic objectives balance the needs of all key stakeholders?

Notes:

N1. "Strategy development" refers to your organization's approach (formal or informal) to preparing for the future. Strategy development might utilize various types of forecasts, projections, options, scenarios, and/or other approaches to envisioning the future for purposes of decision making and resource allocation.

N2. "Strategy" should be interpreted broadly. Strategy might be built around or lead to any or all of the following: new products, services, and markets; revenue growth via various approaches, including acquisitions; and new partnerships and alliances. Strategy might be directed toward becoming a preferred supplier, a local supplier in each of your major customers' markets, a low-cost producer, a market innovator, and/or a high-end or customized product/service provider.

N3. Challenges [2.1b (2)] addressed in your strategy might include rapid response, customization, lean or virtual manufacturing, rapid innovation, web-based supplier/customer relationship management, and product/service quality. Responses to Item 2.1 should focus on your specific challenges—those most important to your business success and to strengthening your organization's overall performance.

N4. Item 2.1 addresses your overall organizational strategy, which might include changes in services, products, and product lines. However, the Item does not address product and service design; you should address these factors in Item 6.1.

This Item [2.1] looks at how the organization sets strategic directions and develops strategic objectives, with the aim of strengthening overall performance and competitiveness.

The first part of this Item [2.1a(1)] asks the organization to describe its strategic planning process and identify the key participants, key steps, and planning time horizons. This helps examiners understand the steps and data used in the planning process. It is usually a good idea to provide a flowchart of the planning process. This helps examiners understand how the planning process works without wasting valuable space in the application.

Organizations must consider the key factors that affect its future success. These factors cover external and internal influences on the organization. Each factor must be addressed and outlined to show how relevant data and information are gathered and analyzed. Although the organization is not limited to the number of factors it considers important in planning, the six factors identified in Item 2.1a(2) must be addressed unless a valid rationale can be offered as to why the factor is not appropriate. Together, these six factors will cover the most important variables for any organization's future success.

- The planning process should examine all the key influences, risks, challenges, and other requirements that might affect the organization's future opportunities and directions—taking as long-term a view as possible. This approach is intended to provide a thorough and realistic context for the development of a customer- and market-focused strategy to guide ongoing decision making, resource allocation, and overall management.

- This planning process should cover all types of businesses, competitive situations, strategic issues, planning approaches, and plans. The requirement calls for a future-oriented basis for action but does not specifically require formalized planning, planning departments, planning cycles, or a specified way of visualizing the future. Even if the organization is seeking to create an entirely new business situation, it is still necessary to set and to test the objectives that define and guide critical actions and performance.

- This Item also focuses on identifying the factors and actions the organization must take to achieve a leadership position in a competitive market. This usually requires ongoing revenue growth and improvements in operational effectiveness. Achieving and sustaining a leadership position in a competitive market requires a view of the future that includes not only the markets or segments in which the organization competes, but also how it competes. How it competes presents many options and requires understanding of the organization's and competitors' strengths and weaknesses. No specific time horizon for planning is required by the Criteria; the thrust of this Item is finding ways to create and ensure sustained competitive leadership.

- In order to maintain competitive leadership, an increasingly important part of strategic planning requires processes to project the competitive environment accurately. Such projections help detect and reduce competitive threats, shorten reaction time, and identify opportunities. Depending on the size and type of business, maturity of markets, pace of change, and competitive parameters (such as price or innovation rate), organizations might use a variety of modeling, scenario, or other techniques and judgments to project the competitive environment.

The second part of this Item [2.1b] asks for a summary of the organization's key strategic objectives and the timetable for accomplishing them. It also asks how these objectives address the challenges outlined in the Organizational Profile.

- The purpose of the timetable is to provide a basis for projecting the path that improvement is likely to take. This allows the organizations' leaders to monitor progress more accurately. Consider Figure 25. The performance goal four years into the future is to achieve a level of performance of 100. Currently the organization is at 20. At the end of year one, the organization achieved a performance level of 40, represented by the circle symbol. It appears that that level of performance is on track toward the goal of 100. However, the path from the current state to the future state is rarely a straight line. Unless the expected trajectory is known (or at least estimated), it is not possible to evaluate the progress accurately. Without timetables or trajectories, leaders are forced to default to use best guess or intuition as a basis for comparing actual, measurable progress against expected progress.

In Figure 26, the planned trajectory is represented by the triangle symbols. When compared with the current level of performance (the circle symbol),

it is clear that there is a performance shortfall of approximately 30.

In Figure 27, the planned trajectory is represented by the square symbols. When compared with the current level of performance (the circle symbol), it is clear that the performance is ahead of schedule.

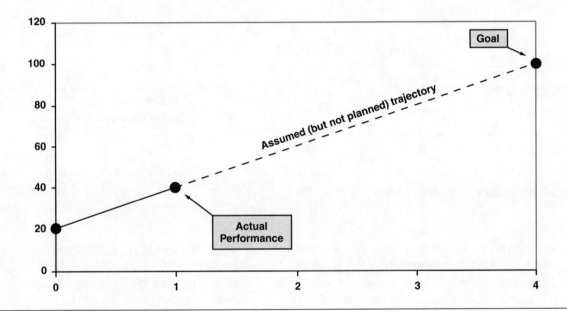

Figure 25 Assumed trajectory.

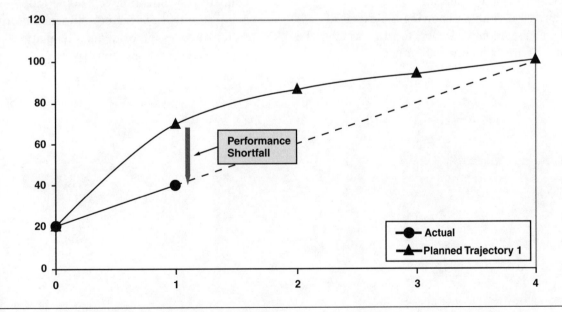

Figure 26 Planned trajectory 1—Peformance shortfall.

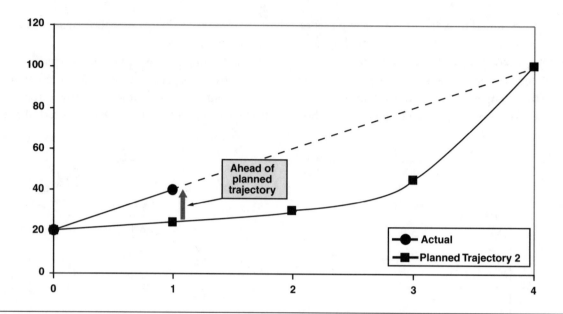

Figure 27 Planned trajectory 2—Ahead of plan.

There are several possible decisions that leaders could make based on this information. It might mean that the original estimates/goals were low and should be reset. It might also mean that the process did not need all of the resources it had available. These resources may be better used in areas where performance is not ahead of schedule.

In any case, without knowing the expected path toward a goal, it requires leaders to guess whether the level of progress is appropriate or not.

- Finally, the last part of this Item requires the organization to evaluate the options it considered in the strategic planning process to ensure it responded fully to the six factors identified in Item 2.1a(2) that were most important to business success. This last step helps the organization "close the loop" to make sure that the factors influencing organization success were adequately analyzed and support key strategic objectives.

2.1 Strategy Development

How the organization sets strategic direction to define and strengthen competitive position

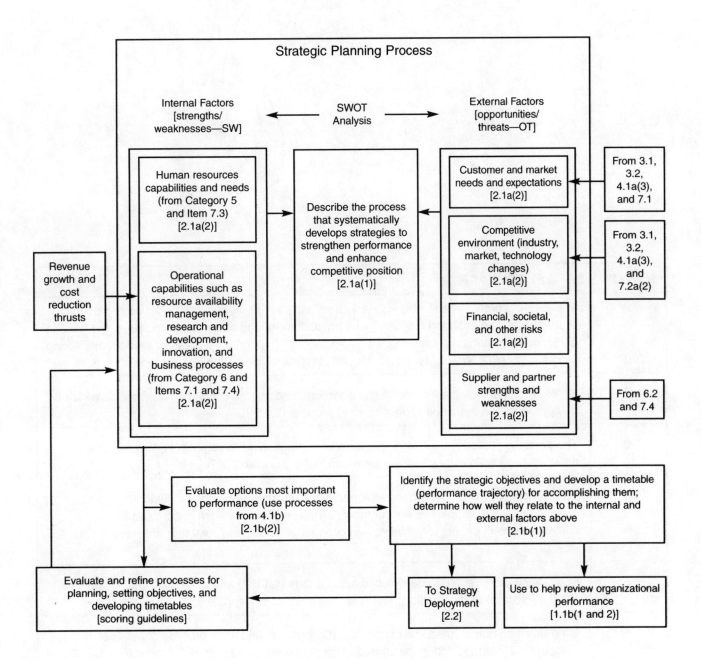

2.1 Strategy Development Item Linkages

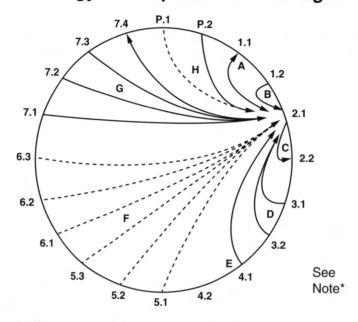

NATURE OF RELATIONSHIP	
A	The planning process [2.1] includes seniors as part of their responsibilities for setting direction, expectations, and ensuring a strong focus on customers and employee empowerment [1.1a]. In addition, the timelines or performance trajectory [2.1b(1)] provide a basis for leaders monitoring progress [1.1b(1)]. Without timelines it is difficult to determine if the organization is on track.
B	Public health, environmental, waste management, and related concerns [1.2a] are considered, as appropriate, in the strategy development process [2.1a(2)].
C	The planning process [2.1a] produces a set of strategic objectives [2.1b(1)] that must be converted into action plans that are deployed to the workforce [2.2a].
D	The planning process [2.1] includes information on current and potential customer requirements and the projected competitive environment [3.1], as well as intelligence obtained from customer-contact people (complaints and comments) [3.2a] and customer satisfaction data [3.2b].
E	Key organizational and competitive comparison data [4.1a(3)] and analytical data, including various forecasts and projections [4.1b], are used for planning [2.1a(2)].
F	Information on human resource capabilities [Category 5] and work process capabilities [Category 6] is considered in the strategic planning process as part of the determination of internal strengths and weaknesses. To avoid cluttering diagrams 5.1–6.3, these arrows will not be repeated there.

Continued

NATURE OF RELATIONSHIP		*continued*
G	Customer-focused, financial, and market results [7.1 and 7.2], and human resource and organization effectiveness results [7.3 and 7.4], are used in the planning process [2.1a(2)] to set strategic objectives [2.1b(1)]. In addition, results in 7.4a(2) must specifically report on progress toward achieving the strategic objectives.	
H	Employee educational levels, diversity, and other characteristics [P.1a(3)] may affect the determination of human resource strengths and weaknesses as a part of the strategic planning process [2.1a(2)]. The competitive environment defined in P.2a should also be examined as part of the strategy development process [2.1a(2)].	

*Note: The many inputs to strategy development will not all be repeated on other linkage diagrams to avoid clutter.

IF YOU DON'T DO WHAT THE CRITERIA REQUIRE...

Item Reference	Possible Adverse Consequences
2.1a(1)	Without clearly defined short- and longer-term planning horizons, it may be difficult to properly align the analysis and collection of market and industry forecast data to support effective planning. The shorter the planning horizon, the easier it is to be accurate in forecasting. However, the planning horizon must be at least as long as the time it takes the organization to design, develop, and deliver new products and services required by customers and markets. For example, if the design-delivery cycle time is seven years (as it was in the U.S. automobile industry), then to be effective an organization must be able to forecast or anticipate customer and market requirements seven years out—which is difficult to do accurately. Alternatively, the organization could reduce its design-delivery cycle time to less than 24 months (as it is with the Japanese automobile industry), reduce the required strategic planning horizon, and be able to more accurately anticipate customer and market requirements.
2.1a(2)	The failure to address the six key factors (customer and market means; competitive environment; technological and other changes that might affect operations; internal strengths and weaknesses; supplier and partner strengths and weaknesses; and external risks such as financial, societal, and regulatory) usually results in a flawed strategic plan—a plan that has overlooked an element critical to future success. For example, an organization may fail to achieve strategic objectives if it assumed (incorrectly) that a key supplier would be able to deliver critical components at a certain time. Likewise, a strategic plan that doesn't adequately account for the arrival of competitive offerings or new technologies in the marketplace can be faced with major hurdles (consider the impact of the digital watch on the traditional Swiss watch industry). Failing to consider or incorrectly forecasting these six elements may result in a strategic plan that cannot be achieved.
2.1b(1)	Knowing whether the strategy is unfolding as expected is critical to the successful performance or the organization and the leadership. The failure to develop a timetable with clearly defined targets for accomplishing strategic objectives makes it extremely difficult for leaders to effectively monitor organizational performance [as required by Item1.1b(1)]. Without defined milestones, leaders must guess whether the rate of progress is appropriate or not. Without clear timelines or trajectories for growth, leaders frequently assume the path between current state and desired state (goals) is linear. Data indicate that the actual path is almost never linear; so the assumptions of linearity that leaders make in the absence of clear timelines and trajectories are usually incorrect.
2.1b(2)	Strategy development is an ongoing, dynamic process. It is often a difficult process that takes a considerable amount of time to complete initially and then requires continual attention to address a rapidly changing marketplace. However, if leaders fail to ensure that planning has fully addressed organizational challenges and ensure that the strategic objectives effectively balance the needs of all key stakeholders, the plan may be ineffective and the time it took to develop the plan may be wasted.

2.1 STRATEGY DEVELOPMENT—SAMPLE EFFECTIVE PRACTICES

A. Strategy Development Process

- Business goals, strategies, and issues are addressed and reported in measurable terms. Strategic objectives consider future requirements needed to achieve organizational leadership after considering the performance levels that other organizations are likely to achieve in the same planning time frame.

- The planning and objective-setting process encourages input (but not necessarily decision making) from a variety of people at all levels throughout the organization.

- Data on customer requirements, key markets, benchmarks, supplier and partner, human resource, and organizational capabilities (internal and external factors) are used to develop business plans.

- Plans and the planning process itself are evaluated each cycle for accuracy and completeness—more often if needed to keep pace with changing business requirements.

- Opportunities for improvement in the planning process are identified systematically and carried out each planning cycle.

- Refinements in the process of planning, plan deployment, and receiving input from work units have been made. Improvements in plan cycle time, plan resources, and planning accuracy are documented.

B. Strategic Objectives

- Strategic objectives are identified and a timetable (or planned growth trajectory) for accomplishing the objectives are set.

- Options to obtain best performance for the strategic objectives are systematically evaluated against the internal and external factors used in the strategy development process.

- The process of setting timelines or trajectories and the accuracy of the projections are analyzed and referred.

- Best practices from other providers, competitors, or outside benchmarks are identified and used to provide better estimates of trajectories.

2.2   Strategy Deployment (45 points)
Approach/Deployment Scoring

Describe how your organization converts its strategic objectives into action plans. Summarize your organization's action plans and related key performance measures/indicators. Project your organization's future performance on these key performance measures/indicators.

Within your response, include answers to the following questions:

a.   Action Plan Development and Deployment

(1) How do you develop and deploy action plans to achieve your key strategic objectives? Include how you allocate resources to ensure accomplishment of your action plans.

(2) What are your key short- and longer-term action plans? Include key changes, if any, in your products/services, your customers/markets, and how you operate.

(3) What are your key human resource plans that derive from your short- and longer-term strategic objectives and action plans?

(4) What are your key performance measures/indicators for tracking progress relative to your action plans? How do you ensure that your overall action plan measurement system achieves organizational alignment and covers all key deployment areas and stakeholders?

b.   Performance Projection

What are your performance projections for your key measures/indicators for both your short- and longer-term planning time horizons? How does your projected performance compare with competitors' performance, key benchmarks, goals, and past performance, as appropriate?

Notes:

N1. Action plan development and deployment are closely linked to other Items in the Criteria. Examples of key linkages are:
- Item 1.1 for how your senior leaders set and communicate directions
- Category 3 for gathering customer and market knowledge as input to your strategy and action plans and for deploying action plans
- Category 4 for information and analysis to support your key information needs, to support your development of strategy, to provide an effective basis for your performance measurements, and to track progress relative to your strategic objectives and action plans
- Category 5 for your work system needs; employee education, training, and development needs; and related human resource factors resulting from action plans
- Category 6 for process requirements resulting from your action plans
- Item 7.4 for specific accomplishments relative to your organizational strategy

N2. Measures/indicators of projected performance (2.2b) might include changes resulting from new business ventures; business acquisitions; new value creation; market entry and shifts; and significant anticipated innovations in products, services, and technology.

The first part of this Item [2.2a] looks at how the organization translates its strategic objectives (which were identified in item 2.1b) into action plans to accomplish the objectives and to enable assessment of progress relative to action plans. Overall, the intent of this item is to ensure that strategies are deployed at all levels throughout the organization to align work for goal achievement.

The first part of this Item [2.2a] calls for information on how action plans are developed and deployed. This includes spelling out key performance requirements and measures, as well as allocating resources and aligning work throughout the organization. Leaders must develop action plans that address the key strategic objectives (which were developed using the processes in Item 2.1). Organizations must summarize key short- and longer-term action plans. Particular attention is given to products/services, customers/markets, how the organization operates, and key human resource plans that will enable accomplishment of strategic objectives and action plans.

The organization should provide the key measures/indicators used in tracking progress relative to the action plans. The organization should also describe how these measures or indicators are used to achieve organizational alignment and coverage of all key work units and stakeholders.

Accomplishing action plans requires resources and performance measures, as well as the alignment of work unit and supplier/partner plans. Of central importance in this Area is how alignment and consistency are achieved—for example, via key processes and key measurements. Alignment and consistency are intended also to provide a basis for setting and communicating priorities for ongoing improvement

activities—part of the daily work of all work units. Also required are the key measures and/or indicators used in tracking progress relative to the action plans, how they are communicated, and how strategic objectives, action plans, and performance are aligned. Action plans include human resource plans that support the overall strategy.

Without effective alignment, routine work and acts of improvement can be random and serve to suboptimize organizational performance. In Figure 28, the arrows represent the well-intended work carried out by employees of organizations who lack a clear set of expectations and direction. Each person, each manager, and each work unit works diligently to achieve goals they believe are important. Each is pulling hard—but not necessarily in ways that ensure performance excellence. This encourages the creation of "fiefdoms" within organizations.

With a clear, well-communicated strategic plan, it is easier to know when daily work is out of alignment. The large arrow in Figure 29 represents the strategic plan pointing the direction the organization must take to be successful and achieve its mission and vision. The strategic plan and accompanying measures make it possible to analyze work and business practices to know when they are not aligned and to help employees, including leaders, to know when adjustments are required.

A well-deployed and understood strategic plan helps everyone in the organization distinguish between random acts of improvement and aligned improvement. Random acts of improvement give a false sense of accomplishment and rarely produce optimum benefits for the organization. For example, a decision to improve a business process that is not

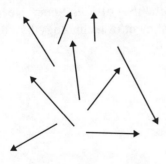

Figure 28 Nonaligned Work.

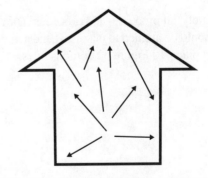

Figure 29 Strategic Direction.

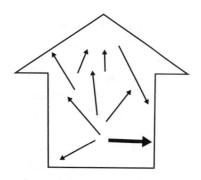

Figure 30 Random Improvement.

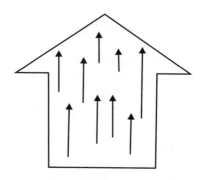

Figure 32 Systematic Alignment.

aligned with the strategic plan (as the small bold arrow in Figure 30 represents) usually results in a wasteful expenditure of time, money, and human resources—improvement without benefiting customers or enhancing operating effectiveness.

On the other hand, by working systematically to strengthen processes that are aligned with the strategic plan, the organization moves closer to achieving success, as Figure 31 indicates.

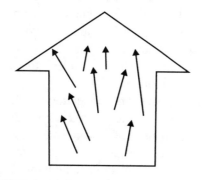

Figure 31 Moving Toward Alignment.

Ultimately, all processes and procedures of an organization should be aligned to maximize the achievement of strategic plans, as Figure 32 demonstrates.

Key changes in products/services or customers/markets might include Web-based or e-commerce initiatives, integrated within or separate from current business.

Critical action plan resource requirements include human resource plans that support the overall strategy. Examples of possible human resource plan elements are:

- Redesign of work organization and/or jobs to increase employee empowerment and decision making

- Initiatives to promote greater labor-management cooperation, such as union partnerships

- Initiatives to foster knowledge sharing and organizational learning

- Modification of compensation and recognition systems to recognize team, organizational, stock market, customer, or other performance attributes

- Education and training initiatives, such as developmental programs for future leaders, partnerships with universities to help ensure the availability of future employees, and/or establishment of technology-based training capabilities

Finally, the second part of this Item [2.2b] asks the organization to provide a projection of key performance measures and/or indicators, including key performance targets and/or goals for both short- and longer-term planning time horizons. This projected performance is the basis for comparing past performance and performance relative to competitors and benchmarks, as appropriate.

- Projections and comparisons in this Area are intended to help the organization's leaders improve their ability to understand and track dynamic, competitive performance factors. Through this tracking process, they should be better prepared to take into account its rate of improvement and change relative to competitors and relative to their own targets or stretch goals. Such tracking serves as a key diagnostic management tool.

- In addition to improvement relative to past performance and to competitors, projected perfor-

mance also might include changes resulting from new business ventures, entry into new markets, e-commerce initiatives, product/service innovations, or other strategic thrusts. Without this comparison information, it is possible to set goals that, even if attained, may not result in competitive advantage. More than one high-performing company has been surprised by a competitor that set and achieved more aggressive goals. Consider the following example represented by Figure 31. Imagine that you are ahead of your competition and committed to a 10 percent increase in profit over your base year. After eight years you are twice as profitable. To your surprise, you find that your competitor has increased 20 percent each year. You have achieved your goal, but your competitor has beaten you, making slightly more. After 10 years, the competitor has a significant lead. It is not good enough to achieve your goals unless your goals place you in a competitive position.

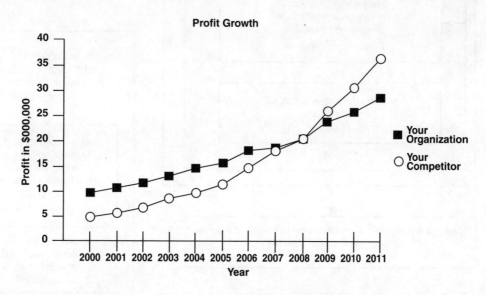

Figure 31

2.2 *Strategy Deployment*

Summary of strategy, action plans, and performance projections; how they are developed, communicated, and deployed.

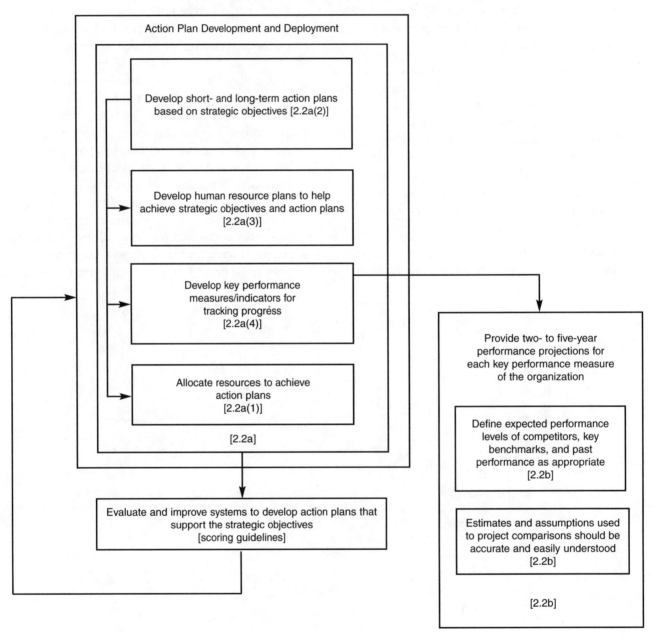

2.2 Strategy Deployment Item Linkages

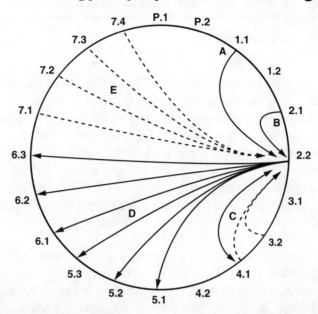

NATURE OF RELATIONSHIP	
A	The leadership team [1.1a(1)] ensures that action plans are aligned throughout the organization with strategic objectives, and that resources are allocated to ensure the actions are accomplished [2.2a(1)].
B	The planning process [2.1] develops the strategic objectives that are converted into action plans to support these objectives [2.2a(1)].
C	The action plans [2.2a(1)] and related performance measures [2.2a(4)] define part of the data that need to be collected to monitor alignment [4.1a], analyzed to support decision making [4.1b], help define requirements for data availability [4.2a] and hardware and software reliability [4.2b], customer relations management [3.2a], and customer satisfaction determination [3.2b]. Benchmarking comparison data [4.1a(3)] and analytical processes [4.1b] are used to set organizational measures and objectives [2.2].
D	Measures, objectives, action plans, and human resource plans [2.2a] are used to drive and align actions to achieve improved performance [Category 6] and develop human resources [Category 5]. It is particularly important that action plans and measures [2.2a], are aligned with and supported by employee feedback, recognition, and reward [5.1a(3)].
E	Results data [Category 7] are used to help determine performance projections for short- and longer-term planning and goal setting [2.2b]. In addition, specific accomplishments related to organizational strategy and actions must be reported in Item 7.4a(2). (To avoid clutter and make the diagrams more readable, these relationships will not be repeated on the Category 7 linkage diagrams.)

	IF YOU DON'T DO WHAT THE CRITERIA REQUIRE...
Item Reference	**Possible Adverse Consequences**
2.2a(1)	The failure to develop action plans to carry out strategic objectives and employ them at all levels of the organization usually means that work may not be aligned to achieve the strategy. Instead, there is a tendency for managers and other employees to focus their work on things they believe are important. This can result in significant resources being spent on activities that do not contribute to the objectives the organization's leaders have determined are critical for its future success. In addition, the failure to allocate resources appropriately to accomplish action plans frequently means that some plans are not accomplished because of insufficient resources, while other plans are accomplished inefficiently because of too many resources. In both cases, the value to the customer and the organization is suboptimized.
2.2a(2)	The inability to articulate and communicate key short- and longer-term action plans usually means those plans do not exist, or they are only expressed as vague generalities. Unclear plans make it more difficult to help employees at all levels of the organization understand what work they must do to help the organization achieve future success. Again, without clear direction from the top, employees will still work hard but their work may be unfocused as they follow their own ideas for appropriate action—everyone is not pulling in the same direction.
2.2a(3)	By definition, "plans" describe activities or actions that have not yet taken place. Many times, in order to achieve plans, employees must possess skills, knowledge, or abilities that they do not currently possess. Without appropriate plans to develop, acquire, or motivate the human resources necessary to carry out desired actions, the organization may not be able to achieve its strategic objectives. Its employees may not have the knowledge, skills, or abilities to carry out the actions required for success in the future.
2.2a(4)	Without appropriate measures or indicators it is difficult for leaders, managers, and employees throughout the organization to determine if they are making appropriate progress or if certain adjustments need to be made. In addition, the absence of measures makes it more difficult to communicate expectations accurately. Unclear expectations increase the likelihood that employees will not understand what they are required to do to achieve strategic objectives. Consider the adage, "what gets measured gets done." Without appropriate measures it is difficult to focus everyone on doing the right things.
2.2b	In the best-performing organizations, strategic goals are designed to enable the organization to win in highly competitive situations. If an organization desires to achieve a leadership position, it must understand where the competition is likely to be in the future before it sets its goals. Unless the organization's leaders understand the likely future performance levels of key competitors (in the same planning horizon), they may set an aggressive goal, achieve that goal, and still lose—finding themselves behind the competition.

2.2 STRATEGY DEPLOYMENT— SAMPLE EFFECTIVE PRACTICES

A. Action Plan Development and Deployment

- Plans are in place to optimize operational performance and improve customer focus using tools such as reengineering, streamlining work processes, and reducing cycle time.

- Actions have been defined in measurable terms, which align with strategic objectives and enable the organization to sustain established leadership positions for major products and services for key customers or markets.

- Strategies to achieve key organizational results (operational performance requirements) are defined.

- Planned performance and productivity levels are defined in measurable terms for key features of products and services.

- Planned actions are challenging, realistic, achievable, and understood by employees throughout the organization. Each employee understands his or her role in achieving strategic and operational goals and objectives.

- Resources are available and committed to achieve the plans (no unfunded mandates). Capital projects are funded according to business improvement plans.

- Plans are absolutely used to guide operational performance improvements. Plans drive budget and action, not the other way around.

- Incremental (short-term) strategies to achieve long-term plans are defined in measurable terms and timelines are in place to help monitor progress.

- Business plans, short- and long-term goals, and performance measures are understood and used to drive actions throughout the organization.

- Each individual in the organization, at all levels, understands how his or her work contributes to achieving organizational goals and plans.

- Plans are followed to ensure that resources are deployed and redeployed as needed to support goals.

- Human resource plans support strategic plans and goals. Plans show how the workforce will be developed to enable the organization to achieve its strategic goals.

- Key issues of training and development, hiring, retention, employee participation, involvement, empowerment, and recognition and reward are addressed as a part of the human resource plan. Appropriate measures and targets for each are defined.

- Innovative strategies may involve one or more of the following:

  - Redesign of work to increase employee responsibility

  - Improved labor-management relations (that is, prior to contract negotiations, train both sides in effective negotiation skills so that people focus on the merits of issues, not on positions. A goal, for example, is to improve relations and shorten negotiation time by 50 percent.)

  - Forming partnerships with education institutions to develop employees and ensure a supply of well-prepared future employees

  - Developing gain-sharing or equity-building compensation systems for all employees to increase motivation and productivity

  - Broadening employee responsibilities; creating self-directed or high-performance work teams

- Key performance measures (for example, employee satisfaction or work climate surveys) have been identified to gather data to manage progress. (Note: Improvement results associated with these measures should be reported in 7.3.)

- The effectiveness of human resource planning and alignment with strategic plans is evaluated systematically.

- Data are used to evaluate and improve performance and participation for all types of employees (for example, absenteeism, turnover, grievances, accidents, recognition and reward, and training participation).

- Routine, two-way communication about performance of employees occurs.

- The process to develop action plans to support strategic objectives is systematically evaluated.

B.   Performance Projection

- Projections of two- to five-year changes in performance levels are developed and used to collect data (measure) and track progress.

- Data from competitors, key benchmarks, and/or past performance form a valid basis for comparison. The organization has valid strategies and goals in place to meet or exceed the planned levels of performance for these competitors and benchmarks.

- Plans include expected future levels of competitor or comparison performance and are used to set and validate the organization's own plans and goals.

- Future plans and projections of performance consider new acquisition, optimum but secure growth, reducing costs through operational excellence processes, and anticipated research and development of innovations internally or among competitors. The accuracy of these projections is mapped and analyzed. Techniques to improve accuracy are developed and implemented.

3 Customer and Market Focus—85 Points

The Customer and Market Focus Category examines how your organization determines requirements, expectations, and preferences of customers and markets. Also examined is how your organization builds relationships with customers and determines the key factors that lead to customer acquisition, satisfaction, and retention and to business expansion.

This Category addresses how the organization seeks to understand the voices of customers and of the marketplace. The Category stresses relationships as an important part of an overall listening, learning, and performance excellence strategy. Customer satisfaction and dissatisfaction results provide vital information for understanding customers and the marketplace. In many cases, such results and trends provide the most meaningful information, not only on customers' views but also on their marketplace behaviors—repeat business and positive referrals.

Customer and Market Focus contains two Items that focus on understanding customer and market requirements, and building relationships and determining satisfaction.

Customer and Market Knowledge

- Determining market or customer segments
- Determining customer information validity
- Determining important product or service features
- Using complaint information and data from potential and former customers

Customer Relationships and Satisfaction

- Make customer contact and feedback easy and useful
- Handle complaints effectively and responsively
- Ensure complaint data are used to eliminate causes of complaints
- Build customer relationships and loyalty
- Systematically determine customer satisfaction and the satisfaction of competitor's customers

3.1 Customer and Market Knowledge (40 points)
Approach/Deployment Scoring

Describe how your organization determines requirements, expectations, and preferences of customers and markets to ensure the continuing relevance of your products/services and to develop new opportunities.

Within your response, include answers to the following questions:

a. Customer and Market Knowledge

(1) How do you determine or target customers, customer groups, and/or market segments? How do you include customers of competitors and other potential customers and/or markets in this determination?

(2) How do you listen and learn to determine key customer requirements (including product/service features) and their relative importance/value to customers' purchasing decisions for purposes of product/service planning, marketing, improvements, and other business development? In this determination, how do you use relevant information from current and former customers, including marketing/sales information, customer retention data, won/lost analysis, and complaints? If determination methods vary for different customers and/or customer groups, describe the key differences in your determination methods.

(3) How do you keep your listening and learning methods current with business needs and directions?

Notes:

N1. Customer groups (3.1a [1]) might include Web-based customers and/or customers with whom you have direct contact. Key product/service features and purchasing decisions might take into account transactional modes and factors such as confidentiality and security.

N2. If your products/services are sold to or delivered to end-use customers via other businesses such as retail stores or dealers, customer groups (3.1a[1]) should include both the end users and these intermediate businesses.

N3. "Product/service features" (3.1a [2]) refers to all the important characteristics of products/services and to their performance throughout their full lifecycle and the full "consumption chain." This includes all customers' purchase experiences and other interactions with your organization. The focus should be on features that affect customer preference and repeat business—for example, those features that differentiate your products and services from competing offerings. Those features might include price, reliability, value, delivery, customer or technical support, and the sales relationship.

N4. Listening/learning (3.1a [2]) might include gathering and integrating Web-based data and information that bear upon customers' purchasing decisions. Keeping your listening and learning methods current with business needs and directions (3.1a [3]) also might include use of current and new technology, such as Web-based data gathering.

This Item [3.1] looks at the organization's key processes for gaining knowledge about its current and future customers and markets, in order to offer relevant products and services, understand emerging customer requirements and expectations, and keep pace with changing markets and marketplaces. Processes required by Item 3.1 permit the organization to gather intelligence about its customers and competition. It is a critical starting place for determining direction and strategic planning.

This information is intended to support marketing, business development, and planning. In a rapidly changing competitive environment, many factors may affect customer preference and loyalty and the interface with customers in the marketplace, making it necessary to listen and learn on a continuous basis. To be effective, such listening and learning strategies need to have a close connection with the organization's overall business strategy. For example, if the organization customizes its products and services, the listening and learning strategy needs to be backed by a capable information system—one that rapidly accumulates information about customers and makes this information available where needed throughout the organization or elsewhere within the overall value chain.

The organization must have a process for determining or segmenting key customer groups and markets. To ensure that a complete and accurate picture of customer requirements and concerns is obtained, organizations should consider the requirements of potential customers, including competitors' customers. (Note: a potential customer is a customer the organization wants but is currently being served by a competitor.) The organization should show how these determinations include relevant information from current and former customers. In addition, the organization should tailor its listening and learning techniques to different customer groups and market segments. A relationship or listening strategy might work with some customers, but not with others.

- Information sought should be sensitive to specific product and service requirements and their relative importance or value to the different customer groups. This determination should be supported by use of information and data, such as complaints and gains and losses of customers.

- In addition to defining customer requirements, organizations must determine key requirements and drivers of purchase decisions and key product/service features. In other words, the organization must be able to prioritize key customer requirements and drivers of purchase decisions. These priorities are likely to be different for different customer groups and market segments. Knowledge of customer groups and market segments allows the organization to tailor listening and learning strategies and marketplace offerings, to support marketing strategies, and to develop new business.

- In a rapidly changing competitive environment, many factors may affect customer preference and loyalty. This makes it necessary to listen and learn on a continuous basis. To be effective as an organization, listening and learning need to be closely linked with the overall business strategy and strategy planning process.

- E-commerce is changing the competitive arena rapidly. This may significantly affect the relationships with customers and the effectiveness of listening and learning strategies. It may also force the organization to redefine customer groups and market segments.

- A variety of listening and learning strategies are commonly used by top-performing organizations. Increasingly, companies interact with customers via multiple modes. Some examples of listening and learning strategies include:

  - Close integration with key customers

  - Rapid innovation and field trials of products and services to better link research and development (R&D) and design to the market

  - Close tracking of technological, competitive, and other factors that may bear upon customer requirements, expectations, preferences, or alternatives

  - Defining the customers' value chains and how they are likely to change

  - Focus groups with leading-edge customers

– Use of critical incidents, such as complaints, to understand key service attributes from the point of view of customers and customer-contact employees

– Interviewing lost customers to determine the factors they use in their purchase decisions

– Survey/feedback information, including information collected on the Internet

– Won/lost analysis relative to competitors

Finally, the organization must have a system in place to improve its customer listening and learning strategies to keep current with changing business needs and directions. If the organization competes in a rapidly changing environment, it may need to evaluate and improve its customer listening and learning strategies more frequently. The organization should be able to demonstrate that it has made appropriate improvements to ensure its techniques for understanding customer requirements and priorities keeps pace with changing business needs.

3.1 Customer and Market Knowledge

How the organization determines longer-term requirements, expectations, and preferences of target or potential customers and markets to anticipate their needs and to develop business opportunities

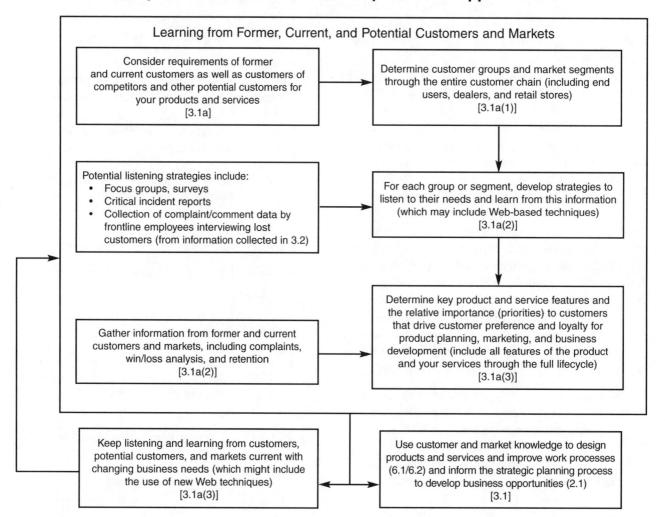

3.1 Customer and Market Knowledge Item Linkages

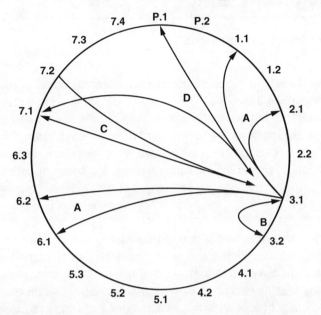

NATURE OF RELATIONSHIP	
A	Information about current and future customer and market requirements [3.1] is used for strategic planning [2.1a(a)], to design products and services [6.1a(2)], to revise work processes [6.1(3)] and business processes [6.2a(2, 3)], and to help leaders set directions for the organization [1.1a(1)].
B	Customer complaints [3.2a(3)] are used to help assess current customer expectations and refine requirements [3.1a(2)]. Information about customer requirement priorities [3.1a(2)] is used to build instruments and better target questions to assess customer satisfaction [3.2b(1)].
C	Customer satisfaction data and complaint trends [7.1a] and market growth data [7.2a(2)] are used to help validate customer expectations and refine requirements [3.1]. In addition, processes to gather intelligence about customer requirements [3.1] are used to define and produce customer satisfaction results [7.1].
D	The customer and market groups reported in P.1b(1) were determined using the processes described in 3.1a(1 & 2). The information in P.1b(1) helps examiners identify the kind of results, broken out by customer and market segment, which should be reported in Item 7.1.

IF YOU DON'T DO WHAT THE CRITERIA REQUIRE...	
Item Reference	**Possible Adverse Consequences**
3.1a(1)	The failure to classify or group customers, customer groups, or markets into meaningful segments may make it difficult to identify and differentiate key requirements that may be critical to one group but not another. For example, frequent or high-volume customers may have different expectations than infrequent or small customers. Dealers may have different requirements than end users. Unless these differences are understood it may be difficult for the organization to customize information collection techniques as well as programs, products, and services according to the needs and expectations of different groups of customers.
3.1a(2)	Different techniques may be needed to understand the requirements of different groups of customers. The failure to listen and learn about the key customer requirements for products and services, especially those features that are most important to customer purchasing decisions, may make it difficult to design and develop those products and services that are most likely to delight (or even satisfy) customers and increase market share. In addition to gathering feedback directly from current and former customers, complaint and lost customer data may provide additional insights into unmet requirements and present opportunities. If an organization does not know why it lost or gained customers, it makes it more difficult to keep customers.
3.1a(3)	The failure to systematically evaluate the processes used to listen and learn about customer requirements may make it difficult to identify specific areas needing change. For example, it does not do much good to create a survey to identify customer requirements if the questions asked on the survey are not the right questions. Incorrect information generated by this survey may cause the organization to design and deliver the wrong products or services. Furthermore, it does not do much good to use a written survey tool when face-to-face interviews may be a better way to acquire accurate and actionable information. The failure to evaluate the effectiveness of the approaches used to identify and prioritize customer requirements may make it difficult to keep up with changing customer and market needs and gather critical information necessary for strategic planning [Item 2.1a(2)] as well as the design and development of new products and services [Item 6.1a(2)].

3.1 CUSTOMER AND MARKET KNOWLEDGE—SAMPLE EFFECTIVE PRACTICES

A. Customer and Market Knowledge

- Various systematic methods are used to gather data and identify current requirements and expectations of customers (for example, surveys, focus groups, and the use of Web-based systems).

- Key product and service features are defined. Product and service features refer to all important characteristics and to the performance of products and services that customers experience or perceive throughout their use. Factors that bear on customer preference and loyalty—for example, those features that enhance or differentiate products and services from competing offerings—are defined in measurable terms.

- Customer requirements are identified or grouped by customer segments. These segments are consistently used for planning, data analysis, product and service design, production, and delivery devises, and for reporting and monitoring progress.

- Customer data such as complaints and gains or losses of customers are used to support the identification or validation of key customer requirements.

- Fact-based, systematic methods are used to identify the future requirements and expectations of customers. These are tested for accuracy and estimation techniques are improved.

- Customers of competitors are considered and processes are in place to gather expectation data from potential customers.

- Effective listening and learning strategies include:

  - Close monitoring of technological, competitive, societal, environmental, economic, and demographic factors that may bear on customer requirements, expectations, preferences, or alternatives

  - Focus groups with demanding or leading-edge customers

  - Training of frontline employees in customer listening

  - Use of critical incidents in product or service performance or quality to understand key service attributes from the point of view of customers and frontline employees

  - Interviewing lost customers

  - Won/lost analysis relative to competitors

  - Analysis of major factors affecting key customers

- Tools such as forced- or paired-choice analysis are used (where customers select between options A and B, A and C, B and C, and so forth). Using this technique, organizations quickly prioritize requirements and focus on delivering those that make the greatest impact on satisfaction, repeat business, and loyalty.

- Methods to listen and learn from customers are evaluated and improved through several cycles. Examples of factors that are evaluated include:

  - The adequacy and timeliness of customer-related information

  - Improvement of survey design

  - Approaches for getting reliable and timely information—surveys, focus groups, customer-contact personnel

  - Improved aggregation and analysis of information

- Best practices for gathering customer requirements and forecasting are gathered and used to make improvements.

3.2   Customer Relationships and Satisfaction (45 points)
Approach/Deployment Scoring

Describe how your organization builds relationships to acquire, satisfy, and retain customers and to develop new opportunities. Describe also how your organization determines customer satisfaction.

Within your response, include answers to the following questions:

a.   Customer Relationships

(1) How do you build relationships to acquire and satisfy customers and to increase repeat business and positive referrals?

(2) How do you determine key customer contact requirements and how they vary for differing modes of access? How do you ensure that these contact requirements are deployed to all people involved in the response chain? Include a summary of your key access mechanisms for customers to seek information, conduct business, and make complaints.

(3) What is your complaint management process? Include how you ensure that complaints are resolved effectively and promptly and that all complaints are aggregated and analyzed for use in improvement throughout your organization and by your partners, as appropriate.

(4) How do you keep your approaches to building relationships and providing customer access current with business needs and directions?

b.   Customer Satisfaction Determination

(1) How do you determine customer satisfaction and dissatisfaction and use this information for improvement? Include how you ensure that your measurements capture actionable information that predicts customers' future business with you and/or potential for positive referral. Describe significant differences in determination methods for different customer groups.

(2) How do you follow-up with customers on products/services and transactions to receive prompt and actionable feedback?

(3) How do you obtain and use information on your customers' satisfaction relative to customers' satisfaction with competitors and/or benchmarks, as appropriate?

(4) How do you keep your approaches to determining satisfaction current with business needs and directions?

Notes:

N1. Customer relationships (3.2a) might include the development of partnerships or alliances with customers.

N2. Determining customer satisfaction and dissatisfaction (3.2b) might include use of any or all of the following: surveys, formal and informal feedback, use of customer account histories, complaints, and transaction completion rates. Information might be gathered on the Internet, through personal contact or a third party, or by mail.

N3. Customer satisfaction measurements might include both a numerical rating scale and descriptors for each unit in the scale. Actionable customer satisfaction measurements provide useful information about specific product/service features, delivery, relationships, and transactions that bear upon the customers' future actions—repeat business and/or positive referral.

N4. Your customer satisfaction and dissatisfaction results should be reported in Item 7.1.

The Item on page 122 [3.2] describes processes that examine the impact of products and services on customer relationships and satisfaction. In particular, this Item looks at the organization's processes for building customer relationships and determining customer satisfaction, with the aim of acquiring new customers, retaining existing customers, and developing new opportunities. Relationships provide an important means for organizations to understand and manage customer expectations and to develop new business. Also, customer-contact employees may provide vital information to build partnerships and other longer-term relationships with customers.

Overall, Item 3.2 emphasizes the importance of obtaining actionable information, such as feedback and complaints from customers. To be actionable, the information gathered should meet two conditions:

- Customer responses should be tied directly to key product, service, and business processes, so that opportunities for improvement are clear

- Customer responses should be translated into cost/revenue implications to support the setting of improvement and change priorities

The first part of this Item [3.2a(1)] looks at the organization's processes for providing easy access for customers and potential customers to seek information or assistance and/or to comment and complain.

- This access makes it easy to get timely information from customers about issues that are of real concern to them. Timely information, in turn, is transmitted to the appropriate place in the organization to drive improvements or new levels of product and service.

- Information from customers should be actionable. To be actionable, organizations should be able to tie the information to key business processes, and be able to determine cost/revenue implications for improvement priority setting.

Organizations must also determine key customer-contact requirements, how these vary for different modes of access, and make sure all employees who are involved in responding to customers understand these requirements. As part of this response, the organization is asked to describe key access mechanisms for customers to seek information, conduct business, and make complaints. Also important is how customer-contact requirements are deployed along the entire response chain.

- Customer-contact requirements essentially refer to customer expectations for service after contact with the organization has been made. Typically, the organization translates customer-contact requirements into customer service standards. Customer-contact requirements should be set in measurable terms to permit effective monitoring and performance review.

- A good example of a measurable customer-contact requirement might be the customer expectation that a malfunctioning computer would be back online within 24 hours of the request for service. Another example might be the customer requirement that a knowledgeable and polite human being is available within 10 minutes to resolve a problem with software. In both cases, a clear requirement and a measurable standard were identified.

- A bad example of a customer service standard might be "we get back to the customer as soon as we can." With this example, no standard of performance is defined. Some customer-contact representatives might get back to a customer within a matter of minutes. Others might take hours or days. The failure to define precisely the contact requirement makes it difficult to allocate appropriate resources to meet that requirement consistently.

- These customer service standards must be deployed to all employees who are in contact with customers. Such deployment needs to take account of all key points in the response chain— all units or individuals in the organization that make effective interactions possible. These standards then become one source of information to evaluate the organization's performance in meeting customer-contact requirements.

Organizations should capture, aggregate, analyze, and learn from the complaint information and comments they receive. A prompt and effective response and solutions to customer needs and desires are a source of satisfaction and loyalty.

- Effective complaint management requires the prompt and courteous resolution of complaints. This leads to recovery of customer confidence. Customer loyalty and confidence is enhanced when problems are resolved by the first person the customer contacts. In fact, prompt resolution of problems helps to ensure higher levels of loyalty than if the customer never had a problem in first place. Even if the organization ultimately resolves a problem, the likelihood of maintaining a loyal customer is reduced by 10 percent when that customer is referred to another place or person in the organization.[1]

- The organization must also have a mechanism for learning from complaints and ensuring that design/production/delivery process employees receive information needed to eliminate the causes of complaints. Effective elimination of the causes of complaints involves aggregation of complaint information from all sources for evaluation and use in overall organizational improvement—both design and delivery stages (see Items 6.1, 6.2, and 6.3).

- Complaint aggregation, analysis, and root cause determination should lead to effective elimination of the causes of complaints and to priority setting for process, product, and service improvements. Successful outcomes require effective deployment of information throughout the organization.

For long-term success, organizations should build strong relationships with customers since business development and product/service innovation increasingly depend on maintaining close relationships with customers.

- Organizations should keep approaches to all aspects of customer relationships current with changing business needs and directions, since approaches to and bases for relationships may change quickly.

[1]From the article, "Basic Facts on Customer Complaint Behavior and the Impact of Service on the Bottom Line," by John Goodman. First published in *Competitive Advantage* (June 1999): pp. 1–5. The article can be read at http://www.e-satisfy.com/pdf/basicfacts.pdf.

- Organizations should also develop an effective process to determine the levels of satisfaction and dissatisfaction for the different customer groups, including capturing actionable information that reflects customers' future business and/or positive referral intentions. Satisfied customers are a requirement for loyalty, repeat business, and positive referrals.

The second part of this Item [3.2b] looks at how the organization determines customer satisfaction and dissatisfaction.

- The organization must gather information on customer satisfaction and dissatisfaction, including any important differences in approaches for different customer groups or market segments. This highlights the importance of the measurement scale in determining those factors that best reflect customers' market behaviors—repurchase, new business, and positive referral. The organization must keep its approaches to determining customer satisfaction current with changing business needs and directions. Changing business needs and directions might include new modes of customer access, such as the Internet. In such cases, key contact requirements might include online security for customers and access to personal assistance.

- The organization should systematically follow-up with customers regarding products, services, and recent transactions to receive feedback that is prompt and actionable. Prompt feedback enables problems to be identified quickly to help prevent them from recurring.

- The organization should determine the satisfaction levels of the customers of competitors in order to identify threats and opportunities to improve future performance. Such information might be derived from the organization's own comparative studies or from independent studies. The factors that lead to customer preference are of critical importance in understanding factors that drive markets and potentially affect longer-term competitiveness and are particularly helpful during strategic planning.

The customer satisfaction data gathered from the complaint management process in Item 3.2a ensure timely resolution of problems and can help recover or build customer loyalty. Data from the complaint processes in Item 3.2a are collected at the customer's convenience. However, data collected by survey or similar means, as required by Item 3.2b, produce information at the convenience of the organization. Customers complain when they have a problem. They do not tend to hold their complaint until the organization finds it convenient to ask them.

Although the complaint-type customer feedback (from Item 3.2a) is timely, it is often difficult to develop reliable trend data. The processes in Item 3.2b make it easier to track satisfaction over time. Both techniques are required to fully understand the dynamics that build loyalty, retention, and positive referral. To be effective, both techniques should be used to drive improvement actions.

3.2 Customer Relationships and Satisfaction

How customer satisfaction is determined, relationships strengthened, and current products and services enhanced to support customer- and market-related planning

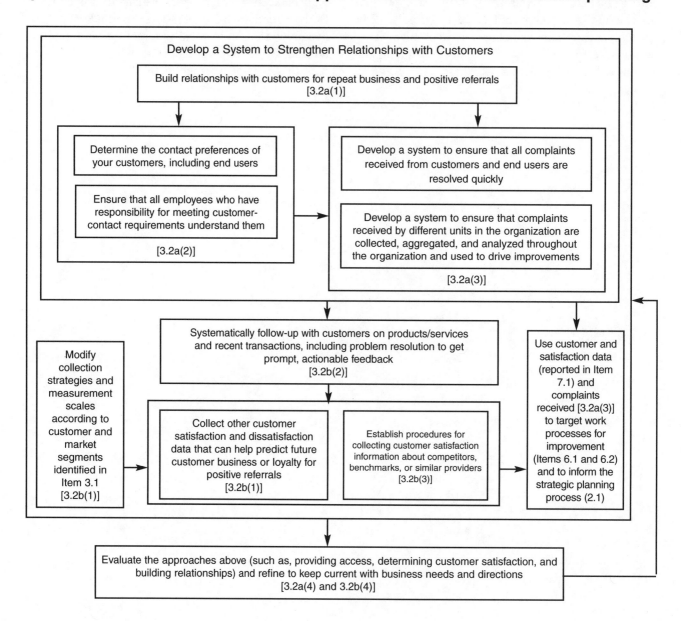

3.2 Customer Relationships and Satisfaction Item Linkages

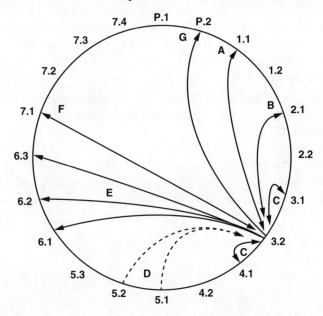

NATURE OF RELATIONSHIP	
A	Priorities and customer-contact requirements (service standards) for customer service personnel [3.2a(1)] are driven by top leadership [1.1a(1)]. Leaders [1.1a(1)] personally interact with and build better relationships with customers [3.2a(1)]. They receive useful information from those customers to improve management of decision making.
B	Information about customer satisfaction [3.2b(1)] and complaints [3.2a(3)] collected by customer-contact employees is used in the planning process [2.1a(2)]. In addition, strategic objectives [2.1b(1)] influence customer relationship management [3.2a] and customer satisfaction determination processes [3.2b] by identifying key focus areas.
C	Information concerning customer requirements and expectations [3.1a] and benchmark data [4.1a(3)] are used to help identify, set, and deploy customer contact requirements (service standards) [3.2a(2)]. Customer complaint data [3.2a] are used to help assess customer requirements and expectations [3.1]. Customer relationships data [3.2a(3)] and satisfaction data [3.2b(1)] are analyzed [4.1b] and used to set priorities for action.
D	Training [5.2] and improved flexibility and self-direction [5.1a(1)] should enhance the ability of customer-contact employees [3.2a(2)] to understand requirements and develop the skills to resolve complaints and satisfy customers [3.2a(3)].
E	Information collected through customer relations employees [3.2a(2)] is used to enhance design of products and services and to improve operational, business, and support processes [6.1, 6.2, and 6.3].

Continued

NATURE OF RELATIONSHIP	*continued*
F	Information from customer relations processes [3.2a(3)] can help in the design of customer satisfaction measures [3.2b(1)] and produce data on customer satisfaction [7.1]. In addition, customer satisfaction results data [7.1a(1)] are used to set customer contact requirements (service standards) [3.2a]. Efforts of improved accessibility and responsiveness in complaint management [3.2a] should result in improved complaint response time, effective complaint resolution, and a higher percentage of complaints resolved on first contact. These results should be reported in 7.1.
G	Information about the satisfaction of competitors' customers, which is needed to create the description for P.2a, use processes discussed in Items 3.1a(1) and 3.2b(3).

	IF YOU DON'T DO WHAT THE CRITERIA REQUIRE...
Item Reference	**Possible Adverse Consequences**
3.2a(1)	The failure to build lasting relationships and loyalty with customers makes it easier for customers to "jump ship" when problems arise. Loyal customers are twice as likely to use your products and services than those who are simply satisfied. The TARP Studies have found that the cost to win a new customer versus retain a current customer varies from 2:1 to 20:1.* Without a disciplined approach for building relationships and cultivating loyalty, the benefits of loyal customers become a hit-or-miss opportunity for the organization. For example, in many manufacturing companies today, service is a key differentiator. Products that were once considered specialty items, such as personal computers, are now commodities. Therefore, service can become the factor that differentiates companies and cultivates loyal customers. Furthermore, since it is more costly to acquire a new customer than keep an existing customer, organizations can avoid unnecessary expenses by building relationships and strengthening the loyalty of current customers. Loyal customers are far more likely to provide positive referrals than a dissatisfied or even minimally satisfied customer. *From the article, "Basic Facts on Customer Complaint Behavior and the Impact of Service on the Bottom Line," by John Goodman. First published in *Competitive Advantage* (June 1999) 1–5. The article can be read at http://www.e-satisfy.com/pdf/basicfacts.pdf.
3.2a(2)	Customer contact requirements (sometimes called customer service standards) help define the customers' expectations for service after initiating a contact, question, or complaint. For example, a large direct order computer company surveyed its customers and determined that they expected to have a technician helping them solve their problem within *ten* minutes of making the initial contact. By knowing the customer contact requirements and the hour-to-hour call volume, the organization was able to put enough technicians in place to ensure the average response time was *nine* minutes or less. The failure to understand and meet customer contact requirements and make it easy for customers to contact the organization makes it more difficult to build loyalty and learn quickly about customer problems.
3.2a(3)	Once the organization learns about a customer problem, the speed and efficiency with which it resolves that problem contributes a great deal to customer loyalty and willingness to make positive referrals. The failure to resolve a problem to the customer's satisfaction at the first point of contact almost cuts in half the likelihood of maintaining a loyal customer. In addition, the failure to collect, aggregate, analyze, and use complaint data to drive improvements throughout the organization (and as appropriate to key suppliers or partners), increases the likelihood that the problem will recur again and again. Failing to prevent the problem from recurring directly adds cost but no value to the products or services delivered to customers. Rework associated with repeating problems is a pure waste of resources and can be a significant source of customer dissatisfaction.
3.2a(4)	The failure to systematically evaluate the processes used to build relationships, resolve complaints, and prevent them from recurring may make it difficult to identify specific areas needing change. Making it easy for customers to complain but not resolving those complaints

Continued

	effectively and promptly may create even higher levels of dissatisfaction. Ignorance about the effectiveness of customer access and complaint resolution processes may blind the organization to a problem of its own creation, especially in a highly competitive arena where customer and market requirements can change quickly. Without an ongoing system to evaluate and improve processes to build relationships and satisfy customers, current processes may not be able to keep up with changing business or market demands.
3.2b(1)	The failure to accurately determine customer satisfaction and dissatisfaction may make it difficult for the organization to make timely adjustments in the products and services it offers. Furthermore, if the data collection processes do not help the organization understand what drives customer behavior, the organization may not know until it is too late (the customer goes elsewhere) that they have a serious problem. The failure to predict customer behavior and the likelihood for positive referral also makes it difficult to forecast product demand which may create supply chain difficulties—excessive inventories or excessive delays in restocking. In addition, the failure to take into account differences in customer or market segments and adjust the techniques for collecting customer satisfaction and dissatisfaction data appropriately may cause the organization to collect inaccurate or unreliable information, which threatens the accuracy of the organization's decision making and planning.
3.2b(2)	The longer an organization waits to gather customer satisfaction data, the more time it takes to identify and correct a problem. Organizations that fail to follow up with customers whenever a transaction occurs and learn about problems promptly, increase the likelihood that other customers will experience the same problem because it will not have been identified or corrected. Similarly, organizations that fail to follow up with customers may be unaware of elements that drive satisfaction and loyalty that could be spread to other parts of the organization or to other products and services.
3.2b(3)	By failing to obtain information on the satisfaction of the competitors' customers, the organization may not learn what it must do differently to satisfy and acquire (win over) the customers of its competitors.
3.2b(4)	Organizations that do not evaluate the effectiveness of their techniques to determine customer satisfaction and dissatisfaction run the risk of making bad decisions based on misleading or even useless information. It does not do much good to gather customer satisfaction data unless the organization asks the right questions. Failing to ask the right questions rarely produces accurate, actionable information to support effective decision making. Moreover, the failure to evaluate the effectiveness of the approaches used to assess customer satisfaction may make it difficult to keep up with changing customer and market needs and gather critical information necessary for strategic planning as well as the development of new or improved products and services.

3.2 CUSTOMER RELATIONSHIPS AND SATISFACTION—SAMPLE EFFECTIVE PRACTICES

A. Customer Relationships

- Several methods are used to ensure ease of customer contact, 24 hours a day if necessary (for example, toll-free numbers, pagers for contact personnel, Web sites, e-mail, surveys, interviews, focus groups, electronic bulletin boards).

- Customer-contact employees are empowered to make decisions to address customer concerns.

- Adequate staff are available to maintain effective customer contact.

- Measurable performance expectations are set for employees whose job brings them in regular contact with customers. The performance of employees against these expectations is tracked.

- A system exists to ensure that customer complaints are resolved promptly and effectively by the first point of contact. This often means training customer-contact employees and giving them authority for resolving a broad range of problems.

- Complaint data are tracked, analyzed, and used to initiate prompt corrective action to prevent the problem from recurring.

- Training and development plans and replacement procedures exist for customer-contact employees. These processes have been measured and refined.

- Measurable customer-contact requirements (service standards) have been derived from customer expectations (for example, timeliness, courtesy, efficiency, thoroughness, and completeness).

- Requirements for building relationships are identified and may include factors such as product knowledge, employee responsiveness, and various customer contact methods.

- A systematic approach is in place to evaluate and improve service levels, customer-focused decision making, and customer relationships.

B. Customer Satisfaction Determination

- Several customer satisfaction indicators are used (for example, repeat business measures, praise letters, and direct measures using survey questions and interviews).

- Comprehensive satisfaction and dissatisfaction data are collected and segmented or grouped to enable the organization to predict customer behavior (likelihood of remaining a customer).

- Customer satisfaction and dissatisfaction measurements include both a numerical rating scale and descriptors assigned to each unit in the scale. An effective (actionable) customer satisfaction and dissatisfaction measurement system provides the organization with reliable information about customer ratings of specific product and service features and the relationship between these ratings and the customer's likely market behavior.

- Customer dissatisfaction indicators include complaints, claims, refunds, recalls, returns, repeat services, litigation, replacements, performance rating downgrades, repairs, warranty work, warranty costs, misshipments, and incomplete orders.

- Satisfaction data are collected from former customers.

- Competitors' customer satisfaction is determined using external or internal studies. This information is used to refine services and product features.

- Procedures are in place and evaluated to ensure that customer contact is initiated to follow-up on recent transactions to build relationships. Data from these contacts are used.

- Organization-based or independent organization comparative studies take into account one or more indicators of customer dissatisfaction as well as satisfaction. The extent and types of such studies depend on industry and organization size.

- The process of collecting complete, timely, and accurate customer satisfaction and dissatisfaction data is regularly evaluated and improved. Customer preferences, by customer segment, are considered when designing procedures to determine satisfaction levels. Some prefer surveys, others focus groups, and others prefer face-to-face interactions. Several improvement cycles are evident.

4 Information and Analysis—90 Points

> The Information and Analysis Category examines your organization's information management and performance measurement systems and how your organization analyzes performance data and information.

Information and Analysis is the main point within the criteria for all key information to effectively measure performance and manage the organization, and to drive improvement of performance and competitiveness.

This category is like the "motherboard" on a personal computer. All information flows into and out of it. In the simplest terms, Category 4 is the "brain center" for the alignment of the organization's operations and its strategic objectives. Moreover, since information and analysis might themselves be a source of competitive advantage and productivity growth, the category also may have strategic value and its capabilities should be considered as part of the strategic planning process.

Information and Analysis evaluates the selection, management, and effectiveness of use of information and data to support processes, action plans, and the performance management system. Systems to analyze, review, capture, store, retrieve, and distribute data to support decision making are also evaluated.

Measurement and Analysis of Organizational Performance

- This Item looks at the mechanical processes associated with data collection, information, and measures (including comparative data) for planning, decision making, improving performance, and supporting action plans and operations.

- The Item also looks at the analytical processes used to make sense out of the data. It also looks at how these analyses are deployed throughout the organization and used to support organization-level review, decision making, and planning.

Information Management

- This Item looks at how the organization ensures that needed data and information are accessible to employees, suppliers and partners, and customers as needed and appropriate to support decision making. The data system must provide for and ensure data integrity, reliability, accuracy, timeliness, security, and confidentiality.

- This Item also seeks to ensure that hardware and software are reliable and user-friendly throughout the organization. In many organizations, people with minimal computer skills must be able to access and use data to support decision making.

4.1 Measurement and Analysis of Organizational Performance (50 points)
Approach/Deployment Scoring

Describe how your organization provides effective performance management systems for measuring, analyzing, aligning, and improving performance at all levels and in all parts of your organization.

Within your response, include answers to the following questions:

a. Performance Measurement

(1) How do you gather and integrate data and information from all sources to support daily operations and organizational decision making?

(2) How do you select and align measures/indicators for tracking daily operations and overall organizational performance?

(3) How do you select and ensure the effective use of key comparative data and information?

(4) How do you keep your performance measurement system current with business needs and directions?

b. Performance Analysis

(1) What analyses do you perform to support your senior leaders' organizational performance review and your organization's strategic planning?

(2) How do you communicate the results of organizational-level analysis to work group and/or functional-level operations to enable effective support for decision making?

(3) How do you align the results of organizational-level analysis with your key business results, strategic objectives, and action plans? How do these results provide the basis for projections of continuous and breakthrough improvements in performance?

Notes:

N1. Performance measurement is used in fact-based decision making for setting and aligning organizational directions and resource use at the work unit, key process, departmental, and whole organization levels.

N2. Comparative data and information sources (4.1a [3]) include benchmarking and competitive comparisons. "Benchmarking" refers to identifying processes and results that represent best practices and performance for similar activities, inside or outside your organization's industry. Competitive comparisons relate your organization's performance to that of competitors in your markets.

N3. Analysis includes examining trends; organizational, industry, and technology projections; and comparisons, cause-effect relationships, and correlations intended to support your performance reviews, help determine root causes, and help set priorities for resource use. Accordingly, analysis draws upon all types of data: customer-related, financial and market, operational, and competitive.

N4. The results of organizational performance analysis should contribute to your senior leaders' organizational performance review in 1.1b and organizational strategic planning in Category 2.

N5. Your organizational performance results should be reported in Items 7.1, 7.2, 7.3, and 7.4.

The Item on page 134 [4.1] looks at to the mechanical aspects of the selection, management, and use of data and information for performance measurement and analysis in support of organizational planning and performance improvement. The processes and systems required by this item:

- Provide a key foundation for consistently good decision making.

- Serve as a central collection and analysis point in the management system to guide the organization's process management toward the achievement of key business results and strategic objectives.

The first part of this Item [4.1a] requires the organization to select and use measures to better track daily operations and enhance decision-making accuracy. It should select and integrate measures for monitoring overall organizational performance.

- Data alignment and integration are key concepts for successful implementation of the performance measurement system. They are viewed in terms of extent and effectiveness of use to meet performance assessment needs. Alignment and integration include how measures are aligned throughout the organization, how they are integrated to yield organizationwide measures, and how performance measurement requirements are deployed by senior leaders to track work group and process level performance on key measures targeted for organizationwide significance and/or improvement.

- Comparative data should be selected and used to help drive performance improvement. These requirements address the major components of an effective performance measurement system.

- Performance data and information are especially important in business networks, alliances, and supply chains. Once determining the data and information requirements, the organization should determine data and information requirements of the strategic planning and goal-setting process.

The organization should show how competitive comparisons and benchmarking data are selected and used to help drive performance improvement.

- The use of competitive and comparative information is important to all organizations. The major premises for using competitive and comparative information are: (1) the organization needs to know where it stands relative to competitors and best practices; (2) comparative and benchmarking information often provides the impetus for significant ("breakthrough") improvement or change; and (3) preparation for comparing performance information frequently leads to a better understanding of the processes and their performance. Benchmarking information also may support business analysis and decisions relating to core competencies, alliances, and outsourcing.

- Effective selection and use of competitive comparisons and benchmarking information require: (1) determination of needs and priorities; (2) criteria for seeking appropriate sources for comparisons—from within and outside the organization's industry and markets; and (3) use of data and information to set stretch targets and to promote major, nonincremental improvements in areas most critical to the organization's competitive strategy.

The last part of Item 4.1a examines how the organization's performance measurement system kept current with changing business needs. This involves ongoing evaluation and demonstrated refinement.

The second part of this Item [4.1b] examines how the organization analyzes data to support decision making. Isolated facts and data do not usually provide an effective basis for setting organizational priorities and effective decision making. Accordingly, close alignment is needed between analysis and organizational performance review and between analysis and organizational planning. This ensures that analysis is relevant to decision making and that decision making is based on relevant data and information.

Effective decision making usually requires leaders to understand cause-effect connections among and between processes and business/performance results. Process actions and their results may have many resource implications. High-performing organizations find it necessary to have support systems that provide an effective analytical basis for decisions because resources for improvement are limited and cause-effect connections are often unclear. In addition, organizations must have the ability to perform effective analyses to support senior leaders' assessment of overall organizational performance and strategic planning. Moreover, the results of organizational-level analysis must be effectively communicated by leaders to support decision making throughout the organization and ensure those decisions are aligned with business results, strategic objectives, and action plans. Accordingly, systematic processes must be in place for analyzing all types of data and to determine overall organizational health, including key business results, action plans, and strategic objectives. In addition, organizations must evaluate the effectiveness of its analytical processes and make improvements based on the evaluation.

Facts, rather than intuition, are used to support most decision making at all levels based on the analyses conducted to make sense out of the data collected. Analyses that organizations typically conduct to gain an understanding of performance and needed actions vary widely depending on the type of organization, size, competitive environment, and other factors. These analyses help the organization's leaders understand the following:

- How product and service improvement correlates with key customer indicators such as customer satisfaction, customer retention, and market share.

- Cost/revenue implications of customer-related problems and effective problem resolution.

- Interpretation of market share changes in terms of customer gains and losses and changes in customer satisfaction.

- The impact of improvements in key operational performance areas such as productivity, cycle time, waste reduction, new product introduction, and defect levels.

- Relationships between employee/organizational learning and value added per employee.

- Financial benefits derived from improvements in employee safety, absenteeism, and turnover.

- Benefits and costs associated with education and training, including Internet-based, or e-learning, opportunities.

- Benefits and costs associated with improved organizational knowledge management and sharing.

- How the ability to identify and meet employee requirements correlates with employee retention, motivation, and productivity.

- Cost/revenue implications of employee-related problems and effective problem resolution.

- Individual or aggregate measures of productivity and quality relative to competitors.

- Cost trends relative to competitors.

- Relationships among product/service quality, operational performance indicators, and overall financial performance trends as reflected in indicators such as operating costs, revenues, asset utilization, and value added per employee.

- Allocation of resources among alternative improvement projects based on cost/benefit implications or environmental/community impact.

- Net earnings derived from quality, operational, and human resource performance improvements.

- Comparisons among business units showing how quality and operational performance improvement affect financial performance.

- Contributions of improvement activities to cash flow, working capital use, and shareholder value.

- Profit impacts of customer retention.

- Cost/revenue implications of new market entry, including global market entry or expansion.

- Cost/revenue, customer, and productivity implications of engaging in and/or expanding e-commerce/e-business and use of the Internet and intranets.

- Market share versus profits.

- Trends in economic, market, and shareholder indicators of value.

The availability of electronic data and information of many kinds (for example, financial, operational, customer-related, accreditation/regulatory) and from many sources (for example, internal, third-party, and public sources; the Internet; Internet tracking software) permits extensive analysis and correlations. Effectively utilizing and prioritizing this wealth of information are important to the success of top-performing organizations.

4.1 *Measurement and Analysis of Organizational Performance*

How the organization selects, manages, analyzes, and uses information and data to support decision making for key processes and to improve performance at all levels and parts of the organization

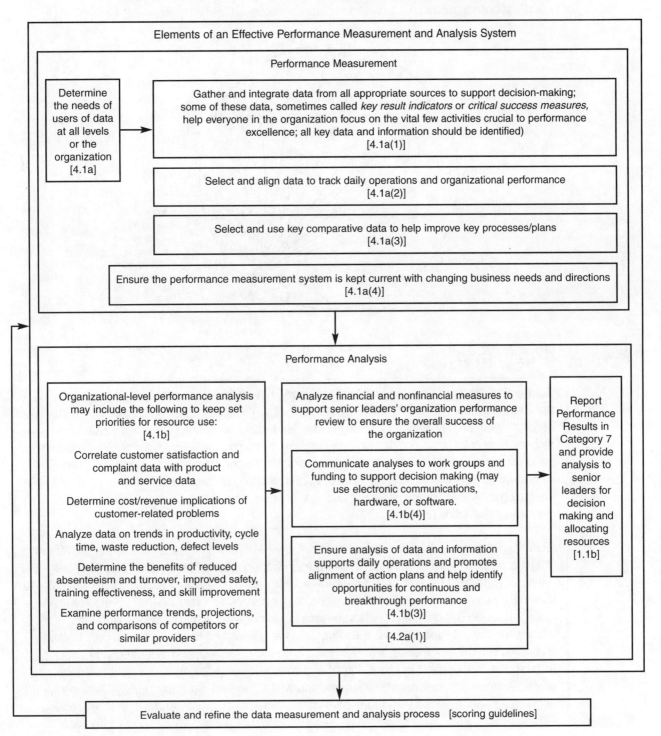

Elements of an Effective Performance Measurement and Analysis System

Performance Measurement

Determine the needs of users of data at all levels or the organization [4.1a]

Gather and integrate data from all appropriate sources to support decision-making; some of these data, sometimes called *key result indicators* or *critical success measures,* help everyone in the organization focus on the vital few activities crucial to performance excellence; all key data and information should be identified) [4.1a(1)]

Select and align data to track daily operations and organizational performance [4.1a(2)]

Select and use key comparative data to help improve key processes/plans [4.1a(3)]

Ensure the performance measurement system is kept current with changing business needs and directions [4.1a(4)]

Performance Analysis

Organizational-level performance analysis may include the following to keep set priorities for resource use: [4.1b]

Correlate customer satisfaction and complaint data with product and service data

Determine cost/revenue implications of customer-related problems

Analyze data on trends in productivity, cycle time, waste reduction, defect levels

Determine the benefits of reduced absenteeism and turnover, improved safety, training effectiveness, and skill improvement

Examine performance trends, projections, and comparisons of competitors or similar providers

Analyze financial and nonfinancial measures to support senior leaders' organization performance review to ensure the overall success of the organization

Communicate analyses to work groups and funding to support decision making (may use electronic communications, hardware, or software. [4.1b(4)]

Ensure analysis of data and information supports daily operations and promotes alignment of action plans and help identify opportunities for continuous and breakthrough performance [4.1b(3)]

[4.2a(1)]

Report Performance Results in Category 7 and provide analysis to senior leaders for decision making and allocating resources [1.1b]

Evaluate and refine the data measurement and analysis process [scoring guidelines]

4.1 *Measurement and Analysis of Organizational Performance Item Linkages*

Information and Analysis [Category 4] is the "brain center" of the integrated management system and the conduit for data to support better decision making at all levels. Therefore, Item 4.1 links with all other items. The following summarizes the key relationships:

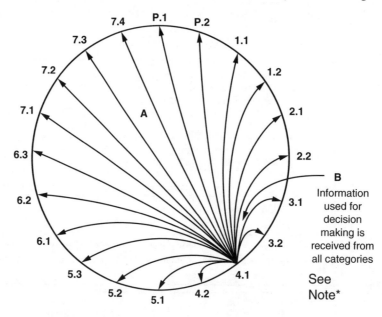

NATURE OF RELATIONSHIP	
A	Data and information are collected and analyzed [4.1] and made available [4.2] for developing the Organizational Profile [P.1 and P.2], planning [2.1a(2)], setting strategic objectives [2.1b(1)], benchmarking priority setting [4.1], day-to-day leadership decisions [1.1], setting public responsibility standards (regulatory, legal, ethical) for community involvement [1.2], reporting performance results [7.1, 7.2, 7.3, and 7.4], improving work processes [6.1, 6.2, 6.3] and human resource systems [5.1, 5.2, and 5.3], determining customer requirements [3.1], managing customer complaints and building customer relations [3.2a], and determining customer satisfaction [3.2b].
B	Data and information used to support analysis, decision making, and continuous improvement [4.1] are received from all processes. Information from customer satisfaction data [7.1] are analyzed [4.1b] and used to help determine ways to assess customer requirements [3.1a(2)], to determine standards or required levels of customer service and relationship development [3.2a(2)], and to design instruments to assess customer satisfaction [3.2b(1)]. Data and information are received from the following areas and analyzed to support decisions: human resources capabilities, including work system efficiency, initiative, and self-direction [5.1a(1)]; training and development needs [5.2a(2)] and effectiveness [5.2a(4)]; and safety, retention, absenteeism, organizational effectiveness, and well-being and satisfaction [5.3]. Data are aggregated and analyzed [4.1] to improve work processes [6.1, 6.2, and 6.3] that will reduce

Continued

NATURE OF RELATIONSHIP	*continued*
	cycle time, waste, and defect levels. Performance data from all parts of the organization are integrated and analyzed [4.1] to assess performance in key areas such as customer-related performance [7.1], operational performance [7.4], financial and market performance [7.2], and human resource performance [7.3], relative to competitive performance in all areas.

*Note: Because the information collected and used for decision-making links with all other Items, all
of the linkage arrows will not be repeated on the other Item maps. Only the most relevant will be repeated.

IF YOU DON'T DO WHAT THE CRITERIA REQUIRE...	
Item Reference	**Possible Adverse Consequences**
4.1a(1)	The failure to systematically gather appropriate data and information from throughout the organization to support the daily operational and organizational decision making can create an environment where decisions are typically based on intuition, gut feel, or guesswork. Furthermore, information gathered in this way may ignore some of the linkages critical to sustaining high performance in an organization. Decisions based on intuition or guesswork tend to be highly variable, which introduces error. Furthermore, in an environment where decisions are based on intuition it is usually the boss' intuition that drives the decision—which can lead to the disengagement of the people in the organization. Decisions made in this manner erode the organization's efforts to promote employee empowerment and innovation [Item 1.1a(2)]. Finally, the failure to integrate data and information may make it difficult to monitor overall organizational performance. Disjointed, nonintegrated data are difficult to consolidate and report in a manageable, easy to understand "dashboard" to support effective decision making.
4.1a(2)	Data and information provide a basis for decision making at all levels of the organization: top leaders use the data to make decisions about the direction of the organization, and employees use data to make decisions about operational matters. Unless measures are selected and aligned to provide the right information, at the right time, in the right format, the decisions of the leaders and the employees are likely to be suboptimized. Moreover, although, the failure to gather appropriate data tends to reduce decision-making quality, spending resources to gather data and information that do not support decision making throughout the organization (useless data) typically adds unnecessary cost. It is difficult to collect the right data and information if the organization has failed to determine what data are needed to support decision making at all levels. In addition, the failure to collect appropriate information makes it more difficult to monitor performance against goals [Item 1.1b(1)], effectively communicate expectations throughout the organization [Item 1.1a(1)], and deploy actions needed to carry out strategy [Item 2.2a].
4.1a(3)	The failure to collect and effectively use the right comparative data makes it difficult for the organization to learn and take appropriate action. Learning from the best helps provoke an understanding of what systems and processes may be required to make quantum leaps in performance as well as the levels that must be reached to achieve a leadership position [Item 2.2b]. For example, comparisons showing that the organization's projected performance outpaces the industrial *average* will have little meaning if the *best* competitor's rate of improvement is greater. Furthermore, if an organization collects comparative data from world-class benchmarks, but does not effectively use comparative data for planning [Item 2.1a(2)], to identify areas needing breakthrough performance, or set improvement priorities [Item 1.1b(2)] then it is simply wasting resources. If an organization does not collect comparative performance outcome data it is not able to determine if its own rate of progress is sufficient to keep it ahead of the competition or evaluate the strength of its own performance results [required by Category 7].

Continued

IF YOU DON'T DO WHAT THE CRITERIA REQUIRE... *(continued)*	
4.1a(4)	Organizations that fail to improve the speed and accuracy of decision making typically do not perform well in a competitive environment. Without a process to evaluate the information system and how well it responds to the needs of the business, organizations may not know they are collecting insufficient or incorrect data and information. In addition, organizations may not know if the data effectively support daily operations and organizational decision making. They may not know if the resources spent to collect benchmarking and comparison data are producing appropriate benefits.
4.1b(1)	The lack of a system to analyze and make sense out of raw data may make it difficult for senior leaders to understand cause-and-effect relationships, root causes of problems, and the impact of various processes on performance outcomes. This may make it more difficult for leaders to identify specific areas within the organization where improvement is required. It also makes it more difficult for leaders to effectively set priorities. Consider the following examples: (a) without a cost-benefit analysis it is more difficult to determine whether project A or project B should receive support, because it is difficult to know which project is likely to be of greater benefit to the organization; (b) calculating C_{pk} (the capability of a process) helps leaders understand the extent to which their key processes are in control or need adjustment (the raw run data cannot support this kind of decision making); and (c) failing to understand root causes makes it more difficult to prevent problems from recurring, which adds cost but not value.
4.1b(2)	Employees and managers at all levels of the organization need useful information to support decision making. The failure to ensure that people at every level understand the impact that their work has on overall organizational performance makes it more difficult for them to identify and understand why they need to perform at certain agreed levels and why change may need to occur. Without this information, employees and managers throughout the organization must rely on intuition or incomplete data to support decision making—typically reducing the accuracy of those decisions and, in some cases, suboptimizing the overall performance of the organization.
4.1b(3)	Strategy identifies the things an organization must do to be successful in the future. Many actions must be taken in an organization to ensure strategic objectives are achieved. Data analysis helps leaders understand critical relationships between actions and outcomes to effectively allocate resources and achieve desired results. The failure to examine and understand the relationship between performance outcomes, action plans, and strategic objectives may cause senior leaders to make inappropriate decisions about the allocation of limited resources. This means that the organization may not realize the maximum benefit from the expenditure of those resources. For example, failing to understand the correlation between product and service quality improvement and improved customer satisfaction and retention may cause the leader to divert resources to less important activities.

4.1 MEASUREMENT AND ANALYSIS OF ORGANIZATIONAL PERFORMANCE—SAMPLE EFFECTIVE PRACTICES

A. Performance Measurement

- Above all, data and information are favored as a decision-making support tool, rather than a quick and easy reliance on intuition or "gut feel."

- Data collected at the individual worker level are consistent across the organization to permit consolidation and organizationwide performance monitoring.

- Quality and operational data are collected and routinely used for management decisions.

- Internal and external data are used to describe customer satisfaction and product and service performance.

- The cost of quality (including rework, delay, waste, scrap, errors) and other financial concerns are measured for internal operations and processes.

- Data are maintained on employee-related issues of satisfaction, morale, safety, education and training, use of teams, and recognition and reward.

- Supplier performance data are maintained.

- Employees, customers, and suppliers are involved in validating data.

- A systematic process exists for data review and improvement, standardization, and easy employee access to data. Training on the use of data systems is provided as needed.

- Data used for management decisions' focus on critical success factors are integrated with work processes for the planning, design, and delivery of products and services.

- Users of data help determine what data systems are developed and how data are accessed.

- A systematic process is in place for identifying and prioritizing comparative information and benchmark targets.

- Research has been conducted to identify best-in-class organizations, which may be competitors or noncompetitors. Critical business processes or functions are the subject of benchmarking. Activities such as those that support the organization's goals and objectives, action plans, and opportunities for improvement and innovation are the subject of benchmarking. Benchmarking also covers key products, services, customer satisfiers, suppliers, employees, and support operations.

- The organization reaches beyond its own business to conduct comparative studies.

- Benchmark or comparison data are used to improve the understanding of work processes and to discover the best levels of performance that have been achieved. Based on this knowledge, the organization sets goals or targets to stretch performance as well as drive innovations.

- Any systematic process is in place to improve the use of benchmark or comparison data in the understanding of all work processes.

B. Performance Analysis

- Systematic processes are in place for analyzing all types of data and to determine overall organizational health, including key business results, action plans, and strategic objectives. Part of the process is a method to evaluate the effectiveness of the analysis process and improve upon it.

- Facts, rather than intuition, are used to support most decision making at all levels based on the analyses conducted to make sense out of the data collected.

- The analysis process itself is analyzed to make the results more timely and useful for decision making for quality improvement at all levels.

- Analysis processes and tools, and the value of analyses to decision making, are systematically evaluated and improved.

- Analysis is linked to work groups to facilitate the decision making (sometimes daily) throughout the organization.

- Analysis techniques enable meaningful interpretation of the cost and performance impact of organization processes. This analysis helps people at all levels of the organization make necessary trade-offs, set priorities, and reallocate resources to maximize overall organization performance.

4.2   Information Management (40 points)
Approach/Deployment Scoring

Describe how your organization ensures the quality and availability of needed data and information for employees, suppliers/partners, and customers.

Within your response, include answers to the following questions:

a.   **Data Availability**

(1)   How do you make needed data and information available? How do you make them accessible to employees, suppliers/partners, and customers, as appropriate?

(2)   How do you ensure data and information integrity, reliability, accuracy, timeliness, security, and confidentiality?

(3)   How do you keep your data and information availability mechanisms current with business needs and directions?

b.   **Hardware and Software Quality**

(1)   How do you ensure that hardware and software are reliable and user friendly?

(2)   How do you keep your software and hardware systems current with business needs and directions?

Notes:

N1.   Data availability (4.2a) is of growing importance as the Internet and e-business/e-commerce are used increasingly for business-to-business and business-to-consumer interactions and intranets become more important as a major source of organization-wide communications.

N2.   Data and information access [4.2a(1)] might be via electronic and other means.

The first part of this Item [4.2a] examines how the organization ensures the availability of high-quality, timely data and information for all key users—employees, suppliers/partners, and customers. Top-performing organizations make data and information available and accessible to all appropriate users. They ensure that required data and information have all the characteristics users need, including reliability, accuracy, timeliness, and appropriate levels of security and confidentiality.

- As the sources of data and information and the number of users within the organization grow dramatically, systems to manage information technology often require significant resources. Top-performing organizations consider the management of information technology as a strategic imperative. The expanding use of electronic information within organizational operations, more comprehensive knowledge networks, new data from the Internet, and increasing business-to-business and business-to-consumer communications challenges make it absolutely critical that the organization develops systems to ensure data reliability and availability in a user-friendly format.

- Data and information are especially important in business networks, alliances, and supply chains. Information management systems should facili-

tate the use of data and information and should recognize the need for rapid data validation and reliability assurance, given the increasing use of electronic data transfer.

- Organizations must ensure data and information reliability since reliability is critical to good decision making, successful monitoring of operations, and successful data integration for assessing overall performance.

The second part of this Item [4.2b] examines the organization's hardware systems and software to ensure they are reliable and user friendly, facilitating full access and encouraging routine use.

- Processes should be in place to protect against system failure which may damage critical data. This may require redundant systems as well as effective backup and storage of data.

- Processes should be in place to protect against external threats, including attacks from hackers, viral infections, power surges, and other storm-related damage.

Finally, as with the other items required for performance excellence, the organization must systematically evaluate and improve data availability mechanisms, software, and hardware to keep them current with changing business needs and directions.

4.2 Information Management

How the organization ensures the quality and availability of data for employees, key suppliers and partners, and customers

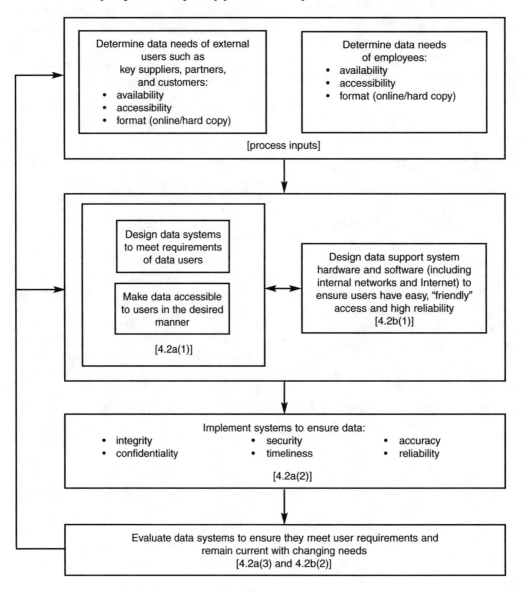

4.2 Information Management Item Linkages

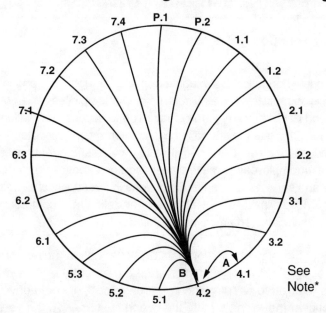

NATURE OF RELATIONSHIP	
A	This Item, Information Management, enables the data flow within the organization and indirectly interacts with all other items (similar to the relationships identified and reported in the Item 4.1 diagram). The simplest way to show these relationships is to tie this Item [4.2] with the Measurement and Analysis of Organizational Performance Item [4.1].
B	In order to ensure that hardware and software systems are reliable and user-friendly [4.2b], information from the following types of system users is gathered: leaders [Category 1]; planners [Category 2]; customer relations and contact staff [Category 3]; information specialists [Category 4]; human resource personnel, managers, and employees [Category 5]; operations workers and managers [Category 6]; and people who monitor and interpret results [Category 7] for use in decision making.

*Note: All of the linkage arrows will not be repeated on the other Item maps. Only the most relevant will be repeated.

\multicolumn{2}{|l|}{**IF YOU DON'T DO WHAT THE CRITERIA REQUIRE...**}	

Item Reference	Possible Adverse Consequences
4.2a(1)	Getting the right information to the right people at the right time and in the right format enables effective decision making. Just as different types of employees in an organization need different data to support decision making, they may need to access information in different ways. Similarly, customers and suppliers may need access to information to facilitate ordering and delivery of required products and services. The failure to provide appropriate access to data may make it more difficult for employees to make timely decisions about work, for customers to place orders for products and services, or lead to disruptions in the supply chain. Providing inappropriate access to individuals inside or outside the organization may compromise data confidentiality and security or even violate certain privacy statutes.
4.2a(2)	Decisions that are made based on data and information may be compromised if the data are inaccurate or unreliable. For example, when a data entry error is made and goes unnoticed (sometimes referred to as "garbage in, garbage out"), it could drive decisions to deliver the wrong product at the wrong time to the wrong customer. At the very least this is likely to cause the product to be returned and restocked, adding cost but not value. The lack of timely information may cause decisions to be delayed inappropriately. Consider, for example, an organization that conducts an employee (or customer) satisfaction survey but does not analyze or make the data available for eight months. This not only sends a message to the organization that employee (or customer) concerns are unimportant, it also makes it difficult to identify real problems that may be contributing to customer dissatisfaction, low worker morale, and poor productivity.
4.2a(3)	In a rapidly changing world, access to information and the use of that information to provide insight and help decision making can provide a strategic advantage. Rapid data availability is becoming more and more critical for business success, especially in e-business situations. In some industries such as banking, a few seconds can make the difference between capitalizing on currency rate fluctuations or being hurt by them. As product and delivery cycle times grow shorter, the need for rapid access to information grows greater. Without evaluating the suitability of data and information systems, and making refinements based on this evaluation, the organization leaves itself open to falling behind and not being able to respond rapidly to changing business needs and directions.
4.2b(1)	The breadth, depth, and speed of decision making continue to increase as artificial intelligence plays a larger and larger role in our lives. Hardware and software are at the heart of this phenomenon. More people than ever before are being asked to interact with computers. In the best-performing organizations, employees frequently use computers to access data and use them to develop relevant analyses that enable better decisions about their work. People with very little computer literacy must now enter and retrieve data from these systems. A user interface that may be easily understood by information management technicians may be incomprehensible to a line worker, customer, or supplier. The failure to

Continued

IF YOU DON'T DO WHAT THE CRITERIA REQUIRE...	*(continued)*
	make these systems reliable and easy to use (user-friendly) makes it difficult, if not impossible, for some people to use them effectively. This may create significant problems for organizations, particularly those venturing into areas where e-commerce plays a larger and larger role. Consider, for example, a bank that wants to expand and promote distance banking via the Internet or through home-to-bank modem connections. If the software is not reliable and *very* user-friendly, many customers may be unwilling or unable to take advantage of these services. This may limit the organization's ability to achieve strategic and/or market share goals that should have been considered during the strategy development process [Item 2.1a(2)].
4.2b(2)	Concerns about security, data loss, sophisticated hackers, and increased customer requirements for better access and availability places steadily increasing demands on hardware and software systems. The failure to keep these systems current may expose them to internal or external threats. For example, the failure to update virus protections frequently and maintain up-to-date, effective firewalls can expose the computer system (and the organization) to catastrophic and costly losses. (Please note that this Item does not require improvements in software and hardware simply for the sake of buying new gadgets. Improvements should help support changing business needs and directions—as a means to an end, not the end itself. This is another example where a cost-benefit data analysis [Item 4.1b] may be crucial to making good decisions about maintaining appropriate software and hardware systems.)

4.2 INFORMATION MANAGEMENT—SAMPLE EFFECTIVE PRACTICES

A. Data Availability

- Users of data help determine what data systems are developed and how data are accessed.

- Every person has access to the data they need to make decisions about their work, from top leaders to individual workers or teams of workers.

- The performance measurement system is systematically evaluated and refined. Improvements have been made to reduce cycle time for data collection and to increase data access, reliability, and use.

- A "sunset" review is conducted to determine what data no longer need to be collected and can be dropped.

- A data integrity and reliability team routinely and randomly checks data. Systems are in place to minimize or prevent human error in data entry and analysis.

- Data systems are benchmarked against best-in-class systems and continually refined.

B. Hardware and Software Quality

- Hardware and software systems have been protected against external threats from hackers, viral threats, water, and electrical damage. Protection systems are updated as appropriate (for example, viral updates are made several times daily).

- Disciplined, automatic file backup occurs. Backup data are stored in a secure, external facility.

- Data are protected against misuse from external sources through encryption and randomly changing user passwords.

- Procedures required to interface with the hardware and software were designed to meet the needs and capabilities of all computer users, to ensure they are not excluded.

5 Human Resource Focus—85 Points

The Human Resource Focus Category examines how your organization motivates and enables employees to develop and utilize their full potential in alignment with your organization's overall objectives and action plans. Also examined are your organization's efforts to build and maintain a work environment and an employee support climate conducive to performance excellence and to personal and organizational growth.

Human Resource Focus addresses key human resource practices—those directed toward creating a high-performance workplace and toward developing employees to enable them and the organization to adapt to change. The category covers human resource development and management requirements in an integrated way, that is, aligned with the organization's strategic directions. Included in the focus on human resources is a focus on the work environment and the employee support climate.

To ensure the basic alignment of human resource management with overall strategy, the Criteria also include human resource planning as part of organizational planning in the Strategic Planning Category. Human resource focus evaluates how the organization enables employees to develop and use their full potential.

Work Systems

- Design, organize, and manage work and jobs to optimize employee performance and potential

- Recognition and reward practices support objectives for customer satisfaction, performance improvement, and employee and organization learning goals

- Identify skills needed by potential employees, recruit, and hire

Employee Education, Training, and Development

- Deliver, evaluate, and reinforce appropriate training to achieve action plans and address organization needs including building knowledge, skills, and abilities to improve employee development and performance

Employee Well-Being and Satisfaction

- Improve employee safety, well-being, development, and satisfaction and maintain a work environment free from distractions to high performance

- Leaders at all levels encourage and motivate employees to reach full potential

- Systematically evaluate employee well-being, satisfaction, and motivation and identify improvement priorities that promote key business results

5.1 Work Systems (35 Points)
Approach/Deployment Scoring

Describe how your organization's work and jobs, compensation, career progression, and related workforce practices motivate and enable employees and the organization to achieve high performance.

Within your response, include answers to the following questions:

a. **Work Systems**

   (1) How do you organize and manage work and jobs to promote cooperation, initiative/innovation, your organizational culture, and the flexibility to keep current with business needs? How do you achieve effective communication and knowledge/skill sharing across work units, jobs, and locations, as appropriate?

   (2) How do you motivate employees to develop and utilize their full potential? Include formal and/or informal mechanisms you use to help employees attain job-and career-related development/learning objectives and the role of managers and supervisors in helping employees attain these objectives.

   (3) How does your employee performance management system, including feedback to employees, support high performance and a customer and business focus? How do your compensation, recognition, and related reward/incentive practices reinforce these objectives?

   (4) How do you accomplish effective succession planning for senior leadership and throughout the organization?

   (5) How do you identify characteristics and skills needed by potential employees? How do you recruit, hire, and retain new employees? How do your work systems capitalize on the diverse ideas, cultures, and thinking of the communities with which you interact (your employee hiring and customer communities)?

Notes:

N1. "Employees" refers to your organization's permanent, temporary, and part-time personnel, as well as any contract employees supervised by your organization. Employees include team leaders, supervisors, and managers at all levels. Contract employees supervised by a contractor should be addressed in business or support processes in Category 6.

N2. "Your organization's work" refers to how your employees are organized and/or organize themselves in formal and informal, temporary, or longer-term units. This might include work teams, process teams, customer action teams, problem-solving teams, centers of excellence, functional units, cross-functional teams, and departments—self-managed or managed by supervisors. "Jobs" refers to responsibilities, authorities, and tasks of individuals. In some work systems, jobs might be shared by a team.

N3. Compensation and recognition (5.1a [3]) include promotions and bonuses that might be based upon performance, skills acquired, and other factors. Recognition includes monetary and nonmonetary, formal and informal, and individual and group mechanisms.

This Item [5.1] looks at the organization's systems for work and job design, compensation, employee performance management, motivation, recognition, communication, and hiring, with the aim of enabling and encouraging all employees to contribute effectively and to the best of their ability. These systems are intended to foster high performance, individual and organizational learning, and adaptation to change.

Work and jobs should be designed in such a way as to allow employees to exercise discretion and decision making, resulting in higher involvement and better performance.

- High-performance work is enhanced by systems that promote employee flexibility, innovation, knowledge and skill sharing, alignment with organizational objectives, customer focus, and rapid response to changing business needs and requirements of the marketplace. Work should support organizational objectives. To achieve high levels of organizational performance, it is essential to fully develop the capabilities of the workforce.

- Developing and sustaining high-performance work systems requires ongoing education and training, and information systems (see Category 4) that ensure adequate information availability. To help employees realize their full potential, many organizations use individual development plans prepared with the input of each employee and designed to address his/her career and learning objectives.

- The ability to respond quickly to changing customer and workplace requirements demands a workforce characterized by initiative and self-direction. Hierarchical, command-and-control management styles work directly against fast response and high-performance capability. After all, the opposite of individual initiative is an environment where managers demand review and approval of decisions that are typically better made by employees doing the work.

- Factors to consider in work and job design include simplification of job classifications, cross-training, job rotation, use of teams (including self-directed teams), and changes in work layout and location.

Effective communication across functions and work units is also important to ensure a focus on customer requirements and to ensure an environment with trust, knowledge sharing, and mutual respect. Leaders and managers throughout the best organizations consistently motivate employees to develop and utilize their full potential as well as share knowledge and information at all levels. Internal barriers to knowledge and skill sharing suboptimize organizational performance.

The best organizations put in place an employee performance management system that provides measurable feedback to employees, supports high-performance objectives, and supports a customer and business focus. Furthermore, employee compensation, recognition, and reward is aligned to support these business objectives. In addition, to make sure all employees understand their responsibilities, systems exist to promote effective communication and cooperation, at all levels of the organization.

- Once the organization determines its key strategic objectives, it should review compensation, reward, and recognition systems to ensure they support those objectives. The failure to do this creates an environment where employees are focused on one set of activities (based on their compensation plan) but the organization has determined that another set of activities (the action plans to achieve the strategic objectives) is necessary for success.

- Compensation and recognition systems must be matched to support the work necessary for business success. Consistent with this, compensation and recognition might be tied to demonstrated skills and/or to peer evaluations. Compensation and recognition approaches also might include profit sharing, team or unit performance awards, and should be linked to the achievement of certain levels of customer satisfaction and loyalty, which are important to business success.

The organization must perform effective succession planning for senior leadership and managers at all levels of the organization. The rate of new knowledge acquisition is accelerating throughout the world. Significantly more new knowledge is causing change to occur faster than ever before in history. To manage effectively in this climate of rapid change, organizations must prepare its future leaders and managers. The best organizations do not wait for vacancy to occur before it thinks about the requirements and skills needed. Succession planning enables organizations to identify future skill needs against current skill gaps, enabling them to recruit and develop the necessary human resources.

Finally, organizations must profile, recruit, and hire employees who will meet skill requirements required to position the organization for future success. Obviously, the right workforce is by key driver of high performance.

- As the pool of skilled talent continues to shrink, it becomes more important than ever for organizations to specifically define the capabilities and skills needed by potential employees of all types and create a work environment to attract them. Accordingly, it is critical to take into account characteristics of diverse populations to make sure appropriate support systems exist that make it possible to attract skilled workers.

5.1 Work Systems

How the organization's work and job design, and compensation and recognition approaches, career progression, and recruitment enable and encourage all employees to contribute effectively to achieving high performance

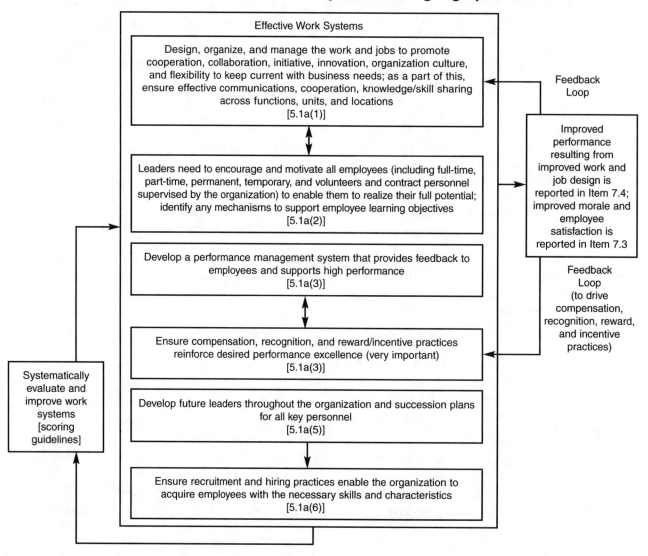

5.1 *Work Systems Item Linkages*

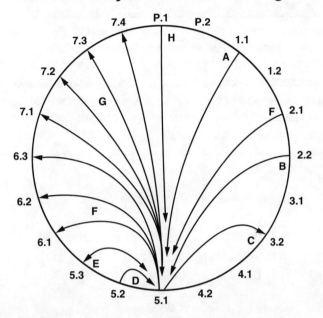

NATURE OF RELATIONSHIP	
A	Top leaders (and subsequently leaders at all levels) [1.1a(2)] set the policies and role model actions essential to improving work and job design to enhance employee empowerment, initiative, self-direction, and flexibility [5.1a(1)].
B	Human resource development plans and goals [2.2a(3)] address ways to improve employee performance and involvement [5.1].
C	Flexibility, initiative, and communication and knowledge sharing [5.1a(1)] are essential to enhance the effectiveness and ability of customer-contact employees to resolve customer concerns promptly [3.2a(3)].
D	Effective training [5.2] is critical to enable employees/managers at all levels to improve skills and improve their ability to manage, organize, and design better work processes [5.1].
E	A safe, secure work climate [5.3] enhances employee participation, self-direction, and initiative [5.1] and vice-versa.
F	Effective performance feedback, compensation, and recognition [5.1a(3)] are essential to improving operational, business, and support processes [6.1, 6.2, and 6.3] and ensuring alignment to overall strategic objectives [2.1b(1)].
G	Compensation, incentives, recognition, and rewards [5.1a(3)] are based in part on performance results [Category 7]. Improvements in work and job design, flexibility, innovation, empowerment, sharing, and communication [5.1a(1)], and developing employee potential [5.1a(2)] result in

Continued

NATURE OF RELATIONSHIP	*continued*
	improved performance and business results [Category 7]. Processes to improve initiative and flexibility [5.1] can enhance all performance results [Category 7].
H	Employee characteristics such as educational levels, workforce and job diversity, the existence of bargaining units, the use of contract employees, and other special requirements [P.1a(3)] help set the context for determining the requirements for knowledge and skill sharing across work units, jobs, and locations [5.1a(1)].

IF YOU DON'T DO WHAT THE CRITERIA REQUIRE...

Item Reference	Possible Adverse Consequences
5.1a(1)	The alignment of strategic objectives and the work to accomplish them is vital to the success and optimum performance of the organization. Once strategic objectives [Item 2.1b(1)] and related actions [Item 2.2a(1)] have been identified and deployed to all levels of the organization, leaders and managers can more effectively organize employees (or they can organize themselves) to carry out the necessary work. In addition, appropriate responsibilities, authorities, and other tasks should be defined to ensure the actions are carried out. If the organization and management of work and jobs are not aligned to support strategic objectives and related actions, the organization may not be able to optimize the work that is done. The failure to promote cooperation among work units often contributes to redundancy and working at cross-purposes. The failure to promote knowledge and skill sharing often forces the organization to duplicate efforts in the search for more effective and efficient processes. The failure to share knowledge also contributes to isolationism within an organization and prevents "pockets of excellence" from spreading. Frequently, employees organized in a hierarchical, command and control environment find individual initiative, innovation, and flexibility stifled, reducing morale and further eroding productivity and responsiveness [Item 5.3b(3)] to changing customer requirements [Item 6.1a(2) and Item 3.2a(3)].
5.1a(2)	An organization that fails to develop and use the full potential of its employees wastes significant resources. This waste can be classified into two categories: the failure to develop existing potential and take advantage of it; and the failure to use skills and abilities that already exist. This waste is equivalent to running an operation at less than optimum capacity; for example, paying an employee for 40 hours of work but asking for only 20 or going out and hiring additional people when the potential for skills development already exists but goes unrecognized. To make matters worse, employees usually recognize when their skills are underused and their productivity suffers further erosion, or they seek job opportunities outside the organization where they can develop and advance more fully, or both.
5.1a(3)	In order to optimize performance, work throughout the organization must be fully aligned to support strategic objectives [Item 2.1b(1)] and related action plans [Item 2.2a(1)]. The action plans should be deployed fully throughout the organization at all levels with appropriate quantitative measures developed to monitor progress [Item 2.2a(4)]. The work of individual employees, when taken together, should enable the organization to achieve its strategic objectives. There are two questions that are fundamental to the work endeavors that employee feedback should address: (1) are the right things being done (the vital few); and (2) are they being done right (correctly).

The failure to provide feedback to employees about their performance may make it more difficult for them to determine if they are doing the right thing in support of business strategy or if they are doing things in the right way (process discipline). It forces them to decide for themselves if they are doing a good job or not. In addition, the failure to provide feedback causes the |

Continued

IF YOU DON'T DO WHAT THE CRITERIA REQUIRE...	*(continued)*

	organization to miss an opportunity to reinforce a customer and business focus. After all, "what gets measured gets done." The alignment of what is "expected" and what is "rewarded" send very strong messages throughout the organization about what is really important. Failing to align appropriate compensation, recognition, rewards, and incentives with the strategic objectives may also contribute to a lack of focus amongst the workforce, allowing employees to substitute their own ideas instead of being driven/guided by the reinforcement of management. Many employees equate compensation with the activities that the organization wants to achieve. For example, if achieving profitability is critical for organization success, the organization typically rewards people for achieving financial goals. Everyone clearly understands the importance of "profit" because their own compensation and rewards are tied to it. Similarly, the failure to provide rewards, recognition, or compensation that supports a customer focus may cause employees to believe that customers are unimportant. Rewards (or the absence of them) drive behavior and motivate people to respond in certain ways.
5.1a(4)	In the face of worldwide shortages of highly skilled employees, an organization's failure to conduct effective succession planning (both for senior leaders and for key positions throughout the organization) could threaten organizational stability in the long-term and create immediate performance problems in the short term. When critical personnel shortages exist within an organization, it is frequently unable to carryout key objectives. If succession planning does not look ahead at least as far as it might take to acquire or train replacement personnel, the organization may lack the talent it needs to fulfill its promises to customers or other key stakeholders.
5.1a(5)	Skill mapping is a process that many high-performing organizations practice to compare the skills it needs to achieve strategic objectives with the skills its workforce currently possesses. When a skill gap is identified, it enables organizations to more effectively make decisions as to whether they need to recruit, hire, or train appropriate employees. The failure to identify characteristics and skills needed by potential employees increases the likelihood of not having appropriate staff in the right places when needed. The failure to capitalize on diverse ideas, cultures, and thinking may limit the organization's ability to be innovative, flexible, and creative [Item 5.1a(1) and Item 1.1a(2)]. This in turn, may limit the organization's ability to meet the challenges of today's highly competitive environment.

5.1 WORK SYSTEMS—SAMPLE EFFECTIVE PRACTICES

A.   Work Systems

- Fully using the talents of all employees is a basic organizational value.

- Managers use cross-functional work teams to break down barriers, improve effectiveness, and meet goals.

- Teams have access to data and are authorized to make decisions about their work (not just make recommendations).

- Employee opinion is sought regarding work design and work processes.

- Prompt and regular feedback is provided to teams regarding their performance. Feedback covers both results and team processes.

- Although lower-performing organizations use teams for special improvement projects (while the "regular work" is performed using traditional approaches), higher-performing organizations use teams and self-directed employees as the way regular work is done.

- Self-directed or self-managed work teams are used throughout the organization. They have authority over matters such as budget, hiring, and team membership and roles.

- A systematic process is used to evaluate and improve the effectiveness and extent of employee involvement.

- Many indicators of employee involvement effectiveness exist, such as the improvements in time or cost reduction produced by teams.

- The performance management system provides feedback to employees that supports their ability to contribute to a high-performing organization.

- Compensation, recognition, and rewards/incentives are provided for generating improvement ideas. In addition, a system exists to encourage and provide rapid reinforcement for submitting improvement ideas.

- Compensation, recognition, and rewards/incentives are provided for results, such as for reductions in cycle time and exceeding target schedules with error-free products or services at less-than-projected cost.

- Employees, as well as managers, participate in creating the compensation, recognition, and rewards/incentives practices and help monitor its implementation and systematic improvement.

- The organization evaluates its approaches to employee performance and compensation, recognition, and rewards to determine the extent to which employees are satisfied with them, the extent of employee participation, and the impact of the system on improved performance (reported in Item 7.3).

- Evaluations are used to make improvements. The best organizations have several improvement cycles. (Many improvement cycles can occur in one year.)

- Performance measures exist for employee involvement, self-direction, and initiative. Goals for these measures are expressed in measurable terms. These measurable goals form at least a good part of the basis for performance recognition.

- Recognition, reward/incentives, and compensation are influenced by customer satisfaction ratings as well as other performance measures.

- A formal system is in place to develop future leaders. This includes providing training and practice in high-performance leadership techniques. Leaders receive specific training and practicing using Baldrige Criteria and performance improvement systems.

- Demonstrated proficiency in the use of the Baldrige performance excellence criteria is a prerequisite to leadership advancement.

- Future leaders serve as examiners in the Baldrige process, state quality award process, or internal award process.

5.2   Employee Education, Training, and Development (25 points)
Approach/Deployment Scoring

Describe how your organization's education and training support the achievement of your overall objectives, including building employee knowledge, skills, and capabilities, and contributing to high performance.

Within your response, include answers to the following questions:

a. Employee Education, Training, and Development

(1) How do education and training contribute to the achievement of your action plans? How does your education and training approach balance short- and longer-term organizational objectives and employee needs, including development, learning, and career progression?

(2) How do you seek and use input from employees and their supervisors/managers on education and training needs and delivery options?

(3) How do you address in your employee education, training, and development your key organizational needs associated with technological change, management/leadership development, new employee orientation, safety, performance measurement/improvement, and diversity?

(4) How do you deliver education and training? Include formal and informal delivery, including mentoring and other approaches, as appropriate. How do you evaluate the effectiveness of education and training, taking into account individual and organizational performance?

(5) How do you reinforce the use of knowledge and skills on the job?

Notes:

N1. Technological change (5.2a [3]) might include computer and Internet literacy.

N2. Education and training delivery (5.2a [4]) might occur inside or outside your organization and involve on-the-job, classroom, computer-based, distance learning, and/or other types of delivery (formal or informal).

This Item [5.2] looks at the organization's system for workforce education, training, and on-the-job reinforcement of knowledge and skills, with the aim of meeting ongoing needs of employees and a high-performance workplace.

To help the organization achieve its high-performance objectives, education and training must be effectively designed, delivered, reinforced on the job, evaluated, and improved. To optimize organization effectiveness, the education and training system should place special emphasis on meeting individual career progression and organizational business needs.

- Education and training needs might vary greatly depending on the nature of the organization's work, employee responsibility, and stage of organizational and personal development. These needs might include knowledge-sharing skills, communications, teamwork, problem solving, interpreting and using data, meeting customer requirements, process analysis and simplification, waste and cycle-time reduction, and priority setting based on strategic alignment or cost/benefit analysis. Education needs also might include basic skills, such as reading, writing, language, and arithmetic.

Organizations should consider job and organizational performance in education and training design and evaluation. Education and training should tie to action plans, and balance short- and longer-term individual and organizational objectives. Employees and their supervisors should help determine training needs and contribute to the design and evaluation of education and training, because these individuals frequently are best able to identify critical needs and evaluate success.

- Education and training delivery might occur inside or outside the organization and could involve on-the-job, classroom, computer-based, distance learning (including Web-based instruction), or other types of delivery. Training also might occur through developmental assignments (including mentoring and apprenticeship) within or outside the organization.

- When evaluating education and training, leaders should identify specific measures of effectiveness as a critical component of evaluation. Such measures might address impact on individual, unit, and organizational performance, impact on

customer-related performance, and cost/benefit analysis of the training.

- Although this Item does not require specific training for customer-contact employees, the Item does require that education and training "keep current with business and individual needs" and "address performance excellence." If an objective of the organization is to enhance customer satisfaction and loyalty, it may be critical to identify job requirements for customer-contact employees and then provide appropriate training to these employees. Such training is increasingly important and common among high-performing organizations. It frequently includes: acquiring critical knowledge and skills with respect to products, services, and customers; skills on how to listen to customers; recovery from problems or failures; and learning how to manage customer expectations effectively.

Frequently, organizations must ensure that training and education contribute to high performance. This may require organizations to provide training in the use of performance excellence tools.

- This training may be similar to the "quality" training organizations provided in the past. Training may focus on the use of performance measures, skill standards, quality control methods, benchmarking, problem-solving processes, and performance improvement techniques.

- This training should also address high-priority needs such as technological change, management/leadership development, new employee orientation, diversity training, safety, and performance measurement and improvement. Succession planning and leadership development [examined in Item 5.1a(4)] typically require organizations to provide specialized training and development to key individuals identified as possible successors.

Finally, unless knowledge and skills acquired in training are reinforced on the job, they are quickly and easily forgotten—even after a few days. Accordingly, leaders, managers, and supervisors throughout the organization must promptly ensure that employees actually use the skills acquired through recent training. In fact, one of the measures of leadership effectiveness may consider the extent to which they reinforce these skills among their employees.

5.2 Employee Education, Training, and Development

How the organization's education and training addresses business objectives, building employee knowledge, skills, and capabilities, and contributes to improving employee performance

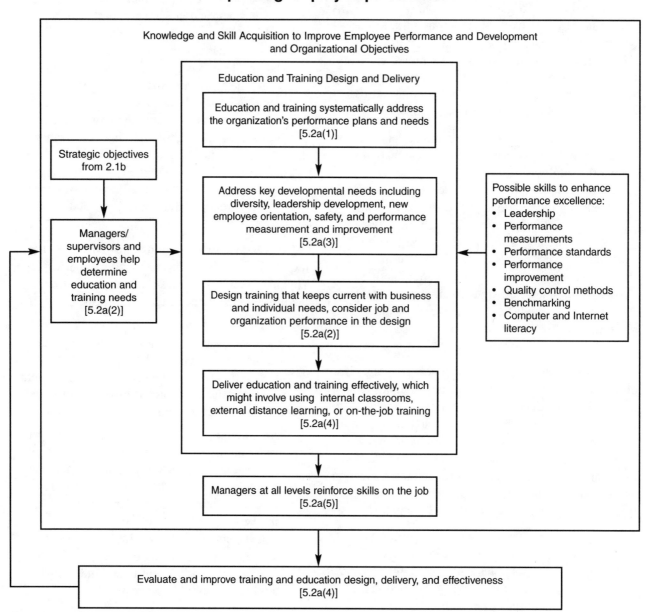

Knowledge and Skill Acquisition to Improve Employee Performance and Development and Organizational Objectives

Education and Training Design and Delivery

Education and training systematically address the organization's performance plans and needs [5.2a(1)]

Strategic objectives from 2.1b

Managers/ supervisors and employees help determine education and training needs [5.2a(2)]

Address key developmental needs including diversity, leadership development, new employee orientation, safety, and performance measurement and improvement [5.2a(3)]

Possible skills to enhance performance excellence:
• Leadership
• Performance measurements
• Performance standards
• Performance improvement
• Quality control methods
• Benchmarking
• Computer and Internet literacy

Design training that keeps current with business and individual needs, consider job and organization performance in the design [5.2a(2)]

Deliver education and training effectively, which might involve using internal classrooms, external distance learning, or on-the-job training [5.2a(4)]

Managers at all levels reinforce skills on the job [5.2a(5)]

Evaluate and improve training and education design, delivery, and effectiveness [5.2a(4)]

5.2 *Employee Education, Training, and Development Item Linkages*

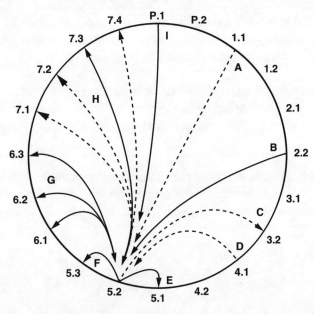

NATURE OF RELATIONSHIP	
A	Leaders [1.1a(2)] are responsible for supporting appropriate skill development of all employees through training and development systems and reinforcing learning on the job [5.2a].
B	Human resource development plans [2.2a(3)] (which were developed to support strategic objectives in [2.1b(1)]) are used to help align training [5.2a(1)] to ensure employees and leaders possess appropriate knowledge, skills, and ability.
C	Training [5.2] can enhance capabilities of customer-contact employees and strengthen customer relationships [3.2a(2 and 3)].
D	Key measures and benchmarking data [4.1] are used to improve training [5.2]. Information regarding training effectiveness [5.2] is analyzed [4.1].
E	Effective training [5.2a(3)] enables managers at all levels to improve their ability to design, organize, and manage better work processes that promote empowerment, innovation, creativity, and sharing [5.1a(1)]; develop employee potential [5.1a(2)]; make performance feedback and recognition and reward more relevant [5.1a(3)]; enhance succession planning [5.1a(4)]; and recruit and retain the best employees [5.1a(5)].
F	Effective training [5.2a(3)] is critical to maintaining and improving a safe, healthful work environment [5.3a] and improved employee motivation and well-being [5.3b].

Continued

NATURE OF RELATIONSHIP		*continued*
G	Training [5.2a(3)] is essential to managing technological change and improving work-in-process effectiveness and innovation [6.1, 6.2, and 6.3]. In addition, training requirements [5.2] are defined in part by process requirements [6.1, 6.2, and 6.3].	
H	Results of improved training and development [5.2] are reported in 7.3. In addition, results pertaining to customer satisfaction [7.1], financial and market performance [7.2], and operational performance [7.4] reflect, in part, and are monitored to assess training effectiveness [5.2a(4)].	
I	Employee characteristics such as educational levels workforce and job diversity, the existence of bargaining units, the use of contract employees, and other special requirements [P.1a(3)] help set the context for determining appropriate training needs by employee segment [5.2a(1)].	

IF YOU DON'T DO WHAT THE CRITERIA REQUIRE...

Item Reference	Possible Adverse Consequences
5.2a(1)	Strategic objectives [Item 2.1b(1)] define what the organization must achieve to be successful in the future. Action plans [Item 2.2a(1)] define the things the organization must do to achieve the strategic objectives. If employees lack the necessary skills to carryout required actions, the strategic plan may fail. Education and training that do not contribute to the achievement of action plans may be a waste of resources. Managers have a responsibility to help employees attain their job- and career-related learning and development objectives [Item 5.1a(2)]. If managers fail to take advantage of appropriate education and training to help employees with work-related development, learning, and career progression, they run the risk of weakening morale and motivation as well as contributing to employee obsolescence. This may adversely impact employee job security and employability and undermine the organization's ability to maintain a viable workforce to compete effectively.
5.2a(2)	Employees and managers who are closest to the work usually understand best what skills are required (and missing) to do the work effectively. Failing to obtain and use input from these employees and their supervisors may result in the development of inappropriate or ineffective education and training opportunities. Providing ineffective or inappropriate training can waste resources in two ways: (1) the cost of paying employees' salary during training, the cost of training facilities, and the cost of instruction; and (2) the cost to the organization of lost productivity while employees are participating in training.
5.2a(3)	Today's best-performing organizations have found that the following six areas are instrumental in optimizing performance and winning in a highly competitive environment: (1) technological change; (2) management development; (3) new employee orientation (acculturation); (4) safety; (5) performance measurement and improvement; and (6) capitalizing on diverse ideas and cultures. The failure to effectively address these factors as a part of employee education, training, and development may adversely affect the organizations ability to achieve its strategic objectives. The failure to keep pace with or lead technology change may make it difficult to establish or maintain a competitive advantage. The failure to develop better managers and leaders may make it more difficult to develop strategic objectives, fully engage employees, and optimize organizational performance. The failure to provide effective employee orientation may make it difficult to get new employees to optimal levels of performance quickly. The failure to understand safety procedures may contribute to higher accident rates, higher compensation claims, and lost productivity. The failure to understand performance measurement and improvement systems is likely to slow or stall organizational improvement and make it extremely difficult to keep pace in a highly competitive environment. The failure to understand and take advantage of diverse ideas and cultures may limit the organization's creativity and innovation, and contribute to falling behind competitors.
5.2a(4)	The failure to deliver education and training using appropriate methods, consistent with the learning styles and needs of the students, usually suboptimizes the effectiveness of training.

Continued

IF YOU DON'T DO WHAT THE CRITERIA REQUIRE...	*continued*

	If students do not acquire relevant knowledge, skills, or abilities from education and training, the organization has wasted resources. If students do learn new skills and acquire new abilities but those new skills and abilities are not used on the job, the organization has also wasted resources. If the students use the new skills and abilities on the job and it makes no difference to organizational performance or career progression, the organization has again wasted resources.
5.2a(5)	If it is worth training an employee to acquire new skills and abilities, it is important to reinforce the use of those new skills when the employee returns to the job. The failure to reinforce the use of recently acquired knowledge and skills on the job may cause those new skills and abilities to become obsolete and quickly forgotten. Accordingly, the cost of training and the cost of lost productivity while the employee is receiving the training represent wasted resources. Most importantly, when the newly acquired skills are not utilized the value of those skills and potential productivity gains are lost. Losses of this nature can materially impact an organization's rate of growth and its ability to achieve strategic objectives.

5.2 EMPLOYEE EDUCATION, TRAINING, AND DEVELOPMENT—SAMPLE EFFECTIVE PRACTICES

A. Employee Education, Training, and Development

- Managers and employees conduct systematic needs analyses to ensure that skills required to perform work are routinely assessed, monitored, and maintained.

- Clear linkages exist between strategic objectives and education and training. Skills are developed based on work demands and employee needs.

- Training plans are developed based on employee input.

- Employee career and personal development options, including development for leadership, diversity, new employee orientation, and safety, are enhanced through formal education and training. Some development uses on-the-job training, including rotational assignments or job exchange programs.

- The organization uses various methods to deliver training to ensure that it is suitable for employee knowledge and skill levels.

- To minimize travel costs, all training is examined to determine if electronic or distance delivery options are viable.

- Training is linked to work requirements, which managers reinforce on the job. Just-in-time training is preferred (rather than just-in-case training) to help ensure that the skills will be used immediately after training.

- Employee feedback on the appropriateness of the training is collected and used to improve course delivery and content.

- The organization systematically evaluates training effectiveness on the job. Performance data are collected on individuals and groups at all levels to assess the impact of training.

- Employee satisfaction with courses is tracked and used to improve training content, training delivery, instructional effectiveness, and the effectiveness of supervisory support for the use of training on the job.

- Training design and delivery is systematically refined and improved based on regular evaluations.

5.3 Employee Well-Being and Satisfaction (25 points)
Approach/Deployment Scoring

Describe how your organization maintains a work environment and an employee support climate that contribute to the well-being, satisfaction, and motivation of all employees.

Within your response, include answers to the following questions:

a. **Work Environment**

How do you improve workplace health, safety, and ergonomics? How do employees take part in improving them? Include performance measures and/or targets for each key environmental factor. Also include significant differences, if any, based on varying work environments for employee groups and/or work units.

b. **Employee Support and Satisfaction**

(1) How do you determine the key factors that affect employee well-being, satisfaction, and motivation? How are these factors segmented for a diverse workforce and for varying categories and types of employees, as appropriate?

(2) How do you support your employees via services, benefits, and policies? How are these tailored to the needs of a diverse workforce and different categories and types of employees, as appropriate?

(3) What formal and/or informal assessment methods and measures do you use to determine employee well-being, satisfaction, and motivation? How do you tailor these methods and measures to a diverse workforce and to different categories and types of employees, as appropriate? How do you use other indicators, such as employee retention, absenteeism, grievances, safety, and productivity, to assess and improve employee well-being, satisfaction, and motivation?

(4) How do you relate assessment findings to key business results to identify priorities for improving the work environment and employee support climate?

Notes:

N1. Specific factors that might affect your employees' well-being, satisfaction, and motivation (5.3b [1]) include: effective employee problem or grievance resolution; safety factors; employees' views of management; employee training, development, and career opportunities; employee preparation for changes in technology or the work organization; the work environment and other work conditions; management's empowerment of employees; information sharing by management; workload; cooperation and teamwork; recognition; services and benefits; communications; job security; compensation; and equal opportunity.

N2. Approaches for employee support (5.3b[2]) might include: providing counseling, career development, and employability services; recreational or cultural activities; nonwork-related education; day care; job rotation or sharing; special leave for family responsibilities or community service; home safety training; flexible work hours and location; outplacement; and retirement benefits (including extended health care).

Continued on next page

5.3   *Employee Well-Being and Satisfaction—continued*

N3. Measures/indicators of well-being, satisfaction, and motivation (5.3b[3]) might include: data on safety and absenteeism, the overall turnover rate, the turnover rate for customer contact employees, employees' charitable contributions, grievances, strikes, other job actions, insurance costs, worker's compensation claims, and results of surveys. Survey indicators of satisfaction might include employee knowledge of job roles, employee knowledge of organizational direction, and employee perception of empowerment and information sharing. Your results relative to such measures/indicators should be reported in Item 7.3.

N4. Setting priorities (5.3b[4]) might draw upon your human resource results presented in Item 7.3 and might involve addressing employee problems based on their impact on your organizational performance.

This Item [5.3] looks at the organization's work environment, the employee support climate, and how employee satisfaction is determined, with the aim of enhancing the well-being, satisfaction, and motivation of all employees, recognizing their diverse needs.

The first part of this Item [5.3a] looks at how the organization provides a safe and healthful work environment for all employees, taking into account their differing work environments and associated requirements. Employees should help identify and improve factors important to workplace safety. Also important is how the organization identifies appropriate measures and targets for key environmental factors so that status and progress can be tracked.

- The organization should be able to show how it includes such factors in its planning and improvement activities. Important factors in this Area include establishing appropriate measures and targets for employee safety and health. Organizations should also recognize that employee groups might experience very different environments and need different services to ensure workplace safety.

- Organizations should also identify appropriate measures and targets for key environmental factors so that status and progress can be tracked.

The second part of this Item [5.3b] looks at how the organization determines key factors that affect employee well-being, satisfaction, and motivation. The organization must provide appropriate services, benefits, and policies to enhance employee well-being, satisfaction, and motivation. The best organizations develop a holistic view of employees as key stakeholders. Most organizations, regardless of size, have many opportunities to contribute to employees' well-being, satisfaction, and motivation. These organizations place special emphasis on the variety of approaches used to satisfy a diverse workforce with differing needs and expectations in order to reduce attrition and increase motivation.

- Examples of services, facilities, activities, and other opportunities are: personal and career counseling; career development and employability services; recreational or cultural activities; formal and informal recognition; non-work-related education; day care; special leave for family responsibilities and/or for community service; home safety training; flexible work hours and benefits packages; outplacement services; and retiree benefits, including extended health care and access to employee services. Also, these services might include career enhancement activities such as skills assessments, helping employees develop learning objectives and plans, and conducting employability assessments.

- As the workforce becomes more diverse (including employees that may work in other countries for multinational companies) it becomes more important to consider and support the needs of those employees with different services.

High-performing organizations also used both formal and informal assessment methods and measures to determine employee well-being, satisfaction, and motivation. These methods and measures are tailored to assess the differing needs of a diverse workforce. In addition, indicators other than employee opinion surveys (for example, employee turnover, grievances, complaints, and absenteeism) are used to support the assessment. Taken together, these methods and measures ensure that assessment findings are relevant and relate to key business results in order to identify key priorities for improvement.

Many factors might affect employee motivation, well-being, and satisfaction. Although satisfaction with pay and promotion potential is important, these factors might not be adequate to understand the factors that contribute to the overall climate for motivation and high performance.

- For this reason, high-performing organizations usually consider a variety of factors that might affect well-being, satisfaction, and motivation, such as effective employee problem and grievance resolution; safety; employee development and career opportunities; employee preparation for changes in technology or work organization; work environment and management support; workload; communication, cooperation and teamwork; job security; appreciation of the differing needs of diverse employee groups; recognition; benefits; compensation; and organizational support for serving customers.

- In addition to direct measurement of employee satisfaction and well-being through formal or informal surveys, some other indicators of satisfaction and well-being include: absenteeism, turnover, grievances, strikes, accidents, lost-time injuries, and worker's compensation claims.

Information and data on the well-being, satisfaction, and motivation of employees are actually used in identifying improvement priorities. Priority setting might draw upon human resource results reported in Item 7.3 and might involve addressing employee problems based on the impact on organizational performance. Factors inhibiting motivation need to be prioritized and addressed. The failure to address these factors is likely to result in even greater problems, which may not only impact human resource results (Item 7.3), but adversely affect customer satisfaction (Item 7.1), financial performance (Item 7.2), and operational excellence (Item 7.4).

5.3 Employee Well-Being and Satisfaction

How the organization maintains a work environment and employee support climate that supports the well-being, satisfaction, and motivation of employees

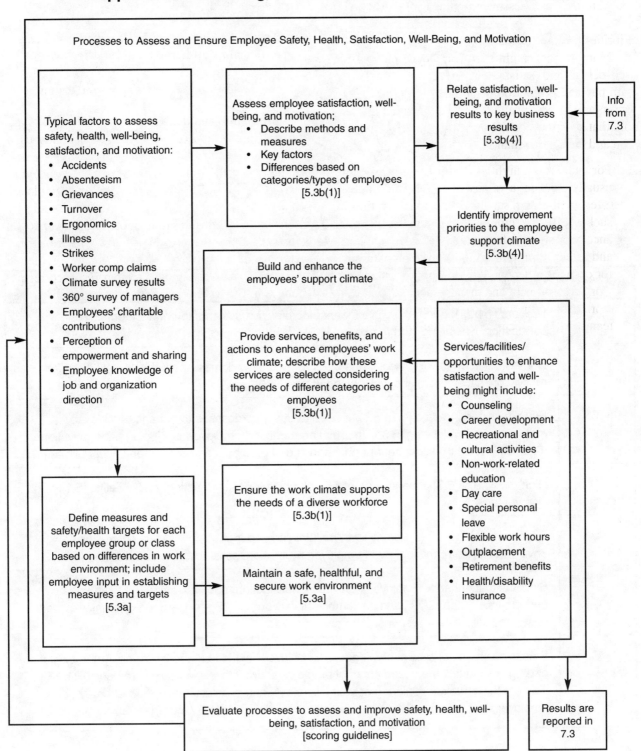

Processes to Assess and Ensure Employee Safety, Health, Satisfaction, Well-Being, and Motivation

Typical factors to assess safety, health, well-being, satisfaction, and motivation:
- Accidents
- Absenteeism
- Grievances
- Turnover
- Ergonomics
- Illness
- Strikes
- Worker comp claims
- Climate survey results
- 360° survey of managers
- Employees' charitable contributions
- Perception of empowerment and sharing
- Employee knowledge of job and organization direction

Assess employee satisfaction, well-being, and motivation;
- Describe methods and measures
- Key factors
- Differences based on categories/types of employees
[5.3b(1)]

Relate satisfaction, well-being, and motivation results to key business results
[5.3b(4)]

Info from 7.3

Identify improvement priorities to the employee support climate
[5.3b(4)]

Build and enhance the employees' support climate

Provide services, benefits, and actions to enhance employees' work climate; describe how these services are selected considering the needs of different categories of employees
[5.3b(1)]

Services/facilities/opportunities to enhance satisfaction and well-being might include:
- Counseling
- Career development
- Recreational and cultural activities
- Non-work-related education
- Day care
- Special personal leave
- Flexible work hours
- Outplacement
- Retirement benefits
- Health/disability insurance

Ensure the work climate supports the needs of a diverse workforce
[5.3b(1)]

Define measures and safety/health targets for each employee group or class based on differences in work environment; include employee input in establishing measures and targets
[5.3a]

Maintain a safe, healthful, and secure work environment
[5.3a]

Evaluate processes to assess and improve safety, health, well-being, satisfaction, and motivation
[scoring guidelines]

Results are reported in 7.3

5.3 Employee Well-Being and Satisfaction Item Linkages

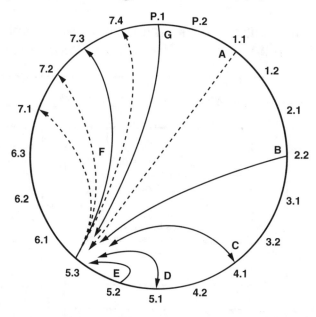

NATURE OF RELATIONSHIP	
A	Leaders [1.1a(2)] are responsible for creating effective systems to enhance employee satisfaction, well-being, and motivation [5.3].
B	Human resource development plans [2.2a(3)] typically address or set the context for safety, motivation, satisfaction, and well-being systems [5.3].
C	Key benchmarking data [4.1a(3)] are used to design processes to enhance employee motivation and well-being [5.3b]. Information regarding employee well-being and motivation [5.3b(3)] is used to gain a better understanding of problems and performance capabilities [4.1].
D	High motivation [5.3] enhances employee participation, self-direction, and initiative [5.1], and vice versa.
E	Effective training [5.2a(3)] is critical to maintaining and improving a safe, healthful work environment [5.3a] and improved employee motivation, satisfaction, and well-being [5.3b].
F	Systems that enhance employee motivation, satisfaction, and well-being [5.3] can boost performance [7.2 and 7.4] and customer satisfaction [7.1]. Specific results of employee well-being and satisfaction systems are reported in 7.3.
G	Employee characteristics such as educational levels, workforce and job diversity, the existence of bargaining units, the use of contract employees, and other special requirements [P.1a(3)] help set the context for tailoring benefits, services, and satisfaction assessment methods for employees according to various types and categories [5.3b(1,2, and 3)].

IF YOU DON'T DO WHAT THE CRITERIA REQUIRE...

Item Reference	Possible Adverse Consequences
5.3a	The failure to improve workplace health, safety, and ergonomics may increase employee accidents and illness, reduce employee effectiveness, and negatively impact morale and motivation. Poor working conditions can distract employees, reduce productivity, and increase errors, rework, cycle time, and waste, to name a few. Failing to involve employees in the identification of potential health, safety, and ergonomics issues may cause the organization to overlook and fail to correct those problems. In addition, if significant variation exists in the work environment for different employee groups or work units, employees are likely to face different workplace health, safety, and ergonomic issues. For example, carpal tunnel syndrome (repetitive stress injuries) may be a problem for people who do substantial keypunching but not for certain employees on the shop floor. Those employees may be more concerned with injury from lifting heavy objects. Accordingly, the failure to define performance measures and establish targets for each key environmental factor and each distinct employee group increases the likelihood the problems will go unnoticed and those employees will be distracted from their work, suboptimizing performance.
5.3b(1)	Factors that affect employee well-being, satisfaction, and motivation can vary significantly from organization to organization or within an organization from site to site, or among different groups of employees in the same organization. The failure to determine the key factors affecting employee well-being, satisfaction, and motivation for each employee group or segment may make it difficult to identify key problems and take appropriate corrective action. The inability to identify and correct these problems can reduce employee morale and motivation which, in turn, hurts productivity and ultimately customer satisfaction.
5.3b(2)	Just as different employee groups may have different needs for safety, different groups of employees may need different support services and benefits to keep them from being distracted in their work. For example, in one company employees located in an extremely rural area lost an entire day of work traveling to a dentist or physician to deal with a toothache or a minor medical problem. Locating a trailer with dental and health professionals near the plant entrance minimized the time employees had to be absent from work due to a medical problem. A sister plant in the same company, located near a major metropolitan area, had plenty of dentists and physicians nearby and determined that its employees would be better served by an in-house exercise and wellness program. When an organization fails to identify and tailor benefits and services to the needs of its diverse workforce, it may increase distractions and reduce optimum employee participation and performance. Suboptimum employee performance hurts productivity.
5.3b(3)	Because the factors that affect employee well-being, satisfaction, and motivation can vary significantly among the diverse groups of employees, if an organization fails to differentiate assessment methods and measures it may not be able to determine accurately the existence of problems and take appropriate corrective action. The failure to identify and correct a

Continued

IF YOU DON'T DO WHAT THE CRITERIA REQUIRE...	*(continued)*
	problem that adversely affects employee well-being, satisfaction, and motivation can contribute to operational inefficiency, waste resources, and reduce product and service quality and customer satisfaction. Failing to consider data that relate to employee well-being and satisfaction such as absenteeism, grievances, and undesired employee attrition may also prevent a problem from being identified and corrected. Finally, the "one size fits all" method of assessing employee well-being and satisfaction (such as the *annual* climate survey) may fail to take into account parts of the organization that may be undergoing change and face more turmoil than other parts of the organization. For organizations that are relatively stable, an annual survey may be appropriate. However, for organizations (or parts of organizations) that face a more volatile, unstable environment, more frequent assessments may be required. The failure to ask the right questions, at the right time, and in the right manner, may prevent the organization from learning about and correcting serious problems that may adversely affect performance and productivity.
5.3b(4)	When deciding what actions to take to improve the work environment (based on the results of appropriate surveys and related data), organizations may waste resources if they do not set priorities for improvement that are likely to optimize business results. In the example above [5.3b(2)], the plant manager could have installed a workout room and shower facilities rather than a health services trailer. However, analysis revealed that exercise facilities would have minimum impact on productivity, where as the health-care trailer would save hundreds of days each year in lost time due to employee absenteeism. Organizations risk wasting resources if they fail to understand the likely impact on business results of the improvement priorities they set in response to employee satisfaction assessment findings.

5.3 EMPLOYEE WELL-BEING AND SATISFACTION— SAMPLE EFFECTIVE PRACTICES

A. Work Environment

• Issues and concerns relating to employee health, safety, and workplace environment are used to design the work environment for all groups of employees. Plans exist to optimize working conditions and eliminate adverse conditions.

• Root causes for health and safety problems are systematically identified and eliminated. Corrective actions are communicated widely to help prevent the problem in other parts of the organization.

• Targets are set and reviewed for all key health, safety, and ergonomic factors affecting the employees' work environment. Employees are directly involved in setting these targets.

B. Employee Support and Satisfaction

• Special activities and services are available for employees. These are quite varied, depending on the needs of different employee categories. Examples include the following:

   – Flexible benefits plan including: health care; on-site day care; dental; portable retirement; education (both work and non-work-related); maternity, paternity, and family illness leave.

   – Group purchasing power program where the number of participating merchants is increasing steadily.

   – Special facilities for employee meetings to discuss their concerns.

• Senior leaders build a work climate that addresses the needs of a diverse workforce. Recruitment and training are tools to enhance the work climate.

• Key employee satisfaction opinion indicators are gathered periodically based on the stability of the organization (organizations in the midst of rapid change conduct assessments more frequently). Supervisors, managers, and leaders take consistent and prompt action to improve conditions identified through these employee satisfaction surveys.

• On-demand electronic surveys are available for quick response and tabulations any time managers need employee satisfaction feedback. Whenever the survey is completed, managers always follow-up promptly to make improvements identified by the survey that relate to key business results.

• Satisfaction data are derived from employee focus groups, e-mail data, employee satisfaction survey results, turnover, absenteeism, stress-related disorders, and other data that reflect employee satisfaction. (A key employee satisfaction indicator is one that reflects conditions affecting employee morale and motivation.)

• Managers use the results of these surveys to focus improvements in work systems and enhance employee satisfaction. Actions to improve satisfaction are clearly tied to assessments so employees understand the value of the assessment, and the improvement initiatives do not appear random or capricious.

• Employee satisfaction indicators are correlated with drivers of business success to help identify where resources should be placed to provide maximum business benefit.

• Methods to improve how employee satisfaction is determined are systematically evaluated and improved. Techniques to actually improve employee satisfaction and well-being are, themselves, evaluated and refined consistently.

6 Process Management—85 Points

The Process Management Category examines the key aspects of your organization's process management, including customer-focused design, product and service delivery, key business, and support processes. This Category encompasses all key processes and all work units.

Process Management is the focal point within the Criteria for all key work processes. Built into the category are the central requirements for efficient and effective process management: effective design; a prevention orientation; linkage to suppliers and partners and a focus on supply chain integration; operational performance; cycle time; and evaluation, continuous improvement, and organizational learning.

Agility, cost reduction, and cycle time reduction are increasingly important in all aspects of process management and organizational design. In simplest terms, agility refers to an organization's ability to adapt quickly and effectively to changing requirements. Depending on the nature of the organization's strategy and markets, flexibility might mean rapid changeover from one product to another, rapid response to changing demands, or the ability to produce a wide range of customized services. Agility might demand special strategies such as implementing modular designs, sharing components, sharing manufacturing lines, and providing specialized training. Agility also increasingly involves outsourcing decisions, agreements with key suppliers, and novel partnering arrangements.

Cost and cycle time reduction often involve many of the same process management strategies as achieving agility. Thus, it is crucial to utilize key measures for these requirements in the overall process management.

Process management contains three Items that evaluate the management of product and service processes, business processes, and support processes.

Product and Service Processes
(considered to be core processes required to produce and deliver the organization's main products and services)

- Design, develop, and introduce products and services to meet customer requirements, operational performance requirements, and market requirements

- Ensure a rapid, efficient, trouble-free introduction

- Manage and continuously improve operating processes

Business Processes
(nonproduct/nonservice processes that are critical to business growth and success)

- Design and perform business processes to meet all requirements

- Use customer feedback, supplier feedback, and in-process measures to control and improve the performance of these processes

- Manage and continuously improve business processes

Support Processes
(provide support to core and business processes)

- Design, develop, and provide products and services to meet internal customer requirements

- Use internal customer feedback and in-process measures to control and improve the performance of these processes

- Manage and continuously improve support processes

6.1   Product and Service Processes (45 points)
Approach/Deployment Scoring

Describe how your organization manages key processes for product and service design and delivery.

Within your response, include answers to the following questions:

a. *Design Processes*

(1) What are your design processes for products/services and their related production/delivery systems and processes?

(2) How do you incorporate changing customer/market requirements into product/service designs and production/delivery systems and processes?

(3) How do you incorporate new technology, including e-technology, into products/services and into production/delivery systems and processes, as appropriate?

(4) How do your design processes address design quality and cycle time, transfer of learning from past projects and other parts of the organization, cost control, new design technology, productivity, and other efficiency/effectiveness factors?

(5) How do you design your production/delivery systems and processes to meet all key operational performance requirements?

(6) How do you coordinate and test your design and production/delivery systems and processes? Include how you prevent defects/rework and facilitate trouble-free and timely introduction of products/services.

b. *Production/Delivery Processes*

(1) What are your key production/delivery processes and their key performance requirements?

(2) How does your day-to-day operation of key production/delivery processes ensure meeting key performance requirements?

(3) What are your key performance measures/indicators used for the control and improvement of these processes? Include how in-process measures and real-time customer and supplier/partner input are used in managing your product and service processes, as appropriate.

(4) How do you perform inspections, tests, and process/performance audits to minimize warranty and/or rework costs, as appropriate? Include your prevention-based processes for controlling inspection and test costs, as appropriate.

(5) How do you improve your production/delivery systems and processes to achieve better process performance and improvements to products/services, as appropriate? How are improvements shared with other organizational units and processes and your suppliers/partners, as appropriate?

Continued on next page

6.1 Product and Service Processes—continued

Notes:

N1. Product and service design, production, and delivery processes differ greatly among organizations, depending on many factors. These factors include the nature of your products and services, technology requirements, issues of modularity and parts commonality, customer and supplier relationships and involvement, and product and service customization. Responses to Item 6.1 should be based upon the most critical requirements for your business.

N2. Responses to Item 6.1 should include how your customers and key suppliers and partners are involved in your design processes, as appropriate.

N3. The results of operational improvements in your product and service design and delivery processes should be reported in Item 7.4. Results of improvements in product and service performance should be reported in Item 7.1.

This Item [6.1] looks at the organization's key product and service design and delivery processes, with the aim of improving marketplace and operational performance.

The first part of this Item [6.1a] looks at key design processes for products and services and their related production and delivery processes. The best organizations have an effective process to address key customer/market requirements as well as requirements for new technology, including e-technology and conducting business through the Internet.

- Design approaches could differ appreciably depending upon the nature of products and services—whether the products/services are entirely new, variants, or involve major or minor process changes. Factors that might need to be considered in design include: safety; long-term performance; environmental impact; "green" manufacturing; measurement capability; process capability; manufacturability; maintainability; variability in customer expectations requiring product/service options; supplier capability; and documentation.

- Effective design also must consider cycle time and efficiency of production and delivery processes. This might involve detailed mapping of manufacturing or service processes and redesigning or reengineering those processes to achieve higher levels of efficiency, as well as to meet changing customer requirements. The best organizations have mechanisms in place that encourage learning from past design projects.

- New technology, including e-technology, should be incorporated into the design of products and services. E-technology might include new ways of electronically sharing information with suppliers/partners, communicating with customers and giving them continuous (24/7) access, and automated information transfer from in-service products requiring maintenance in the field.

- Frequently defective design processes require organizations to capture information from customer complaint data that are collected using the processes described in Item 3.2a. Immediate access to customer complaint data allows the organization to make design or production

changes quickly to prevent problems from occurring or recurring.

- The best performing organizations consider requirements of suppliers and/or business partners at the design stage. This minimizes the chances that important design issues are not achievable because of supplier and/or partner limitations. Similarly, effective design systems take into account all stakeholders in the value chain.

- To enhance design process efficiency, all related design and production activities should be coordinated within top-performing organizations. Coordination of design and production/delivery processes involves all work units and/or individuals who will take part in production/delivery and whose performance materially affects overall process outcome. This might include groups such as research and development (R&D), marketing, design, product/process engineering, and key suppliers. If many design projects are carried out in parallel, or if the organization's products require parts, equipment, and facilities that are used for other products, coordination of resources frequently provides a means to significantly reduce unit costs and time to market.

- Design processes should cover all key operational performance requirements and appropriate coordination and testing to ensure effective product/service launch without need for rework.

The last part of this Item [6.1b] looks at how the organization ensures its production and delivery processes meet key performance requirements consistently.

- The best-performing organizations accurately and completely define key production/delivery processes, their key performance requirements, and key performance measures. These requirements and measures provide the basis for maintaining and improving products, services, and production/delivery processes. These organizations also define how performance relative to these requirements is determined and maintained. Increasingly, these requirements usually include the need for agility—speed and flexibility—to adapt to change.

- Top organizations minimize the need for inspections, tests, and audits to avoid rework and warranty costs, because they have implemented processes to prevent problems from occurring in the first place. Sometimes these processes involve error proofing, which make it impossible to do the wrong thing the wrong way (for example, electrical cords on today's appliances have one plug blade wider than the other to prevent it from being inserted incorrectly into a wall outlet).

- Organizations also use key in-process measurements at critical points in processes to minimize problems and costs that may result from deviations from expected performance. Achieving expected performance frequently requires setting performance levels or standards to guide decision making. When deviations occur, corrective action is required to restore the performance of the process to its design specifications. Depending on the nature of the process, the corrective action could involve technical and/or human considerations. Proper corrective action involves changes at the source (root cause) of the deviation. Effective corrective action minimizes the likelihood of this type of variation occurring again or anywhere else in the organization.

- Finally, the best-performing organizations have a system in place to evaluate and improve production/delivery processes to achieve better process efficiency and better products and services. Better performance means not only better quality from the customers' perspective but also results in better financial and operational performance—such as productivity. A variety of process improvement approaches are commonly used. These approaches include:

  - Sharing successful strategies across the organization

  - Process analysis and research (for example, process mapping, optimization experiments, and error proofing)

  - Benchmarking

  - Using alternative technology

  - Using information from customers of the processes—within and outside of the organization

New process improvement approaches might also involve the use of cost data to evaluate alternatives and set improvement priorities. Taken together, these approaches offer a wide range of possibilities, including complete redesign of key processes to achieve new levels of operational excellence.

6.1 Product and Service Processes

How products and services as well as production/delivery processes are designed, managed, and improved

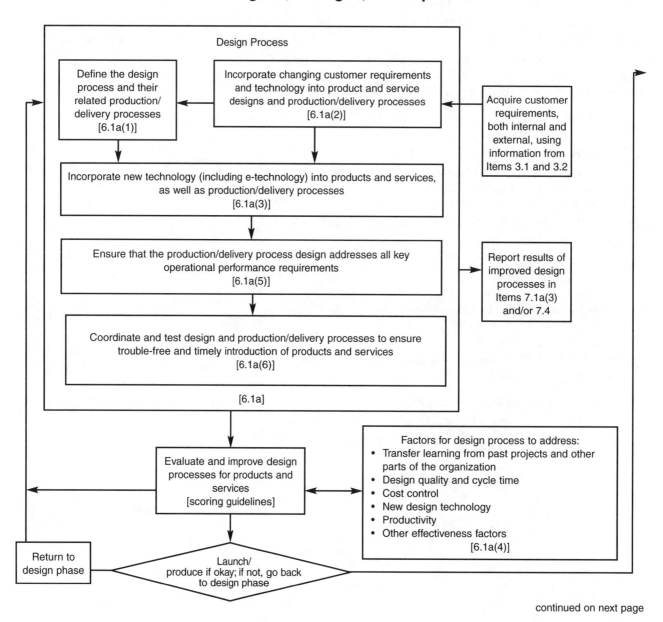

continued on next page

continued from previous page

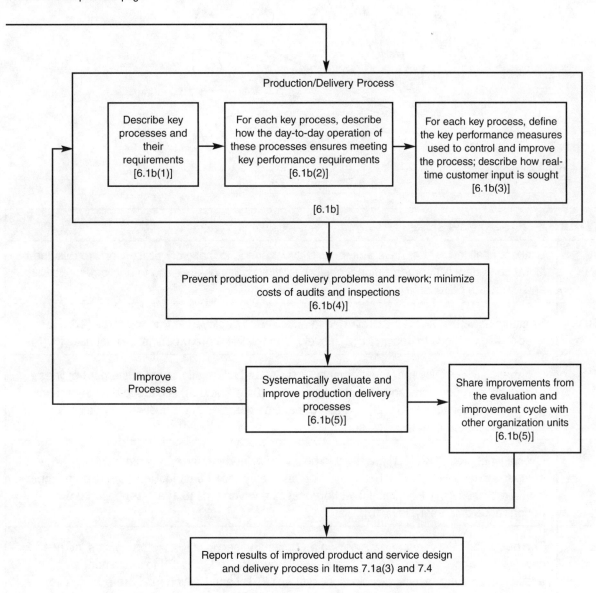

6.1 Product and Service Processes Item Linkages

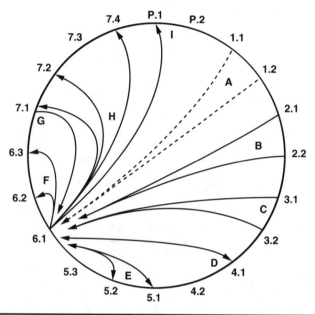

NATURE OF RELATIONSHIP		
A		Leaders at all levels [1.1] have a responsibility for ensuring that work processes are designed [6.1a] consistent with organizational objectives, including those relating to public responsibility and corporate citizenship [1.2a].
B		Strategic objectives [2.1b(1)], converted to actions and deployed to the workforce [2.2a], are used to align actions to design [6.1a], develop, and deliver core products and services [6.1b].
C		Information about customer requirements [3.1a(2)] and information from customer hot lines (complaints) through customer-contact employees [3.2a(2 and 3)] is used to design or modify products and services [(6.1a(2)] and make real-time changes in production and delivery [6.1b(3)] to better meet requirements.
D		Critical work processes [6.1] are used to help identify and prioritize benchmarking or comparison targets [4.1a(3)]. Benchmarking and comparison data [4.1a(3)] are used to improve work processes [6.1]. Priorities for work process improvements [6.1] are set based on performance data analysis [4.1b].
E		The design and delivery of new/modified products and services [6.1] often defines the need for new flexible work systems [5.1a(1)] and skills to be acquired [5.2a(2)] to implement them. In addition, high performance, flexible work systems [5.1a] and training [5.2] are essential to improving work processes [6.1].
F		New or modified design or delivery processes for core business areas [6.1] can help define requirements and set priorities for critical business services [6.2] and support services [6.3].

Continued

NATURE OF RELATIONSHIP		*continued*
G	Information about customer satisfaction [7.1] is used to target improvement efforts in product and service design and development processes [6.1b(3)].	
H	Products and services that are designed to meet customer requirements [6.1a(2 and 5)] and have a trouble-free introduction [6.1a(6)], and consistently meet desired production and delivery requirements [6.1b], should reflect high levels of customer satisfaction [7.1a(1)], loyalty [7.1a(2)], and product and service performance [7.1a(3)]; better operational efficiencies [7.4a(1)], and solid financial results [7.2].	
I	The information in P.1a(1) derives from the delivery processes described in 6.1a and helps set the context for the examiner review of those processes [6.1b(1)].	

IF YOU DON'T DO WHAT THE CRITERIA REQUIRE...	
Item Reference	**Possible Adverse Consequences**
6.1a(1)	The requirements of design processes can vary significantly within an organization based on the nature of the products and services being delivered to customers. Design processes may also vary based on whether the products and services are new or only involve minor variations to current product and service offerings. In any event, a design process that fails to consider the key requirements for products and services, and other factors such as environmental impact, process capability, measurement capability, customer service expectations, supplier capability, and customer documentation requirements (such as found in ISO 9000), may make it difficult or impossible for the organization to achieve desired results (satisfy customers) in an efficient and profitable manner.
6.1a(2)	In an effort to control the design process and ensure consistency, organizations frequently develop elaborate checkpoints or "gates" that must be passed as part of bringing a new product or service into the marketplace. The gates serve a two fold purpose: (1) assuring the focus on customer requirements is maintained throughout the design process and responds to changing customer and market demands, and (2) assuring design maturity is on track. The first deals with fully responding to customer requirements by providing value in the eyes of the customer. The second addresses the ability of the organization to do this in an efficient, effective, and profitable manner. Design processes that are not capable of incorporating changing customer or market requirements into products and services in a timely fashion may find it difficult to remain agile and competitive. For example, an organization that receives customer change requirements at a faster pace than they can implement the changes can be virtually paralyzed. Unwieldy design systems that are unable to meet changing customer requirements often lead to frustrated employees, excessive delay, and ultimately dissatisfied customers and lost business. On the other hand, changing customer requirements—often driven today by the introduction of new technology—can render a design obsolete before it ever gets to market.
6.1a(3)	In today's highly competitive, global economy, speed and agility are important factors that distinguish the best-performing organizations from the rest. The best-performing organizations provide their customers with value faster (speed) and across a wider range of customer areas (agility) than their competition. The speed and agility offered by new technologies enhances that value. As a consequence, the leaders are able to distinguish their organizations in chosen markets, keeping their current customers and acquiring new ones. Increasingly, the failure to use the appropriate technologies limits the organization's ability to keep pace with aggressive competitors. These organizations may have the latest computers but those computers may not be used effectively to accelerate delivery of the things that are important to customers. One Fortune 500 company, learning that its customers placed a premium on accurate bills being delivered on time, acquired and implemented new technology to dramatically speed up its billing cycle. Unfortunately, the billing process itself was not capable of rendering an accurate invoice. Customers received

Continued

IF YOU DON'T DO WHAT THE CRITERIA REQUIRE...	*continued*
	their inaccurate invoices faster than ever. Using technology to accelerate a bad process only produces unsatisfactory results faster. The failure to incorporate the *appropriate* technologies can have significant adverse affects on an organization's ability to bring value to its customers and to operate in an efficient and effective manner.
6.1a(4)	Eliminating unnecessary steps in any work process tends to reduce variation (increasing quality), reduce cycle time, and reduce cost. In addition, learning from the successes and mistakes of others helps prevent employees from repeating the same problems (which add rework, waste, and delay). When designing new products and services and related production and delivery systems, the failure to consider factors such as cost control, new technology, variability, and ways to enhance productivity and efficiency typically adds unnecessary cost, delay, and rework, making it more difficult to meet the increasing demands of customers and the marketplace.
6.1a(5)	Organizations that fail to take into account all key operational performance requirements when designing production and delivery systems frequently find that the system they designed is inadequate. Design flaws produce undesired results and nonconforming products and services. This, in turn, requires even more rework or more people-intensive services, which can add significant delay and prevent the organization from achieving its objectives.
6.1a(6)	Organizations can always tell if a process is producing desired results by waiting for those results and checking to see if the product and service meet customer and operational requirements. Unfortunately, waiting for the end of the process to learn that it has not produced desired results is time consuming and expensive, since most costs may have already been sunk. The earlier an organization can determine if a process is not likely to produced desired results, the earlier it can take corrective action to minimize rework, scrap, delay, and unnecessary cost. If an organization does not test its design processes and related production/delivery systems and is unable to ensure that all work units or individuals are properly coordinated and aligned to produce desired results, it will be unable to avoid the costs of nonconformance (costs arising from the failure to do it right the first time).
6.1b(1)	Organizations that fail to identify the key performance requirements of its production and delivery processes may find it difficult to monitor the day-to-day performance of these processes and ensure desired results are consistently produced. For example, when customers require their goods be *delivered* "on time" they expect to *receive* them at a predetermined time and location. High-performing companies then align their supply chain and internal core production, delivery, and support processes to fulfill those requirements. Problems can arise if requirements are not understood correctly. For example, one Fortune 500 company interpreted "on-time" delivery as a function of when material left its shipping dock. Unfortunately, the time that the parts were shipped did not guarantee they would be received by the customer on time; and a critical order was delivered late (the company had to substantially discount the price to recover). Because the company was internally focused, its leaders did not appreciate the difference between shipping date and the customer-required delivery date. Unless performance

Continued

IF YOU DON'T DO WHAT THE CRITERIA REQUIRE...	*continued*
	requirements for key production and delivery processes are accurately identified and understood, organizations may find it difficult to satisfy its customers and the marketplace.
6.1b(2)	The best-performing organizations are able to consistently deliver products and services that meet key performance requirements. They do this by identifying key processes, monitoring them regularly, and improving then continuously. The failure to ensure consistent day-to-day operation of production and delivery processes increases the likelihood of defects, which contribute to rework, waste, delay, and excessive costs. In the earlier case of the Fortune 500 company with the on-time delivery problems, as part of attacking the problem they established a bar-coding system at retail sites that provided them information on both the timeliness of deliveries and the inventory depletion rate. The company was able predict demand based on the level of remaining inventory and previous ordering behaviors and more consistently ensure that new product was *delivered* on time.
6.1b(3)	Without key measures or indicators of process performance, it is difficult for employees to determine if the process is working as it should. Without in-process measures, employees must generally wait until they receive results at the end of the line to determine if production and delivery processes are working as intended. The failure to collect and analyze in-process data (using tools such as C_{pk} or statistical process control charts), makes it more difficult for employees to know when to adjust a process to make it work better. Inappropriate or unnecessary adjustments can actually increase variation and decrease product quality — the classic statistical problem of "tampering" or "chasing tails."
	Customers can usually determine quickly if the products and services they receive meet (or exceed) their requirements. They are in a good position to provide near real-time feedback that will enable employees to make adjustments to improve product and service production and delivery processes. The failure to gather and use this information in a timely fashion makes it more difficult for organizations to make appropriate changes to reduce rework costs and increase customer satisfaction.
6.1b(4)	Sometimes products and services initially meet customer requirements but fail later in the products/service lifecycle. Organizations that do not gather information about product and service suitability during the expected lifecycle may miss opportunities to modify design, production, or delivery systems and reduce rework costs or warranty claims. The best-performing organizations, however, do not rely on excessive inspection and testing to determine if products and services are likely to meet customer requirements. Instead, these organizations develop processes that prevent problems using tools and techniques such as error proofing. The best that testing or inspection can hope to accomplish is to uncover and correct a problem before the customer receives the product or service. Although this is better than shipping defective products, it is still more costly to fix the problem than to prevent it from happening in the first place.

Continued

IF YOU DON'T DO WHAT THE CRITERIA REQUIRE...	*continued*

6.1b(5)	Organizations that fail to systematically evaluate and improve production and delivery systems and processes often seem to lag behind the competition. Consider two comparable organizations, each using similar processes to develop and deliver similar products and services. Let's also assume that the organizations are equally competitive today. However, one organization has embedded into its work processes an ongoing evaluation and improvement of its design, production, and delivery systems; the other has not. As time passes the first organization begins to see the impact of improved work processes. It is able to produce goods and services faster, better, and cheaper than its competitor. It has been able to pass a portion of its cost savings on to its customers (lowering prices), keeping the rest as increased profit. As a result of better, more timely, and less expensive products, it is acquiring greater market share—at the expense of its competitor—and making its stockholders exceedingly happy as its share price increases. In addition, the first organization has been able to accelerate performance by sharing improvements with other organizational units so they can get better as well. The organization that does not systematically improve continues to fall further and further behind in a highly competitive environment (or as the popular adage acclaims: today, if you're standing still [not continuously improving], you're falling behind).

6.1 PRODUCT AND SERVICE PROCESSES—SAMPLE EFFECTIVE PRACTICES

A. Design Processes

- A systematic, iterative process (such as quality function deployment) is used to maintain a focus on the voice of the customer and convert customer requirements into product or service design, production, and delivery.

- Product design requirements are systematically translated into process specifications, with measurement plans to monitor process consistency.

- The work of various functions is coordinated to bring the product or service through the design-to-delivery phases. Functional barriers between units have been eliminated organizationwide.

- Concurrent engineering is used to operate several processes (for example, product and service planning, R&D, manufacturing, marketing, supplier certification) in parallel as much as possible, rather than operating in sequence. All activities are closely coordinated through effective communication and teamwork.

- Internal process capacity and supplier capability, using measures such as C_{pk}, are reviewed and considered before production and delivery process designs or plans are finalized.

- Market, design, production, service, and delivery reviews occur at defined intervals or as needed.

- Steps are taken (such as design testing or prototyping) to ensure that the production and delivery process will work as designed, and will meet customer requirements.

- Design processes are evaluated and improvements have been made so that future designs are developed faster (shorter cycle time), at lower cost, and with higher quality, relative to key product or service characteristics that predict customer satisfaction.

B. Production/Delivery Processes

- Performance requirements (from Item 6.1a, design processes, and Item 3.1, customer requirements) are set using facts and data and are monitored using statistical or other process control techniques.

- Production and service delivery processes are measured and tracked. Measures (quantitative and qualitative) should reflect or assess the extent to which customer requirements are met, as well as production consistency.

- For processes that produce defects (out-of-control processes), root causes are quickly and systematically identified and corrective action is taken to prevent their recurrence.

- Corrections are monitored and verified. Improvements are shared throughout the organization.

- Processes are systematically reviewed to improve productivity, reduce cycle time and waste, and increase quality.

- Tools are used—such as flowcharting, work redesign, and reengineering—throughout the organization to improve work processes.

- Benchmarking, competitive comparison data, or information from customers of the process (in or out of the organization) are used to gain insight to improve processes.

- Information about customer requirements, complaints, concerns, and reactions to products and services are captured "near real-time" and used directly by workers to improve the production delivery processes.

6.2 Business Processes (25 points)
Approach/Deployment Scoring

Describe how your organization manages its key processes that lead to business growth and success.

Within your response, include answers to the following questions:

a. Business Processes

(1) What are your key business processes for business growth and success?

(2) How do you determine key business process requirements, incorporating input from customers and suppliers/partners, as appropriate? What are the key requirements for these processes?

(3) How do you design and perform these processes to meet all the key requirements?

(4) What are your key performance measures/indicators used for the control and improvement of these processes? Include how in-process measures and customer and supplier feedback are used in managing your business processes, as appropriate.

(5) How do you minimize overall costs associated with inspections, tests, and process/performance audits, as appropriate?

(6) How do you improve your business processes to achieve better performance and to keep them current with business needs and directions? How are improvements shared with other organizational units and processes, as appropriate?

Notes:

N1. Your key business processes are those nonproduct/nonservice processes that are considered most important to business growth and success by your organization's senior leaders. These might include processes for innovation, research and development, technology acquisition, information and knowledge management, supply chain management, supplier partnering, outsourcing, mergers and acquisitions, global expansion, project management, and sales/marketing. The key business processes to be included in Item 6.2 are distinctive to your organization and how you operate.

N2. To provide as complete and concise a response as possible for your key business processes, you might want to use a tabular format identifying the key processes and the attributes of each as called for in questions 6.2a(1)–6.2a(4).

N3. The results of improvements in your key business processes and key business process performance results should be reported in Item 7.4.

This Item [6.2] examines the organization's key nonproduct and nonservice business processes, with the aim of improving business success. A nonproduct/nonservice business process is one that is critical to the future success and business growth of the organization but does not involve actually producing products or services. These processes frequently relate to an organization's strategic objectives and critical success factors. As such, it might be useful to consider them as "strategic business processes." These are not core business activities. However, they may be considered as more critical than ordinary support activities. Key business processes might include the following:

- Processes for innovation, including empowering employees to generate and implement new ideas.

- Research and development, involving dedicated units and distributing R&D responsibility throughout the organization.

- Technology acquisition, which may involve partnering, acquisitions, mergers, invention, or other techniques.

- Information and knowledge management, which goes beyond traditional information technology or information management activities. Knowledge management often supports knowledge transfer and knowledge sharing among all organizational units at all levels and sites within an organization.

- Mergers and acquisitions, including global expansion initiatives.

- Project management, to ensure on-time and consistent development of new programs, products, and services.

- Sales/marketing, to strengthen and expand new markets, including e-commerce.

- Supply chain management, supplier partnering, and outsourcing. For many organizations, supply chain management is an increasingly important factor in achieving productivity and profitability goals and overall business success. Suppliers and partners are receiving increasing strategic attention as organizations reevaluate and outsource their core functions. Accordingly, supply chain management processes typically fulfill two purposes: to help improve the performance of suppliers and partners; and in turn, contribute to better internal operational performance. Supply chain management might include processes for supplier selection, with the aim of reducing the total number of suppliers and increasing preferred supplier and partnering agreements.

Given the diverse nature of these processes, the requirements and performance characteristics might vary significantly for different processes.

For each key business process the organization identifies key design requirements. In top-performing organizations, key business processes are designed and executed to meet all performance requirements incorporating input from customers and suppliers/partners, just as they do for core product and service processes.

In addition, key performance measures are identified and customer and supplier feedback are used to better control and improve the execution of these business processes. As with core production and delivery processes, top-performing organizations minimize costs associated with inspections, tests, and audits through use of prevention-based processes. Finally, as with all other processes, the best organizations improve key business processes to achieve better performance and to keep them current with changing business needs and directions.

6.2 Business Processes

How key nonproduct and nonservice processes that are critical to business growth and success are designed, managed, and improved

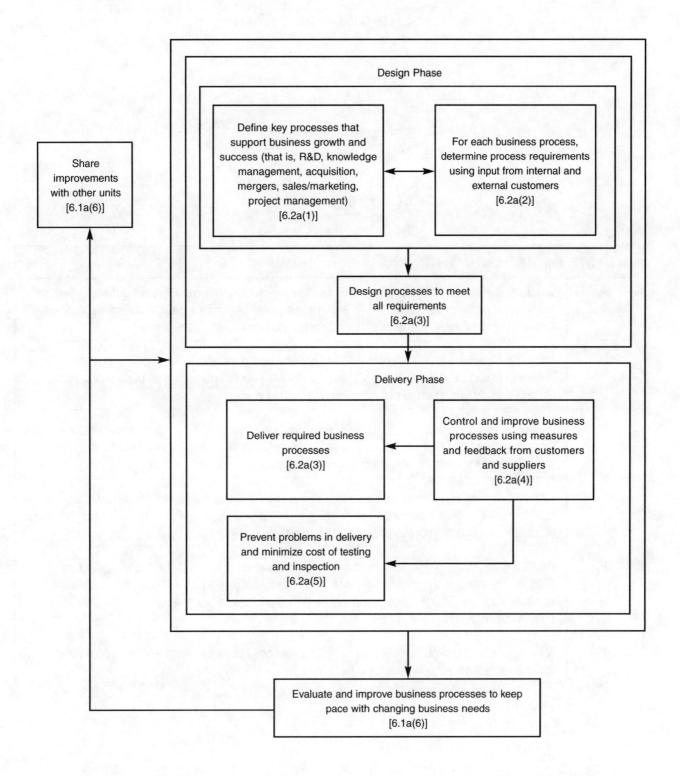

6.2 Business Processes Item Linkages

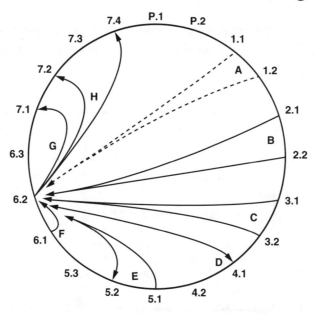

NATURE OF RELATIONSHIP	
A	Leaders at all levels [1.1] have a responsibility for ensuring that business processes critical for growth and success are designed [6.2a(2)] consistent with organizational objectives, including those relating to public responsibility and corporate citizenship [1.2a].
B	Strategic objectives [2.1b(1)], converted to actions and deployed to the workforce [2.2a], are used to align actions to design [6.2a(1, 2, and 3)] and perform critical business services [6.2a(3 and 4)] important to organizational growth and success.
C	Customer requirements data [3.1a(2)], customer questions [3.2a(2)], complaints/complaint resolution [3.2a(3)], and satisfaction/dissatisfaction [3.2b(1, 2, and 3)] are used to identify requirements for critical business processes [6.2a(2)].
D	Critical business processes such as R&D, knowledge management, and information technology [6.2] are used to help identify and prioritize benchmarking targets [4.1a(3)]. Benchmarking data [4.1a(3)] are used to improve critical business processes [6.2].
E	High-performance, flexible work systems and effective recognition [5.1a(1 and 3)] and training [5.2] are essential to improving critical business processes [6.2]. In addition, some business services such as R&D [6.2] can help define new flexible work systems [5.1a] and skills that need to be acquired [5.2a].
F	New or modified design or delivery processes for core business areas [6.1] can help define requirements and set priorities for critical business services [6.2].

Continued

NATURE OF RELATIONSHIP		*continued*
G	Information about customer satisfaction [7.1] is used to target improvement efforts in critical business processes [6.2]. Improved critical business processes [6.2] support organizational growth and success and can be reflected in better product and service performance [7.1a(3)].	
H	Improved critical business processes [6.2] support organizational growth and success and can be reflected in better operational efficiency [7.4] and financial results [7.2].	

IF YOU DON'T DO WHAT THE CRITERIA REQUIRE...

Item Reference	Possible Adverse Consequences
6.2a(1)	The requirements of key business processes can vary significantly within an organization based on the nature of the core products and services that these business processes must support. Senior leaders are responsible for identifying those nonproduct and nonservice process that are critical for business growth and success as key business processes. Once the process has been identified as a "key business process," the requirements of Item 6.2 apply.
6.2a(2)	An organization that fails to accurately identify the performance requirements of its key business processes may find it difficult to design and optimize those processes to meet customer expectations. When business processes fail to meet requirements, resources are wasted and the objectives of the organization may be jeopardized.
6.2a(3)	Organizations that fail to take into account all key operational performance requirements when designing key business processes frequently find that the system they designed is not optimum. Design flaws produce undesired results, as well as nonconforming products and services. These, in turn, require even more rework. The failure to consistently meet the requirements of business process customers may increase the likelihood of downstream problems with the design, production, and delivery of core products and services.
6.2a(4)	Without key measures or indicators of process performance, it is difficult for employees to determine if the process is working as it should. Without in-process measures, employees must generally wait until they get the results at the end of the line to determine if the business processes worked as intended. The failure to collect and analyze in-process data makes it more difficult for employees to know when to adjust a process to make it work better. Inappropriate or unnecessary adjustments can actually increase variation and decrease product quality. Customers can usually determine quickly if the products and services they receive meet (or exceed) their requirements. They are in a good position to provide near real-time feedback that will enable employees to make adjustments to meet requirements. The failure to gather and use this information makes it more difficult for organizations to make timely changes to reduce rework costs and increase customer satisfaction.
6.2a(5)	High-performing organizations do not rely on excessive inspection and testing to determine if business process requirements are likely to be met. Conceptually, the only time to inspect is when the outcome is not known. Instead, these organizations design process controls that let them know how well the process is performing during each of its critical steps. They develop processes that prevent problems using tools and techniques such as error proofing. The best that testing or inspection can hope to accomplish is to uncover and correct a problem before the customer is disrupted. Although this is better than causing problems for customers, it is still more costly to fix the problem than to prevent it from happening in the first place.

Continued

IF YOU DON'T DO WHAT THE CRITERIA REQUIRE...	*continued*

6.2a(6)	Business processes that do not systematically improve continue to fall further and further behind in a highly competitive environment. Unless business process units are systematically and continually improving, they may not be able to effectively provide critical support to core product and service delivery units within the parent organization and may contribute to the erosion of overall capability in the parent organization. Even key business processes may be outsourced as their value becomes substandard. The failure to share effective practices with other organizational support units may cause them to waste time and other resources in redundant work—work that adds cost but not value.

6.2 BUSINESS PROCESSES— SAMPLE EFFECTIVE PRACTICES

A. Business Processes

- Key business services, which are critical to the success of the organization and support core production and delivery activities, are formally identified. These processes may include research and development, knowledge management, technology acquisition and implementation, and acquisitions and mergers to name a few. For each of these key business service areas, a formal process exists to understand customer requirements, translate those requirements into efficient processes, measure their effectiveness, and systematically improve.

- Improvements in key business services are made with the same rigor and concern for the internal and external customer as improvements in core operating processes.

- All key business services are subject to continuous review and improvements in performance and customer satisfaction.

- Systems to ensure process performance are maintained, and customer requirements are met. In-process measures are defined and monitored to ensure early alert of problem.

- Root causes of problems are systematically identified and corrected for processes that produce defects.

- Corrections are monitored and verified. Processes used and results obtained should be systematic and integrated throughout the organization.

- Key business processes are systematically reviewed to improve productivity, reduce cycle time and waste, and increase quality. Improvements in these processes are shared throughout the organization and both core work areas (related to the activities in Item 6.1) and ordinary support processes (related to the activities in Item 6.3).

- Work process simplification or improvement tools are used with measurable sustained results.

- Measurable performance goals are used to drive higher levels of performance.

- Benchmarking, competitive comparison data, or information from customers of the process (in or out of the organization) are used to gain insight to improve processes.

6.3 Support Processes (15 points)
Approach/Deployment Scoring

Describe how your organization manages its key processes that support your daily operations and your employees in delivering products and services.

Within your response, include answers to the following questions:

a. Support Processes

(1) What are your key processes for supporting your daily operations and your employees in delivering products and services?

(2) How do you determine key support process requirements, incorporating input from internal customers, as appropriate? What are the key operational requirements (such as productivity and cycle time) for these processes?

(3) How do you design these processes to meet all the key requirements?

(4) How does your day-to-day operation of key support processes ensure meeting key performance requirements?

(5) What are your key performance measures/indicators used for the control and improvement of these processes? Include how in-process measures and internal customer feedback are used in managing your support processes, as appropriate.

(6) How do you minimize overall costs associated with inspections, tests, and process/performance audits?

(7) How do you improve your support processes to achieve better performance and to keep them current with business needs and directions? How are improvements shared with other organizational units and processes, as appropriate?

Notes:

N1. Your key support processes are those that are considered most important for support of your organization's product/service design and delivery processes and daily operations. These might include finance and accounting, facilities management, legal, human resource, and administration processes.

N2. The results of improvements in your key support processes and key support process performance results should be reported in Item 7.4.

This Item [6.3] looks at the organization's key support processes, with the aim of improving overall operational performance. The organization must ensure its key support processes are designed to meet all internal operational and customer requirements.

The requirements of this Item are similar to the requirements in Items 6.1 and 6.2.

- Support processes are those that support daily operations and product and/or service delivery, but are not usually designed in detail with the products and services. The support process requirements usually do not depend significantly upon product and service characteristics. Instead, support process design requirements usually depend significantly upon internal customer requirements, and they must be coordinated and integrated to ensure efficient and effective linkage and performance.

- Support processes might include finance and accounting, software services, public relations, transportation services, food services, human resource services, legal services, plant and facilities management, and secretarial and other administrative services.

As with core operating processes, described in Item 6.1, the organization must ensure that the day-to-day operation of its key support processes consistently meet the key performance requirements. To do this, in-process measures are defined to permit rapid identification and correction of potential problems. As with other work processes, key support processes should incorporate mechanisms to obtain and use customer feedback to help identify problems and take prompt, corrective action. The organization should also minimize costs associated with inspection, tests, and audits through use of prevention-based processes, as in Items 6.1 and 6.2.

Finally, organizations should systematically evaluate and improve its key support processes to achieve better performance and to keep them current with changing business needs and directions. Top organizations evaluate and improve the performance of key support processes. Four approaches to evaluating and improving support processes are frequently used:

1. Process analysis and research

2. Benchmarking

3. Use of alternative technology

4. Use of information from customers of the processes—within and outside of the organization

Together, these approaches offer a wide range of possibilities, including complete redesign of key processes or steps within the processes.

6.3 Support Processes

How key support processes are designed, managed, and improved to improve daily operations

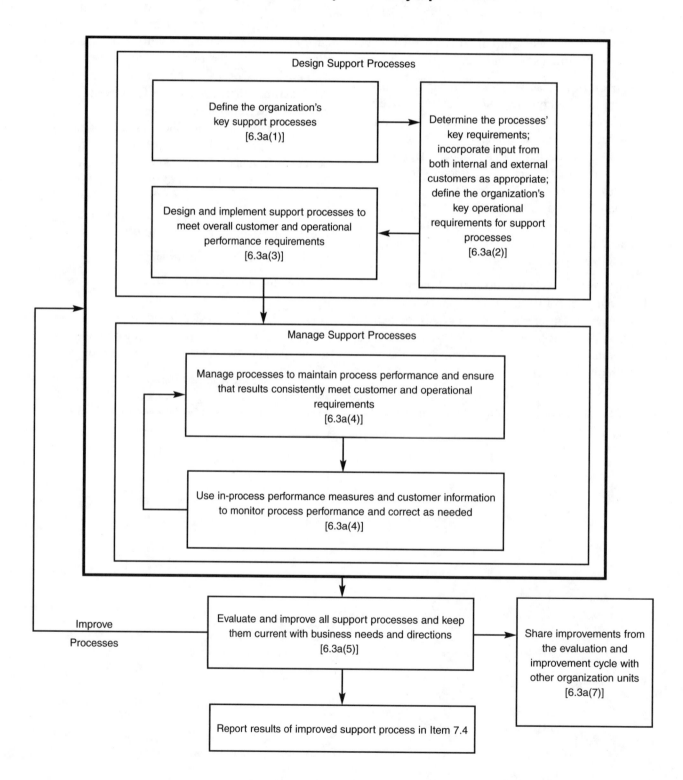

Design Support Processes

Define the organization's
key support processes
[6.3a(1)]

Determine the processes'
key requirements;
incorporate input from
both internal and external
customers as appropriate;
define the organization's
key operational
requirements for support
processes
[6.3a(2)]

Design and implement support processes to
meet overall customer and operational
performance requirements
[6.3a(3)]

Manage Support Processes

Manage processes to maintain process performance and ensure
that results consistently meet customer and operational
requirements
[6.3a(4)]

Use in-process performance measures and customer information
to monitor process performance and correct as needed
[6.3a(4)]

Improve

Processes

Evaluate and improve all support processes and keep
them current with business needs and directions
[6.3a(5)]

Share improvements from
the evaluation and
improvement cycle with
other organization units
[6.3a(7)]

Report results of improved support process in Item 7.4

6.3 Support Processes Item Linkages

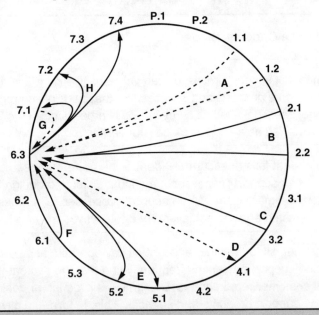

NATURE OF RELATIONSHIP	
A	Leaders at all levels [1.1] have a responsibility for ensuring that support processes are designed [6.2a(2)] consistent with organizational objectives, including those relating to public responsibility and corporate citizenship [1.2a].
B	Strategic objectives [2.1b(1)], converted to actions and deployed to the workforce [2.2a], are used to align actions to design [6.3a(1, 2, and 3)] and perform support services [6.3a(3 and 4)] important to organizational growth and success.
C	Customer questions [3.2a(2)], complaints/complaint resolution [3.2a(3)], and satisfaction/dissatisfaction [3.2b(1, 2, and 3)] are used to identify requirements for support processes [6.3a(2)].
D	Critical work processes in the support area [6.3a] are used to help identify and prioritize benchmarking targets [4.1a(3)]. Benchmarking data [4.1a(3)] are used to improve support work processes [6.3].
E	High-performance, flexible work systems [5.1a(1)] and effective recognition [5.1a(3)] and training [5.2a] are essential to improving support work processes [6.3]. In addition, design and delivery of new/modified support services [6.3] can help define new flexible work systems [5.1a(1)] and skills that need to be acquired [5.2a(2)].
F	New or modified design or delivery processes for core business areas [6.1] can help define requirements and set priorities for support services [6.3].
G	Information about customer satisfaction [7.1a] may be used to help identify improvement efforts and support work processes [6.3].
H	Improved support work processes [6.3a(7)] can lead to better product and service performance [7.1b], operational efficiency [7.4a], and financial results [7.2a].

IF YOU DON'T DO WHAT THE CRITERIA REQUIRE...	
Item Reference	**Possible Adverse Consequences**
6.3a(1)	The requirements of support processes can vary significantly within an organization based on the nature of the core products and services that these business processes must support. If a process has *not* been identified as a key business process or a core product and service process, it is reviewed as a support process under the requirements of Item 6.3.
6.3a(2)	An organization that fails to accurately identify the performance and operational requirements of its support processes may find it difficult to design those processes to meet internal customer expectations. When support processes fail to meet requirements, resources are wasted and the achievement of objectives may be jeopardized.
6.3a(3)	Organizations that fail to take into account all key operational performance requirements when designing support processes frequently find that the system they designed does not meet internal customer requirements. Design flaws produce undesired results and nonconforming support products and services. This, in turn, usually requires even more rework and disrupts core work processes.
6.3a(4)	The failure to consistently meet the requirements of support process customers may increase the likelihood of downstream problems with the design, production, and delivery of core products and services.
6.3a(5)	Without key measures or indicators of process performance, it is difficult for employees to determine if a process is working as it should. Without in-process measures, employees must generally wait until they get the results at the end of the line to determine if the support processes worked as intended. The failure to collect and analyze in-process data makes it more difficult for employees to know when to adjust a process to make it work better. Inappropriate or unnecessary adjustments can actually increase variation and decrease product quality. Internal customers can usually determine quickly if the products and services they receive meet requirements. The failure to gather and make timely use of feedback from internal customers makes it more difficult for organizations to reduce rework costs and increase customer satisfaction.
6.3a(6)	High-performing organizations do not rely on excessive inspection and testing to determine if business process requirements are likely to be met. Instead, these organizations develop processes that prevent problems using tools and techniques such as error proofing. The best that testing or inspection can hope to accomplish is to uncover and correct a problem before the internal customer is disrupted. However, it is still more costly to fix the problem than to prevent it from happening in the first place.
6.ab(7)	Support processes that do not improve may cause the support function to become so ineffective that it becomes a good target for outsourcing. These support process units may not be able to effectively provide critical support to core product and service delivery units within the parent organization and may contribute to the erosion of overall capability in the parent organization. The failure to share effective practices with other organizational support units may cause them to waste time and other resources in redundant work—work that adds cost but not value.

6.3   SUPPORT PROCESSES— SAMPLE EFFECTIVE PRACTICES

A.   Support Processes

• Support processes may include: procurement, finance and accounting, human resources, payroll, information technology systems, communications, public relations, legal affairs, maintenance, transportation, food service, facilities management, and training, to name a few. A formal process exists to understand internal customer requirements for these processes, translate those requirements into efficient service delivery, and measure their effectiveness.

• Specific improvements in support services are made with the same rigor and concern for the internal and external customer as improvements in core operating processes.

• All key support services are subject to continuous review and improvements in performance and customer satisfaction.

• Systems to ensure process performance are maintained, and customer requirements are met. In-process measures are defined and monitored to ensure early alert of problem.

• Root causes of problems are systematically identified and corrected for processes that produce defects.

• Corrections are monitored and verified. Processes used and results obtained should be systematic and integrated throughout the organization.

• Support processes are systematically reviewed to improve productivity, reduce cycle time and waste, and increase quality. Ideas are shared throughout the organization.

• Work process simplification or improvement tools are used with measurable sustained results.

• Measurable goals and related actions are used to drive higher levels of performance.

• Benchmarking, competitive comparison data, or information from customers of the process (in or out of the organization) are used to gain insight to improve processes.

7 Business Results—450 Points

> The Business Results Category examines your organization's performance and improvement in the key business areas of customer satisfaction, product and service performance, financial and marketplace performance, human resource results, and operational performance. Also examined are performance levels relative to those of competitors.

The Business Results Category provides a results focus that encompasses customers' evaluation of the organization's products and services, overall financial and market performance, and results of all key processes and process improvement activities. Through this focus, the criteria's dual purposes—superior value of offerings as viewed by customers and the marketplace, superior organizational performance reflected in operational and financial indicators, and organizational and personal learning—are maintained. Category 7 thus provides "real-time" information (measures of progress) for evaluation and improvement of processes, products, and services, aligned with overall organizational strategy.

- Item 4.1 calls for analysis of business results data and information to determine overall organizational performance.

  Together, business results present a balanced scorecard of organizational performance. Historically, businesses have been far too preoccupied with financial performance. Many performance reviews focused almost exclusively on achieving (or failing to achieve) expected levels of financial performance. As such, the results were considered "unbalanced."

- Financial results are considered "lagging" indicators of business success. Financial results are the net of all the good processes, bad processes, satisfied customers, dissatisfied customers, motivated employees, disgruntled employees, effective suppliers, and sloppy suppliers, to name a few. By the time financial indicators become available, bad products and dissatisfied customers have already occurred.

- The second most lagging indicator is customer satisfaction. By definition, customers must experience the product or service before they are in a position to comment on their satisfaction with that product or service. As with financial results, customer satisfaction is affected by many variables including process performance, employee motivation and morale, and supplier performance.

- On the other hand, leading indicators help organizations predict subsequent customer satisfaction and financial performance. Leading indicators include operational effectiveness and employee well-being and satisfaction. Supplier and partner performance, because it affects an organization's own operating performance, is also a leading indicator of customer satisfaction and financial performance.

Taken together, these measures represent a balance between leading and lagging indicators and enable decision makers to identify problems early and take corrective action.

Category 7 requires organizations to report current levels and improvement trends for the following:

- Customer satisfaction and dissatisfaction and product and service quality broken out by appropriate customer groups and market segments

- Financial and marketplace performance

- Human resource performance

- Operational performance

For all of these areas, organizations must include appropriate comparative data to enable examiners to define what "good" means. Otherwise, even though performance may be improving, it is difficult to determine whether the level of performance is good or not.

7.1   Customer-Focused Results (125 points)
Results Scoring

Summarize your organization's key customer-focused results, including customer satisfaction and product and service performance results. Segment your results by customer groups and market segments, as appropriate. Include appropriate comparative data.

Provide data and information to answer the following questions:

a.   Customer Results

(1) What are your current levels and trends in key measures/indicators of customer satisfaction and dissatisfaction, including comparisons with competitors' levels of customer satisfaction?

(2) What are your current levels and trends in key measures/indicators of customer-perceived value, customer retention, positive referral, and/or other aspects of building relationships with customers, as appropriate?

b.   Product and Service Results

What are your current levels and trends in key measures/indicators of product and service performance that are important to your customers?

Notes:

N1. Customer satisfaction and dissatisfaction results reported in this Item should relate to determination methods and data described in Item 3.2.

N2. Measures/indicators of customers' satisfaction with your products/services relative to customers' satisfaction with competitors might include objective information and data from your customers and from independent organizations.

N3. Service performance [7.1b] might include measures of success in providing nontraditional services to customers, such as Internet-based services.

This Item [7.1] looks at the organization's customer-focused performance results, with the aim of demonstrating how well the organization has been satisfying its customers and delivering product and service quality that lead to satisfaction, loyalty, and positive referral.

Organizations must provide data to demonstrate current levels, trends, and appropriate comparisons for key measures and/or indicators of:

• Customer satisfaction, dissatisfaction, and satisfaction relative to competitors

• Customer loyalty (retention), positive referral, and customer-perceived value

• Product and service performance relating to key drivers of customers' satisfaction and retention

Top-performing organizations use all relevant data to determine and help predict the organization's performance as viewed by customers.

• Relevant data and information include: customer satisfaction and dissatisfaction; retention, gains, and losses of customers and customer accounts; customer complaints and warranty claims; customer-perceived value based on quality and price; and awards, ratings, and recognition from customers and independent rating organizations.

• Relevant data and information also include measures of product and service performance that serve as indicators of customers' views and decision making relative to future purchases and relationships. These measures of product and service performance are derived from customer-related information gathered in Items 3.1 and

3.2. Improvements in these measures should show a strong, positive correlation with customer and marketplace improvement measures. The correlation between product/service performance and customer indicators is a critical management tool—a device for defining and focusing on key quality and customer requirements and for identifying product/service differentiators in the marketplace.

Product/service performance results appropriate for recording in this Item might be based upon one or more of the following:

- Internal (organizational) measurements
- Field performance
- Data collected by the organization or for the organization
- Customer surveys on product and service performance
- Attributes that cannot be accurately assessed through direct measurement (for example, ease of use) or when variability in customer expectations makes the customer's perception the most meaningful indicator (for example, courtesy)

7.1 *Customer-Focused Results*

The organization's customer satisfaction and customer dissatisfaction results using indicators of product/service performance that tend to be predictors of customer satisfaction

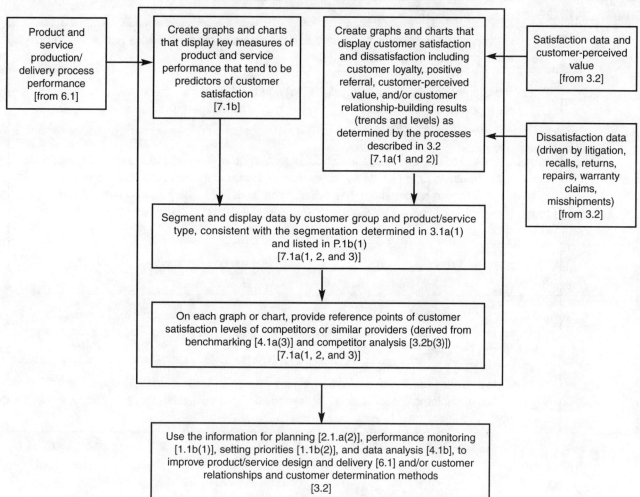

7.1 Customer-Focused Results Item Linkages

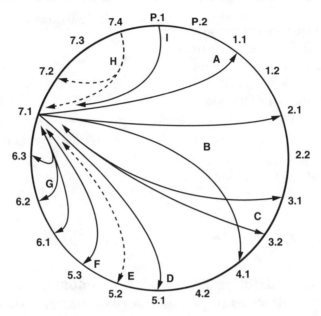

NATURE OF RELATIONSHIP	
A	Data on levels of satisfaction of customers and indicators of product/service performance [7.1] are monitored by leaders at all levels [1.1b(1)].
B	Data on customer satisfaction and loyalty [7.1a] and product/service performance indicators [7.1b] are reported and analyzed [4.1b] to assess operational performance and for strategic planning [2.1a(2)].
C	Processes used to gather intelligence about current customer requirements [3.1a(2)], strength of customer relations [3.2a(1)], and to determine customer satisfaction [3.2b(1)] produce customer satisfaction results data [7.1a]. In addition, customer satisfaction results [7.1] are used to help set customer-contact requirements (service standards) [3.2a(2)] and better understand customer requirements [3.1a(2)].
D	Recognition and rewards [5.1a] should be based, in part, on customer satisfaction results [7.1].
E	Customer satisfaction data [7.1] are monitored, in part, to assess training effectiveness [5.2a(4)]. In addition, results pertaining to customer satisfaction [7.1], reflect, in part, training effectiveness [5.2a(4)].
F	Systems to enhance employee motivation, satisfaction, and well-being [5.3] can produce higher levels of customer satisfaction [7.1] (especially from customer-contact employees) and vice versa.

Continued

NATURE OF RELATIONSHIP		*continued*
G	Data on satisfaction and dissatisfaction of customers [7.1a(1)] are used to help design products and services [6.1a(2)] and to improve operational [6.1b], business [6.2], and support [6.3] processes. These processes [6.1, 6.2 and 6.3] have a direct effect on customer satisfaction/dissatisfaction results [7.1].	
H	Better operational [7.4a] and public responsibility and citizenship [7.4b] results can enhance both financial [7.2a] and market [7.2] results and customer-focused results [7.1].	
I	The information in P.1b(1) helps examiners identify the kind of results, broken out by customer and market segment, that should be reported in Item 7.1.	

IF YOU DON'T DO WHAT THE CRITERIA REQUIRE...	
Item Reference	**Possible Adverse Consequences**
7.1	Failing to provide comparison data makes it difficult for leaders (or Baldrige examiners) to determine if the level of performance reported is good or not. Failing to provide results data for at least most areas of importance to the organization makes it difficult to determine if performance is getting better in key areas. Finally, the failure to provide this information as part of a Baldrige Award assessment is likely to reduce the score and may even prevent an organization from receiving a site visit (during which time additional results data are usually obtained).

7.1 CUSTOMER-FOCUSED RESULTS—SAMPLE EFFECTIVE RESULTS

A. Customer-Focused Results

- Trends and indicators of customer satisfaction and dissatisfaction (including complaint data), segmented by customer groups, are provided in graph and chart form for all key measures. Multiyear data are provided.

- All indicators show steady improvement. (Indicators include data collected in Area 3.2b, such as customer assessments of products and services, customer awards, and customer retention.)

- All indicators compare favorably to competitors or similar providers.

- Graphs and information are accurate and easy to understand.

- Data are not missing.

- Results data are supported by customer feedback, customers' overall assessments of products and services, customer awards, and indicators from design and production/delivery processes of products and services.

B. Product and Service Results

- Data are presented concerning customer dissatisfaction for the most relevant product or service quality indicators collected through the processes described in Item 3.2b (some of which may be referenced in the Organizational Profile).

- Operational data are presented that correlate with, and help predict, customer satisfaction. These data show consistently improving trends and levels that compare favorably with competitors.

- All indicators show steady improvement. (Indicators include data collected in Item 6.1, such as product and service quality levels and on-time delivery.)

- All indicators compare favorably to competitors or similar providers.

- Graphs and information are accurate and easy to understand.

- Data are not missing.

7.2 Financial and Market Results (115 points)
Results Scoring

Summarize your organization's key financial and marketplace performance results, segmented by market segments, as appropriate. Include appropriate comparative data.

Provide data and information to answer the following questions:

a. Financial and Market Results

(1) What are your current levels and trends in key measures/indicators of financial performance, including aggregate measures of financial return and/or economic value, as appropriate?

(2) What are your current levels and trends in key measures/indicators of marketplace performance, including market share/position, business growth, and new markets entered, as appropriate?

Notes:

N1. Responses to 7.2a(1) might include: aggregate measures such as return on investment (ROI), asset utilization, operating margins, profitability, profitability by market/customer segment, liquidity, debt to equity ratio, value added per employee, and financial activity measures.

N2. New markets entered (7.2a [2]) might include offering Web-based services.

This Item [7.2] looks at the organization's financial and market results, with the aim of understanding marketplace challenges and opportunities.

Organizations should provide data demonstrating levels, trends, and appropriate comparisons for key financial, market, and business indicators. Overall, these results should provide a complete picture of financial and marketplace performance.

- Measures reported in this Item are those usually tracked by senior leaders to assess organization-level performance.

- Appropriate financial measures and indicators might include:

  – Revenue

  – Profits

  – Market position

  – Cash-to-cash cycle time

  – Earnings per share

  – Returns

- Marketplace performance measures might include:

  – Market share

  – Measures of business growth

  – New product and geographic markets entered (including exports)

  – Entry into e-commerce markets

  – Percent of sales from new products

7.2 Financial and Market Results

Results of improvement efforts using key measures and/or indicators of financial and market performance

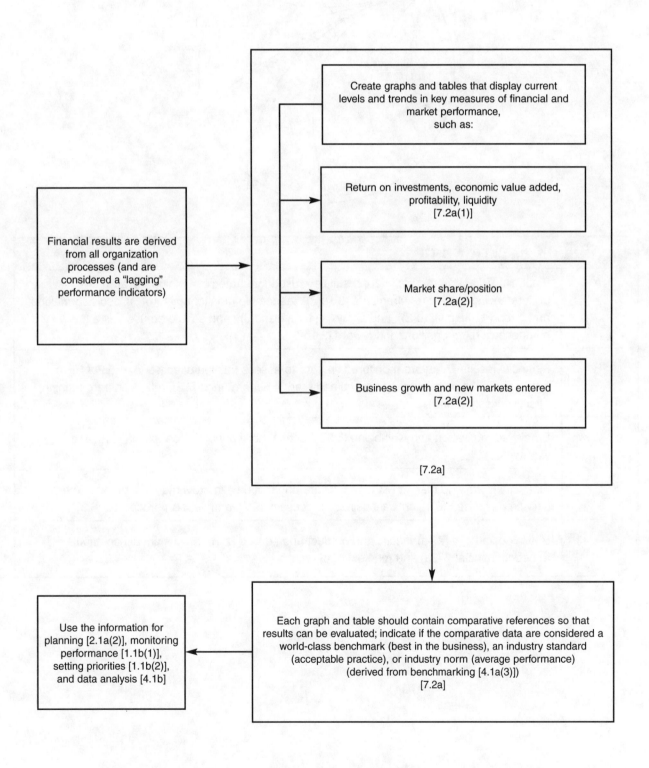

7.2 *Financial and Market Results Item Linkages*

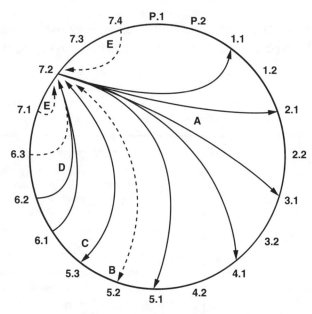

NATURE OF RELATIONSHIP	
A	Financial [7.2a] and market [7.2b] results are used for strategic planning [2.1a(2)]; understanding market requirements [3.1a(2)]; leadership monitoring [1.1b(1)]; decision making and priority setting [1.1b(2)]; and analysis [4.1b(1 and 3)]; and should be used as a basis for compensation, recognition, and reward [5.1b(3)].
B	Financial results [7.2a] are monitored, in part, to assess training effectiveness [5.2a(4)]. In addition, results pertaining to financial and market performance [7.2], reflect, in part, training effectiveness [5.2a(4)].
C	Employee motivation and well-being [5.3] affect financial performance results [7.2], and vice-versa.
D	Financial [7.2a] and market [7.2b] results are enhanced by improvements in product and service processes [6.1], critical business processes [6.2], and support processes [6.3].
E	Better operational [7.4a] results and product and service [7.1b] results should contribute to better financial [7.2a] and market [7.2b] results.

IF YOU DON'T DO WHAT THE CRITERIA REQUIRE...	
Item Reference	**Possible Adverse Consequences**
7.2	Failing to provide comparison data makes it difficult for leaders (or Baldrige examiners) to determine if the level of performance reported is good or not. Failing to provide results data for at least most areas of importance to the organization makes it difficult to determine if performance is getting better in key areas. Finally, the failure to provide this information as part of a Baldrige Award assessment is likely to reduce the score and may even prevent an organization from receiving a site visit (during which time additional results data are usually obtained).

7.2 FINANCIAL AND MARKET RESULTS—SAMPLE EFFECTIVE RESULTS

A. Financial and Market Results

- Key measures and indicators of organization market and financial performance address the following areas:

  - Effective use of materials, energy, capital, and assets

  - Asset utilization

  - Market share, business growth, new markets entered, and market shifting

  - Return on equity

  - Operating margins

  - Pre-tax profit

  - Earnings per share

  - Generating enough revenue to cover expenses (not-for-profit and public sector)

  - Operating within budget (government sector)

- Measures and indicators show steady improvement.

- All key financial and market data are presented.

- Comparative data include industry best, best competitor, and other appropriate benchmarks.

7.3 Human Resource Results (80 Points)
Results Scoring

Summarize your organization's key human resource results, including employee well-being, satisfaction, and development and work system performance. Segment your results to address the diversity of your workforce and the different types and categories of employees, as appropriate. Include appropriate comparative data.

Provide data and information to answer the following questions:

a. Human Resource Results

(1) What are your current levels and trends in key measures/indicators of employee well-being, satisfaction and dissatisfaction, and development?

(2) What are your current levels and trends in key measures/indicators of work system performance and effectiveness?

Notes:

N1. Results reported in this Item should relate to activities described in Category 5. Your results should be responsive to key process needs described in Category 6 and to your organization's action plans and human resource plans described in Item 2.2.

N2. For appropriate measures of employee well-being and satisfaction [7.3a(1)], see Notes to Item 5.3. Appropriate measures/indicators of employee development might include: innovation and suggestion rates, courses completed, learning, on-the-job performance improvements, and cross-training rates.

N3. Appropriate measures/indicators of work system performance and effectiveness [7.3a(2)] might include: job and job classification simplification, job rotation, work layout, and changing supervisory ratios.

This Item [7.3] looks at the organization's human resource results, with the aim of demonstrating how well the organization has created, maintained, and enhanced a positive, productive, learning, and caring work environment.

Organizations should provide data demonstrating current levels, trends, and appropriate comparisons for key measures and/or indicators of employee well-being, satisfaction, dissatisfaction, and development. The best-performing organizations also provide data and information on the organization's work system performance and effectiveness, showing favorable comparisons with industry leaders.

- Results reported might include generic or organization-specific factors.

  - Generic factors might include: safety, absenteeism, turnover, satisfaction, and complaints (grievances). For some measures, such as absenteeism and turnover, local or regional comparisons may be most appropriate.

  - Organization-specific factors are related to the human resource results of employee well-being and satisfaction. These factors might include: extent of training or cross-training, and the extent and success of systems that promote self-directed and empowered employees.

- Results measures reported for work system performance might include: improvement in job classification, job rotation, work layout, and improved employee decision making. Results reported might include input data, such as extent of training, but the main emphasis should be on data that show effectiveness and improvement of outcomes.

7.3 Human Resource Results

Results of human resource improvement efforts using key measures and/or indicators of such performance

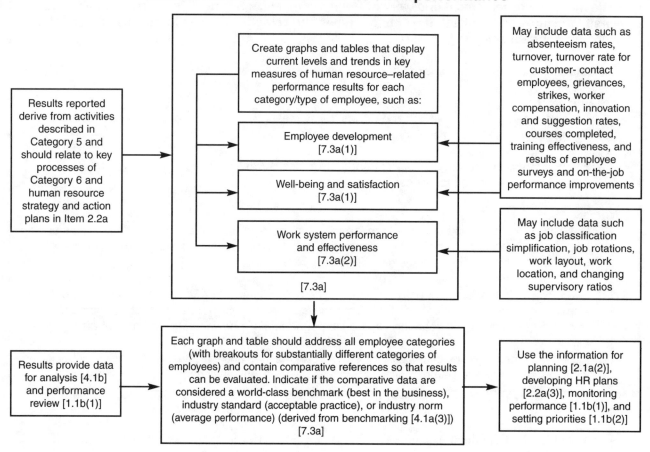

Results reported derive from activities described in Category 5 and should relate to key processes of Category 6 and human resource strategy and action plans in Item 2.2a

Create graphs and tables that display current levels and trends in key measures of human resource–related performance results for each category/type of employee, such as:

Employee development [7.3a(1)]

Well-being and satisfaction [7.3a(1)]

Work system performance and effectiveness [7.3a(2)]

[7.3a]

May include data such as absenteeism rates, turnover, turnover rate for customer- contact employees, grievances, strikes, worker compensation, innovation and suggestion rates, courses completed, training effectiveness, and results of employee surveys and on-the-job performance improvements

May include data such as job classification simplification, job rotations, work layout, work location, and changing supervisory ratios

Results provide data for analysis [4.1b] and performance review [1.1b(1)]

Each graph and table should address all employee categories (with breakouts for substantially different categories of employees) and contain comparative references so that results can be evaluated. Indicate if the comparative data are considered a world-class benchmark (best in the business), industry standard (acceptable practice), or industry norm (average performance) (derived from benchmarking [4.1a(3)]) [7.3a]

Use the information for planning [2.1a(2)], developing HR plans [2.2a(3)], monitoring performance [1.1b(1)], and setting priorities [1.1b(2)]

7.3 Human Resource Results Item Linkages

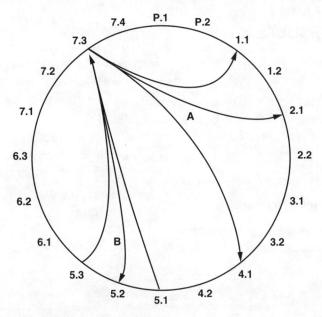

NATURE OF RELATIONSHIP	
A	Human resource results [7.3] are reported and used for planning [2.1], for leader decision making [1.1], to provide feedback to organizational managers [1.1], and analysis [4.1].
B	Human resource results derive from and are enhanced by improving work systems and enhancing flexibility and by strengthening employee recognition systems [5.1], training [5.2], and well-being and satisfaction [5.3]. In addition, human resource results data [7.3] are monitored, in part, to assess training effectiveness [5.2].

IF YOU DON'T DO WHAT THE CRITERIA REQUIRE...	
Item Reference	Possible Adverse Consequences
7.3	Failing to provide comparison data makes it difficult for leaders (or Baldrige examiners) to determine if the level of performance reported is good or not. Failing to provide results data for at least most areas of importance to the organization makes it difficult to determine if performance is getting better in key areas. Finally, the failure to provide this information as part of a Baldrige Award assessment is likely to reduce the score and may even prevent an organization from receiving a site visit (during which time additional results data are usually obtained).

7.3 HUMAN RESOURCE RESULTS—SAMPLE EFFECTIVE RESULTS

A. Human Resource Results

- The results reported in Item 7.3 derive from activities described in Category 5 and the Human Resource Plans and Goals from Item 2.2a.

- Multiyear data are provided to show sustained performance.

- All results show steady improvement.

- Data are not missing. If human resource results are declared important, related data are reported.

- Comparison data for benchmark or competitor organizations are reported, and the organization compares favorably.

- Trend data are reported for employee satisfaction with working conditions, safety, retirement package, and other employee benefits. Satisfaction with management is also reported.

- Trends for declining absenteeism, grievances, employee turnover, strikes, and worker compensation claims are reported.

- Data reported are segmented for all employee categories.

7.4 Organizational Effectiveness Results (120 Points)
Results Scoring

Summarize your organization's key performance results that contribute to the achievement of organizational effectiveness. Include appropriate comparative data.

Provide data and information to answer the following questions:

a. Operational Results

(1) What are your current levels and trends in key measures/indicators of the operational performance of key design, production, delivery, business, and support processes? Include productivity, cycle time, supplier/partner performance, and other appropriate measures of effectiveness and efficiency.

(2) What are your results for key measures/indicators of accomplishment of organizational strategy?

b. Public Responsibility and Citizenship Results

What are your results for key measures/indicators of regulatory/legal compliance and citizenship?

Notes:

N1. Results reported in 7.4a should address your key operational requirements and progress toward accomplishment of your key organizational performance goals as presented in the Organizational Profile and in Items 1.1, 2.2, 6.1, 6.2, and 6.3. Include results not reported in Items 7.1, 7.2, and 7.3.

N2. Regulatory and legal compliance results reported in 7.4b should address requirements described in Item 1.2.

N3. Results reported in Item 7.4 should provide key information for analysis (Item 4.1) and review (Item 1.1) of your organizational performance and should provide the operational basis for customer-focused results (Item 7.1) and financial and market results (Item 7.2).

This Item [7.4] looks at the organization's other key operational performance results, with the aim of achieving organizational effectiveness and key organizational goals, and demonstrating good organizational citizenship. Organizations should provide data in this item if it does not belong in Items 7.1, 7.2, or 7.3.

Results expected in Item 7.4 should report on current levels, trends, and appropriate comparisons for key measures and/or indicators of operational and strategic performance that support the ongoing achievement of results reported in Items 7.1 through 7.3.

- This Item encourages the organization to develop and include unique and innovative measures to track business development and operational improvement. However, all key areas of business and operational performance should be covered by measures that are relevant and important to the organization.

- Measures and/or indicators of operational effectiveness and efficiency might include:

  - Reduced emission levels

  - Waste-stream reductions, by-product use, and recycling

  - Internal responsiveness indicators such as cycle times, production flexibility, lead-times, set-up times, and time to market

  - Business-specific indicators such as innovation rates and increased use of e-technology,

product/process yields, and delivery performance to request

- Supply chain indicators such as reductions in inventory and/or incoming inspections, increases in quality and productivity, improvements in electronic data exchange, and reductions in supply chain management costs

- Third-party assessment results such as ISO 9000 audits

- Indicators of strategic goal achievement

Organizations should also provide data and information on the results of its regulatory/legal compliance and citizenship activities. Measures should include environmental and regulatory compliance and noteworthy achievements in these areas, as appropriate. Results also should include indicators of support for key communities and other public purposes. If the organization has received sanctions or adverse actions under law, regulation, or contract during the past three years, the incidents and current status should be summarized and reported.

Organizations should provide appropriate comparisons for key measures and/or indicators to permit the assessment of the strength or "goodness" of the organization's performance.

7.4 Organizational Effectiveness Results

Results of improvement efforts that contribute to achievement of operational effectiveness

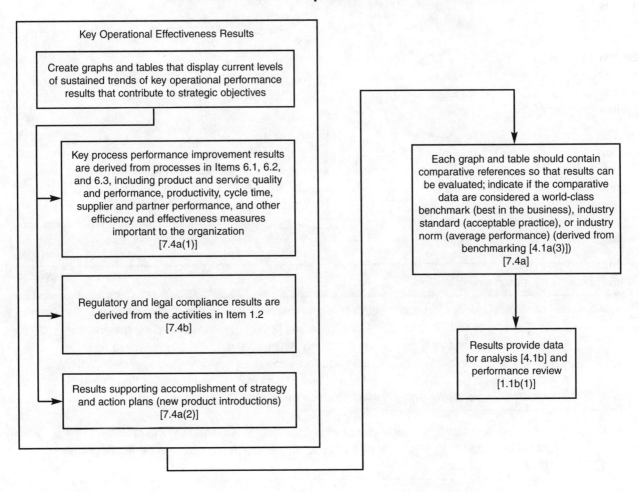

Key Operational Effectiveness Results

Create graphs and tables that display current levels of sustained trends of key operational performance results that contribute to strategic objectives

Key process performance improvement results are derived from processes in Items 6.1, 6.2, and 6.3, including product and service quality and performance, productivity, cycle time, supplier and partner performance, and other efficiency and effectiveness measures important to the organization
[7.4a(1)]

Regulatory and legal compliance results are derived from the activities in Item 1.2
[7.4b]

Results supporting accomplishment of strategy and action plans (new product introductions)
[7.4a(2)]

Each graph and table should contain comparative references so that results can be evaluated; indicate if the comparative data are considered a world-class benchmark (best in the business), industry standard (acceptable practice), or industry norm (average performance) (derived from benchmarking [4.1a(3)])
[7.4a]

Results provide data for analysis [4.1b] and performance review
[1.1b(1)]

7.4 *Organizational Effectiveness Results Item Linkages*

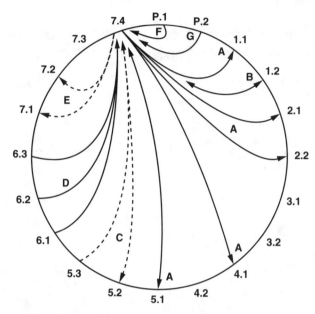

NATURE OF RELATIONSHIP	
A	Operational results and public citizenship and responsibility results [7.4] are reported and used for planning [2.1a(2)], setting strategic objectives [2.1b(1)], management improvement, performance monitoring and decision making [1.1b], analysis [4.1b], and reward and recognition determination [5.1a(3)]. In addition, processes to improve employee initiative and flexibility [5.1a(1)] and better alignment of recognition and reward to desired performance outcomes [5.1a(3)] will enhance performance results [7.4].
B	Results for regulatory and legal compliance and citizenship, related to the activities in Item 1.2, should be reported in 7.4b. In addition, these results are monitored to determine if process changes are needed.
C	Employee motivation, satisfaction, and well-being [5.3] affect product and service performance results [7.4]. In addition, results pertaining to operational performance [7.4] reflect, in part, and are monitored to assess training effectiveness [5.2a(4)].
D	Designing products and services to meet customer requirements [6.1a(2 and 3)] and improved product and service delivery and consistency [6.1b], business processes [6.2a], and support service processes [6.3a] affect product and service performance outcomes [7.4a(1)].
E	Organizational effectiveness results [7.4] provide the basis for financial and market results [7.2] and customer-focused results [7.1].

Continued

NATURE OF RELATIONSHIP	*continued*
F	The regulatory requirements described in P.1a(5), and the key suppliers and dealers listed in P.1b(2), create an expectation that related performance results will be reported in 7.4b and 7.4a respectively.
G	Progress in achieving strategic challenges, as described in P.2b, should be reported in Item 7.4a(2). [Note that the strategic challenges identified in P.2b should be consistent with the strategic objectives in 2.1b(1).]

IF YOU DON'T DO WHAT THE CRITERIA REQUIRE...	
Item Reference	**Possible Adverse Consequences**
7.4	Failing to provide comparison data makes it difficult for leaders (or Baldrige examiners) to determine if the level of performance reported is good or not. Failing to provide results data for at least most areas of importance to the organization makes it difficult to determine if performance is getting better in key areas. Finally, the failure to provide this information as part of a Baldrige Award assessment is likely to reduce the score and may even prevent an organization from receiving a site visit (during which time additional results data are usually obtained).

7.4 ORGANIZATIONAL EFFECTIVENESS RESULTS—SAMPLE EFFECTIVE RESULTS

A. Operational Results

- Indices and trend data are provided in graph and chart form for all operational performance measures identified in 1.1, 6.1, 6.2, and 6.3, relevant organizational goals (2.2), and the key business factors identified in the Organizational Profile and not reported elsewhere in Category 7. Multiyear data are reported.

- Most to all indicators show steady improvement.

- Product and service quality measures and indicators address requirements such as accuracy, timeliness, and reliability. Examples include defect levels, repeat services, meeting product or service delivery or response times, and availability levels. However, if these measures predict customer satisfaction, they should be moved to Item 7.1.

- Operational performance measures address:

  - Productivity, efficiency, and effectiveness, such as productivity indices, waste reduction, energy efficiency, and product/service design improvement measures

  - Cycle-time reductions

- Comparative data include industry best, best competitor, industry average, and appropriate benchmarks. Data are also derived from independent surveys, studies, laboratory testing, or other sources.

- Data are not missing. (For example, do not show a steady trend from 1996 to 2000, but leave out 1998.)

- Data are not aggregated since aggregation tends to hide poor performance by blending it with good performance. Charts and graphs break out and report trends separately.

B. Public Responsibility and Citizenship Results

- Indices and trend data are provided in graph and chart form for all regulatory and legal compliance requirements identified in Item 1.2.

- Operational performance measures address public responsibilities such as environmental improvements.

- Data indicate most measures of regulatory compliance exceed requirements. Performance is leading the industry. No sanctions or violations have been reported.

- Resources allocated to support key communities, consistent with business strategy, demonstrate positive desired results, increasing in effectiveness over time.

Tips on Preparing a Baldrige Award Application

Applications are put together by every conceivable combination of teams, committees, and individual efforts, including consultants. There is no "right" or "best" way to do it. There are, however, lessons that have been learned and are worth considering because they contribute to people and organizations growing and improving.

Author's Note: Gathering process information from across the organization is essential to prepare an accurate and complete Baldrige application. Over the past several years, I have helped many organizations conduct assessments and apply for awards. During this time, I prepared a Microsoft® Word template to help writing teams gather information and prepare to write. The application template provided on a CD that is included with this book facilitates the collection of critical information and makes it easier to write a Baldrige application.

The thoughts that follow are intended to generate conversation and learning. They are not intended to present a comprehensive treatment of the subject.

Getting the Fingerprints of the Organization on the Application

How do we put together a "good" application? To be "good" from a technical perspective, it must be both accurate and respond fully to the requirements of the criteria.

To be effective, the application must be more than technically accurate. The organization must feel a sense of commitment and ownership for the application. Ownership requires a role for people throughout the organization as well as top leadership. The actual "putting of words on paper" can be accomplished in a variety of ways. However, ignoring this larger question of ownership exposes the organization to developing a sterile, disjointed, or unrecognizable document that discounts its value as a vehicle of growth.

The Spirit and Values in an Application

Like it or not, the team or individual that is responsible for developing an application will be closely watched by everyone in the organization. The people coordinating the development of the application need to be perceived as "walking the talk." They need to be seen as believers and role models for what is being written. In the midst of the pressure of putting together an application, a few values have to be continuously brought to the forefront:

- Continuous improvement must be fully embedded into all management processes and work processes.

- The application describes the system used to run the business. This includes not just a description of the pieces, but also the linkages among the activities that make the organization function effectively.

- Put your best foot forward, but do not exaggerate—don't perfume the pig.

Core Values and Recurring Themes

In a document as complex and fact-filled as an application, make sure key messages are clearly communicated. There are 11 Core Values and the application must address all of them. The organization needs to decide at the onset what key messages drive business success. These key messages must pop out from each category and tie together the entire application. This is one of the reasons it becomes so important to design and write the Overview early and well. Too many applicants ignore the importance of the Overview as an organizing tool. The Overview must clearly identify those things that are important to the business, important to its customers, and important to the future of the business. These selected themes need to serve as a constant reminder as the application is developed. We are often asked, "How many themes should an organization focus on?" The answer really depends on how many the organization actually uses. Try developing three.

Tests for Reasonableness

During the development of an application there are "tests" that need to be conducted periodically with two groups of people: the senior executive team and customer-contact employees.

With senior executive teams the issue is the rate of growth of those items undergoing intensive improvement efforts and under the direct sponsorship of senior executives. Every Baldrige application effort uses the occasion to drive significant business process improvements throughout the organization. The development of an application offers an opportunity to review these initiatives. Each initiative is usually an improvement on an existing process and therefore a candidate for inclusion in an application to demonstrate progress.

At the customer-contact level, the issue is a "reality check." Does the application as written reflect the way the business is run? Several things happen at this level when people are given the opportunity to review a developing application:

- Frontline people should get an opportunity to comment on how closely the write-up reflects reality. It provides the writer(s) the opportunity to calibrate those words with reality.

- It forces the customer-contact employee to take a "roof top" view—which can be a learning experience in itself.

- It forces the writer to walk in the shoes of the individual contributor—again learning.

Test the Application

As an application comes together, a question asked by everyone—particularly the leadership team—is, "How well are we doing, what's the score?" Although the real value of an application is continuous improvement, the competitive nature of people also comes to the forefront. After all, its that spirit that helps drive us to higher levels of excellence. Nurture that spirit.

The best means of getting an objective review is to have people familiar with the Baldrige process examine the application. It is surprising how differently outsiders sometimes view the workings of the business we have just written about and know so well. The important aspect of this review is obviously the skill of the reviewers or examiners. The value to the organization is threefold:

- An early assessment—which sets expectations and eliminates surprises.

- An opportunity for an early start on improvement initiatives.

- A test of understandability by outsiders—which every application ultimately has to pass.

Take Time to Celebrate/ Continuously Improve

Developing an application is tough work. At the end of the day it is: (1) a document highlighting the accomplishments and future aspirations of the organization, (2) a plan for getting there, and (3) an operations manual for new people entering the business.

At key milestones in the development of an application, it is important to take time to celebrate the accomplishments just completed. The celebration should be immediate, inclusive, and visible. Such a celebration raises questions within the organization, it raises eyebrows, and it raises expectations—all of which are critical when trying to change and improve the overall performance of the organization. It also presents a perfect opportunity to promote improvement initiatives.

Some Closing Thoughts

In the words of David Kearns, former CEO of Xerox and one of the greatest leaders of performance excellence in the world, "Quality is a journey without an end." Every company today is faced with the struggle to bring about change—and the pace quickens each year. Baldrige is a mechanism that can help focus the energy for change in a most productive manner. Used properly it can help companies breakout of restrictive paradigms and continue on the journey to top levels of performance excellence.

2002 CRITERIA RESPONSE GUIDELINES

The guidelines given in this section are offered to assist Criteria for Performance Excellence users in responding most effectively to the requirements of the 18 Criteria Items. Writing an application for the Baldrige Award involves responding to these requirements in 50 or fewer pages.

The guidelines are presented in three parts:

1. General Guidelines regarding the criteria booklet, including how the Items are formatted

2. Guidelines for Responding to Approach/Deployment Items

3. Guidelines for Responding to Results Items

General Guidelines

Read the entire Criteria booklet.

The main sections of the booklet provide an overall orientation to the criteria, including how responses are to be evaluated for self-assessment or by Award Examiners. You should become thoroughly familiar with the following sections:

- Criteria for Performance Excellence
- Scoring Information
- Glossary of Key Terms
- Category and Item Descriptions

Review the Item format and understand how to respond to the Item requirements.

The Item format shows the different parts of Items, the significance of each part, and where each part is placed. It is especially important to understand the Areas to Address and the Item Notes. Each Item is classified as either Approach-Deployment or Results depending on the type of information required.

Item requirements are presented in question format, sometimes with modifying statements. Responses to an Item should contain answers to all questions and modifying statements; however, each question need not be answered separately. Responses to multiple questions within a single Area to Address may be grouped as

appropriate to the organization. The CD accompanying this book contains a restatement of the criteria in declarative sentences, not questions. Many have found this makes it easier to understand the many different requirements that are embedded in the criteria.

Start by preparing the Organizational Profile.

The Organizational Profile is the most appropriate starting point for initiating a self-assessment or for writing an application. The Organizational Profile is intended to help everyone—including Criteria users, application writers, and reviewers—to understand what is most relevant and important to the organization's business and to its performance.

In addition, read the information describing the linkages, sample effective practices, and process flow diagrams presented in this book. In particular, be certain to understand how the various requirements of the Criteria are integrated into a comprehensive management system. Then gather data using the electronic application template provided with this book.

GUIDELINES FOR RESPONDING TO APPROACH/DEPLOYMENT ITEMS

The Criteria focus on key performance results. However, results by themselves offer little diagnostic value. For example, if some results are poor or are improving at rates slower than the competition's, it is important to understand why this is so and what might be done to accelerate improvement.

The purpose of Approach/Deployment Items is to permit diagnosis of the organization's most important processes—the ones that enable fast-paced performance improvement and contribute to key business results. Diagnosis and feedback depend heavily upon the content and completeness of Approach-Deployment Item responses. For this reason, it is important to respond to these Items by providing key process information.

Understand the Meaning of "How"

Items requesting information on approach and deployment include questions that begin with the word "how." Responses should outline key process information such as methods, measures, deployment, and evaluation/improvement/learning factors.

Responses lacking such information, or merely providing an example, are referred to in the Scoring Guidelines as anecdotal information and are worth little to nothing.

Understand the Meaning of "What"

Two types of questions in Approach-Deployment Items begin with the word "what." The first type of question requests basic information on key processes and how they work. Although it is helpful to include who performs the work, merely stating who does not permit diagnosis or feedback. The second type of question requests information on what your key findings, plans, objectives, goals, or measures are. These questions set the context for showing alignment in your performance management system. For example, when you identify key strategic objectives, your action plans, human resource development plans, some of your results measured, and results reported in Category 7 should be expected to relate to the stated strategic objectives.

Describe your system for meeting the requirements of each item. Ensure that methods, processes, and practices are fully described. Use flowcharts to help examiners visualize your key processes.

Show That Activities Are Systematic

Ensure that the response describes a systematic approach, not merely an anecdotal example. Systematic approaches are repeatable, predictable, and involve the systematic use of data and information for evaluation, subsequent improvement, and learning. In other words, the approaches are consistent over time, build in learning and evaluation, and show maturity. Scores above 50 percent rely on clear evidence that approaches are systematic, evaluated, and refined.

Show Deployment

Ensure that the response gives clear and sufficient information on deployment. For example, one must be able to distinguish from a response whether an approach described is used in one, some, most, or all parts of the organization. If the process you describe is widely used in the organization be sure to state where it is deployed.

Deployment can be shown compactly by using summary tables that outline what is done in different parts of the organization. This is particularly effective if the basic approach is described in a narrative.

Show Focus, Consistency, and Integration

The response demonstrates that the organization is focused on key processes and on improvements that offer the greatest potential to improve business performance and accomplish organization action plans.

There are four important factors to consider regarding integration:

1. The Organizational Profile should make clear what is important

2. The Strategic Planning Category, including the strategic objectives and action plans, should highlight areas of greatest focus and describe how strategy alignment is accomplished

3. Descriptions of organizational-level analysis and review (Items 4.1 and 1.1) should show how the organization analyzes and reviews performance information to set priorities

4. The Process Management Category should highlight product, service, support, and supplier processes that are key to overall performance

Integrating systems required in the Approach/Deployment Items and tracking corresponding measures in the Results Items should improve business performance.

Respond Fully to Item Requirements

Ensure that the response fully addresses all important parts of each Item and each Area to Address. Missing or incomplete information will be interpreted by examiners as a system deficiency—a gap in approach and/or deployment. All areas should be addressed and checked in final review. Individual components of an Area to Address may be addressed individually or together.

Cross-Reference When Appropriate

Each Item response should, as much as possible, be self-contained. However, some responses to different Items might be mutually reinforcing. It is then appropriate to refer to the other responses, rather than to repeat information. In such cases, key process information should be given in the Item requesting this information. For example, employee education and training should be described in detail in Item 5.2. References elsewhere to education and training would then reference, but not repeat, this detail.

Use a Compact Format

Applicants should make the best use of the 50 application pages permitted. Use flowcharts, tables, and "bulletized" presentation of information.

Refer to the Scoring Guidelines

The evaluation of item responses is accomplished by consideration of the Criteria Item requirements and the maturity of the organization's approaches, breadth of deployment, and strength of the improvement process relative to the scoring guidelines. Therefore, applicants need to consider both the criteria and the Scoring Guidelines in preparing responses. *In particular, remember that in order to score over 50 percent, organizations must demonstrate consistent evaluation and corresponding improvements at least for the basic Item requirements. The Scoring Guidelines make this requirement applicable to all Items in Categories 1 through 6. Even if the Criteria questions for the Item do not ask for a description of techniques, it will help the examiners give you full credit for your processes if an explanation is provided to show how the processes are systematically evaluated and refined.*

GUIDELINES FOR RESPONDING TO RESULTS ITEMS

The Baldrige Criteria place great emphasis (and 45 percent of the score) on results. All Results Items remain in Category 7 for 2002. Items 7.1, 7.2, 7.3, and 7.4 call for results related to all key requirements, stakeholders, and goals.

Focus on Reporting Critical Results

Results reported should cover the most important requirements for business success highlighted in the Organizational Profile and the Strategic Planning and Process Management Categories, and included in responses to other Items, such as Human Resource Focus (Category 5) and Process Management (Category 6).

Four key requirements for effective presentation of results data include the following:

1. Trends show directions of results and rates of change

2. Performance levels show performance on some meaningful measurement scale

3. Comparisons show how trends or levels compare with those of other, appropriately selected organizations

4. Breadth and importance of results show that all important results are included

No Minimum Time

No minimum period of time is required for trend data. However, results data might span five years or more for some results. Trends might be much shorter for some of the organization's more recent improvement activities. Because of the importance of showing deployment and focus, new data should be included even if trends and comparisons are not yet well established. However, it may be better to report four quarterly measures covering a one-year period than two measures for beginning and end of year. The four measures help to demonstrate a sustained trend (if one exists).

Compact Presentation

Many results can be reported compactly by using graphs and tables. Graphs and tables should be labeled for easy interpretation. Results over time or compared with others should be "normalized"—presented in a way (such as use of ratios) that takes into account various size factors. For example, reporting safety trends in terms of lost workdays per 100 employees would be more meaningful than total lost workdays, if the number of employees has varied over the time period or if you are comparing your results to organizations varying in size from yours.

Link Results with Text

Descriptions of results and the results themselves should be in close proximity in the application. Trends that show a significant positive or negative change should be explained. Use figure numbers that correspond to Items. For example, the third figure for Item 7.1 should be 7.1-3. (See Figure 34.)

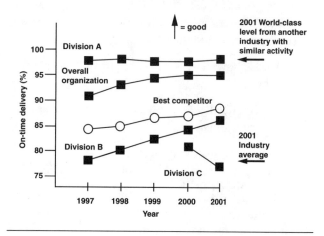

Figure 34 On-time delivery performance.

Figure 34 illustrates data an applicant might present as part of a response to Item 7.1, Customer-Focused Results. In the Organizational Profile and in Item 3.1, the applicant has indicated on-time delivery as a key customer requirement.

Using the graph, the following characteristics of clear and effective data presentation are illustrated:

- A figure number is provided for reference to the graph in the text.

- Both axes and units of measure are clearly labeled.

- Trend lines report data for a key business requirement—on-time delivery.

- Results are presented for several years.

- Appropriate comparisons are clearly shown.

- The organization shows, using a single graph, that its three divisions separately track on-time delivery.

- If different segments or components exist, show each as a separate measure. Avoid aggregating data when the segments are meaningful.

- An upward-pointing arrow appears on the graph, indicating that increasing values are "good." (A downward-pointing arrow would indicate that decreasing values are "good.") The "desired direction" arrows may seem obvious to the authors of the application but some desired directions are not obvious to examiners who are not familiar with certain data displays.

To help interpret the scoring guidelines, the following comments on the graphed results in the sample above would be appropriate.

- The current overall organization performance level is very good to excellent. This conclusion is supported by the comparison with competitors and with a world-class level.

- The organization exhibits an overall excellent improvement record.

- Division A is the current performance leader—showing sustained high performance and a slightly positive trend. Division B shows rapid improvement. Its current performance is near that of the best industry competitor, but trails the world-class level.

- Division C—a new division—is having early problems with on-time delivery. (The applicant should analyze and explain the early problems in the application text.) Its current performance is not yet at the level of the best industry competitor.

Complete Data

Be sure that results data are displayed for all relevant customer, financial, market, human resource, operational performance, and supplier performance characteristics. If you identify relevant performance measures and goals in other parts of the analysis (for example, Categories 1 through 6), be sure to include the results of these performance characteristics in Category 7. As each relevant performance measure is identified in the assessment process, create a blank chart and label the axes.

Define all units of measure, especially if they are industry-specific or unique to the applicant. As data are collected, populate the charts. If expected data are not provided in the application, examiners may assume that the trends or levels are not good. Missing data drive the score down in the same way that poor trends do.

After you complete all of the data in Category 7, review the Organizational Profile and the processes described in Categories 1 through 6. Make a list of all of the results that an examiner would expect to find in Category 7. Then cross-check this list with the data provided in Category 7. If any "Expected" data are missing, be sure to add the appropriate charts or graphs.

Break Out Data

This point, mentioned earlier, bears repeating: avoid aggregating the data. Where appropriate, break data into meaningful components. If you serve several different customer groups, display performance and satisfaction data for each group. As Figure 35 demonstrates, only one of the three trends is positive, although the average is positive. Examiners will seek component data when aggregate data are reported. Presenting aggregate data instead of meaningful component data is likely to reduce the score.

Data and Measures

Comparison data are required for all items in Category 7. These data are designed to demonstrate how well the organization is performing. To judge performance excellence, one must possess comparison data. In Figure 36, performance is represented by the line connecting the squares. Clearly the organization is improving, but how "good" is it? Without comparison data, answering that question is difficult.

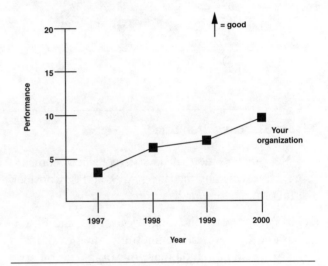

Figure 36 Getting better.

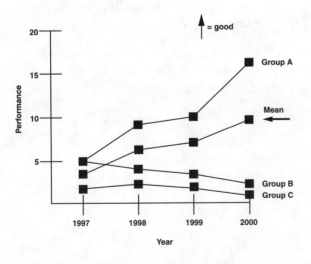

Figure 35 Breakout group data.

Now consider the chart with comparison data added (Figure 37).

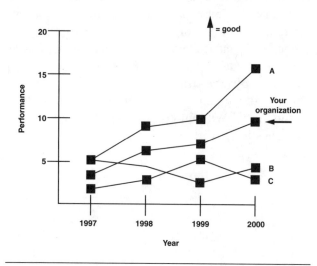

Figure 37 Comparison data.

Note the position of three hypothetical comparisons, represented by the letters A, B, and C. Consider the following two scenarios:

1. If A represents the industry average and both B and C represent competitors, then examiners would conclude that your organization's performance was substandard, even though it is improving.

2. If A represents a best-in-class (benchmark) organization and B represents the industry average, then examiners would conclude that your organizational performance is very good.

In both scenarios, the organizational performance remained the same, but the examiner's perception of it changed based on changes in comparison data.

Measures

Agreeing on relevant measures is a difficult task for organizations in the early phases of quality and performance improvement. The task is easier if the following guidelines are considered:

• Clearly define customer requirements. Clear customer requirements are easier to measure. Clearly defined customer requirements require probing and suggesting. For example, the customer of a new computer wants the equipment to be reliable. After probing to find what "reliable" means, we discover that: (1) the customer expects it to work all of the time; (2) prompt appearance by a repair technician at the site if it does stop working; (3) immediate access to parts; and (4) the ability to fix it right the first time.

• For each of the four requirements defined, identify a measure. For example, mean-time between failures is one indicator of reliability, but it does not account for all of the variation in customer satisfaction. Since the customer is concerned with run-time, we must assess how long it took the repair technician to arrive at the site, diagnose the problem, and fix it. Measures include time in hours, days, weeks between failures, time in minutes between the service call and the computer regaining capability (time to fix), time in minutes waiting for parts, and the associated costs in terms of cash and worker effort.

• Collect and report data. Several charts might be required to display these factors, or one chart with several lines.

Scoring System

The scoring of responses to Criteria Items (Items) and Award applicant feedback are based on three evaluation dimensions:

1. Approach
2. Deployment
3. Results

Criteria users need to furnish information relating to these dimensions. Specific factors for these dimensions are described as follows:

Approach

Approach refers to how you address the Item requirements—the method(s) used. The factors used to evaluate approaches include:

- Appropriateness of the methods to the requirements

- Effectiveness of use of the methods. Degree to which the approach:

  - Is repeatable, integrated, and consistently applied

  - Embodies evaluation/improvement/learning cycles

  - Is based on reliable information and data

- Alignment with organizational needs

- Evidence of beneficial innovation and change

Deployment

Deployment refers to the extent to which your approach is applied to all requirements of the Item.

The factors used to evaluate deployment include:

- Use of the approach in addressing Item requirements relevant and important to your organization

- Use of the approach by all appropriate work units

Results

Results refers to outcomes in achieving the purposes given in the Item.

The factors used to evaluate results include:

- Current performance

- Performance relative to appropriate comparisons and/or benchmarks

- Rate and breadth of performance improvements

- Linkage of results measures to important customer, market, process, and action plan performance requirements identified in the Organizational Profile and in Approach/Deployment Items

Item Classification and Scoring Dimensions are classified according to the kinds of information and/or data you are expected to furnish relative to the three evaluation dimensions. The two types of Items and their designations are:

1. Approach/Deployment (for all Items in Categories 1–6)

2. Results (for all Items in Category 7)

Approach and Deployment are linked to emphasize that descriptions of Approach should always indicate the Deployment—consistent with the specific requirements of the Item. Although Approach and Deployment dimensions are linked, feedback to award applicants reflects strengths and/or opportunities for improvement in either or both dimensions.

Results Items call for data showing performance levels, relevant comparative data, and improvement trends for key measures/indicators of organizational performance. Results Items also call for data on breadth of performance improvements, that is, on how widespread your improvement results are. This is directly related to the Deployment dimension; if improvement processes are widely deployed, there should be corresponding results. A score for a Results Item is thus a composite based upon overall performance, taking into account the rate and breadth of improvements and their importance.

Importance as a Scoring Factor

The three evaluation dimensions described above are critical to evaluation and feedback. However, evaluation and feedback also considers the importance of your reported Approach, Deployment, and Results to your key business factors. The areas of greatest importance should be identified in the Organizational Profile and in the narrative for Items, such as 2.1 (Strategy Development), 2.2 (Strategy Deployment), 3.1 (Customer and Market Knowledge), 3.2 (Customer Relationships and Satisfaction), 4.1 (Measurement and Analysis of Organizational Performance), 5.1 (Work Systems), 5.3 (Employee Well-Being and Satisfaction), 6.1 (Product and Service Processes), 6.2 (Business Processes), 6.3 (Support Processes), and Category 7 (Business Results). Your key customer requirements and key strategic objectives and action plans are particularly important.

Assignment of Scores to Your Responses

Baldrige Award Examiners observe the following guidelines in assigning scores to applicants' responses:

- All Areas to Address should be included in the Item response. Also, responses should reflect what is important to the organization.

- In assigning a score to an Item, an Examiner first decides which scoring range (for example, 50 percent to 60 percent) best fits the overall Item response. Overall "best fit" does not require total agreement with each of the statements for that scoring range. Actual score within the range depends upon an Examiner's judgment of the closeness of the Item response in relation to the statements in the next higher and next lower scoring ranges.

- An Approach/Deployment Item score of 50 percent represents an approach that meets the overall objectives of the Item and that is deployed to the principal activities and work units covered in the Item. Higher scores reflect maturity (cycles of improvement), integration, and broader deployment.

- A Results Item score of 50 percent represents a clear indication of improvement trends and/or good levels of performance in the principal results areas covered in the Item. Higher scores reflect better improvement rates and/or levels of performance, and better comparative performance as well as broader coverage and integration with business requirements.

SUPPLEMENTARY SCORING GUIDELINES

Author's note: Many examiners and organizations have found the official scoring guidelines to be vague, although they have been improved considerably since the earlier years of the Award. The official scoring guidelines, presented in 20 percent increments, may increase the difficulty of reaching consensus on a score and increase scoring variation. To resolve this problem, I developed the following supplemental scoring guidelines. Many organizations and state award programs have used these guidelines for several years and found that they make the consensus process easier and produce comparable scores.

Approach/Deployment

1. For each Approach/Deployment Item, first determine the appropriate level on the approach scale. This sets the upper possible score the applicant may receive on the Item.

2. Then read the corresponding level on the deployment scale. For example, if the approach level is 40 percent, read the 40 percent standard on the deployment scale where one would expect "several work units are in the early stages of deployment," and "progress in achieving the primary purposes of the Item is not inhibited." If that is the case, the final score is 40 percent.

3. However, if the deployment score is lower than the approach score then it establishes the lower range of possible final scores for the

Item. The actual final score will be between the low and high scores. For example, if "many major gaps exist and progress is significantly inhibited," the lowest possible score would be 10 percent. This final score must be between 40 and 10 percent (for example, 10, 20, 30, or 40 percent).

4. Never increase an approach score based on better deployment.

5. Scoring Approach/Deployment Items are presented on the pages immediately following this scoring section.

Results

1. For Results Items, base your assessment only on the standards described on the results scale. Do not consider Approach or Deployment standards at all.

2. Determine the extent to which performance results are positive, complete, and at high levels relative to competitors or similar providers or an industry standard.

3. To determine the extent to which all important results are reported, examiners should develop a list of the key measures the applicant indicates are important. Start with the measures listed in the overview section. Then add to the key measures list based on key data reported in Item 2.1 and the goals in 2.2, as well as measures that may be mentioned in Categories 5 and 6. Key measures can be reported anywhere in an application.

Baldrige Scoring Guidelines **Approach/Deployment**	
0%	• No systematic approach evident; information is anecdotal
10% to 20%	• The beginning of a systematic approach to the basic purposes of the Item is evident • Major gaps exist in deployment that would inhibit progress in achieving the basic purposes of the Item • Early stages of a transition from reacting to problems to a general improvement orientation are evident
30% to 40%	• An effective, systematic approach, responsive to the basic purposes of the Item, is evident • The approach is deployed, although some areas or work units are in early stages of deployment • The beginning of a systematic approach to evaluation and improvement of basic Item processes is evident
50% to 60%	• An effective, systematic approach, responsive to the overall purposes of the Item, is evident • The approach is well deployed, although deployment may vary in some areas or work units • An act-based, systematic evaluation and improvement process is in place for improving the efficiency and effectiveness of key processes • The approach is aligned with basic organizational needs identified in the other Criteria Categories
70% to 80%	• An effective, systematic approach, responsive to the multiple requirements of the Item and your current and changing business needs, is evident • Approach is well-deployed, with no significant gaps • A fact-based, systematic evaluation and improvement process and organizational learning/sharing are key management tools; there is clear evidence of refinement and improved integration as a result of organizational-level analysis and sharing • The approach is well-integrated with organizational needs identified in the other Criteria Categories
90% to 100%	• An effective, systematic approach, fully responsive to all the requirements of the Item and all your current and changing business needs, is evident • The approach is fully deployed without significant weaknesses or gaps in any areas or work units • A very strong, fact-based, systematic evaluation and improvement process and extensive organizational learning/sharing are key management tools; strong refinement and integration, backed by excellent organizational-level analysis and sharing, are evident • The approach is fully integrated with organizational needs identified in the other Criteria Categories

Supplemental Scoring Guidelines		
Score	**Approach**	**Deployment**
0%	No systematic approach evident; anecdotal information.	Anecdotal, undocumented.
10%	Early beginning of a systematic approach consistent with the basic purposes of the Item is somewhat evident. Mostly reactive approach to problems. Many key requirements of the Item not addressed. In the earliest stages of transitioning from reacting to problems to a general improvement orientation.	Many major gaps exist in deployment. Progress in achieving basic purposes of Item is significantly inhibited.
20%	A partially systematic but beginning approach consistent with the basic purposes of the Item is evident. Generally reactive to problems. Some key requirements of the Item not addressed. In the early stages of transitioning from reacting to problems to a general improvement orientation.	Some major gaps exist in deployment. Progress in achieving basic purposes of Item is noticeably inhibited.
30%	An effective, systematic approach responsive to the basic purposes of the Item is somewhat evident. A few key requirements of the Item are not addressed. Beginning of a systematic approach to evaluation but little, if any, improvement of basic Item processes is evident. Random improvements may have been made.	The approach is generally deployed although several units are in the earliest stages of deployment. Progress in achieving primary purposes of Item is minimally inhibited.
40%	An effective, systematic approach responsive to the basic purposes of the Item is clearly in place. Several minor requirements of the Item are not addressed. Beginning of a systematic approach to evaluation and improvement of basic Item processes is evident. Random improvements may have been made.	The approach is deployed although several units are in the early stages of deployment. Progress in achieving primary purposes of Item is not inhibited.
50%	An effective, systematic approach responsive to the overall purposes of the Item and changing business needs is fully developed. Some minor requirements of the Item are not addressed. Fact-based improvement system is in place for basic Item processes that includes process evaluation in key areas (but no refinements based on this evaluation are in place). Random improvements may have been made. The approach is aligned with some basic organization needs identified in the other Criteria Categories.	No major gaps in deployment exist that inhibit progress in achieving primary purposes of Item, although deployment may vary in some areas or work units. Some work units still in the early stages of deployment.
60%	An effective, systematic approach responsive to the overall purposes of the Item is clearly in place. A few minor requirements of the Item not addressed. Fact-based improvement system is in place for the basic requirements of the Item, including at least one evaluation cycle completed, including some systematic refinement based on the evaluation in key areas. The approach is aligned with the most basic organization needs identified in the other Criteria Categories.	No major gaps in deployment exist that inhibit progress in achieving primary purposes of Item, although deployment may vary in some areas or work units. A few work units still in the early stages of deployment.
70%	An effective systematic approach, responsive to many of the multiple purposes of the Item, is clearly in place. Organizational learning and sharing are frequently used management tools at many levels. Some systematic evaluation and evidence of refinements and improved integration result from organization-level analysis and learning. The approach is aligned and well-integrated with many overall organization needs identified in the other Criteria Categories.	Approach is well-deployed with some work units in the middle to advanced stages. No significant gaps exist that inhibit progress in achieving the purposes of Item.
80%	An effective, systematic approach, responsive to most of the multiple purposes of the Item and current and changing business needs, is clearly in place. Organizational learning and sharing are frequently used management tools at most levels. Considerable, systematic evaluation and evidence of refinements and integration result from organization-level analysis and learning. The approach is aligned and well-integrated with most overall organization needs identified in the other Criteria Categories.	Approach is well-deployed with many work units in the advanced stages. No gaps exist that inhibit progress in achieving the purposes of Item.
90%	An effective, systematic approach, responsive to all of the multiple purposes of the Item and current and changing business needs is in place. Considerable, systematic evaluation; and extensive refinements; and improved organizational sharing and learning are key management tools at most levels. Some innovative processes are evident with strong refinement and integration supported by substantial organization-level analysis and sharing.	Approach is fully deployed with most work units in the advanced stages. No significant gaps or weaknesses exist in any areas or work units.
100%	An effective, systematic approach, fully responsive to all of the multiple purposes of the Item and all current and changing business needs, is clearly in place. Considerable, systematic evaluation; clear evidence of extensive refinements; and improved organizational sharing and learning are key management tools at all levels. Many innovative processes are evident with strong refinement and integration supported by excellent organization-level analysis and sharing.	Approach is fully deployed with most to all work units in the advanced stages. No significant gaps or weaknesses exist in any areas or work units.

Baldrige Scoring Guidelines Results	
0%	• There are no results or poor results in areas reported
10% to 20%	• There are some improvements and/or early good performance levels in a few areas • Results are not reported for many to most areas of importance to your organization's key business requirements
30% to 40%	• Improvements and/or good performance levels are reported in many areas of importance to your organization's key business requirements • Early stages of developing trends and obtaining comparative information are evident • Results are reported for many to most areas of importance to your organization's key business requirements
50% to 60%	• Improvement trends and/or good performance levels are reported for most areas of importance to your organization's key business requirements • No pattern of adverse trends and no poor performance levels are evident in areas of importance to your organization's key business requirements • Some trends and/or current performance levels—evaluated against relevant comparisons and/or benchmarks—show areas of strength and/or good to very good relative performance levels • Business results address most key customer, market, and process requirements
70% to 80%	• Current performance is good to excellent in areas of importance to your organization's key business requirements • Most improvement trends and/or current performance levels are sustained • Many to most trends and/or current performance levels—evaluated against relevant comparisons and/or benchmarks—show areas of leadership and very good relative performance levels • Business results address most key customer, market, process, and action plan requirements
90% to 100%	• Current performance is excellent in most areas of importance to your organization's key business requirements • Excellent improvement trends and/or sustained excellent performance levels are reported in most areas • Evidence of industry and benchmark leadership is demonstrated in many areas • Business results fully address key customer, market, process, and action plan requirements

Supplemental Scoring Guidelines	
Score	**Scoring Results**
0%	No results or poor results in areas reported.
10%	Results not reported for most areas of importance to the organization's key requirements. Limited positive results and/or limited good performance levels are evident for a few areas.
20%	Results not reported for many areas of importance to the organization's key requirements. Some positive results and/or early good performance levels are evident for a few of these areas.
30%	Results are reported for many areas of importance to the organization's key requirements. Improvements and/or good performance levels are evident for many areas of importance to the organization's key requirements. Early stages of developing trends but little or no comparative information has been obtained.
40%	Results are reported for most key areas of importance to the organization's key requirements. Improvements and good performance levels are evident for many areas of importance to the organization's key requirements. Early stages of developing trends and obtaining comparative information.
50%	Results are reported for most key customer, process, and action plan requirements. Some positive trends and/or good performance levels—evaluated against relevant comparisons or benchmarks—show a few areas of strength or good relative performance levels. No pattern of adverse trends and no poor performance levels in areas of importance to key organization requirements.
60%	Results are reported for most customer, process, and action plan requirements. Many positive trends and/or good performance levels—evaluated against relevant comparisons and benchmarks—show some areas of strength and good relative performance levels. No pattern of adverse trends and no poor performance levels in areas of importance to key organization requirements.
70%	Results are reported for most key customer, process, and action plan requirements. Current performance is good in many areas important to key organization requirements. Most improvement trends and/or current performance levels are sustained and many of these—evaluated against relevant comparisons and/or benchmarks—show some areas of leadership and very good relative performance levels.
80%	Results are reported for most key customer, process, and action plan requirements. Current performance is excellent in many areas important to key organization requirements. Most improvement trends and/or current performance levels are sustained and most of these—evaluated against relevant comparisons and/or benchmarks—show areas of leadership and very good relative performance levels.
90%	Results fully address key customer, process, and action plan requirements. Current performance is excellent in most areas important to key organization requirements. Most improvement trends or current performance levels are sustained and most of these—evaluated against relevant comparisons or benchmarks—show areas of industry or benchmark leadership in many areas.
100%	Results fully address key customer, process, and action plan requirements. Current performance is excellent in most areas important to key organization requirements. Excellent improvement trends and current performance levels are sustained and—evaluated against relevant comparisons and benchmarks—show industry or benchmark leadership in many areas.

APPROACH/DEPLOYMENT TERMS

Systematic

Look for evidence of a system—a repeatable, predictable process that uses data and information to promote improvement and learning—that is used to fulfill the requirements of the Item. Briefly describe the system. Be sure to explain how the system works. You must communicate the nature of the system to people who are not familiar with it. This is essential to achieve the 30 percent scoring threshold.

Integrated

Determine the extent to which the system is integrated or interconnected with other elements of the overall management system. Show the linkages across categories for key themes such as those displayed earlier for each Item. Consider the extent to which the work of senior leaders is integrated. For example:

1. Senior executives (Item 1.1) are responsible for shaping and communicating the organization's values and performance expectations throughout the leadership system and workforce.

2. They develop relationships with key customers (Item 3.2) and monitor customer satisfaction (Item 7.1) and organization performance (Items 7.2, 7.3, and 7.4).

3. Leaders must convert goals and strategic objectives into measurable milestones and timelines to serve as a basis for monitoring performance (Item 1.1b(1)) and setting improvement priorities (Item 1.1b(2)).

3. This information, when properly analyzed (Item 4.1), helps them plan and monitor progress better and make more informed decisions to optimize customer satisfaction and operational and financial performance.

4. With this in mind, senior executives participate in strategy development (Item 2.1) and ensure the alignment of the workplace to achieve strategic objectives (Item 2.2).

5. Senior executives may also become involved in supporting new structures to improve employee performance (Item 5.1), training effectiveness (Item 5.2), and employee well-being and satisfaction (Item 5.3).

Similar relationships (linkages) exist between other items. Highlight these linkages to demonstrate integration.

Prevention-Based

Prevention-based systems are characterized by actions to minimize or prevent the recurrence of problems. In an ideal world, all systems would produce perfect products and flawless service. Since that rarely happens, high-performing organizations are able to act quickly to recover from a problem (fight the fire) and then take action to identify the root cause of the problem and prevent it from surfacing again. The nature of the problem, its root cause, and appropriate corrective action is communicated to all relevant employees so that they can implement the corrective action in their area before the problem arises.

Continuous Improvement

Continuous improvement is a bedrock theme. It is the method that helps organizations keep their competitive edge. Continuous improvement involves evaluation and improvement of processes crucial to organizational success. Evaluation and improvement completes the high-performance management cycle. Continuous improvement evaluations can be complex, data-driven, statistical processes, or as simple as a focus group discussing what went right, what went wrong, and how it can be done better. The key to optimum performance lies in the pervasive evaluation and improvement of all processes. By practicing systematic, pervasive, continuous improvement, time becomes the organization's ally. Consistent evaluation and refinement practices with correspondingly good deployment can drive the score to 60 percent or 70 percent, and higher.

Complete

Each Item contains one or more Areas to Address. Many Areas to Address contain several parts. Failure to address all areas and parts can push the score lower. If an Area to Address or part of an Area does not apply to your organization, it is important to explain why. Otherwise, examiners may conclude that the system is incomplete.

Anecdotal

If your assessment describes a process that is essentially anecdotal and does not fully address the Criteria, it is worth very little (0 to 10 points).

Deployment

The extent to which processes are widely used by organization units affects scoring. For example, a systematic approach that is well-integrated, evaluated consistently, and refined routinely may be worth 70 percent to 90 percent. However, if that process is not in place in all key parts of the organization, the 70 percent to 90 percent score will be reduced, perhaps significantly, depending on the nature and extent of the gap.

Major gaps are expected to exist at the 0 to 20 percent level. At the 30 percent and higher levels, no major gaps exist, although some units may still be at the early stages of development. At the 70 percent to 80 percent level, no major gaps exist and the approach is well-integrated with organizational needs identified in other parts of the criteria.

Summary

For each Item examined, the process is rated as follows:

- *Anecdotal*: 0 to 10 percent

- *Beginnings of a Systematic Approach* (perhaps just planned, piloted, or recently implemented): 10 percent to 20 percent

- *Effective, Systematic Approach with the Beginnings of a Process to Evaluate and Improve* (planned or piloted): 30 to 40 percent

- *Effective, Systematic, with Fact-Based Evaluation Process in Place*: 50 percent

- *Integrated*: 70 percent to 100 percent

- *Refined*: 60 percent to 100 percent

- *Widely used, with No Significant Gaps in Deployment*: 70+ percent

Systematic, integrated, prevention-based, and continuously improved systems that are widely used are generally easier to describe than undeveloped systems. Moreover, describing activities or anecdotes does not convince examiners that an integrated, prevention-based system is in place. In fact, simply describing activities and anecdotes suggests that an integrated system does not exist. However, by tracing critical success threads through the relevant Items in the Criteria, the organization demonstrates that its system is integrated and fully deployed.

To demonstrate system integration, pick several critical success factors and show how the organization manages them. For example, trace the leadership focus on performance.

- Identify performance-related data that are collected to indicate progress against goals (Item 4.1).

- Show how performance data are analyzed (Item 4.1) and used to set work priorities (Item 1.1).

- Show how performance effectiveness is considered in the planning process (Item 2.1) and how work at all levels is aligned to increase performance (Item 2.2).

- Demonstrate the impact of human resource management (Item 5.1) and training (Item 5.2) on performance and show how both tie to the strategy and human resource plans (Item 2.2).

- Show how design, development, production, delivery, business, and support processes (Items 6.1, 6.2, and 6.3) are enhanced to improve results.

- Report the results of improved performance (Items 7.1, 7.2, 7.3, and 7.4) and be sure all key results are reported with key comparative or benchmark data included.

- Determine how improved performance affects customer satisfaction levels (Item 7.1).

- Show how customer concerns (Item 3.1 and 3.2) are used to drive the selection of key measures (Item 4.1) and impact design and delivery processes (Item 6.1).

Note that the application is limited to 50 pages, not including the five-page Organizational Profile. This may not be sufficient to describe in great detail the approach, deployment, results, and systematic integration of all of your critical success factors, goals, or key processes. Thus, you must pick the most important few, indicate them as such, and then thoroughly describe the threads and linkages throughout the application.

Self-Assessments of Organizations and Management Systems

Baldrige-based self-assessments of organization performance and management systems take several forms, ranging from rigorous and time intensive to simple and somewhat superficial. This section discusses the various approaches to organizational self-assessment and the pros and cons of each. Curt Reimann, the first director of the Malcolm Baldrige National Quality Award Office and the closing speaker for the 10th Quest for Excellence Conference, spoke of the need to streamline assessments to get a good sense of strengths, opportunities for improvement, and the vital few areas to focus leadership and drive organizational change. Three distinct types of self-assessment will be examined: the written narrative, the Likert scale survey, and the behaviorally anchored survey.

Full-Length Written Narrative

The Baldrige application development process is the most time-consuming organizational self-assessment process. To apply for the Baldrige Award, applicants must prepare a 50-page written narrative to address the requirements of the performance excellence Criteria. In the written self-assessment, the applicant is expected to describe the processes and programs it has in place to drive performance excellence. The Baldrige application process serves as the vehicle for self-assessment in most state-level quality awards. The process has not changed since the national quality award program was created in 1987 (except for reducing the maximum page limit from 85 to 50 pages). (Author's Note: The CD attached to the back cover of this book contains a document designed to facilitate the collection of information within an organization to serve as a basis for a complete and thorough written application.)

Over the years, three methods have been used to prepare the full-length, comprehensive written narrative self-assessment.

1. The most widely used technique involves gathering a team of people to prepare the application. The team members are usually assigned one of the seven Categories and asked to develop a narrative to address the Criteria requirements of that Category. The Category writing teams are frequently subdivided to prepare responses Item by Item. After the initial draft is complete, an oversight team consolidates the narrative and tries to ensure processes are linked and integrated throughout. Finally, top leaders review and scrub the written narrative to put the best spin on the systems, processes, and results reported.

2. Another technique is similar to that described above. However, instead of subdividing the writing team according to the Baldrige Categories, the team remains together to write the entire application. In this way, the application may be more coherent and the linkages between business processes are easier to understand. This approach also helps to ensure consistency and integrity of the review processes. However, with fewer people involved, the natural "blind spots" of the team may prevent a full and accurate analysis of the management system. Finally, as with the method described above, top leaders review and scrub the written narrative.

3. The third method of preparing the written narrative is the least common and involves one person writing for several days to produce the application. Considering the immense amount of knowledge and work involved, it is easy to understand why the third method is used so rarely.

With all three methods, external experts are usually involved. Baldrige Award recipients usually reported they hired consultants to help them finalize their application by sharpening its focus and clarifying linkages.

Pros:

- Baldrige-winning organizations report that the discipline of producing a full-length written self-assessment (Baldrige application) helped them learn about their organization and identify opportunities for improvement before the site visit team arrived. The written narrative self-assessment process clearly helped focus leaders on their organization's strengths and opportunities for improvement—provided that a complete and honest assessment was made.

- The written narrative self-assessment also provides rich information to help examiners conduct a site visit (the purpose of which is to verify and clarify the information contained in the written self-assessment).

Cons:

- Written narrative self-assessments are extremely time- and labor-intensive. Organizations that use this approach for Baldrige or state applications or for internal organizational review report that it requires between approximately 2000 and 4000 person-hours of effort—sometimes much more. People working on the self-assessment are diverted from other tasks during this period.

- Because the application is closely scrutinized and carefully scrubbed, and because of page limits, it may not fully and accurately describe the actual management processes and systems of the organization. Decisions based on misleading or incomplete information may take the organization down the wrong path.

- Although the written self-assessment provides information to help guide a site visit, examiners cannot determine the depth of deployment because only a few points of view are represented in the narrative.

- Finally, and perhaps most importantly, the discipline and knowledge required to write a meaningful narrative self-assessment is usually far greater than that possessed within the vast majority of organizations. Even the four 1997 Baldrige winners hired expert consultants to help them prepare and refine their written narrative.

Short Written Narrative

Two of the most significant obstacles to writing a useful full-length written narrative self-assessment are poor knowledge of the performance excellence Criteria and the time required to produce a meaningful assessment. If people do not understand the Criteria, it takes significantly longer to prepare a written self-assessment. In fact, the amount of time required to write an application/assessment is inversely related to the knowledge of the Criteria possessed by the writers. The difficulty associated with writing a full-length narrative has prevented many organizations from participating in state, local, or school award programs.

To encourage more organizations to begin the performance improvement journey, many state award programs developed progressively higher levels of recognition, ranging from "commitment" at the low end, through "demonstrated progress," to "achieving excellence" at the top of the range. However, even with progressive levels of recognition, the obstacle of preparing a 50-page written narrative prevented many from engaging in the process. To help resolve this problem, several state programs permit applicants who seek recognition at the lower levels to submit a 7- to 20-page "short" written narrative self-assessment. (Most states still require applicants for the top-level award to complete a full-length written self-assessment.) The short form ranges from requiring a one page description per category to one page per Item (hence the 7- to 20-page range in length).

Pros:

- It clearly takes less time to prepare the short form.

- Because of the reduced effort required to complete the self-assessment, more organizations are beginning the process of assessing and improving their performance.

Cons:

- The short form provides significantly less information to help examiners prepare for the site visit. Although it does take less time to prepare than the full-length version, the short form still requires several hundred hours of team preparation.

- The short form is usually closely scrutinized and carefully scrubbed just as its full-length cousin. This reduces accuracy and value to both the organization and examiners.

- The knowledge required to write even a short narrative prevents organizations in the beginning stages from preparing an accurate and meaningful assessment.

- Finally, there is not enough information presented in the short form to understand the extent of deployment of the systems and processes covered by the Criteria.

The Survey Approach

Just about everyone is familiar with a Likert scale survey. These surveys typically ask respondents to rate, on a scale of 1 to 5, the extent to which they strongly disagree or strongly agree with a comment.

The following is an example of a simple Likert scale survey item:

Senior leaders effectively communicate values and customer focus.				
1	2	3	4	5
Strongly Disagree				Strongly Agree

A variation on the simple Likert scale survey item has been developed in an attempt to improve consistency among respondents. Brief descriptors have been added at each level as shown below in the descriptive Likert scale survey item:

Senior leaders effectively communicate values and customer focus.				
1	2	3	4	5
None	Few	Some	Many	Most

Pros:

- The Likert scale survey is quick and easy to administer. People from all functions and levels within the organization can provide input.

Cons:

- Both the simple and the descriptive Likert scale survey items are subject to wide ranges of interpretation. One person's rating of "2" and another person's rating of "4" may actually describe the same systems or behaviors. This problem of scoring reliability raises questions about the accuracy and usefulness of both the simple and the descriptive survey techniques for conducting organizational self-assessments. After all, a quick and easy survey that produces inaccurate data still has low value. That is the main reason why states have not adopted the Likert scale survey as a tool for conducting the self-assessments, even for organizations in the beginning stages of the quality journey.

The Behaviorally Anchored Survey

A behaviorally anchored survey contains elements of a written narrative and a survey approach to conducting a self-assessment. The method is simple. Instead of brief descriptors such as "strongly agree/strongly disagree" or "none-few-some-many-most," a more complete behavioral description is presented for each level of the survey scale. Respondents simply identify the behavioral description that most closely fits the activities in the organization. In addition, by asking the respondent to describe briefly the processes used by the organization to do what the Baldrige Criteria require, we can simulate the kind of information collected on a site visit, checking deployment and process integration. A sample is shown on the next page.

Improving Leadership Effectiveness Throughout the Organization [1.1b(3)]

1F How well do all parts of the organization make sure that its products, services, and business operations do not hurt the public? Are there effective systems in place to meet regulatory and legal requirements and follow ethical business practices?

1 **Not Evident** ☐	Leaders do not check their own effectiveness.
2 **Beginning** ☑	A few leaders and managers generally use financial and budget results, but no employee feedback, to check their own effectiveness.
3 **Basically Effective** ☐	Some leaders and managers use financial and budget results and a little employee feedback to check their own effectiveness. They use this information to set personal improvement goals.
4 **Mature** ☐	Many leaders and managers use financial and budget results, other performance results, and employee feedback to check their own effectiveness. They use this information to set personal improvement goals. Some have improved their own effectiveness. The leadership improvement system is checked.
5 **Advanced** ☐	Most leaders and managers use financial and budget results, other key performance results, and employee feedback to evaluate their own effectiveness. They use this information to set personal improvement goals. Many have improved their own effectiveness. The system to evaluate and improve leadership effectiveness is routinely checked and some refinements have been made.
6 **Role Model** ☐	Nearly all leaders and managers use key performance results and employee feedback to evaluate their own effectiveness. They use this information to set personal improvement goals. Most have improved their own effectiveness. The system to evaluate and improve leadership effectiveness is routinely checked and ongoing refinements have been made.
? or Not Applicable ☐	I do not have enough information to answer this question or it is not applicable to my organization.

Describe ways that your leaders and managers use employee feedback or performance results to improve their own effectiveness. Suggest ways they can improve.

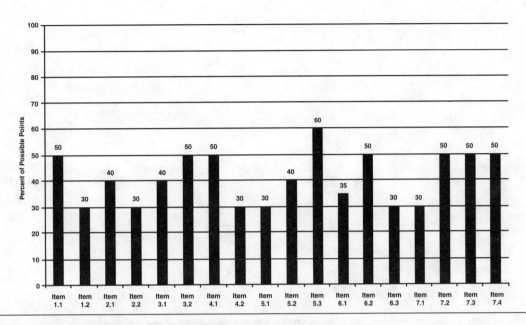

Figure 38 Sample Organization Overall Percent Scores By Item.

Since the behavioral descriptions in the survey combine the requirements of the Criteria with the standards from the scoring guidelines, it is possible to produce accurate Baldrige-based scores for Items and Categories for the entire organization and for any subgroup or division.

Figure 38 provides sample scores for the entire organization and for two job classifications. The chart below shows the percent scores, on a 0 to 100 scale, for each Item. This helps users determine, at a glance, the relative strengths and weaknesses.

Figure 39 shows the ratings by subgroup, in this case, position of senior leaders and employees. On the previous graph, Item 1.1, Leadership System, reflected a rating of 50 percent. However, according to the breakout below, senior leaders believe the

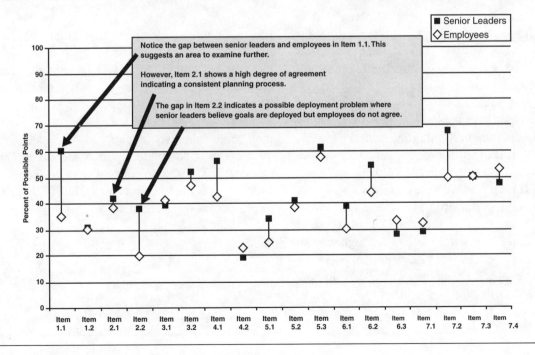

Figure 39 Sample organization position percent scores by item.

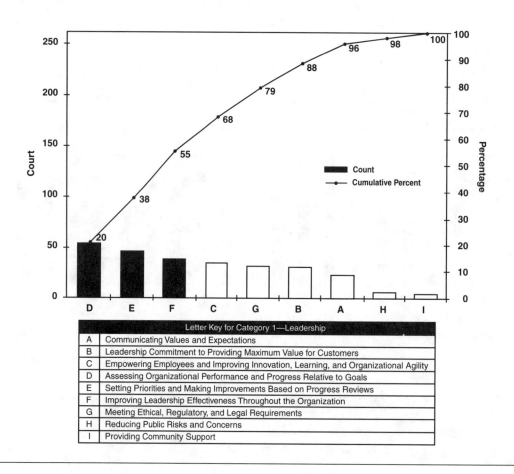

Letter Key for Category 1—Leadership

A	Communicating Values and Expectations
B	Leadership Commitment to Providing Maximum Value for Customers
C	Empowering Employees and Improving Innovation, Learning, and Organizational Agility
D	Assessing Organizational Performance and Progress Relative to Goals
E	Setting Priorities and Making Improvements Based on Progress Reviews
F	Improving Leadership Effectiveness Throughout the Organization
G	Meeting Ethical, Regulatory, and Legal Requirements
H	Reducing Public Risks and Concerns
I	Providing Community Support

Figure 40 Category 1 - Leadership: Analysis of Areas Most Needing Improvement.

processes are much stronger (over 60 percent) than employees (less than 35 percent). This typically indicates incomplete systems development or poor deployment of existing systems and processes required by the Item.

The Pareto diagram in Figure 40 presents data reflecting the areas respondents believed were most in need of improvement. Continuing with the leadership example, it is clear that respondents believe that leaders need to do a better job of assessing organizational performance and progress relative to goals (Theme D), setting priorities and making improvements based on progress reviews (Theme E), and improving leadership effectiveness throughout the organization (Theme F). This helps examiners focus on which areas in leadership may be the most important opportunities for improvement.

Figure 41 allows examiners to determine what type of employee identified the various improvement priorities. Look at "D" and "F" below and you will see that employees identified the need to improve these areas by a 2 to 1 margin over senior managers. This tends to indicate a deployment gap and suggests that senior managers are not perceived as effective as they believe themselves to be.

Finally, a complete report of the comments and explanations of the respondents can be prepared and used by examiners and organization leaders for improvement planning.

1. Leadership

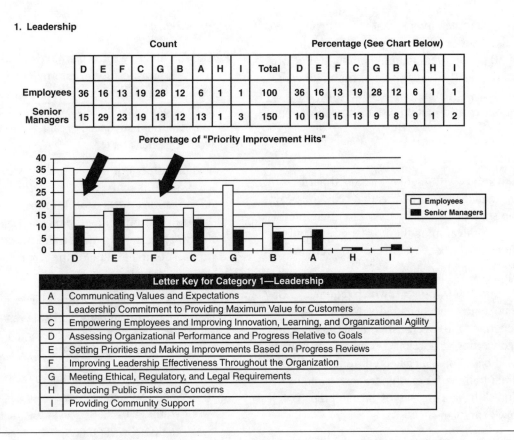

					Count										Percentage (See Chart Below)					
	D	E	F	C	G	B	A	H	I	Total	D	E	F	C	G	B	A	H	I
Employees	36	16	13	19	28	12	6	1	1	100	36	16	13	19	28	12	6	1	1
Senior Managers	15	29	23	19	13	12	13	1	3	150	10	19	15	13	9	8	9	1	2

	Letter Key for Category 1—Leadership
A	Communicating Values and Expectations
B	Leadership Commitment to Providing Maximum Value for Customers
C	Empowering Employees and Improving Innovation, Learning, and Organizational Agility
D	Assessing Organizational Performance and Progress Relative to Goals
E	Setting Priorities and Making Improvements Based on Progress Reviews
F	Improving Leadership Effectiveness Throughout the Organization
G	Meeting Ethical, Regulatory, and Legal Requirements
H	Reducing Public Risks and Concerns
I	Providing Community Support

Figure 41 Priority Improvemnt Counts and Percentages—By Position for the Leadership Category.

Pros:

- Descriptive behavioral anchors increase the consistency of rating. That is, one respondent's rating of "2" is likely to reflect the same observed behaviors as another respondent's rating of "2."

- Although completing a behaviorally anchored survey requires more reading than a Likert scale survey, the amount of time and cost required to complete it is still less than 10 percent of the time and cost required to prepare a written narrative.

- Because it is easy and simple to use, the behaviorally anchored survey does not impose a barrier to participation as does the written narrative. States and companies who use surveys with properly written behavioral anchors find the accuracy of the assessmnt to be as good and in many cases better than that achieved by the full-length narrative self-assessment, and significantly better than Likert scale or short narrative

assessments. By obtaining input from a cross-section of functions, locations, and grade levels throughout the organization, a performance profile can be developed which not only identifies strengths and opportunities for improvement, but deployment gaps as well—something the written narrative assessments rarely provide.

- For organizations doing business throughout the world, the behaviorally anchored survey—translated into the native language of respondents—permits far greater input than the written narrative.

- Modern techniques involving surveying through Internet access created an easy way to survey a large, global company.

- Accurate survey data, based on behavioral anchors, can be used to compare or benchmark organizations within and among industries, and can also support longitudinal performance studies.

• Finally, examiners report that the effort required to analyze survey data and plan a site visit is about 50 percent less than the amount of effort required to analyze and prepare for a site visit based on a written narrative. Moreover, they report better information regarding deployment.

Cons:

• Organizations with highly developed performance management systems that seek to apply for top state or national recognition may prefer to practice developing the full-length narrative self-assessment because it is usually required.

• Examiners who are comfortable with the Baldrige application review process, which requires 25 or more hours to conduct an individual review of a full-length narrative self-assessment, initially find it disconcerting to develop comments and plan a site visit based on data gathered from a survey. Different training for examiners is required to develop skills at using survey data to prepare feedback and plan site visits.

NOTE: The preceding report summary of a behaviorally anchored self-assessment survey written by Mark L. Blazey is administered only by the National Council for Performance Excellence, Winooski, Vermont. Readers may contact them by calling Wendy Steager at 802-655-1922 or by writing to NCPE, One Main Street, Winooski, VT 05404. Several state quality awards and many private sector organizations are using this type of assessment instead of the written narrative form of evaluation. NCPE is the only organization authorized to administer this assessment tool and produce reports as described above. Any other use is not permitted.

In conclusion:

• The full-length written narrative self-assessment is costly. It provides useful information both to examiners and the organizations completing it. The process of completing the written self-assessment can help more advanced organizations to focus and work together as a team.

• The usefulness of the short form written self-assessment is marginal, especially for beginning organizations; little useful information is provided to examiners and managers/employees of the organization. However, because it takes less time to complete, one of the barriers to participation is lowered.

• Concerns over the accuracy and inter-rater reliability of the simple and descriptive Likert scales make their use in conducting effective organizational assessments of management systems marginal.

• The behaviorally anchored survey with comments from respondents combines the benefits of survey speed with the accuracy and completeness of a well-developed written narrative self-assessment. In addition, the behaviorally anchored survey can identify gaps in deployment unlike the written narrative self-assessment and is less costly and faster to administer than the written narrative.

A complete copy of many business, education, and health care surveys can be obtained from the National Council for Performance Excellence, One Main Street, Winooski, Vermont 05404 (802-655-1922). Their Web site is: www.PerformanceExcellence.com .

Following is a sample of a behaviorally anchored survey.

2002
Baldrige Business

Organizational Self-Assessment, Behaviorally Anchored Version

Customized Demographic Profile

Each participating organization completes a customized demographic profile (a generic sample follows). In this way, survey data can be analyzed by these variables to help pinpoint specific areas needing improvement. This allows the extent of use (deployment) of management systems to be examined.

Please circle one selection from EACH column below to indicate your position within the organization.

Position	Location	Function	Org.	Years of Service
– **Executive** – **Manager** – **Supervisor** – **Technician** – **Individual Contributor**	– **North** – **South** – **East** – **West** – **HQ**	– **Engineering** – **Sales** – **Human Resources** – **Finance** – **Quality** – **Marketing** – **Materials Planning** – **Manufacturing** – **Supply Management** – **Info Technology** – **Other**	– **1** – **2** – **3** – **4** – **5** – **Other**	– **0 < 1** – **1 < 3** – **3 < 5** – **5 < 10** – **10+**

BALDRIGE IN-DEPTH INSTRUCTIONS

This survey consists of 62 themes or questions that relate to the 2002 Baldrige Performance Excellence Criteria. It is organized into seven "sections," one for each of the seven Performance Excellence Criteria Categories.

- To the best of your knowledge, select a rating (1 to 6) that describes the level of development in your organization. Note that all of the elements of a statement must be true before you can select that level. If one or more is not true, you must go to a lower level. After you have selected the rating level, please enter the value in the empty box to the right of the row of statements.

- ➡️ Accuracy Tip: The rating scale involves your assessment about the extent of use of the required management processes. The following definitions should help you rate this consistently:
  - ✔ Few   less than 15%
  - ✔ Some   15% to less than 30%
  - ✔ Many   30% to less than 50%
  - ✔ Most   50% to less than 80%
  - ✔ Nearly All   80% to less than 99%
  - ✔ All   100%

- ➜ Time Saving Tip: Start reading at level 3. If all parts of the statement are true, go to level 4, if not, drop back to read level 2. After a few answers, save even more time by starting at the number you select most often. Don't waste time by reading from row 1 each time (unless most of your answers are 1).

- If you do not know an answer, enter NA (Not Applicable/Does Not Apply) or ? (Don't Know). If you are unsure of the meaning of a word or phrase, please check the glossary at the end of this booklet.

- After all statements in the first category (Leadership) have been rated, go to the last page in the Leadership Category. Follow the directions and identify two areas you believe most need improvement in your organization now. Then, go back to the space below each row of statements you identified as vital to improve. Describe briefly the activities your organization conducts that relate to the topic. Also, please suggest steps that your organization or its leaders could take to improve the processes. Your thoughtful comments are as helpful as the rating itself. If you want to comment on more themes, please do so.

- Continue in the same way to complete all seven Categories.

SUMMARY OF CATEGORY 1: LEADERSHIP

This sample assessment looks at one question in the Leadership Category (see sample question at Figure 42). The full-length assessment of Leadership contains nine questions covering the following themes:

The first part (six questions 1A through 1F) looks at how senior leaders set directions and seek future opportunities to help guarantee the long-term success of the organization. Senior leaders should express clear values and set high-performance expectations that address the needs of all stakeholders.

- You are asked how senior leaders set directions, communicate and deploy values and performance expectations, and take into account the expectations of customers and other stakeholders. This includes how leaders create an environment for innovation, learning, knowledge sharing, and organizational agility. You also are asked how senior leaders review organizational performance, what key performance measures they regularly review, and how review findings are used to drive improvement and change, including your leaders' effectiveness.

The second part (three questions 1G through 1I) looks at how well the organization meets its responsibilities to the public and how the organization practices good citizenship.

- You are asked how the organization addresses current and future impacts on society in a proactive manner and how it ensures ethical business practices in all stakeholder interactions. The impacts and practices are expected to cover all relevant and important areas—products, services, and operations.

- You also are asked how the organization, senior leaders, and employees identify, support, and strengthen key communities as part of good citizenship practices.

Leadership Commitment to Providing Maximum Value for Customers

1B. How serious are top leaders about providing maximum value to customers and stakeholders? Do they make it clear that producing value for all customers and stakeholders is critical for success?

Not Evident
1. Leaders focus on short-term business issues, not on value for customers.

Beginning
2. A few leaders are just beginning to focus on value for customers.

Basically Effective
3. Some leaders focus occasionally on value for customers through their written and verbal communication.

Mature
4. Many leaders and managers focus on providing maximum value to customers. They sometimes talk with customers and check on the effectiveness of activities that focus on customer value.

Advanced
5. Most leaders and managers focus on providing maximum value to customers. They regularly talk with customers and check on the effectiveness of customer value activities. They sometimes make improvements.

Role Model
6. Nearly all leaders and managers focus on providing maximum value to customers. They frequently talk with customers and regularly check on the effectiveness of customer value activities. They make ongoing improvements.

NA. *Not Applicable*
I do not have enough information to answer this question.

Figure 42 Sample Leadership Question.

SUMMARY OF CATEGORY 2: STRATEGIC PLANNING

This sample assessment looks at one question in the Strategic Planning Category (see sample question at Figure 43). The full-length assessment of Strategic Planning contains seven questions covering the following themes:

The first part (three questions 2A through 2C) looks at how the organization develops its strategic plans (see sample question at Figure 43). The category stresses that customer-driven quality and operational performance excellence are key strategic issues that need to be integral parts of the organization's overall planning. Specifically:

- Customer-driven quality is a strategic view of quality. The focus is on the drivers of customer satisfaction, customer retention, new markets, and market share—key factors in competitiveness, profitability, and business success

- Operational performance improvement contributes to short- and longer-term productivity, growth, and cost/price competitiveness. Building operational capability—including speed, responsiveness, and flexibility—represents an investment in strengthening your competitive fitness.

The second part (four questions 2D through 2G) looks at the way work processes support the organization's strategic directions, to help make sure that priorities are carried out.

- The organization must translate its strategic objectives into action plans to accomplish the objectives. The organization must also be able to assess the progress of action plans. The aim is to ensure that strategies are understood and followed by everyone in the organization to help achieve goals.

Developing Action Plans Based on Strategic Objectives

2D. How well do the organization's action plans support its strategic objectives? Do the action plans help all parts of the organization pull together (align) to carry out its strategic objectives? Are appropriate resources allocated to carry out the actions?

Not Evident
1. The organization does not develop specific action plans to support strategic objectives.

Beginning
2. The organization has developed action plans to support a few strategic objectives. Resources are not allocated to achieve desired actions.

Basically Effective
3. The organization has developed action plans to support some strategic objectives. Resources are generally allocated to achieve desired actions.

Mature
4. The organization has developed action plans to support many strategic objectives in regards to its products/services, customers/markets, HR requirements, and resource allocation. Resources are specifically allocated to achieve desired actions. The action plans and resources are sometimes checked to see how well they support objectives.

Advanced
5. The organization has developed action plans to support most strategic objectives in regards to its products/services, customers/markets, HR requirements, and resource allocation. Resources are specifically allocated to achieve desired actions. The action plans and resources are regularly checked to see how well they support objectives and improvements are sometimes made.

Role Model
6. The organization has developed action plans to support all strategic objectives in regards to its products/services, customers/markets, HR requirements, and resource allocation. Resources are specifically allocated to achieve desired actions. The action plans and resources are regularly checked to see how well they support objectives. They are consistently improved to strengthen key products and services.

NA. **Not Applicable**
I do not have enough information to answer this question.

Figure 43 Sample Strategic Planning Question.

SUMMARY OF CATEGORY 3: CUSTOMER AND MARKET FOCUS

This sample assessment looks at one question in the Customer and Market Focus Category (see sample question at Figure 44). The full-length assessment of Customer and Market Focus contains 11 questions covering the following themes:

The first part (four questions 3A through 3D) looks at how the organization tries to understand what the customers and the marketplace wants. The organization must learn about customers and markets to help make sure you understand new customer requirements, offer the right products and services, and keep pace with changing customer demands and increasing competition.

- You are asked how the organization determines key customer groups and how it segments the markets.

- You are asked how the organization determines the most important product/service features.

- Also, you are asked how the organization improves the way it listens and learns from customers so that it keeps current with changing business needs.

The second part (seven questions 3E through 3K) looks at how well the organization builds good relationships with customers to get repeat business and positive referrals. You are also asked how the organization gets data on customer satisfaction and dissatisfaction for customers and competitors' customers.

- You are asked how the organization makes it easy for customers and potential customers to get information or assistance and/or to comment and complain.

- You are asked how the organization gathers, analyzes, and learns from complaint information to increase customer satisfaction and loyalty.

- You are asked how the organization builds relationships with customers, since success depends on maintaining close relationships with customers.

- You are asked how the organization determines the satisfaction and dissatisfaction for different customer groups because satisfied customers are necessary for loyalty, repeat business, and positive referrals.

- Finally, you are asked how the organization follows up with customers, and how it determines customer satisfaction relative to competitors so that it may improve future performance.

Understanding What Customers Value Most in Products and Services

3D.   How well does the organization determine what product and service features your customers value the most? How do you know what factors drive their purchasing decisions?

Not Evident
1. The organization does not use a strategic planning process. Leaders' opinions seem to drive plans.

Beginning
2. The organization does not collect data to determine why customers make purchase decisions. It intuitively understands preferences of its customers.

Basically Effective
3. The organization collects and analyzes data to determine why some customers make purchase decisions and what few product and service features these customers value.

Mature
4. The organization collects and analyzes data to determine why many customers make purchase decisions and what product and service features these customers value. It sometimes checks how well the process works.

Advanced
5. The organization collects and analyzes data to determine why most customers make purchase decisions and what product and service features these customers value for most of the product/service lifecycle. It often checks how well the process works and sometimes makes improvements.

Role Model
6. The organization collects and analyzes data to determine why nearly all customers make purchase decisions and what product and service features these customers value for the entire product/service lifecycle. It regularly checks how well the process works and makes ongoing improvements.

NA.   ***Not Applicable***
I do not have enough information to answer this question.

Figure 44 Sample Customer and Market Focus Question.

SUMMARY OF CATEGORY 4: INFORMATION AND ANALYSIS

This sample assessment looks at one question in the Information and Analysis Category (see sample question at Figure 45). Information and Analysis is the "brain center" of an effective management system. Appropriate information and analysis are used to improve decision making at all levels to achieve high levels of performance. Effective measures, properly deployed, also help align the organization's operations to achieve its strategic goals.

The full-length assessment of Customer and Market Focus contains nine questions covering the following themes:

The first part (six questions 4A through 4F) looks at the selection, management, use, and analysis of data and information to support effective decision making at all levels. Data and information guide decision making to help the organization achieve key business results and strategic objectives. Information and analysis systems serve as a key foundation for achieving and sustaining peak performance.

- The organization must build an effective performance measurement system. It must select and integrate the right measures for tracking daily operations and use those measures for monitoring overall organizational performance. The organization must also make sure that data and information are accurate and reliable.

- Competitive comparisons and benchmarking (best practices) information should be used to help drive performance improvement.

- The organization should evaluate and improve the performance measurement system to keep it current with changing business needs.

- Data and information concerning processes and results (outcomes) from all parts of the organization must be analyzed to support the senior leaders' assessment of overall organizational health, organizational planning, and daily operations.

- Analyses must be communicated to support decision making at all levels of the organization.

- Finally, these analyses must be closely aligned with key business results and strategies to ensure the analysis is relevant to support effective decision making.

The second part (three questions 4G through 4I) looks at how the organization ensures the quality and availability of data and information to support effective decision making for employees, suppliers and partners, and customers.

- The organization must ensure data and information are available, accessible, reliable, accurate, timely, secure, and confidential, as appropriate.

- For data that are captured, stored, analyzed, and/or accessed through electronic means, the organization must ensure hardware and software reliability and user friendliness.

All of these systems must be evaluated and enhanced to ensure they remain current with changing business needs and directions.

Selecting Measures to Track Daily Operations and Overall Organizational Performance

4B. How well does the organization select and align appropriate measures throughout the organization to effectively track daily operations and overall organizational performance?

Not Evident
1. The organization does not collect data to track how well it performs.

Beginning
2. The organization collects data to track financial performance but very few other areas of business performance.

Basically Effective
3. The organization collects data to understand some areas of organizational performance such as financial, market, customer satisfaction, and operational.

Mature
4. The organization collects data to understand many areas of organizational performance such as financial, market, customer satisfaction, operational, and human resources. The organization sometimes checks usefulness of the data.

Advanced
5. The organization collects data to understand most areas of organizational performance such as financial, market, customer satisfaction, operational, human resources, and supplier effectiveness. The organization regularly checks how well the data enable tracking and promote alignment at the different levels and sometimes makes improvements.

Role Model
6. The organization collects data to understand nearly all areas of organizational performance including financial, market, customer satisfaction, operational, human resources, and supplier effectiveness. The organization regularly checks how well the data enable tracking and promote alignment throughout the organization and makes ongoing improvements.

NA. *Not Applicable*
I do not have enough information to answer this question.

Figure 45 Sample Information and Analysis Question.

SUMMARY OF CATEGORY 5: HUMAN RESOURCE FOCUS

This sample assessment looks at one question in the Human Resource Focus Category (see sample question at Figure 46).

The full-length assessment of Human Resource Focus contains 11 questions covering the following themes:

The first part (six questions 5A through 5F) looks at how well the organization's systems for work and job design, compensation, motivation, recognition, and hiring help all employees reach peak performance.

- You are asked how the organization designs work and jobs to empower employees to exercise initiative, innovation, and decision making, resulting in high performance.

- You are asked how the organization compensates, recognizes, and rewards employees to support its high-performance objectives (strategic objectives) as well as ensuring a customer and business focus.

- Finally, you are asked how the organization recruits and hires employees who will meet its expectations and needs. The right workforce is an enabler of high performance.

The second part (two questions 5G and 5H) looks at how well education and training meets the needs of employees.

- You are asked how education and training are designed, delivered, reinforced on the job, and evaluated.

- You are also asked about how well the organization provides training in performance excellence, which includes succession planning and leadership development, at all levels.

The third part (three questions 5I through 5K) looks at the organization's work environment, its employee support climate, and how the organization determines employee satisfaction, with the aim of fostering the well-being, satisfaction, and motivation of all employees.

- You are asked how the organization's work environment for all employees is safe and healthful.

- You are asked how the organization enhances employee well-being, satisfaction, and motivation for all employee groups.

- Finally, you are asked how the organization assesses employee well-being, satisfaction, and motivation, and how it relates assessment findings to key business results to set improvement priorities.

Providing Feedback, Compensation, and Recognition to Support High-Performance Goals and a Customer and Business Focus

5D. How well do managers and supervisors at all levels provide feedback to employees and make sure pay, reward, and recognition support high performance and a customer and business focus? [Note that compensation and recognition might include promotions and bonuses based on performance, skills acquired, and other factors contributing to high-performance goals. Recognition may be provided to individuals and/or groups and includes monetary and nonmonetary and formal and informal techniques.]

Not Evident
1. The organization does not provide effective feedback to employees or tie pay or recognition to performance.

Beginning
2. The organization provides effective feedback about performance to a few employees. It rarely ties pay and recognition to performance.

Basically Effective
3. The organization provides effective feedback about performance to some employees. It ties pay and recognition to some high performance.

Mature
4. The organization provides effective feedback about performance to many employees. It ties pay and recognition to many high-performance goals. The organization sometimes checks its processes.

Advanced
5. The organization provides effective feedback about performance to most employees. It ties pay and recognition to most high-performance, customer-focus, and business goals and strategies. The organization regularly checks the effectiveness of its feedback and compensation processes and improvements are sometimes made.

Role Model
6. The organization provides effective feedback about performance to nearly all employees. It ties pay and recognition to nearly all high-performance, customer-focus, and business goals and strategies. The organization regularly checks its feedback and compensation processes and makes ongoing improvements.

NA. *Not Applicable*
I do not have enough information to answer this question.

Figure 46 Sample Human Resource Focus Question.

SUMMARY OF CATEGORY 6: PROCESS MANAGEMENT

This sample assessment looks at one question in the Process Management Category (see sample question at Figure 47). The full-length assessment of Process Management contains 11 questions covering the following themes:

Process Management is the focal point for all key work processes. The first part (six questions 6A through 6F) looks at the organization's product and service design and delivery processes.

- You are asked how customer/market requirements are addressed in the design process.

  You are also asked how cost control, cycle time, and learning from past design projects are addressed. You should make sure that design processes actually work as expected.

- Production/delivery processes must work consistently. Performance measures should be designed to get an early alert of potential problems so you can take prompt action to correct the problem.

- Finally, you are asked how the organization improves its production/delivery processes to achieve better processes and products/services.

The middle part (two questions 6G and 6H) examines the design and delivery of key business processes such as innovation, research and development, technology acquisition, information and knowledge management, supply chain management, supplier partnering, outsourcing, mergers and acquisitions, global expansion, project management, and sales and marketing.

- You are asked how key business processes are determined using input from customers and suppliers/partners as appropriate.

- You must effectively control and improve these business processes using in-process measures and customer and supplier feedback, as appropriate.

- Finally, you are asked how the organization improves its business processes to achieve better performance.

The last part (three questions 6I through 6K) examines the organization's key support processes, with the aim of improving overall operational performance.

- You are asked how key support processes are designed to meet all the requirements of internal and external customers.

- The day-to-day operation of key support processes should meet the key requirements.

  In-process measures and internal customer feedback should be used to get an early alert of problems.

- Finally, you are asked how the organization improves its key support processes to achieve better performance.

Designing Products and Services

6A.   How well does the organization design products and services, as well as related production and delivery systems, that meet current and changing customer requirements? To what extent does the organization incorporate changing customer and market requirements into product and service designs and into production and delivery systems/processes? Does an effective process exist to ensure that the production and delivery systems that were designed will meet all key operational performance requirements?

Not Effective
1. The organization does not have a standard design process.

Beginning
2. The organization uses a standard design process for a few key products and services. The design process does not include customer input.

Basically Effective
3. The organization uses a standard design process for some key products and services. The design process uses some customer input.

Mature
4. The organization has a standard design process for many key products and services. The design process uses customer and supplier input. The effectiveness of these processes is sometimes checked to make sure they meet many requirements.

Advanced
5. The organization has a standard design process for most key products and services, design, production, and delivery processes. The design process uses adequate customer and supplier input to incorporate changing customer and market requirements. These processes are regularly checked to make sure they meet most key operational requirements. Improvements are sometimes made.

Role Model
6. The organization has a standard design process for nearly all key products and service design and production and delivery processes. The design process uses adequate customer and supplier input to incorporate changing customer and market requirements. The effectiveness of these processes is regularly checked to make sure they meet nearly all key operational requirements and ongoing improvements are made.

NA.   *Not Applicable*
I do not have enough information to answer this question.

Figure 47 Sample Process Management Question.

SUMMARY OF CATEGORY 7: BUSINESS RESULTS

This sample assessment looks at one theme in the Business Results Category (see sample question at Figure 48). The full-length assessment of Business Results contains four questions covering the following themes:

The Business Results Category looks for the results produced by the management systems. Results range from lagging performance outcomes such as customer satisfaction, market share, and financial performance to predictive or leading outcomes such as internal operating measures and human resource results. Together, these lagging and leading results create a set of balanced indicators of organizational health, commonly called a "balanced scorecard."

- The first theme (question 7A) looks at how well the organization has been satisfying customers and delivering product and service quality that lead to satisfaction and loyalty.

- The second theme (question 7B) looks at the strength of the organization's financial and market results.

- The third theme (question 7C) looks at how well the organization has been creating and maintaining a positive, productive, learning, and caring work environment.

- The fourth theme (question 7D) looks at the organization's other key operational performance results, to determine the strength of its organizational effectiveness and compliance with applicable laws and regulations.

Customer-Focused Results

7A.   What are the trends and results for customer satisfaction and dissatisfaction? These include customer loyalty indicators, measures of customer-perceived value, customer retention, positive referral, and product and service performance. [Results data may come from internal measures as well as data from customers and independent organizations such as Consumer Reports, J.D. Powers, and so on.]

Not Evident
  1. No results or poor results.

Beginning
  2. Key results are not reported. Good performance levels and improvement in a few areas.

Basically Effective
  3. Many key results are reported and address many areas important to the business. Good performance levels or improvement in some areas. Beginning to develop trends and get comparison data.

Mature
  4. Most key results are reported and address most advanced Balanced Scorecard requirements. Good performance levels or improvement in many areas when compared to industry average.

Advanced
  5. Most key results are reported and address most key customer, market, process, and Balanced Scorecard requirements. No adverse trends or poor performance in key areas. Good to very good performance levels or improvement in most areas when compared to benchmarks or industry average.

Role Model
  6. Most key results are reported and address most key customer, market, process, and Balanced Scorecard requirements. Good to excellent performance levels and sustained improvement in most areas when compared to benchmarks. Leads the industry in some areas.

NA.   *Not Applicable*
  I do not have enough information to answer this question.

Figure 48 Sample Process Management Question.

The Site Visit

INTRODUCTION

Many people and organizations have asked about how to prepare for site visits. This section is intended to help answer those questions and prepare the organization for an on-site examination. It includes rules of the game for examiners and what they are taught to look for. As we all know, the best preparation for this type of examination is to see things through the eyes of the trained examiner.

Before an organization can be recommended to receive the Malcolm Baldrige National Quality Award, it must receive a visit from a team of business assessment experts from the National Board of Examiners. Approximately 25 percent to 30 percent of organizations applying for the Baldrige Award in recent years have received these site visits.

The Baldrige Award site visit team usually includes at least two senior examiners—one of whom is designated as team leader—and three to six other examiners. In addition, the team is accompanied by a representative of the National Quality Award Office and a representative of the American Society for Quality (ASQ), which provides administrative services to the Baldrige Award Office under contract.

The site visit team usually gathers at a hotel near the organization's headquarters on the Sunday morning immediately preceding the site visit. During the day, the team makes final preparations and plans for the visit.

Each team member is assigned lead responsibility for one or more categories of the Award Criteria. Each examiner is usually teamed with one other examiner during the site visit. These examiners usually conduct the visit in pairs to ensure the accurate recording of information.

Site visits usually begin on a Monday morning and last one week. By Wednesday or Thursday, most site visit teams will have completed their on-site

review. They retire to the nearby hotel to confer and write their reports. By the end of the week, the team must reach consensus on the findings and prepare a final report for the panel of judges.

Purpose of Site Visits

Site visits help clarify uncertain points and verify self-assessment (that is, application) accuracy. During the site visit, examiners investigate areas most difficult to understand from self-assessments, such as the following:

- Deployment: How widely a process is used throughout the organization

- Integration: Whether processes fit together to support Performance Excellence

- Process ownership: Whether processes are broadly owned, simply directed, or micromanaged

- Employee involvement: Whether the extent to which employees' participation in managing processes of all types is optimized

- Continuous improvement maturity: The number and extent of improvement cycles and resulting refinements in all areas of the organization and at all levels

Characteristics of Site Visit Issues

Examiners look at issues that are an essential component of scoring and role model determination. They have a responsibility to:

- Clarify information that is missing or vague

- Verify significant strengths identified from the self-assessment

- Verify deployment of the practices described in the self-assessment

Examiners will:

- Concentrate on cross-cutting issues
- Examine data, reports, and documents
- Interview individuals and teams
- Receive presentations from the applicant organization

Examiners are not permitted to conduct their own focus groups or surveys with customers, suppliers, or dealers or disrupt work processes. Conducting focus groups or surveys would violate confidentiality agreements as well as be statistically unsound.

Discussions with the Applicant Prior to the Site Visit

Prior to the official Baldrige Award site visit, all communication between the applicant organization and its team must be routed through their respective single points of contact. Only the team leader may contact the applicant on behalf of the site visit team prior to the site visit. This helps ensure consistency of message and communication for both parties. It prevents confusion and misunderstandings.

The team leader should provide the applicant organization with basic information about the

---

Typically Important Site Visit Issues

- Role of senior management in leading and serving as a role model
- Degree of involvement and self-direction of employees below upper management
- Comprehensiveness and accessibility of the information system
- Utility and validity of available data
- Extent that facts and data are used in decision making
- Degree of emphasis on customer satisfaction
- Extent of systematic approaches to work processes
- Deployment and integration of quality principles and processes
- Training effectiveness
- Use of compensation, recognition, and rewards to promote key values
- Extent that strategic plans align organizational work
- Extent of the use of measurable goals at all levels in the organization
- Evidence of evaluation and improvement cycles in all work processes and in system effectiveness
- Improvement levels in cycle times and other operating processes
- Extent of integration of all processes—operational and support
- Level of maturity of improvement initiatives
- Extent of benchmarking effort
- Level of supplier involvement in performance improvement activities
- Uncovering improvements since the submission of the application (self-assessment) and receiving up-to-date business results

process. This includes schedules, arrival times, and equipment and meeting room needs.

Applicant organizations usually provide the following information prior to the site visit team's final planning meeting at the hotel on the day before the site visit starts:

- List of key contacts

- Organization chart

- Facility layout

- Performance data requested by examiners

The team leader, on behalf of team members, will ask for supplementary documentation to be compiled (such as results data brought up to date) to avoid placing an undue burden on the organization at the time of the site visit.

The site visit team will select sites that allow them to examine key issues and check deployment in key areas. This information may or may not be discussed with the applicant prior to the site visit. Examiners will need access to all areas of the organization.

Conduct of Site Visit Team Members (Examiners)

Examiners are not allowed to discuss findings with anyone but team members. Examiners may not disclose the following to the applicant:

- Personal or team observations and findings

- Conclusions and decisions

- Observations about the applicant's performance systems, whether in a complimentary or critical way

Examiners may not discuss the following with anyone:

- Observations about other applicants

- Names of other award program applicants

Examiners may not accept trinkets, gifts, or gratuities of any kind (coffee, cookies, rolls, breakfast, and lunch are okay), so applicant organizations should not offer them. At the conclusion of the site visit, examiners are not permitted to leave with any of the applicant's materials including

logo items or catalogs—not even items usually given to visitors.

Examiners will dress in appropriate business attire unless instructed otherwise by the applicant organization.

Opening Meeting

An opening meeting will be scheduled to introduce all parties and set the structure for the site visit. The meeting is usually attended by senior executives and the self-assessment writing team. The opening meeting usually is scheduled first on the initial day of the site visit (8:30 or 9:00 a.m.). The team leader generally starts the meeting, introduces the team, and opens the site visit. Overhead slides and formal presentations are usually unnecessary.

The applicant organization usually has one hour to present any information it believes important for the examiners to know. This includes time for a tour, if necessary.

Immediately after the meeting, examiners usually meet with senior leaders and those responsible for preparing sections of the self-assessment (application) since those people are likely to be at the opening meeting.

Conducting the Site Visit

The team will follow the site visit plan, subject to periodic adjustments according to its findings.

The site visit team will need a private room to conduct frequent caucuses. Applicant representatives are not present at these caucuses. The team will also conduct evening meetings at the hotel to review the findings of the day, reach consensus, write comments, and revise the site visit report.

If, during the course of the site visit, someone from the applicant organization believes the team or any of its members are missing the point, the designated point of contact should inform the team leader or the Baldrige Award Office monitor. Also, someone who believes an examiner behaved inappropriately should inform the designated point of contact, who will inform the team leader or the award office monitor.

Employees should be instructed to mark every document given to examiners with the name and work location of the person providing the document. This will ensure that it is returned to the proper person. Records should be made of all material given to team members.

Organizational personnel may not ask examiners for opinions and advice. Examiners are not permitted to provide any information of this type during the site visit.

Team Leader's Site Visit Checklist

This checklist provides a summary of activities required of site visit team leaders.

Preparation

- Size of team and length of visit determined, with starting and ending date and time selected

- All team members receive copies of consensus report

- Team notified of starting/ending times and locations

- Background information on new team members (if any) received

- Category lead and team pairing assignments made for each team member

- New team members complete review of narrative

- Site visit notebooks prepared

- Individual team members prepare assigned site visit issues

- Subteam members exchange site visit issues for comments

- Revised site visit issues received from subteams

- Site visit issues reviewed by team leader and comments sent to subteams

- Team asked to revise site visit themes or issues (as appropriate)

Previsit Meeting

- Examiner introductions/reintroductions

- Site visit issues and themes reviewed and approaches outlined

- Sites selected to visit and logistics reviewed

- Specific requests for first day listed (interviews and data)

- Caucus plans established

Continued on next page

Team Leader's Site Visit Checklist—continued

Conduct of Visit

- Opening presentation conducted
- Followed site visit plan
- Revised plan as required
- Caucused frequently
- Maintained records of findings
- Maintained records of applicant documents received
- Answered all selected site issues; developed information on site visit themes
- Closing meeting conducted

Site Visit Report

- Team completed site visit issues
- Team completed Item and category summary forms
- Team completed overall summary form
- Team initiated report
- Report copied; original given to award office representative before leaving site
- Leader kept copy, narrative, and other notes (or a back-up person has material)
- Collected and returned all applicant material prior to leaving site
- Collected all narratives, materials, and notes; sent or given to award office

Feedback Report

- Senior examiner/feedback author collected feedback points during site visit
- Senior examiner/feedback author reviewed feedback points with team during site visit report writing session
- Reviewed feedback report completed before leaving site and sent to award office

GENERIC SITE VISIT QUESTIONS

Examiners must verify or clarify the information contained in an application, whether or not the examiners have determined a process to be a strength or an opportunity for improvement. Examiners must verify the existence of strengths as well as clarify the nature of each significant opportunity for improvement.

Before and during the site visit review process, examiners formulate a series of questions based on the Baldrige Performance Excellence Criteria. Because the site visit must verify or clarify all significant aspects of the organization's performance management systems against the criteria, it is possible to identify a series of generic questions that examiners are likely to ask during the site visit process. Of course, all questions should be tailored to the specific key factors of the organization to be most relevant. The questions in the following section are presented to help prepare applicants and examiners for the assessment process.

Category 1—Leadership

1   (To top leaders) How do you set direction and guide the organization? Please share with us the mission, vision, and values of this organization.

- What are your organization's top priorities?

- How do you ensure that all your employees know this?

- How do you know how effective you are at communicating your commitment to the vision and values?

- How you know your messages to employees are clear and understood?

2. How do you, as a leader, see your role in supporting processes to ensure Performance Excellence?

- How do you role model the behaviors you want your managers and other employees to emulate?

- What do the leaders personally do to lead this organization? What do you do that visibly displays to employees throughout the organization your personal involvement and com-

mitment to the vision and values? How do you promote innovation?

- How you ensure that middle managers promote employee empowerment and innovation throughout the organization?

3. What is the process used to monitor the performance of your organization? How does it relate to the organization's strategic business plan? Do measurable goals exist? How are they monitored? How often?

- What are the key success factors (or key result areas, critical success factors, key business drivers) for your organization, and how do you use them to drive Performance Excellence?

- What percentage of your time is spent on performance review and improvement activities? How do you review performance to assess the organization's health, competitive performance, and progress? What key performance measures do senior leaders regularly review?

- How do top priorities and opportunities for innovation reflect organizational review findings? Have you set or changed priorities for innovation and resource allocation? Please give examples of how this is done. How do you ensure that these priorities and opportunities for innovation are used throughout the organization? (After you identify a top priority for innovation, ask the leader to provide specific examples of how he or she ensures these are implemented and aligned throughout the organization, as appropriate.) To what extent do these priorities and innovation opportunities involve support from key suppliers and/or partners? (Pick one example of a priority and ask the leader to help you understand how the organization works with affected suppliers or partners.)

4. What is your process for evaluating the effectiveness of the leadership system? How do you include or use employee feedback in the evaluation?

- Please identify specific examples where the senior leadership improved the leadership system as a result of these evaluations. How do managers evaluate and improve their personal leadership effectiveness? How is employee feedback used here?

What are the criteria for promoting managers within the organization?

- How are you making managers accountable for performance improvement, employee involvement, and customer satisfaction objectives? (Look at some samples of managers evaluations [chosen at random] and check to see if they reflect refinements based on organizational performance review findings and employee feedback.)

- How have you improved the process over the years of evaluating managers?

5. What do you do to anticipate public concerns over the possible impact of your organization? How do you determine what risks the public faces because of your products, services, and operations? What are some examples of risks you have identified? What have you done to reduce the risk or threat to the public? How do you know you are successful in these areas? How do you measure progress?

- What are the biggest environmental issues your organization faces? As a corporate citizen, what is your process for contributing to and improving the environment and society?

- How do you know that your processes for protecting the public are effective? How have you improved these processes?

- What are some ways your organization ensures that employees act in an ethical manner in all business transactions? How is this monitored to ensure compliance? How do you ensure complete and accurate financial recordkeeping?

- How do you know that the processes you have in place for identifying and supporting key communities are appropriate? How you know the resource issues allocated for these purposes are appropriately used?

Category 2—Strategic Planning

1. When was the last time the strategic plan was updated? How recent is it?

2. Were you involved in the strategic planning process? What was your role? How does the overall process for developing strategy work? (If the person was involved in the planning process ask them to recite how the process works without referring to written documentation. We must determine whether a consistent planning process is in place that meets the requirements of the criteria—we are not testing the ability of senior leaders to read a written document.) What factors did you consider in the development of your strategic plan?

- How does your strategic plan address supplier and/or partner capabilities? The competitive environment? The impact of new technology?

- How do you consider the needs of all key customers (or other appropriate stakeholders) in the development of the strategic plan? How do you balance requirements when they are conflicting?

- How do you identify resources needed to prepare for new opportunities and requirements? How are wishes addressed?

- Are the strategic objectives for your organization derived from this plan? If not, from where do they come? (Obtain a list of strategic objectives.)

3. How often do you review progress of your key strategic objectives? Please show me the timelines or projections for achieving each objective. Can you tell from this information where you expect to be on each objective next quarter? Next year? In two years? (Note: the frequency of review should be consistent with the review processes described in Item 1.1b(1). For example, if progress toward achieving the customer satisfaction objectives is reviewed quarterly by the senior leadership team, then quarterly milestones should be defined to permit effective review. In addition, the timelines reported under

2.1b(1) should identify the measurable levels of performance that are expected during these reviews.)

4. How do you make sure that goals, objectives, and action plans are understood and used throughout the organization to drive and align work?

   - How do you ensure that organizational, work unit, and individual actions and resources are aligned at all levels? (Pick a strategy that the leader has indicated is important to organizational success. Then ask the leader what actions he or she has determined are critical to achieve the strategy. From the list of actions, pick one or two and ask the leader to explain specifically how resources were allocated to ensure these plans would be accomplished. Then ask how the leader checks to determine if appropriate resources were allocated. Ask if any improvements have been made in this process over the past few years. Repeat this line of questioning at different levels in the organization to check alignment.)

5. Describe your long- and short-term plans to meet the development, education, and training needs of the organization that are necessary to carry out the strategic plans. What are the measures of progress to meet these human resource plans?

   - Summarize the organization's plans that might relate to work design, innovation, rapid response, compensation and recognition, employee development and training, recruitment, health, safety, ergonomics, special services, and employee satisfaction.

   - How do these plans optimize the use of human resources?

   - How do these plans align with the strategic plan?

   - What are examples of changes to the human resource plans based on inputs from the strategic planning in the following areas: recruitment, training, compensation, rewards, incentives, fringe benefits, programs?

6. What is (summarize) your process for evaluation and improvement of the strategic planning and plan deployment process, including the human resource planning process?

   - What are examples of improvements made as a result of this evaluation process? Where and when did they occur?

7. Who do you consider to be your top competitors, and how does your planned performance (goals) compare to theirs and/or similar providers?

   - How do you determine who your top competitors are?

8. What are your specific goals and objectives? Please provide a copy of your short- and longer-range performance projections. How did you go about establishing these projections? How do these projections compare with your competitors' projections for the same time period? What assumptions did you use to determine where your competitors are likely to be in the same planning horizon as your organization? How accurate have these projections been in the past? What have you done to improve the accuracy of projecting future performance of your competitors?

Category 3—Customer and Market Focus

1. Who are your key customers, customer groups, or market segments? What was your reason for grouping them this way? How do you know what your customers expect of you? How does your organization determine short- and long-term customer requirements for each of the customer groups are segments? How do you know what the customers of your competitors are getting (or want)? How have you used this knowledge?

2. What are the key requirements of your customers (break out by segment or group)?

   - How do you differentiate key requirements from less important requirements?

   - How do you anticipate requirements and prepare to meet them?

- How do you evaluate and improve processes for determining customer requirements? Provide some examples of improvements that unit made in the past few years.

3. How do you provide easy access for your customers to obtain information and assistance or complain? What do you expect to learn from customer complaints?

  - What is your process for handling customer complaints? What do you do with the complaint or comment data? (Ask to see some sample complaints and follow the data trail. Determine how the data are analyzed and used to drive improvements.)

  - What does "prompt and effective resolution of a complaint" mean to your organization? What processes do you have in place to ensure complaints are resolved at the first point of contact in the organization? What skills and authority do your customer contact employees need to resolve complaints promptly and effectively? How do you check to determine if your complaint resolution processes are effective or not? What improvements have you made in these processes over the past few years?

  - Describe your process for follow-up with customers. What do you do with feedback from customers regarding products and services? What triggers follow-up action?

  - What are the customer-contact requirements or service standards? How were they determined? How do you know if standards are being met?

  - How do you evaluate and improve the customer-relationship process? What are some improvements you've made to the way you strengthen customer relationships and loyalty? How did you decide they were important to make, and when were they made?

4. What are your key measures for customer satisfaction and dissatisfaction? How do these measures provide information on likely future market behavior (loyalty, repurchase, and referrals)?

- How do you measure customer satisfaction and dissatisfaction? Do you measure satisfaction/dissatisfaction for all key customer groups/segments? What are your customer groups or segments? How do you determine them? How do you differentiate them in regard to products and services you offer? What process do you use to ensure the objectivity and validity of customer satisfaction data? What do you do with the information?

- What customer satisfaction information do you have about your competitors or benchmarks? What do you do with this information? How do employees use this information in their regular work? What action do they take as a result?

- How do you know appropriate action is taken in response to customer satisfaction data?

- How do you go about improving the way you determine customer satisfaction and dissatisfaction? Please provide some examples of how you have improved these techniques over the past several years.

Category 4—Information and Analysis

1. What are the major performance indicators critical to running your organization?

2. How do you determine whether the information you collect and use for decision making is complete, timely, reliable, accessible, and accurate? What is the process you use to determine the relevance of the information to organizational goals and action plans?

  - What criteria do you use for data selection? How do you ensure that all data collected meet these criteria?

  - Describe how you obtain feedback from the users of the information. How is this feedback used to make improvements?

3. You have told us what your top priorities are. How do you benchmark against these? Please describe how needs and priorities for selecting comparisons and benchmarking are determined.

Show us samples of comparative studies. Picking some at random, determine:

- Why was the area selected for benchmarking?

- How did you use competitive or comparative performance data?

- How are the results of your benchmarking efforts used to set appropriate goals?

- How are the results of your benchmarking efforts used to improve work processes?

- How do you evaluate and improve your benchmarking processes?

4. Please share with us an example of analysis of information important to organizational performance review and strategic planning:

- How are data analyzed to determine relationships between customer information and financial performance; operational data and financial performance; or operational data and human resource requirements and/or performance?

- What data and analyses do you use to understand your people, your customers, and your market to help with strategic planning?

- How widely are these analyses used for decision making at functional or workgroup levels?

- What are you doing to improve the analysis process and make it more useful for organizational and operational decision making?

5. How do you make sure that data and information needed to support decision making at all levels of the organization are available, timely, and accurate?

- What are the data security requirements you believe are critical to your system? (For example, certain statutes and regulations, such as the Family and Education Rights and Privacy Act , may require certain levels of security and data protection.) How do you guarantee data and system security and confidentiality?

- How do you make sure that your hardware and software systems meet the needs of all users? How do you determine whether the software and hardware are "user-friendly?"

(Identify what groups use the hardware/software system. Randomly pick a group and ask how the organization makes sure these people can easily use the hardware and software. Then randomly ask some people in a group how their "user-friendliness" requirements were identified and met.)

- What kind of reliability problems have you experienced with your hardware and software? How have you resolved them? What have you done to prevent these types of problems from happening again?

- Please show how you make sure software and hardware are up-to-date. What derives decisions to change or upgrade systems?

Category 5—Human Resource Focus

1. What do you do to ensure effective communication and knowledge sharing among employees and work units?

- What do you do to encourage initiative and self-directed responsibility among employees in their regular work and jobs? What authority do employees have to direct their own actions and make decisions about their work? (To employees) What authority do you have to make decisions about your work, such as resolving problems, improving work processes, and communicating across departments? (To managers) How do you empower employees? What are some examples of processes you have used to evaluate and enhance opportunities for employees to take individual initiative and demonstrate self-directed responsibility in designing and managing their work? Show examples of actions taken and improvements made. When were they made?

- How do your senior leaders, managers, and supervisors encourage employees to develop and put to use their full potential? What are the key areas of concern? (To employees, ask) What does the organization do to enhance your job and career development?

2. Describe your approach to employee recognition and compensation. What specific reward and recognition programs are utilized? How does the organization link recognition, reward, and compensation to achieve high-performance objectives (which are usually stated as strategic objectives or goals)? How does your approach reinforce achievement of goals and objectives?

   • (General question for employees) How have you been recognized for contributing to achieving organization action plans?

3. Describe your recruitment and hiring practices. How do you obtain employees with essential skills, culture, diverse ideas, and critical thinking skills? How do you make sure these skills, diverse ideas, and cultures are used to maximum advantage within your organization?

4. What replacement strategy or process do you have in place for key leaders and employees/employee groups throughout the organization? (For example, if the organization knows key senior leaders or a group of engineers/technicians are scheduled to retire, determine what it is doing to fill the gap this retirement makes?)

5. What ongoing training is provided for your employees?

   • How is your training curriculum designed and delivered? How do you integrate employee, supervisor, and manager feedback into the design and delivery of your training program? What methods are used to determine what training should be offered and how it should be delivered? (Ask related follow-up questions to supervisors, managers, and employees to determine the extent their needs for development, learning, and career progression were identified/considered when designing the education and training approach.)

   • How does your training program affect operational performance goals? How do you know your training improves your business results? Show examples.

   • After you determine the key groups or segments of employees within the organization

ask the following question: What training and education do you provide to ensure that you meet the needs of all categories of employees? What training does a new employee receive to obtain the knowledge and skills necessary for success and high performance, including leadership development?

   • How do you address key training needs, such as new employee orientation, safety, and diversity?

   • How does training and education address Performance Excellence skills needed, such as quality control, benchmarking, and performance measurement?

   • If applicable, how do employees in remote locations participate in training programs?

   • What is your system for improving training? Please give us some examples of improvements made and when they were made.

   • How do you make sure that the knowledge and skills acquired during training are actually used and reinforced on the job? Provide some examples (then select from this list and follow-up to determine how skills are reinforced on the job).

6. What are your standards for employee health and safety? How were they derived? How are you performing against those standards? How do you make sure that your approach to health and safety address the needs of all employee groups?

   • How do you determine that you have a safe and healthy work environment? How do you measure this? What have you done to improve workplace health, safety, and ergonomics?

   • What are your procedures for systematic evaluation and improvement of workplace health, safety, and ergonomics?

7. What services, facilities, activities, and benefits are most important to your workforce? How did you determine these were the most important? Are they the same for all groups or segments of the workforce? If not, how have the services and

benefits been modified or tailored to meet the needs of different groups or categories of employees?

8. What are the key elements that affect employee well-being, satisfaction, and motivation? How did do you determine that these were the key elements? Are the elements the same for all groups of employees? If not, how do they differ?

- How is employee satisfaction measured? (If a survey is used, ask how they know they are asking the right questions on a survey. Unless they have already told you, ask for some specific examples about how they use other information such as employee retention, absenteeism, grievances, safety, and productivity data to assess and improve employee well-being, satisfaction, and motivation.) What do you do with the information? Provide examples.

- What do you do to improve employee satisfaction systematically? Please give us some examples of improvements.

- When you identify the priorities for improving the work environment to promote employee well-being, satisfaction, and motivation, what factors do you consider? What are the top three or four improvement priorities? (Pick one and ask the leader) What specific finding from the employee satisfaction survey or other assessment tool did the organization use to identify this priority action? How is this priority for improving work environment likely to affect key business results?

- How do you ensure that managers throughout the organization work to improve the climate for employee well-being, satisfaction, and motivation?

- What improvements have you made in the process of determining employee satisfaction, well-being, and motivation?

Category 6—Process Management

1. What new program, product, or service have you designed in the past one to two years? (Pick one) What is your process for designing this new or revised product or service to ensure that customer requirements are met? Please walk me through the steps.

- What customer or market requirements changed during the design or development phase? (If any changed, ask how design changes are handled. If they indicated that no customer or market requirements changed, ask what they would do in case requirements did change.)

- What new design technologies, including e-technology, have you used in recent product/service and production/delivery of the projects?

- How do you test new products or services before they are introduced to be sure they perform as expected and meet all customer and operational requirements? What have you done to prevent errors in the design process? What kinds of problems or troubles have you had with past introductions of new products and services? Provide examples of how you've learned from these problems and prevented them in subsequent product/service designs.

- How do you evaluate and improve the process for designing new products/services, and make improvements in cycle time, cost control, productivity, and other effectiveness or efficiency factors? Please provide some examples of improvements and when they were made. What process do you have in place to make sure that lessons learned in one part of the organization (or from past improvement efforts) are transferred to others in the organization to save time and prevent rework?

2. What are your key production and delivery processes and their requirements, including quality and performance indicators?

- What steps have you taken to improve the effectiveness/efficiency of key work processes, including cycle time?

- What are the processes by which you produce and deliver these products and services to ensure that customer expectations are met or exceeded?

- Once you determine that a process may not be meeting measurement goals or performing according to expectations, what process do you use to determine root cause and to bring about process improvement?

- Please give an example of how a customer request or complaint resulted in an improvement of a current process or the establishment of a new process. How often do customers change their requirements? How do you respond to these changes? How has this process been refined to respond more quickly, especially when customer requirements change more often?

3. Please share with us your list of key business processes, requirements, and associated performance measures, including in-process measures. (Remember that key business processes include critical processes necessary for business growth and success.) For example, if supply chain management is designated as a key business process, the following series of questions may be useful: What process is in place for managing your supplier chain? Who are your most important [key] suppliers? How do you establish and communicate to your key suppliers the key requirements they must meet so that your needs are met? What are the key performance requirements? Please explain how you measure your suppliers performance and provide feedback to help them improve.

- What are the steps you have taken to design your key business processes to ensure they meet all performance requirements? How do you determine the types of services and outputs needed? How do your key business processes interact with and add value to your operational processes to enhance business growth and success?

- How does your organization maintain and enhance the performance of key business processes? Share some examples of processes used to determine root causes of problems and how you prevent recurrence of problems.

- How is performance of business services systematically evaluated and refined? Please provide some examples.

4. Please share with us your list of key support processes, requirements, and associated process measures, including in-process measures:

- How is performance of support services systematically evaluated and refined? Please provide some examples.

- What are the steps you have taken to design your key support processes? How do you determine the types of services needed? How do your support services interact with and add value to your operational processes?

- How does your organization maintain the performance of key support services? Share some examples of processes used to determine root causes of support problems and how you prevent recurrence of problems. How do you monitor costs of these processes? How have you reduced costs? Please give examples.

Category 7—Business Results

The Performance Excellence Criteria require organizations to report performance results in the areas of customer-focused results (7.1), financial and market results (7.2), human resource results (7.3), and organizational effectiveness results (7.4). Normally, applicants are careful to display "good" results but sometimes omit results data that are not as good. The scoring guidelines award more points if results are provided for "*most* areas of importance to the organization's key business requirements."

Accordingly, Examiners must be able to determine what results *should* be provided that are important to the organization's success. To evaluate Category 7 properly, Examiners should first develop a list of the results that they "expect" to be provided in Category 7 based on what the organization indicated was important to its success. Then, by comparing their list of "expected" results to the results provided in the application, Examiners can determine what important results are missing.

Usually these key expected results can be found in the Organizational Profile, strategic goals [Item

2.1b], the list of actions required to achieve strategic objectives [Item 2.2a(1)], the priority customer requirements [Item 3.1a(2)], or other places in the application. The following is an example of the table of expected results. The first three columns identify, by Item, what results are expected and the location in the application of information that created the expectation for results. The last two columns identify

where the results were displayed in the application and provide notations about whether the performance was improving and whether comparison data were provided to help judge the strength or goodness of the performance.

Examiners should prepare this analysis in table format as Figure 49 shows.

Item Reference	Expected Result	Reference	Actual Result	Comparison Data
Identify the area in Category 7 that the result should appear (i.e., 7.1b)	Provide a name or label for the expected result.	List the source in the application where you learned about the importance of the result to the organization.	Indicate if the result data were provided (yes/no) and whether the results show improvement (+) or not (-).	Indicate whether the organization has provided comparison data from other relevant organizations (yes/no) and whether results are good relative to those organizations (+) or not (-).
Sample				
Completed Prior to Analyzing Category 7			Completed Based on Category 7 Data Provided	
7.1b	Customer Group "A" Requirements			
7.1b	Price	Org Profile p. ii; and 2.1b, p.11	Data were provided in Fig. 7.1-1 and show improvement (+)	Comparison data were provided (yes-industry mean) and they do better than average (+)
7.1b	Service	OP p. iii; and 2.1b, p.12	Data were provided in Fig. 7.1-2 and show improvement (+)	Comparison data were provided (yes-industry best competitor) and they do better than them (++)
7.1b	Product Performance	OP p. iii and 2.1b, p.12	Data were provided in Fig. 7.1-2 and show flat performance (~)	No comparative data provided (no)

Figure 49 Table of Expected Results.

1. What are the customer satisfaction trends and product/service performance levels at this time? [Links to P.1b and Items 3.1, 3.2 and 6.1]

   - Please show a breakout of data by customer group or segment.

   - How do these customer satisfaction trends and levels compare with those of your competitors or similar providers?

   - What are your current levels and trends for customer loyalty, positive referral, customer-perceived value, and relationship building?

   - What are your current levels and trends for how customers perceive your products and service performance?

   - What are key product and service characteristics that are most critical to customer satisfaction?

2. What are the current levels and trends showing financial or marketplace performance or economic value?

   - Please provide data on key financial measures, such as return on investment (ROI), operating profits (or budget reductions as appropriate), or economic value added.

   - Please provide data on market share or business growth, as appropriate. Identify new markets entered and the level of performance in those markets.

   - How do these trends compare with those of your competitors or similar providers?

3. What are the current levels and trends showing the effectiveness of your human resource practices? [Links to processes in Category 5]

   - Please provide data on key indicators, such as safety/accident record, absenteeism, turnover by category and type of employee/manager, grievances, and related litigation.

   - How do these trends compare with those of your competitors or similar providers?

4. Please show us your supplier/partner performance data trends and current levels for each key indicator, such as on-time delivery, error rate, and reducing costs. [Links to supply chain issues in Item 6.2]

   - How does performance on these key indicators compare to your competitors, other providers, or benchmarks?

5. How do you measure the quality of your products and services? [Links to Item 6.1]

   - Please show us your performance data.

   - What are current levels and trends for key design, production, delivery and support process performance?

   - What are current level and trends for production and cycle time for design, delivery, and production?

   - How do you know which factors are most important to your customers? [Links to Item 3.1 and P.1b]

   - How does your performance on these key indicators compare to your competitors, other providers, or benchmarks?

6. How do you measure support service effectiveness and efficiency? [Links to Item 6.3]

   - Please show us your performance data.

   - How do you know what the key performance indicators should be?

   - How does your performance on these key indicators compare to your competitors, other providers, or benchmarks?

7. How do you measure operating effectiveness and efficiency?

   - Please show us your performance data.

   - How do you know what the key performance indicators should be? [Links to P.1 and P.2 and Items 1.1, 2.2, 6.1, 6.2, and 6.3]

   - How does your performance on these key indicators compare to your competitors, other providers, or benchmarks?

   - What are your results for regulatory/legal compliance and citizenship? [Links to Item 1.2]

   - To what extent have you accomplished your organizational strategy or strategic objectives?

General Cross-Cutting Questions to Ask Employees

- Who are your customers?

- What are the organization's mission, vision, and values?

- What is the strategic plan for the organization? What are the organization's goals, and what role do you play in helping to achieve the goals?

- What kind of training have you received? Was it useful? Who decided what training you should receive? What kind of on-the-job support did you get for using the new skills you learned during training?

- What kinds of decisions do you usually make about your work and the work of the organization? What data or information do you use to help make these decisions? Is this information easily available to help make decisions easier?

- What activities or work are recognized or rewarded? Is achieving customer satisfaction a critical part of your job? Are your rewards and/or recognition determined in part on achieving certain customer satisfaction levels? If so, explain how this works.

Glossary

Action Plans

Action plans refer to specific actions that respond to short- and longer-term strategic objectives. Action plans include details of resource commitments and time horizons for accomplishment. Action plan development represents the critical stage in planning when strategic objectives and goals are made specific so that effective, organizationwide understanding and deployment are possible. In the Criteria, deployment of action plans includes creation of aligned measures for work units. Deployment might also require specialized training for some employees or recruitment of personnel.

An example of an action plan element for a supplier in a highly competitive industry might be to develop and maintain a price leadership position. Action plans could entail design of efficient processes, analysis of resource and asset use, and creation of a cost-accounting system, aligned for the organization as a whole. It might also involve use of a cost-accounting system that provides activity-level cost information to support day-to-day work. Unit and/or team training should include priority setting based on costs and benefits. Organization-level analysis and review should emphasize overall productivity growth. Ongoing competitive analysis and planning should remain sensitive to technological and other changes that might greatly reduce operating costs for the organization or its competitors.

Alignment

Alignment refers to consistency of plans, processes, information, resource decisions, actions, results, analysis, and learning to support key organizationwide goals. Effective alignment requires common understanding of purposes and goals and use of com-plementary measures and information for planning, tracking, analysis, and improvement at three levels: the organizational level, the key process level, and the work unit level.

Analysis

Analysis refers to assessments performed by an organization or its work units to provide a basis for effective decisions. Overall organizational analysis guides process management toward achieving key business results and toward attaining strategic objectives. Despite their importance, individual facts and data do not usually provide an effective basis for actions or setting priorities. Actions depend upon understanding cause/effect relationships. Understanding such relationships comes from analysis of facts and data.

Anecdotal

Anecdotal refers to process information that lacks specific methods, measures, deployment mechanisms, and evaluation/improvement/learning factors. Anecdotal information frequently uses examples and describes individual activities rather than systematic processes.

An anecdotal response to how senior leaders deploy performance expectations might describe a specific occasion when a senior leader visited all company facilities. On the other hand, a systematic approach might describe the communication methods used by all senior leaders to deliver performance expectations on a regular basis, the measures used to assess effectiveness of the methods, and the tools and techniques used to evaluate and improve the communication methods.

Approach

Approach refers to how an organization addresses the Baldrige Criteria Item requirements—the methods and processes used by the organization. Approaches are evaluated on the basis of the appropriateness of the methods or processes to the Item requirements, effectiveness of their use, and their alignment with organizational needs.

Asset Productivity

Asset productivity refers to he productive use that is made of an organization's assets. An overall measure of asset productivity could be made by dividing the total sales/revenue/budget by total asset value. In addition, specific asset productivity can be determined by making similar calculations against a specific asset or set of assets, such as a specific plant, production line, or even the productivity of land assets (acreage).

Basic Requirements

Basic requirements refers to the most central theme of an Item. Basic requirements are the fundamental or essential requirements of that Item. In the Criteria, the basic requirements of each Item are presented as an introductory sentence(s) printed in bold.

Benchmarks and Benchmarking

Benchmarks refers to processes and results that represent best practices and performance for similar activities, inside our outside an organization's industry. Organizations engage in benchmarking activities to understand the current dimensions of world-class performance and to achieve discontinuous (nonincremental) or breakthrough improvement.

Benchmarks are one form of comparative data. Other comparative data organizations might use include industry data collected by a third party (frequently industry averages), data on competitors' performance, and comparisons with similar organizations in the same geographic area.

Benchmarking refers to processes and results that represent best practices and performance for similar activities, inside or outside an organization's industry. *Benchmarking* is a process by which an organization compares its performance against that of other organizations, determines how those organizations achieved higher performance levels, and uses the information to improve its own performance. Although it is difficult to benchmark some processes directly in some businesses, many of the things one organization does are very similar to things that others do. For example, most organizations move information and tangible products, pay people, train them, appraise their performance, and more. A key to successful benchmarking is to identify the process elements of work and find others who are the best at that process.

Continuous Improvement

Continuous improvement refers to the ongoing improvement of products, programs, services, or processes by small increments or major breakthroughs.

Customer

Customer refers to an organization or person who receives or uses a product or service. The customer may be a member or part of another organization or the same organization, or an end user.

Cycle Time

Cycle time refers to time performance—the time required to fulfill commitments or to complete tasks. Time measurements play a major role in the Criteria because of the great importance of time performance to improving competitiveness. In the Criteria booklet, cycle time refers to all aspects of time performance. Other time-related terms in common use are setup time, lead time, order fulfillment time, changeover time, delivery time and time to market, and other key process times.

Data

Data refer to numerical information used as a basis for reasoning, discussion, determining status, decision making, and analysis.

Deployment

Deployment refers to the extent to which an organization's approach is applied to the requirements of a Baldrige Criteria Item. Deployment is evaluated on the basis of the breadth and depth of application of the approach to relevant processes and work units throughout the organization.

Effective

Effective refers to how well an approach, a process, or a measure addresses its intended purpose. Determining effectiveness requires the evaluation of how well a need is met by the approach taken, its deployment, or the measure used.

Effectiveness

Effectiveness refers to the extent to which a work process produces intended results.

Efficiency

Efficiency refers to the effort or resources required to produce desired results. More efficient processes require fewer resources than do less efficient processes.

Employee Involvement

Employee involvement refers to a practice within an organization whereby employees regularly participate in making decisions on how their work is done, including making suggestions for improvement, planning, goal setting, and monitoring performance.

Empowerment

Empowerment refers to giving employees the authority and responsibility to make decisions and take actions. Empowerment results in decisions being made closest to the "front line," where work-related knowledge and understanding reside.

Empowerment is aimed at enabling employees to satisfy customers on first contact, to improve processes and increase productivity, and to better the organization's business results. Empowered employees require information to make appropriate deci-sions; thus, an organizational requirement is to provide that information in a timely and useful way.

Goals

Goals refer to a future condition or performance level that one intends to attain. Goals can be both short and longer term. Goals are ends that guide actions. Quantitative goals, frequently referred to as "targets," include a numerical point or range. Targets might be projections based on comparative and/or competitive data. The term "stretch goals" refers to desired major, discontinuous (non-incremental) or break-through improvements, usually in areas most critical to your organization's future success.
Goals can serve many purposes, including:

- clarifying strategic objectives and action plans to indicate how success will be measured

- fostering teamwork by focusing on a common end

- encouraging "out-of-the-box" thinking to achieve a stretch goal providing a basis for mea-suring and accelerating progress

High-Performance Work

High-performance work, a term used in the Item descriptions and comments, refers to work approaches systematically pursuing ever-higher levels of overall organizational and human performance, including quality, productivity, innovation rate, and time performance. High-performance work results in improved service for customers and other stakeholders.

Approaches to high-performance work vary in form, function, and incentive systems. Effective approaches generally include cooperation between management and the workforce, including workforce bargaining units; cooperation among work units, often involving teams; self-directed responsibility (some-times called empowerment); input to planning; individual and organizational skill building and learning; learning from other organizations; flexibility in job design and work assignments; a flattened organizational structure, where decision making is decentralized and decisions are made closest to the "front line;" and effective use of performance measures, including comparisons. Many high-performance work systems use monetary and nonmonetary incentives based upon factors such as organizational performance, team and/or individual contributions, and skill building. Also, high-performance work approaches usually seek to align the design of organizations, work, jobs, employee development, and incentives.

How

How refers to the process that an organization uses to accomplish its mission requirements. In responding to "how" questions in the Approach-Deployment Item requirements, process descriptions should include information such as methods, measures, deployment, and evaluation/improvement/learning factors.

Indicator

Indicator refers to the two or more measurements are required to provide a more complete picture of performance. For example, the number of complaints is an indicator of dissatisfaction, not an exclusive measure of it. Cycle time is a discrete measure of the time it takes to complete a process. However, it is only one indicator of process effectiveness. Other indicators may include measures of rework, waste, and defects.

Innovation

Innovation refers to making meaningful change to improve products, services, and/or processes and create new value for stakeholders. Innovation involves the adoption of an idea, process, technology, or product that is considered new or new to its proposed application.
Successful organizational innovation is a multistep process that involves development and knowledge sharing, a decision to implement, implementation, evaluation, and learning. Although innovation is often associated with technological innovation, it is applicable to all key organizational processes that would benefit from breakthrough improvement or change in approach or outputs.

Integrated

Integrated refers to the interconnections between the processes of a management system. For example, to satisfy customers an organization must understand their needs, convert those needs into designs, produce the product or service required, deliver it, assess ongoing satisfaction, and adjust the processes accordingly. People need to be trained or hired to do the work, and data must be collected to monitor progress. Performing only a part of the required activities is disjointed and not integrated.

Integration

Integration refers to the harmonization of plans, processes, information, resource decisions, actions, results, analysis, and learning to support key organization-wide goals. Effective integration is achieved when the individual components of a performance management system operate as a fully interconnected unit.
See the definition of "alignment" for the description of this related term.

Inter-rater Reliability

Inter-rater reliability refers to the degree to which multiple raters, observing the same phenomenon, will give it the same rating. If they do, it has high inter-rater reliability; if not, it has low inter-rater reliability.

Leadership System

Leadership system refers to how leadership is exercised, formally and informally, throughout the organization—the basis for and the way that key decisions are made, communicated, and carried out. It includes structures and mechanisms for decision making; selection and development of leaders and managers; and reinforcement of values, directions, and performance expectations.
An effective leadership system respects the capabilities and requirements of employees and other stakeholders, and it sets high expectations for performance and performance improvement. It builds loyalties and teamwork based on the organization's values and the pursuit of shared goals. It encourages and supports initiative and appropriate risk taking, subordinates the organization to purpose and function, and avoids chains of command that require long decision paths. An effective leadership system includes mechanisms for the leaders to conduct a self-examination, receive feedback, and improve.

Levels

Levels refer to numerical information that places or positions an organization's results and performance on a meaningful measurement scale. Performance levels permit evaluation relative to past performance, projections, goals, and appropriate comparisons.

Measures

Measures refer to numerical information that quantifies (measures) input, output, and performance dimensions of processes, products, services, and the overall organization.

Mission

Mission refers to the overall function of an organization. The mission answers the question, "What is this organization attempting to accomplish?" The mission might define customers or markets served, distinctive competencies, or technologies used.

Multiple Requirements

Multiple requirements refer to the individual questions Criteria users need to answer within each Area to Address. These questions constitute the details of an Item's Area(s) to Address. See the definition of "overall requirements" for more information on Areas to Address.

Overall Requirements

Overall requirements refer to the specific Areas Criteria users need to address when responding to the central theme of an Item. Overall requirements address the most significant features of the Item requirements. In the Criteria, the overall requirements of each Item are introduced in blue text and assigned a letter of designation for each Area to Address.

Performance

Performance refers to output results information obtained from processes, products, and services that permits evaluation and comparison relative to goals, standards, past results, and to others. Performance might be expressed in nonfinancial and financial terms.

Operational performance refers to organizational, human resource, and supplier performance relative to effectiveness and efficiency measures and indicators. Examples include cycle time, productivity, waste reduction, and regulatory compliance. Operational performance might be measured at the work unit level, the key process level, and the organization level.

Product and service quality refers to operational performance relative to measures and indicators of product and service requirements, derived from customer preference information. Product and service quality measures should correlate with, and allow the organization to predict, customer satisfaction. Examples of product and service quality include reliability, on-time delivery, defect levels, and service response time. For example, consider a coffee shop that serves breakfast coffee. Product and service quality indicators and measures may include time to serve, time to process payment, freshness (time between brewing and serving), bitterness (acidity measured by pH level), heat (temperature), and strength (ratio of coffee to water and grind coarseness). Taken together, these measures can predict customer satisfaction. In 2002, these results are evaluated as part of Item 7.1.

Customer-focused performance refers to performance relative to measures and indicators of customers' perceptions, reactions, and behaviors, and to measures and indicators of product and service characteristics important to customers. Examples include customer retention, complaints, customer survey results, product reliability, on-time delivery, defect levels, and service response time.

Financial and marketplace performance refers to performance using measures of cost, revenue, and market position, including asset utilization, asset growth, and market share. Examples include returns on investments, value added per employee, debt to equity ratio, returns on assets, operating margins, cash-to-cash cycle time, and other profitability and liquidity measures. Financial measures are generally tracked throughout the organization.

Human resource performance relates to the activities in Category 5. Human resource performance measures usually include absenteeism, employee satisfaction ratings, safety incidents, turnover rates, strikes, worker grievances, and compensation claims.

Performance Excellence

Performance excellence refers to an integrated approach to organizational performance management that results in (1) delivery of ever-improving value to customers, contributing to marketplace success; (2) improvement of overall organizational effectiveness and capabilities; and (3) organizational and personal learning. The Baldrige Criteria for Performance Excellence provide a framework and an assessment tool for understanding organizational strengths and opportunities for improvement and thus for guiding planning efforts.

Performance Projections

Performance projections refer to estimates of future performance or goals for future results. Projections may be inferred from past performance, may be based on competitors' performance, or may be predicted based on changes in a dynamic marketplace. Projections integrate estimates of your organization's rate of improvement and change, and they may be used to indicate where breakthrough improvement or change is needed. Thus, performance projections serve as a key planning management tool.

Prevention-Based

Prevention-based refers to seeking the root cause of a problem and preventing its recurrence rather than merely solving the problem and waiting for it to happen again (a reactive posture).

Process

Process refers to linked activities with the purpose of producing a product or service for a customer (user) within or outside the organization. Generally, processes involve combinations of people, machines, tools, techniques, and materials in a systematic series of steps or actions. In some situations, processes might require adherence to a specific sequence of steps, with documentation (sometimes formal) of procedures and requirements, including well-defined measurement and control steps.

In many service situations, particularly when customers are directly involved in the service,

process is used in a more general way—to spell out what must be done, possibly including a preferred or expected sequence. If a sequence is critical, the service needs to include information to help customers understand and follow the sequence. Service processes involving customers also require guidance to the providers of those services on handling contingencies related to customers' likely or possible actions or behaviors.

Some organizations do not recognize the importance of the services they provide. Consider the coffee shop again. If the focus is only on making the best coffee and the service is poor—making customers wait too long—the coffee shop will lose customers. Delivering service value must be considered as important to success as delivering product value.

In knowledge work such as strategic planning, research, development, and analysis, process does not necessarily imply formal sequences of steps. Rather, process implies general understandings regarding competent performance such as timing, options to be included, evaluation, and reporting. Sequences might arise as part of these understandings.

Productivity

Productivity refers to measures of efficiency of the use of resources. Although the term is often applied to single factors such as staffing (labor productivity), machines, materials, energy, and capital, the productivity concept applies as well to total resources used in producing outputs. Overall productivity—sometimes called total factor productivity—is determined by combining the productivities of the different resources used for an output. The combination usually requires taking a weighted average of the different single factor productivity measures, where the weights typically reflect costs of the resources. The use of an aggregate measure of overall productivity allows a determination of whether or not the net effect of overall changes in a process—possibly involving resource trade-offs—is beneficial.

Effective approaches to performance management require understanding and measuring single factor and overall productivity, particularly in complex cases with a variety of costs and potential benefits.

Purpose

Purpose refers to the fundamental reason that an organization exists. The primary role of purpose is to inspire an organization and guide its setting of values. Purpose is generally broad and enduring. Two organizations in different businesses could have similar purposes, and two organizations in the same business could have different purposes.

Refinement

Refinement refers to the result of a systematic process to analyze performance of a system and improve it.

Results

Results refer to outcomes achieved by an organization in addressing the purposes of a Baldrige Criteria Item. Results are evaluated on the basis of current performance; performance relative to appropriate comparisons; rate, breadth, and importance of performance improvements; and relationship of results measures to key organizational performance requirements.

Root Cause

Root cause refers to the original cause or reason for a condition. The root cause of a condition is that cause which, if eliminated, guarantees that the condition will not recur.

Senior Leaders

Senior leaders refer to an organization's senior management group or team. In many organizations, this consists of the head of the organization and those who directly report to him or her.

Service Standard (Customer-Contact Requirements)

Service standard refers to a set, measurable level of performance. For example, an objective of an organization might be "prompt customer service." A customer-contact requirement or service standard would stipulate how prompt the service should be—

"Equipment will be repaired within 24 hours," or "The phone will be answered by a person on or before the second ring."

Stakeholder

Stakeholder refers to an individual or group that is or might be affected by an organization's actions and success. Examples of key stakeholders include customers, partners, stockholders, and local/professional communities.

Strategic Challenges

Strategic challenges refers to those pressures that exert a decisive influence on an organization's likelihood of future success. These challenges frequently are driven by an organization's future competitive position relative to other providers of similar products or services. While not exclusively so, strategic challenges generally are externally driven. However, in responding to externally driven strategic challenges, an organization may face internal strategic challenges.

External strategic challenges may relate to customer or market needs/expectations; product/service or technological changes; or financial, societal, and other risks. Internal strategic challenges may relate to an organization's capabilities or its human or other resources.

See the definition of "strategic objectives" for the relationship between strategic challenges and the strategic objectives an organization articulates to address key challenges.

Strategic Objectives

Strategic objectives refer to an organization's stated aims or responses to major change opportunities and/or the fundamental challenges the organization faces. Strategic objectives are generally externally focused, relating to significant customer, market, product/service, or technological opportunities and challenges. Broadly stated, they are what an organization must change or improve to remain or become competitive. Strategic objectives set an organization's longer-term directions and guide resource allocations and redistributions.

System

System refers to a set of well-defined and well-designed processes for meeting the organization's quality and performance requirements.

Systematic

Systematic refers to approaches that are repeatable and predictable, rather than anecdotal and episodic. Systematic approaches use data and information so that improvement and learning are possible. Approaches are systematic if they build in the opportunity for evaluation and learning, and thereby permit a gain in maturity. As organizational approaches mature, they become more systematic and reflect cycles of evaluation and learning. A systematic approach also integrates other approaches to ensure high levels of efficiency, effectiveness, and alignment.

Trends

Trends refer to numerical information that shows the direction and rate of change for an organization's results. Trends provide a time sequence of organizational performance.

A minimum of three data points generally is needed to begin to ascertain a trend. The time period for a trend is determined by the cycle time of the process being measured. Shorter cycle times demand more frequent measurement, while longer cycle times might require longer periods before a meaningful trend can be determined.

Examples of trends called for by the Criteria include data related to customer and employee satisfaction and dissatisfaction results, product and service performance, financial performance, marketplace performance, and operational performance, such as cycle time and productivity.

Value

Value refers to the degree of worth relative to cost and relative to possible alternatives of a product, service, process, asset, or function.

Organizations frequently use value considerations to determine the benefits of various options relative to their costs, such as the value of various product and service combinations to customers. Organizations seek to deliver value to all their stakeholders. This frequently requires balancing value for customers and other stakeholders, such as stockholders, employees, and the community.

Values

Values refers to the guiding principles and/or behaviors that embody how the organization and its people expected to operate. Values reflect and reinforce the desired culture of an organization. Values support and guide the decision making of every employee, helping the organization to accomplish its mission and attain its vision in an appropriate manner.

Vision

Vision refers to the desired future state of an organization. The vision describes where an organization is headed, what it intends to be, or how it wishes to be perceived.

Work Systems

Work systems refer to how your employees are organized into formal or informal units; how job responsibilities are managed; and your processes for compensation, employee performance management, recognition, communication, hiring and succession planning. Organizations designed work systems to align their components to enable and encourage all employees to contribute effectively and to the best of their ability.

Waste Reduction

Waste reduction refers to what is obtained from redesigning a product to require less material or from recycling waste to produce useful products.

Clarifying Confusing Terms

Comparative Information vs. Benchmarking

Comparative information includes benchmarking and competitive comparisons. Benchmarking refers to collecting information and data about processes and performance results that represent the best practices and performance for similar activities inside or outside the organization's business or industry. Competitive comparisons refer to collecting information and data on performance relative to direct competitors or similar providers.

For example, a personal computer manufacturer, ABC Micro, must store, retrieve, pack, and ship computers and replacement parts. ABC Micro is concerned about shipping response time, errors in shipping, and damage during shipping. To determine the level of performance of its competitors in these areas, and to set reasonable improvement goals, ABC Micro would gather competitive comparison data from similar providers (competitors). However, these performance levels may not reflect best practices for storage, retrieval, packing, and shipping.

Benchmarking would require ABC Micro to find organizations that carry out these processes better than anyone else and examine both their processes and performance levels, such as the catalog company L.L. Bean.

Benchmarking seeks best-practices information. Competitive comparisons look at competitors, whether or not they are the best.

Customer-Contact Employees

Customer-contact employees are any employees who are in direct contact with customers. They may be direct service providers or answer complaint calls. Whenever a customer makes contact with an organization, either in person or by phone or other electronic means, that customer forms an opinion about the organization and its employees. Employees who come in contact with customers are in a critical position to influence customers for the good of the organization, or to its detriment.

Customer Satisfaction vs. Customer Dissatisfaction

One is not the inverse of the other. The lack of complaints does not indicate satisfaction although the presence of complaints can be a partial indicator of dissatisfaction. Measures of customer dissatisfaction can include direct measures through surveys as well as complaints, product returns, and warranty claims.

Customer satisfaction and dissatisfaction are complex to assess. Customers are rarely "thoroughly" dissatisfied, although they may dislike a feature of a product or an aspect of service. There are usually degrees of satisfaction and dissatisfaction.

Data vs. Information

Information can be qualitative and quantitative. Data are information that lend themselves to quantification and statistical analysis. For example, an incoming inspection might produce a count of the number of units accepted, rejected, and total shipped. This count is considered data. These counts add to the base of information about supplier quality.

Education vs. Training

Training refers to learning about and acquiring job-specific skills and knowledge. Education refers to the general development of individuals. An organization might provide training in equipment maintenance for its workers, as well as support the education of workers through an associate degree program at a local community college.

Empowerment and Involvement

Empowerment generally refers to processes and procedures designed to provide individuals and teams the tools, skills, and authority to make decisions that affect their work—decisions traditionally reserved for managers and supervisors.

Empowerment as a concept has been misused in many organizations. For example, managers may pretend to extend decision-making authority under the guise of chartering teams and individuals to make recommendations about their work, while continuing to reserve decision-making authority for themselves.

This practice has given rise to another term—involvement—which describes the role of employees who are asked to become involved in decision making, without necessarily making decisions. Involvement is a practice that many agree is better than not involving employees at all, but still does not optimize their contribution to initiative, flexibility, and fast response.

Measures and Indicators

The award criteria do not make a distinction between measures and indicators. However, some users of these terms prefer the term indicator; (1) when the measurement relates to performance, but is not a direct or exclusive measure of such performance, for example, the number of complaints is an indicator of dissatisfaction, but not a direct or exclusive measure of it; and (2) when the measurement is a predictor (leading indicator) of some more significant performance, for example, gain in customer satisfaction might be a leading indicator of market share gain.

Operational Performance and Predictors of Customer Satisfaction

Operational performance processes and predictors of customer satisfaction are related but not always the same. Operational performance measures can reflect issues that concern customers as well as those that do not. Operational performance measures are used by the organization to assess effectiveness and efficiency, as well as predict customer satisfaction.

In the example of the coffee shop, freshness is a key customer requirement. One predictor of customer satisfaction might be the length of time, in minutes, between brewing and serving to guarantee freshness and good aroma. The standard might be 10 minutes or less to ensure satisfaction. Coffee more than 10 minutes old would be discarded.

A measure of operational effectiveness might be how many cups were discarded (waste) because the coffee was too old. The customer does not care if the coffee shop pours out stale coffee, and therefore, that measure is not a predictor of satisfaction. However, pouring out coffee does affect profitability and should be measured and minimized.

Ideally, an organization should be able to identify enough measures of product and service quality to predict customer satisfaction accurately and monitor operating effectiveness and efficiency.

Performance Requirements vs. Performance Measures

Performance requirements are an expression of customer requirements and expectations. Sometimes performance requirements are expressed as design requirements or engineering requirements. They are viewed as a basis for developing measures to enable the organization to determine, generally without asking the customer, whether the customer is likely to be satisfied.

Performance measures can also be used to assess efficiency, effectiveness, and productivity of a work process. Process performance measures might include cycle time, error rate, or throughput.

Support Services

Support services are those services that support the organization's product and service delivery core operating processes. Support services might include finance and accounting, management information services, software support, marketing, public relations, personnel administration (job posting, recruitment, and payroll), facilities maintenance and management, secretarial support, and other administration services.

Of course, if an organization is in business to provide a traditional support service such as accounting, then accounting services provided to its external customers become its core work/operating process and are no longer considered a support service. Internal accounting services would continue to be considered a support service.

In the human resources area (Category 5), the criteria require organizations to manage their human resource assets to optimize performance. However, many human resources support services might also exist such as payroll, travel, position control, recruitment, and employee services. These processes must be designed, delivered, and refined systematically according to the requirements of Item 6.3.

Teams and Natural Work Units

Natural work units reflect the people that normally work together because they are a part of a formal work unit. For example, on an assembly line, three or four people naturally work together to install a motor in a new car. Hotel employees who prepare food in the kitchen might constitute another natural work unit.

Teams may be formed of people within a natural work unit or may cross existing (natural) organization boundaries. To improve room service in a hotel, for example, some members of several natural work units such as the switchboard, kitchen workers, and waiters may form a special team. This team would not be considered a natural work unit. It might be called a cross-functional work team because its members come from different functions within the organization.

Appendix A: A Global View of Quality

This section describes Quality/Performance Awards from around the globe. It describes their purpose, goals, strategies, models, and core values. Much of the research for this section is based on the references at the end of the section. In addition to recognizing the contribution of these organizations and sponsors, phone numbers or e-mails are listed for our readers so they may pursue more in-depth research on global awards.

There are about 50 National Quality Organizations around the world:

- Central and Eastern Europe—18 percent

- Western and North Europe—32 percent

- South Europe and Mediterranean—12 percent

- Central and South America and Caribbean—18 percent

- North America—6 percent

- Asia—10 percent

- Africa—4 percent

The large majority of all the above organizations have these common goals:

- To raise the level and quality of management in organizations

- To support the competitiveness of industry in their country

- To share knowledge and best practices

- To increase emphasis on the methods of quality

Quality Awards around the world are based in whole or in part on one of three basic models: The Baldrige Model, The Deming Model, and the European Quality Award Model (which, in itself, ties to the Baldrige model). The Malcolm Baldrige National Quality Award was founded in 1987 and authorized by the U.S. Congress to recognize Service, Small Business, and Manufacturing companies. Of the worldwide quality awards, 41 percent use the Baldrige Model in part or whole as the basic foundation for their award.

The Deming Prize, the longest standing of the awards, was established in 1951 by a resolution of the Union of Japanese Scientists and Engineers (JUSE) and named after the great leader in quality, W. Edwards Deming. The Deming Prize was, and continues to be, primarily used in Japan (although several years ago, representatives of the Japanese government benchmarked the Baldrige process and have created a Baldrige-based national quality award). Four percent of the awards (India and Japan's JUSE Award) are based on this model today. (Reference: JUSE Tokyo, Japan +81-3-5379-1227.)

The European Quality Award (EQA) was initiated in 1992 to recognize high levels of commitment to quality. It was applied particularly by European organizations and has become increasingly popular. Fifty-five percent of quality award organizations use this Baldrige-based quality award in whole or in part as the foundation for their award.

Both the European and Malcolm Baldrige Award have common or very similar core values:

EQA Value	Malcolm Baldrige Value
Customer focus	Customer driven
Supplier partnerships	Valuing employees and partners
People development and involvement	Organizational and personal learning
Processes and facts	Management by fact
Continuous improvement and innovation	Managing for innovation
Leadership and consistency of purpose	Visionary leadership
Public responsibility	Public responsibility and citizenship
Results oriented	Focus on results and creating value

The following core values were included in over 50 percent of the worldwide awards. The Baldrige value follows in parenthesis.

- Customer Orientation (Customer Driven)

- Continuous Improvement (Organizational and Personal Learning but was formerly called Continuous Improvement and Learning)

- Participation by Everyone (Valuing Employees and Partners)

- Committed Leadership (Visionary Leadership)

- Process Orientation (Managing for Innovation)

- Long-Range Perspective (Focus on the Future)

- Public Responsibility (Public Responsibility and Citizenship)

- Management by Facts (Management by Fact)

- Prevention (No clear corresponding value, but Agility corresponds in part)

- Learn from Others (Organizational and Personal Learning)

Although most awards have review cycles to improve their models, they are not annual as is the Malcolm Baldrige. The EQA, for example, is updating its model in 2000 but it is not yet finalized. Therefore, the following comparison is to its most recent model (1996). Between the two awards, 96 percent of the organizations use one of these models in whole or in part as a basis for their awards.

References on Quality Awards

The Deming Prize Guide for Overseas Companies, 1996. Union of Japanese Scientists and Engineers (JUSE). Telephone: +81-3-5379-1227 (Japan), Fax +81-3-5379-1227.

Quality for Excellence and Prosperity, 1998. Hong Kong Management Association HKMA Quality Award. Telephone: 2774 8569/2766 3303 (Hong Kong).

The European Quality Award, 1996. European Foundation for Quality Management. Telephone: +32 2 775 35 11 (Brussels).

Bases Del Premo Nacional A La Calidad, 1996. Republica Argentina. Telephone/Fax: (541) 326-6104 (Argentina). Private Sector Award.

Australian Business Excellence Framework, 1999. Web site: www.apc.org.au .

State of the Quality Organisation: A Comparative Review of the Organisations, Their Products and Service and Quality Awards Programs, 1998. Report sponsored by the Swedish International Development Agency, Swedish Institute for Quality, and the Xerox Corporation. More details may be obtained via e-mail to sari@recomate.se or telephoning +46 31 53 00 (Sweden).

Comparing the European Quality Award Model with the Baldrige Criteria

European Quality Award Requirements	1.1	1.2	2.1	2.2	3.1	3.2	4.1	4.2	5.1	5.2	5.3	6.1	6.2	6.3	7.1	7.2	7.3	7.4
Leadership: How the behavior and actions of the executive team and all other leaders inspire, support, and promote a culture of Total Quality Management. Leaders:																		
1a. visibly demonstrate their commitment to a culture of Total Quality Management	●																	
1b. support improvement and involvement by providing appropriate resources and assistance	●		●															
1c. are involved with customers, suppliers, and other external organizations	●			●														
1d. recognize and appreciate people's efforts and achievements	●								●									
Policy and Strategy: How the organization formulates, deploys, reviews its policy and strategy, and turns it into plans and actions. Policy and strategy are:																		
2a. based on information which is relevant and comprehensive			●				●	●										
2b. developed			●															
2c. communicated and implemented	●			●														
2d. regularly updated and improved			●	●														
People Management: How the organization releases the full potential of its people. People:																		
3a. resources are planned and improved				●														
3b. capabilities are sustained and developed									●	●	●							
3c. agree on targets and continuously review performance	●			●					●		●					●		
3d. are involved, empowered, and recognized									●									
3e. and the organization have an effective dialogue	●								●									
3f. are cared for											●							
Resources: How the organization manages resources effectively and efficiently. How:																		
4a. financial resources are managed	●			●			●					●	●	●				
4b. information resources are managed				●									●					
4c. supplier relationships and materials are managed												●	●					●
4d. buildings, equipment, and other assets are managed												●	●	●				
4e. technology and intellectual property are managed				●			●					●	●	●				
Processes: How the organization identifies, manages, reviews, and improves its processes. Processes:																		
5a. key to the success of the business are identified	●		●		●	●	●											
5b. are systematically managed	●											●	●	●				
5c. are reviewed and targets are set for improvement	●			●			●					●	●	●				
5d. are improved using innovation and creativity											●	●	●	●				
5e. are changed and the benefits evaluated											●	●	●	●				
Customer Satisfaction: What the organization is achieving in relation to the satisfaction of its external customers.																		
6a. the customers' perception of the organization's products, services, and customer relationships					●	●	●	●							●			
6b. additional measurements relating to the satisfaction of the organization's customers					●	●	●	●							●			
People Satisfaction: What the organization is achieving in relation to the satisfaction of its people.																		
7a. the people's perception of the organization									●	●	●						●	
7b. additional measurements relating to people satisfaction				●					●	●	●						●	
Impact on Society: What the organization is achieving in satisfying the needs and the expectations of the local, national, and international community at large (as appropriate). This includes the perception of the organization's approach to quality of life, the environment, the preservation of global resources, and the organization's own internal measures of effectiveness. It will include its relations with authorities and bodies which affect and regulate its business.																		
8a. society's perception of the organization		●																
8b. additional measurements of the organization's impact on society		●					●											●
Business Result: What the organization is achieving in relation to its planned business objectives and in satisfying the needs and expectations of everyone with a financial interest or stake in the organization.																		
9a. financial measurements of the organization's performance																●		
9b. additional measurements of the organization's performance																		●

Additional correlations between the Baldrige and European Quality Award criteria might exist, depending on the interpretation of where results of some support areas are reported.

Appendix B: Comparing Baldrige and ISO 9000:2000—A Maturity/Excellence Model versus a Compliance Model

This section compares two different processes that examine business systems. One is based on compliance to very specific standards and the other is an excellence model—based on the extent of effective use of a complex management system. This section first addresses the key similarities and then the fundamental differences in the processes.

The International Organization for Standardization (ISO) has expanded its focus with its ISO 9000 series. This series focuses on quality assurance and management and describes management system standards. A major factor in the development and use of ISO 9000 were the European organizations in building a common market. ISO 9000 is intended to be an enabler of global trade. It makes it easier for different countries to communicate processes required to meet customer requirements for products and services. ISO 9000 standards assist users through stages of signing a contract, to designing of products and services, through manufacturing and follow-up. It applies to hardware, software, services, and process industries. It is a tool that documents internal processes to meet customer requirements.

Similarities between ISO 9001:2000 and the Baldrige Criteria for Performance Excellence:

- Purpose is business improvement

- Require some form of improvement cycle

- Have some sort of follow-up review or evaluation

- Valuable to customer

The Baldrige Performance Excellence Criteria are different than certification programs such as ISO in intent, design, and process. Compliance, certification, or licensure programs seek to ensure that minimum levels of performance are maintained.

While both ISO and Baldrige are designed to enhance quality, ISO is a standards-based, baseline quality assurance program. The aim is to create confidence between suppliers and their clients. ISO has its roots in the objective of setting minimum thresholds of performance. When met or exceeded, ISO Certification confers the right to trade internationally and between companies. This is certainly an important purpose since it forces low performers to meet higher standards.

The Baldrige Criteria, in contrast, strive to encourage and provide a developmental scale to assess peak performance. Vigorous commitment to improvement by all levels of the organization is pervasive in the Criteria. This encourages companies to raise their performance persistently, from the beginning stages of approach and use, to a mature organization where effective approaches are continuously refined and fully integrated and deployed. The objective is ever-improving world-class performance, not compliance with minimum standards for certification.

The seven Baldrige Criteria describe a highly interdependent management system—a system necessary for top performance. Their real power is found in the synergy of their linkages. It is through this integration that the possibility of enterprisewide improvement comes within reach. As organizations commit to more effective approaches, use them fully and improve them continuously, they move up on the maturity scale. ISO, in contrast, has a "checklist" of individual standards that organizations use to achieve certification and be in compliance.

The Baldrige Criteria compel companies to identify strategic and stretch targets. In the case of small businesses and manufacturing, the objective is to continuously improve, to become the industry's benchmark in terms of product and service, and to sustain impressive results as measured by customer and stakeholder satisfaction, market penetration and performance, outcomes, financial performance, and other measures important to your organization.

Summary of Key Differences

Topic	ISO 9001:2000	Baldrige
Value to customer	Generic quality management system to create confidence between suppliers and clients.	Provides feedback report to guide organization's senior leaders in setting priorities for performance improvement.
	Regulatory or mandated conformity assessment for some organizations.	Recognition for excellence.
Model includes	All of the planned and systematic activities to meet quality requirements within a quality system.	Integrated management system aimed at long-term improvements of all elements of the system.
Assessment	International Standards are developed by ISO Conformity; assessment done by suppliers and clients, not ISO.	Scoring is a complex consensus process where the Malcolm Baldrige Award Office trains and selects evaluators to examine the performance of the entire management system, including: effectiveness of approach, extent of deployment, results, and continuous evaluation and improvement.
	Certification and Registration done by "third party" assessment services.	Score from 0% (no systems at all) to 100% on 1000 (world-class) points in increments of 10%.
Goal	Meet baseline standards.	Be the best.
Sample Assessment Items	ANSI/ISO/ASQ Q9001:2000 4.1 Management responsibilities • Define a quality policy. Your policy should describe your organization's attitude towards quality. • Define the organizational structure that you will need in order to manage your quality system. • Define quality system responsibilities, give quality system personnel the authority to carry out these responsibilities, and ensure that the interactions between these personnel are clearly specified. Also, make sure that all of this is well-documented.	Item 1.1: Organizational Leadership Describe how senior leaders guide your organization and review organizational performance. (a) Senior leadership direction (1) How do senior leaders set, communicate, and deploy organizational values, performance expectations, and a focus on creating and balancing value for customers? Include communication and deployment through your leadership structure and to all staff.
Geography	Certificates issued in at least 121 countries.	United States-based companies and organizations.

Summary

ISO standards-based assessments and Baldrige assessments are valuable for improving performance. ISO has just completed the process of revising their 9000 series standards and including more requirements from the Baldrige Criteria to strengthen their minimum standards. ISO is particularly useful in enabling better communication between countries and organizations involved in international trade. The Baldrige Criteria are intended to promote system-wide optimum organizational performance.

Appendix C: 2002 Systems Required for Performance Excellence

The following section is intended for use by leaders of the organization and its units as a management tool. It defines responsibilities and management systems that are drawn from the 2002 Criteria for Performance Excellence. It can be used as a relatively simple way to focus on the Criteria requirements. Some organizations use this type of information to guide the work of management champions. Organizational leaders at various levels can use the following section for setting objectives and requirements rather than having to translate questions into statements. These statements can be used in conjunction with the Category champion descriptions to further define the areas of responsibility and focus for each Category champion.

1 Leadership

Senior leaders must address values and performance expectations, as well as focus on customers and other stakeholders, empowerment, innovation, learning, and organizational directions. In addition, the organization must address its responsibilities to the public and support its key communities.

1.1 *Organizational Leadership*

Senior leaders must effectively and systematically guide the organization and review organizational performance.

a. Senior Leadership Direction

Senior leaders must clearly set, communicate, and deploy organizational values, performance expectations, and focus on creating and balancing value for customers and other stakeholders through your leadership structure to all employees.

Senior leaders must establish and support employee empowerment and innovation, organizational agility, and organizational and employee learning.

Senior leaders must set clear directions and seek future opportunities for the organization.

b. Organizational Performance Review

Senior leaders must systematically review organizational performance and capabilities to assess organizational success, competitive performance, and progress relative to performance goals and changing organizational needs.

Key performance measures that are regularly reviewed by senior leaders must be defined.

Senior leaders must systematically translate organizational performance review findings into priorities for improvement and opportunities for innovation.

Key recent performance review findings, priorities for improvement, and opportunities for innovation must be known and documented. They must be understood throughout the organization and, as appropriate, by affected suppliers/partners to ensure organizational alignment.

Senior leaders and managers or supervisors at all levels throughout the organization must regularly use organizational performance review findings and employee feedback to improve their leadership effectiveness.

1.2 *Public Responsibility and Citizenship*

Your organization must address its responsibilities to the public and practice good citizenship.

a. Responsibilities to the Public

The organization must systematically examine and address the impacts on society of its products, services, and operations. Key practices, measures, and targets must be identified and they should meet or exceed regulatory and legal requirements for minimizing risks associated with all products, services, and operations.

The organization must have a system in place to anticipate public concerns with current and future products, services, and operations. This system must address these concerns in a proactive manner.

The organization must have a system in place to ensure ethical business practices are followed in all stakeholder transactions and interactions.

b. Support of Key Communities

The organization, its senior leaders, and employees must actively support and strengthen the organization's key communities. A systematic process must be in place to identify key communities and determine appropriate areas of emphasis for organizational involvement and support, consistent with organizational business objectives.

2   Strategic Planning

The organization must have a clear strategy development process, including a process to develop strategic objectives, action plans, and related human resource plans. In addition, a system must be in place to make sure everyone understands these plans and tracks performance against them. Strategic objectives define the things the organization must do to be successful in the future.

2.1 Strategy Development

The organization must have a process to determine how to strengthen organizational performance and improve competitive position. Key strategic objectives need to be defined in measurable terms.

 a. Strategy Development Process

A clear strategic planning process must be in place. All key steps and key participants in the process should be defined (and preferably docu-

mented, although such documentation is not required by the Baldrige Criteria).

The strategic planning process must acquire and consider relevant data and information for all key factors. It must specifically address how each of the following factors relates to the organization and what the organization must do to be successful in the future:

• Customer and market needs/expectations, including new product/service opportunities;

• Competitive environment and capabilities relative to competitors;

• The use of new technology and other key changes that might affect either the products and services offered or how the organization operates;

• Key internal strengths and weaknesses, including human and other resources. This might also include operational capability and resource availability;

• Supplier and/or partner strengths and weaknesses; and

• Financial, societal, and other potential risks.

b. Strategic Objectives

The organization must have a timetable or planned performance trajectory for accomplishing all strategic objectives. Goals and key targets should be defined in measurable terms.

The organization must assess how well the strategic objectives respond to the six key factors above that are most important to the organization's success.

In addition, the strategic objectives must address all organizational challenges.

2.2   Strategy Deployment

The organization must make certain all managers and employees understand the strategy and their personal role in carrying it out. Action plans and related performance measures must be clearly defined. Project the performance of these key measures into the future.

a.   Action Plan Development and Deployment

Systematically develop action plans to implement key strategic objectives. Key short- and longer-term action plans should be defined. Identify key changes, if any, in products/services and/or customers/markets and explain the reasons for the changes to employees throughout the organization.

Develop a system to allocate resources throughout the organization to ensure they are aligned with strategic objectives and that your overall action plan is achieved.

Define key human resource requirements and plans, based on strategic objectives and action plans the organization must implement to ensure it has the human resources to carry out the plan.

Define key performance measures and/or indicators for tracking progress relative to action plans. Systematically communicate and deploy strategic objectives, action plans, and performance measures/indicators throughout the organization to achieve overall organizational alignment of work and resources.

b. Performance Projection

Define the short-and longer-term (two- to five-year) projections for key performance measures and/or indicators.

Determine the projected performance of competitors and key benchmarks, as appropriate, for the same time period as the organization's projected goals. The basis for these comparisons must be clear and may include key benchmarks, goals, and past performance (both the organization's performance and competitors' performance).

3 Customer and Market Focus

The organization must determine requirements, expectations, and preferences of customers and markets. In addition, the organization must build relationships with customers and determine their satisfaction.

3.1 Customer and Market Knowledge

The organization must determine requirements, expectations, and preferences of customers and markets to ensure the relevance of current products/services and to develop new opportunities.

a. Customer and Market Knowledge

Systematically determine target customers, customer groups, and/or market segments. Specifically consider the requirements of customers of competitors and other potential customers and/or markets when determining how best to segment customer groups.

Systematically listen and learn from current, former, and potential customers to determine key requirements and drivers of purchase decisions. If determination methods differ for different customers and/or customer groups, define the key differences and show how your techniques for learning about the requirements of these groups vary according to real differences among the customer groups.

Systematically determine and/or project key product/service features and identify their relative importance/value to customers for purposes of current and future marketing, product planning, and other business developments, as appropriate. Use relevant information from current and former customers, including marketing/sales information, customer retention, won/lost analysis, and complaints in this determination.

Evaluate and improve your listening and learning methods to keep them current with changing business needs and directions.

3.2 Customer Relationships and Satisfaction

The organization must determine the satisfaction of customers and build relationships to retain current business and to develop new opportunities.

a. Customer Relationships

Systematically build relationships with customers to ensure repeat business and/or positive referral. As a part of strengthening relationships, provide easy access to facilitate the ability of customers to conduct business, seek assistance and information, and complain.

Determine key customer-contact requirements and systematically ensure all employees involved in the customer-response chain (all employees that come in contact with customers) understand and adhere to these contact requirements.

Establish a systematic complaint management process to ensure that complaints are resolved effectively and promptly (ideally at the first point of contact). Ensure that all complaints received are aggregated and analyzed for use in overall organizational improvement, and where appropriate to help business partners improve performance.

Evaluate and improve approaches to provide customer access and build relationships to keep current with changing business needs and directions.

b. Customer Satisfaction Determination

Implement systematic processes, take measurements, and collect data to determine customer satisfaction and dissatisfaction. Ensure that measurements capture actionable information that reflects customers' future business and/or potential for positive referral. Define any significant differences in processes or methods for different customer groups and/or market segments.

Systematically follow-up with customers on products/services and recent transactions so the organization can receive prompt and actionable feedback for use in improving products and services and preventing future problems.

Obtain and use information on customer satisfaction relative to competitors and/or benchmarks, as appropriate, to improve your offerings and support strategic planning.

Evaluate and improve approaches to customer satisfaction determination to keep them current with changing business needs and directions.

4 Information and Analysis

The organization must have a performance measurement system and a way to analyze performance data and information.

4.1 Measurement and Analysis of Organizational Performance

The organization must provide effective performance measurement systems for understanding, aligning, and improving performance at all levels and in all parts of the organization.

a. Performance Measurement

Ensure the major components of the organization's performance measurement system includes the following key factors:

- Select measures/indicators that support decision making related to daily operations

- Select and integrate measures/indicators to ensure complete data are available to track overall organizational performance in areas key to business success

- Select key comparative data and information and effectively use the data to set goals and improve work processes throughout the organization

- Evaluate and improve the performance measurement system to keep it current with changing business needs and directions

b. Performance Analysis

The organization must analyze performance data and information to assess and understand overall organizational performance. In particular, analyze data that examines the overall success of the organization, including key business results and strategic objectives to support senior executives' organizational performance review and planning.

Systematically ensure that the results of organizational-level analysis are communicated to work group and/or functional-level operations to enable effective support for decision making at all levels throughout the organization.

Ensure that the analysis effectively supports daily operational decision making throughout the organization, and ensure that measures align with action plans. The results of these analyses should provide a basis for determining targets for continuous and breakthrough improvements in organizational performance.

4.2   *Information Management*

The organization must make high-quality data available when needed for employees, suppliers/partners, and customers to facilitate decision making.

a. Data Availability

Systematically make data and information available and readily accessible to employees, suppliers and partners, and customers appropriate to their needs.

Ensure data and information integrity, reliability, accuracy, timeliness, security, and confidentiality as appropriate. Some data may require significantly more security and confidentiality protections and other data. Similarly, some decisions may require data that are more accurate and reliable than others. Some decisions may also require data near real-time.

Systematically evaluate and refine data systems to ensure they are current with changing business needs and directions.

b. Hardware and Software Quality

Design, develop, or acquire hardware and software and related systems that are reliable and easy-to-use throughout the organization.

Systematically evaluate and refine hardware and software systems to ensure that they are current with changing business needs and directions.

5   Human Resource Focus

The organization must enable employees to develop and utilize their full potential, aligned with the organization's objectives. In addition, the organization must build and maintain a work environment and an employee support climate conducive to Performance Excellence, full participation, and personal and organizational growth.

5.1   *Work Systems*

The organization's work and job design, compensation, career progression, and related workforce practices must enable employees to achieve high performance in all operations.

a. Work Systems

Design, organize, and manage work and jobs to promote cooperation and collaboration, individual initiative, organizational culture, innovation, and flexibility to keep current with business needs. Ensure effective communication, cooperation, and knowledge/skill sharing across work units, functions, and locations, as appropriate.

Ensure that managers and supervisors encourage and motivate employees to develop and utilize their full potential and encourage and support employees in job- and career-related development/learning objectives.

Ensure that the employee performance management system, including feedback to employees, supports high performance (which is usually defined by the strategic objectives). Also ensure that compensation, recognition, and related reward/incentive practices systematically reinforce high performance.

Put processes in place to develop future leaders (also called succession planning) at all levels throughout the organization, including senior leadership.

Systematically identify characteristics and skills needed by potential employees; and recruit and hire new employees to fill skill gaps. When examining key performance requirements, consider the need to capitalize on the diverse ideas, cultures, and thinking of people in the communities within which you operate and conduct business.

5.2   *Employee Education, Training, and Development*

The organization's education and training must support the achievement of business objectives; build employee knowledge, skills, and capabilities; and contribute to improved employee performance.

a. Employee Education, Training, and Development

Ensure that the organization's system for education and training contributes to the achievement of action plans. Education and training should appropriately address short- and long-term organizational and employee needs, including development, learning, and career progression.

Seek and use input from employees and their supervisors/managers to design and set education and training needs and expectations.

Design education and training to ensure it keeps current with business and individual needs. Include how job and organizational performance are used in education and training design and evaluation.

Deliver, evaluate, and improve formal and informal education, training, and learning, as appropriate.

Systematically address key developmental and training needs of the entire workforce, including diversity training, management/leadership development, new employee orientation, and safety, as appropriate.

Ensure that training and education address topics including technological change, management and leadership development, new employee orientation, safety, performance measurements, performance improvement, and diversity, as appropriate.

Systematically reinforce knowledge and skills on the job at all levels of the organization.

5.3 *Employee Well-Being and Satisfaction*

The organization must maintain a work environment and an employee support climate that contribute to the well-being, satisfaction, and motivation of all employees.

a. Work Environment

Systematically assess and improve workplace health, safety, and ergonomics. Ensure employees take part in identifying these factors and in improving workplace safety. Ensure performance measures and/or targets are in place for each key environmental factor. Also identify significant differences in requirements, if any, based on different work environments for employee groups and/or work units.

b. Employee Support and Satisfaction

Systematically determine the key factors that affect employee well-being, satisfaction, and motivation. Ensure that these factors consider and are segmented to reflect a diverse workforce and different categories and types of employees as appropriate.

Enhance employees' work climate via services, benefits, and policies. Ensure these enhancements are selected and tailored to meet the needs of different categories and types of employees and individuals, as appropriate.

Develop and implement formal and/or informal assessment methods and measures to systematically determine employee well-being, satisfaction, and motivation. Methods and measures should be tailored to examine the needs of a diverse workforce and to different categories and types of employees. In addition, use such indicators as employee turnover, absenteeism, grievances, and productivity to assess and improve employee well-being, satisfaction, and motivation.

When deciding what improvements to make, relate employee climate assessment findings to key business results to identify work environment and employee support climate improvement priorities that produce the biggest benefit for the business.

6 Process Management

The organization must have a process management system, including customer-focused design, product and service delivery, key business, and support processes that involve all work units.

6.1 *Product and Service Processes*

The organization must effectively manage key product and service design and delivery processes.

a. Design Processes

A clear design process for products/services and their related production/ delivery processes must be in place. Design processes must be capable of systematically incorporating changing customer/market requirements into product/service designs and production/delivery systems and processes.

Systematically incorporate new technology into products/services and into production/delivery systems and processes, as appropriate.

Ensure that design processes systematically and thoroughly address design quality and cycle time, transfer of learning from past projects and other parts of the organization, cost control, new design technology, productivity, and other efficiency/effectiveness factors.

Evaluate production/delivery process design to ensure it effectively accommodates all key operational performance requirements.

Systematically evaluate, coordinate, and test design and production/delivery processes to ensure capability for trouble-free and timely introduction of products/services.

b. Production/Delivery Processes

Key production/delivery processes and their key performance requirements are well-known and clearly defined.

Day-to-day operation of key production/delivery processes consistently meets key performance requirements.

Key performance measures and/or indicators are used for the control and improvement of key work processes. Real-time customer input is used to improve work processes.

Evaluate and improve production/delivery processes to achieve better process performance and improvements to products/services, as appropriate. Improvements are consistently shared with other organizational units and processes, as appropriate, throughout the organization.

6.2 Business Processes

The organization must effectively manage its key business processes. (These are determined by the senior leader as critical to enhance business growth and success. As such, it might be useful to consider them as "strategic business processes." These are considered non-product and non-service processes, which means that they are not core business activities. However, they are more critical than ordinary support activities.)

a. Business Processes

A systematic process is in place to determine key business process requirements, incorporating input from customers and suppliers/partners, as appropriate. Key operational requirements (such as productivity and cycle time) for the processes are clearly defined.

Processes are designed to meet all the key requirements.

The day-to-day operations of key business processes are effectively controlled to consistently meet key performance requirements. Define and use in-process measures and/or customer feedback in your support processes.

Prevent problems to not only reduce rework and non-value-adding activities, but minimize overall costs associated with inspections, tests, and process or performance audits.

Evaluate and improve business processes to achieve better performance and to keep them current with business needs and directions, as appropriate. Improvements are routinely shared with other organizational units and processes, as appropriate.

6.3 Support Processes

The organization must effectively manage its key support processes.

a. Support Processes

A systematic process is in place to determine key support process requirements, incorporating input from internal customers. Key operational requirements (such as productivity and cycle time) for the key support processes are clearly defined and used to guide decision making to improve performance.

Processes are designed to meet all the key requirements.

The day-to-day operations of key support processes consistently meet key performance requirements. Define and use in-process measures and/or customer feedback in your support processes.

Prevent problems to not only reduce rework and non-value-adding activities, but minimize overall costs associated with inspections, tests, and process or performance audits.

Evaluate and improve support processes to achieve better performance and to keep them current with business needs and directions, as appropriate. Improvements are routinely shared with other organizational units and processes, as appropriate.

7 Business Results

The organization's performance and improvement in key business areas must include: customer satisfaction, product and service performance, financial and marketplace performance, human resource results, supplier and partner results, and operational performance. In addition, the organization must track and improve performance levels relative to competitors.

7.1   *Customer-Focused Results*

The organization's customer-focused results must include customer satisfaction and product and service performance results. Results must be segmented by customer groups and market segments, as appropriate, and include appropriate comparative data to enable examiners to determine the "goodness" or strength of the performance outcomes.

a. Customer-Focused Results

Display data regarding current levels and trends in key measures and/or indicators of customer satisfaction, dissatisfaction, and satisfaction relative to competitors.

Display data regarding current levels and trends in key measures and/or indicators of customer loyalty, positive referral, customer-perceived value, and/or customer relationship building, as appropriate.

b. Product and Service Results

Display data regarding current levels and trends in key measures and/or indicators of product and service performance.

7.2   *Financial and Market Results*

The organization's key financial and marketplace performance results must be grouped and displayed by market segments, as appropriate. Comparative data should be provided to enable examiners to determine the "goodness" or strength of the performance outcomes.

a. Financial and Market Results

Display data regarding current levels and trends in key measures and/or indicators of financial performance. Include aggregate (overall organizational) measures of financial return and/or economic value, as appropriate.

Display data regarding current levels and trends in key measures and/or indicators of marketplace performance. Include market share/position, business growth, and new markets entered, as appropriate.

7.3   *Human Resource Results*

The organization's human resource results must include employee well-being, satisfaction, development, and work system performance. Segment results by types and categories of employees, as appropriate. Include appropriate comparative data to enable examiners to determine the "goodness" or strength of the performance outcomes.

a. Human Resource Results

Display data regarding current levels and trends in key measures and/or indicators of employee well-being, satisfaction and dissatisfaction, and development.

Display data regarding current levels and trends in key measures and/or indicators of work system performance and effectiveness.

7.4   *Organizational Effectiveness Results*

The organization's key operational performance results that contribute to the achievement of organizational effectiveness must be reported. Include appropriate comparative data to enable examiners to determine the "goodness" or strength of the performance outcomes.

a. Operational Results

Display data regarding current levels and trends in key measures and/or indicators of key design, production, delivery, and support-process performance. Include productivity, cycle time, waste, rework, scrap, delay, and other appropriate measures of effectiveness and efficiency.

Display data regarding results for key measures and indicators of accomplishment of organizational strategy.

b. Public Responsibility and Citizenship Results

Display data regarding results for key measures and/or indicators of regulatory and legal compliance and citizenship.

About the Author

Mark L. Blazey, Ed.D.

Mark Blazey is the president of Quantum Performance Group, Inc.—a management consulting and training firm specializing in organization assessment and high-performance systems development. Dr. Blazey has an extensive background in quality systems. For five years he served as a Senior Examiner for the Malcolm Baldrige National Quality Award. He also served as the lead judge for the quality awards for New York State, Vermont, and Aruba, and a judge for the Wisconsin Forward Award. Dr. Blazey has participated on and led numerous site visit teams for national, state, and company-private quality awards and audits over the past 13 years.

Dr. Blazey trains thousands of quality award examiners and judges for state and national quality programs including the Alabama Quality Award, Delaware Quality Award, Illinois Lincoln Award for Business Excellence, Kentucky Quality Award, Minnesota Quality Award, New York State Quality Award, Pennsylvania Quality Leadership Award, Nebraska Quality Award, Vermont Quality Award, Wisconsin Forward Award, Aruba Quality Award, Costa Rica Quality Award, and the national Workforce Excellence Network Award for Performance Excellence, as well as managers and examiners for schools, health care organizations, major businesses, and government agencies. He has set up numerous Baldrige-based programs to enhance and assess performance excellence for all sectors and types of organizations; many of which have subsequently received State and Baldrige recognition.

Dr. Blazey has written many books and articles on quality, including the ASQ Quality Press best-seller *Insights to Performance Excellence*, and co-authored *Insights to Performance Excellence in Education* and *Insights to Performance Excellence in Health Care*. He is a member and Certified Quality Auditor of the American Society for Quality.

Dr. Blazey may be contacted via email at Blazey@QuantumPerformance.com or by telephone at 315-986-9200. He encourages feedback, recommendations, and questions about this book.

Index

Note: Italicized page numbers indicate illustrations.

A

accountability, 46
action plans, 111–12
actionable information, 127
ADAC Laboratories of California, 13
agility, as core value, 25
alignment, of work unit, 111–12
Ames Rubber Corporation, 14
application,
    2002 Application template, CD-ROM
    instructions, CD-ROM
    preparation for, 233–40
AT&T Transmission Sales Business
    Unit, 14
award categories, and point values, 71
award criteria
    organization of, 70
    See also Baldrige criteria; criteria
award criteria framework, 68–70
award cycle fees, CD-ROM
award winners, CD-ROM

B

Baldrige criteria
    versus certification programs, 305–7
    2002 Award criteria, CD-ROM
    See also award criteria; criteria
beginning implementation, 6
behaviorally anchored survey, 253–58
    sample, 259–72
benchmarking data, 46
BI, 12–13
Boeing Airlift and Tanker, 13
brain center, 69
business results, 49–50, 69
    required performance excellence
        systems, 316
Business Results, Category 7, 209–31
    7.1 Customer-Focused Results
        Adverse Consequences, 214

discussion, 210–11
        Item Linkages, 212–13
        Sample Effective Results, 215
        Scoring, 210
    7.2 Financial and Market Results
        Adverse Consequences, 219
        discussion, 216–17
        Item Linkages, 218
        Sample Effective Results, 220
        Scoring, 216
    7.3 Human Resource Results
        Adverse Consequences, 223
        discussion, 221–22
        Item Linkages, 223
        Sample Effective Results, 224
        Scoring, 221
    7.4 Organizational Effectiveness
        Results
        Adverse Consequences, 230
        discussion, 226–27
        Item Linkages, 228–29
        Sample Effective Results, 231
        Scoring, 225

C

Cadiallac, 13
CEO skills, 5
CEO survey, 3–5
change management, 44, 53–56
Chugach School District, 9–10
Clarke American Checks, 9
competency gaps, 4
competition, 5
complaint information, 127–28
compliance model, versus
    maturity/excellence model,
    Appendix B, 305–7
contacts, state and regional awards,
    CD-ROM
contephobia, 46
continuous improvement, 72–73, 248
core training, 37
core values, 21–30
    agility, 25
    customer-driven excellence, 22

focus on results and creating value,
    29
focus on the future, 26
management by fact, 27
managing for innovation, 26
organizational and personal learning,
    23
public responsibility and citizenship,
    28
systems perspective, 30
valuing employees and partners, 24
visionary leadership, 21
Corning Telecommunications Products
    Division, 13
cost reduction, 3
criteria
    changes from 2001, 73–74
    key characteristics of, 72–73
    worldwide use of, 14
    See also award criteria; Baldrige
        criteria
critical skills, 37
customer and market focus, 45–46
    required performance excellence
        systems, 311
Customer and Market Focus, Category 3,
    119–35
    3.1 Customer and Market Knowledge
        Adverse Consequences, 124
        discussion, 121–22
        Item Linkages, 123
        Sample Effective Practices, 125
        Scoring, 120
    3.2 Customer Relationships and
        Satisfaction
        Adverse Consequences, 133–34
        discussion, 127–30
        Item Linkages, 131–32
        Sample Effective Practices, 135
        Scoring, 126
customer requirements, 16
customer satisfaction, 128–29
customer-driven excellence, as core
    value, 22
cycle-time reduction, 3

D

Dana Corporation-Spicer Driveshaft Division, 12
dashboard, to monitor progress, 18–19
Deming Prize, 301
Deming, W. Edwards, 1
DRIP, 46
driver triad, 68

E

eligibility forms, CD-ROM
eligibility guidelines, CD-ROM
employee feedback, 43–44
employee management, 4
employee performance management, 157
employee satisfaction, 48
European Quality Award (EQA), 301–2
    compared to Baldrige, 303

F

fear, 46
focus on the future, as core value, 26

G

global view, of quality, Appendix A, 301–3
globalization, 3
Globe Metallurgical, 14
glossary, 289–96
good citizenship, 92–93
guidelines, for criteria response, 235–40
    Approach/Deployment Items, 235–37
    data and measures, 238–40
    general, 235
    Results Items, 237–38

H

Hendricks, Kevin B., 5–9
human resource focus, 47–48
    required performance excellence systems, 313–14
Human Resource Focus, Category 5, 155–79
    5.1 Work Systems
        Adverse Consequences, 161–62
        discussion, 157–58
        Item Linkages, 159–60
        Sample Effective Practices, 163
        Scoring, 156
    5.2 Employee Education, Training, and Development
        Adverse Consequences, 169–70
        discussion, 165–66
        Item Linkages, 167–68
        Sample Effective Practices, 171
        Scoring, 164

    5.3 Employee Well-Being and Satisfaction
        Adverse Consequences, 177–78
        discussion, 173–75
        Item Linkages, 176
        Sample Effective Practices, 179
        Scoring, 172–73

I

If Japan Can, Why Can't We? 1
implementation cycle, of quality management, 6
information and analysis, 46
    required performance excellence systems, 312–13
Information and Analysis, Category 4, 137–54
    4.1 Measurement and Analysis of Organizational Performance
        Adverse Consequences, 144–45
        discussion, 139–41
        Item Linkages, 142–43
        Sample Effective Practices, 146–47
        Scoring, 138
    4.2 Information Management
        Adverse Consequences, 152–53
        discussion, 149–50
        Item Linkages, 151
        Sample Effective Practices, 154
        Scoring, 148
innovation, managing for, as core value, 26
integrated management systems, 15–20
integrated systems, 248
International Organization for Standardization (ISO), 305
ISO 9000, 305

K

KARLEE Company, 12
knowledge management, 3

L

leadership actions, 51–52
leadership, 19, 42–44
    required performance excellence systems, 309–10
Leadership, Category 1, 81–97
    1.1 Organizational Leadership
        Adverse Consequences, 87–88
        discussion, 83–84
        Item Linkages, 85–86
        Sample Effective Practices, 89–90
        Scoring, 82
    1.2 Public Responsibility and Citizenship
        Adverse Consequences, 96

    discussion, 92–94
    Item Linkages, 95
    Sample Effective Practices, 97
    Scoring, 91
learning, organizational and personal, as core value, 23
lessons learned, 38–50
    business results, 49–50
    customer and market focus, 45–46
    human resource focus, 47–48
    information and analysis, 46
    leadership, 42–44
    process management, 48–49
    strategic planning, 44
Likert scale survey, 253
Link, Albert N., 14
Los Alamos National Bank, 12

M

Malcolm Baldrige National Quality Award (MBNQA)
    compared to EQA, 301, 303
    economic impact of, 14
    establishment of, 1–2
management by fact, as core value, 27
Management Effectiveness Survey, 56, 57–58
manufacturing, 4
market size, 5
mature implementation, 6
maturity/excellence model, versus compliance model, Appendix B, 305–7
motivated people, 16–17

N

"The Nation's CEOs Look to the Future," 3–5

O

Operations Management International (OMI), 12
optimum performance, 15
organizational and personal learning, as core value, 23
Organizational Profile, 75–79
    importance of, 75
    P.1 Organizational Description, 76
        Item Linkages, 77
    P.2 Organizational Challenges, 78
        Item Linkages, 79

P

Pal's Sudden Service, 11–12
Pearl River School District (PRSD), 10–11
performance excellence, systems required for (Appendix C)
    business results, 316
    customer and market focus, 311
    human resource focus, 313–14
    information and analysis, 312–13
    leadership, 309–10
    process management, 314–15
    strategic planning, 310–11
performance excellence standards, 63–66
performance improvement council, 31–37
    business results champion, 37
    customer value champion, 34–35
    human resources focus champion, 35–36
    information and analysis champion, 35
    organizational leadership champion, 32–33
    process management champion, 36–37
    strategic planning champion, 33–34
performance requirements, of managers, 59–62, 67
plan–do–check–act (PDCA), 73
point values, and award categories, 71
potential customers, definition of, 121
prevention-based systems, 248
process management, 48–49
    required performance excellence systems, 314–15
Process Management, Category 6, 181–207
    6.1 Product and Service Processes
        Adverse Consequences, 190–93
        discussion, 184–87
        Item Linkages, 188–89
        Sample Effective Practices, 194
        Scoring, 182–83
    6.2 Business Processes
        Adverse Consequences, 200–1
        discussion, 196–97
        Item Linkages, 198–99
        Sample Effective Practices, 201
        Scoring, 195
    6.3 Support Processes
        Adverse Consequences, 206
        discussion, 203–4
        Item Linkages, 205
        Sample Effective Practices, 207
        Scoring, 202

processes, 17–18
public responsibility and citizenship, as core value, 28

Q

quality, use of word, 42–43

R

Regional Quality Award Contacts, CD-ROM
research study, Hendricks and Singhal, 5–9
results, focus on, as core value, 29
Ritz-Carlton Hotel Company, 13

S

scoring system, 241–49
    Approach/Deployment Items, 248–49
    dimensions, 241–42
    supplementary scoring guidelines, 243–47
Scott, John T., 14
self-assessments, 251–58
    behaviorally anchored survey, 253–58
    full-length written narrative, 251–52
    short written narrative, 252–53
    survey approach, 253
Singhal, Vinod R., 5–9
site visit, 273–88
    characteristics of, 273–74
    conduct of examiners, 275
    conducting, 275–76
    general employee questions, 288
    generic questions, by category, 278–87
    important issues, 274
    preceding discussions, 274–75
    purpose of, 273
    team leader's checklist, 276–77
Solectron Corporation, 14
stakeholders, 5
State Quality Award contacts, CD-ROM
STMicroelectronics, 13
stock prices, of award winners, 7–9
strategic planning, 44
    required performance excellence systems, 310–11

Strategic Planning, Category 2, 99–118
    2.1 Strategy Development
        Adverse Consequences, 108
        discussion, 102–5
        Item Linkages, 106–7
        Sample Effective Practices, 109
        Scoring, 101
    2.2 Strategy Deployment
        Adverse Consequences, 116
        discussion, 111–14
        Item Linkages, 115
        Sample Effective Practices, 117–18
        Scoring, 110
strategies, execution of, 5
strategy, 19
Sunny Fresh Foods, 13
supply chains, 4
systems, 248
systems perspective, as core value, 30

T

terms, clarification of, 297–99
Texas Nameplate Company, 13
training, 47
trends, in business environments, 3–5

U

U.S. Congress, 14
University of Wisconsin-Stout, 11
upward feedback, 55–58

V

valuing employees and partners, as core value, 24
visionary leadership, as core value, 21

W

Wainwright Industries, 13
winners, list of, CD-ROM
work core, 68
work results, 16
written narratives, 251–53

X

Xerox, 38